At the Risk of Being Heard

AT THE RISK OF BEING HEARD

Identity, Indigenous Rights, and Postcolonial States

With a Foreword by Winona LaDuke

Edited by Bartholomew Dean and Jerome M. Levi

The University of Michigan Press
Ann Arbor

2010   2009   2008   2007   7   6   5   4

A CIP catalog record for this book is available from the British Library.

Library of Congress Cataloging-in-Publication Data

At the risk of being heard : identity, indigenous rights, and
     postcolonial states / edited by Bartholomew Dean and Jerome M.
Levi ; with a foreword by Winona LaDuke.
          p.   cm.
     Includes bibliographical references and index.
     ISBN 0-472-09736-9 (alk. paper) — ISBN 0-472-06736-2 (pbk. : alk.
paper)
          1. Indigenous peoples—Civil rights.   2. Indigenous peoples—
     Ethnic identity.   3. Indigenous peoples—Government relations.
     4. Human rights.   5. Postcolonialism.   I. Dean, Bartholomew, 1963–
     II. Levi, Jerome M., 1957–

     GN380 .A85   2003
     306'.08—dc21   2002152248

The royalties for this book are being donated to Cultural Survival. For more information on promoting the rights, voices, and visions of indigenous peoples, please see www.cs.org.

ISBN 978-0-472-09736-4 (alk. paper)
ISBN 978-0-472-06736-7 (pbk. : alk. paper)

For Michelle and Tara

Contents

Foreword

In the colonial to neocolonial alchemy, gold changes to scrap metal and food to poison. We have become painfully aware of the mortality of wealth which nature bestows and imperialism appropriates.

—Eduardo Galeano, *Open Veins of Latin America*

I recall a conversation with a chief from Clayquod Sound in British Columbia. He was from a community that valued its forest and its culture, but found that a huge logging company, MacMillan Bloedel, along with the Canadian government, valued this same forest. He tells me, "There is no such thing as small talk with a cannibal. You can talk about this and that, but in the end, it always gets down to the same thing. . . . That is what it is like talking to the Canadian government. It always gets down to the same thing . . . the government wants what we have."

We are in the new millennium, roughly five hundred years after most of the colonialist expansion into every region of the world, whether colonialism through the military, economic expansion, religious expansion of Christianity, or the spread of the paradigm of science. Here we are, and as my friend Oscar Rodriguez, an Apache from West Texas used to tell me in our college days, "it's tough being an Indian in the nuclear age." Add to that all the ages since. In short, what masquerades as a postcolonial paradigm is often only a new form or new derivation of colonialism, with the attendant struggles of native peoples for the same things: to control our destiny, to control our lives, our land, and to continue our life ways in relative peace.

In the pages of this book there are many stories telling elements of these struggles worldwide—from Australia to Africa, and from Asia to the Americas. As is recounted here, indigenous peoples, whether from Malaysia or the Amazon rainforest, all share similar struggles when it comes to the politics of identity and the challenges they face in articulating their rights. Many of the readers of this text may be more familiar with the struggles of Native people for identity in the United States and Canada, where Eugenics, Blood Quantums, and adoption have become the new mechanisms to cause the elimination of nations of indigenous peoples. Or perhaps readers may be acquainted with the more subtle identity struggles over the issues of mascots, and the controversy over who has the right to determine the representation of a people: the peoples themselves, or the colonizer.

There are also many struggles over the new forms of colonialism—biocolonialism—whether through the Human Genome Diversity Project, or the invasion into the remaining reservoirs of genetic and biological diversity in plants and other forms of life patenting. In the face of globalization, new patents, and the world trade agreements, these issues are very intimate issues of self-determination and, indeed, survival for many nations of people, as they see the potential of having their genetic stock patented, and owned, by someone in a colonizing country. These times are also intimate times of struggles over the heart of spirit and the new ways to appropriate spirit through the appropriation and desecration of sacred sites—as in the United States at places like Zuni, where the people work to protect the Great Salt Mother, or at Great Horned Butte, where those who conduct their vision quests must now compete with rock climbers, or at any myriad of places where people pray and some entity wants to place a championship golf course.

It is, hard, in the end, being an Indian in the postcolonial paradigm. And it is hard having a conversation with a cannibal. Some things change and some stay the same. But in the end, five hundred years after the invention of the colonial paradigm, one can say for sure, that we are still here, we are still struggling, and we intend to survive. In these pages are some of our voices, and we will be heard.

—Winona LaDuke

Acknowledgments

Every narrative is a story of journey. This compilation of essays represents the intellectual journey of a number of leading scholars whose work spans the globe. Since the book's inception, there have been many people and institutions that have generously supported and encouraged its completion. While the volume stems from an Invited Presidential Session we organized at the Annual Meeting of the American Anthropological Association in Washington, D.C., in December 1997, its inspiration began while we were still graduate students. At Harvard University, we were fortunate to be members of the intellectually vibrant Department of Anthropology. We learned firsthand the value of a critically engaged scholarship and were tempered by our teachers, who embodied the Boasian principles of anthropology as a public intellectual enterprise. The opportunity to continue the dialogue following the AAA meeting in 1997 was provided by a series of subsequent intellectual encounters, including the American Ethnological meetings in Toronto in 1998, Carleton College's Chesley Lecture in 1998 and 2000, Harvard University's Weatherhead Center Conference on Indigenous Peoples in 2000, and the Cátedra Andrés Bello in Lima in 2000.

We would like to thank the following individuals, among others, for their contributions to the realization of this book: Benedict Anderson, Kalman Applbaum, Tara AvRuskin Levi, Jonathan Benthall, Manuel Burga Díaz, Robert Bye, Gisela Canepa Koch, Beverly Davenport Sypher, Jim Fisher, Paul Gelles, Ken George, F. Allan Hanson, Olivia Harris, Peter Herlihy, Michael Herzfeld, Laura Hobson Herlihy, Jean Jackson, John Janzen, Paula Lackie, Stephen Lewis, David and Pia Maybury-Lewis, Michelle McKinley, Beth McKinsey, Claudia Molinari, Sally Falk Moore, Joane Nagel, Stephen Nugent, Susan Quay, James Regan, Raul Romero Cevallos, Chris Steiner, Donald Stull, Jacoba Sucher, Howard Sypher, Evon Vogt, Nur Yalman, Akira Yamamoto, and Alan Kolata and Arjun Appadurai of the University of Chicago's Globalization Project. We thank Nate Greenberg for his efforts in making the global map.

This volume benefited from the charitable input of students and faculty at a number of institutions, particularly Carleton College; the University of Kansas; Universidad Nacional Mayor de San Marcos; and Goldsmiths College, University of London. Financial and logistical support from the following is most gratefully acknowledged: Amazonian Peoples' Resources Initiative; the Bush Foundation; Cultural Survival; Carleton College (Presidential Subvention Fund and College Faculty Development Endowment); Minga-Perú; NEH-Minnesota Humanities Commission; Resource Center of the Americas; Royal Anthropological Institute Fellowship in Urgent Anthropology; and the University of Kansas (Department of Anthropology, General Research Fund, Center for Latin American Studies, International Studies, and Hall Center for Humanities).

The book has been enriched by the generous and insightful comments of a number of anonymous reviewers and the fantastic editorial team at the University of Michigan Press, including Ingrid Erickson, Ellen McCarthy, Kevin Rennells, Nancy Trotic, Ann Marie Schultz, Liz Suhay, and Susan Whitlock. Thanks to one and all.

Bartholomew Dean, Lima, Peru
Jerome M. Levi, Northﬁeld, Minnesota
June 2002

Introduction

Jerome M. Levi and Bartholomew Dean

This book assesses the risk of articulating the rights claims of indigenous peoples in the face of state-sanctioned as well as insurgent violence, ethnocide, socioeconomic injustice, and flagrant human rights violations. Indigenous peoples, and in some cases their supporters, encounter considerable risks in being heard advocating for indigenous rights. This is evident in the controversial allegations surrounding the veracity of Nobel laureate Rigoberta Menchú's life story (1984; see Stoll 1998; cf. Nelson 1999; Canby 1999; and Stavans 1999).[1] In some instances, the stakes involve more than questions of testimonial legitimacy; they are literally a matter of life and death. From the killing fields of East Timor to the impoverished reservations of the United States, indigenous peoples are all too often caught in the crossfire between competing political and commercial interests seeking a foothold in their territories. Squeezed by global avarice for their natural resources, fearful of military might, and threatened by dominant groups' intolerance of their distinctive ways of life, indigenous peoples stand at a critical point in history.

At the same time, however, there has been a notable shift in the political landscape over the last twenty-five years. Today there is greater recognition than ever before of the need for nation-states to accommodate difference. This has had particular resonance for the struggles of indigenous peoples, especially their right to self-determination. Indeed, as Rodolfo Stavenhagen recently observed, "[i]ndigenous autonomy is the flavour of the month. People are talking about it all around the world and there are new and instructive experiences in many countries, despite the issue being an old and persistent one" (2000, 10). A growing readiness to acknowledge the rights of indigenous peoples is reflected in the changing sensibilities in the international community. The International Decade of the World's Indigenous People (1995–2004) was proclaimed by the United Nations High

Commissioner for Human Rights and resolved by the General Assembly in December 1993. Many countries have already signed into law the International Labor Organization's 1989 Indigenous and Tribal Peoples Convention (No. 169). This document is of monumental significance, "because it is the first international instrument that explicitly rejects the integrationalist approach which has sustained government policies towards indigenous peoples for decades" (Díaz Polanco and Sánchez 2000, 83).

Meanwhile, other international legal agreements—such as the Draft United Nations Declaration on the Rights of Indigenous Peoples, the draft of the Inter-American Declaration on the Rights of Indigenous Peoples, and the Draft Declaration of Principles for the Defense of the Indigenous Nations and Peoples of the Western Hemisphere—are nearing completion. Thus, for the first time in history, there is a growing global awareness that indigenous peoples are entitled to rights and recognition they have long been denied. From the earthen patios of Chiapas, Mexico, to the Palais Wilson in Geneva, indigenous peoples are mobilizing new social movements and ethnic federations both within and between states in order to take advantage of these historic political openings. Nevertheless, while doing so they confront certain risks—and not only from the expected sources of political, military, or economic repression.

In recognition of the profoundly paradoxical nature of indigenous identity, cultural authenticity, and human rights discourse, we have called this collection of essays *At the Risk of Being Heard.* The contributors to this volume consider the various risks of articulating, hearing, and silencing indigenous peoples' rights-based claims. Enunciation of indigenous rights claims can be hazardous because it may signal a willingness to concede the autonomy of subaltern groups to the power and adjudication of larger, dominant polities (Minow 1995). Yet if indigenous peoples remain silent or absent from new translocal arenas of power, hidden in jungles or mountains, lying low in their ancestral homelands or new "refuge regions," they risk being invisible to those allies and sources that would aid them in their struggles for political, economic, and cultural survival (Levi 1999b). While indigenous peoples' failure to voice the abuse of their rights invites more violations and mistreatment, the more that indigenous people are seen and heard outside of popularly conceived traditional contexts (i.e., the more they become savvy about the media, politically skilled, linked to the international community, the more they risk being seen as "inauthentic." In being heard as political actors, indigenous peoples begin to slip out of the "savage slot" (Trouillot 1991)—whether noble, natural, primitive, or romantic—in spite of the fact that this is the rhetorical position from which they derive much of their symbolic capital, moral authority, and political clout. In rejecting political agency, indigenous people are more likely to retain claims to their cultural authenticity, but they are also more likely to forfeit power and potentially endanger their very existence in the face of heavy-handed exploitation by repressive state regimes.

Consumerism, the ineluctable allure of the foreign, and mass telecommunications have made the ostensibly traditional cultural products of indigenous peoples available to a much wider global audience. This affords indigenous peoples (and ethnic minorities) both opportunities and challenges. New technologies such as the Internet and the digitization of information provide indigenous peoples and those living at the margins of nation-states with an opportunity to advance public acknowledgment of alternative cultural practices and distinctive worldviews. This can legitimize indigenous peoples' struggles for cultural autonomy by providing the subaltern with a forum for the mobilization of public support. Notwithstanding this political benefit, increased global access to the cultural products of indigenous peoples also carries great risks for the continued survival of local systems of knowledge and customary practices (Dean 2001). What is the risk of being heard in an era that has witnessed the Ottomans' attempted extermination of the Armenians, the Holocaust, and the horrific "ethnic cleansings" in Kosovo and Rwanda—to name but a few of the more flagrant examples of genocide that have blighted the globe in just the last century?

In charting the shifting political climate for the rights of indigenous peoples in specific regions of the globe, our book assesses the trade-offs between authenticity and political participation. In the final analysis, we maintain that those who would force a choice between authenticity and political participation traffic in stereotypes and perpetuate a false dichotomy. Nevertheless, the controversy surrounding questions of indigenous identity and the rights accorded those claiming "indigenousness" has compounded the crisis in the idea of the nation as a sovereign and bounded entity (Maybury-Lewis 1997b; Anderson 1998). This book speaks to the problems and prospects posed by this postcolonial scenario and explores what measures can be taken to enhance the integrity and cultural survival of the world's indigenous peoples. The contributors all grapple with a series of interrelated questions. Who exactly are "indigenous peoples"? What specific rights do they have? What is the proper balance between individual rights and public welfare? Can nation-states, particularly when they are often the ones denying human rights, guarantee the enforcement of indigenous peoples' rights? What can and should be the role of activists, advocates, anthropologists, and others concerned with the welfare of the world's indigenous peoples?

The initial impetus for this volume came from a presidential session convened at the 1997 Annual Meeting of the American Anthropological Association to celebrate the twenty-fifth anniversary of Cultural Survival, an organization founded to defend the human rights and cultural autonomy of indigenous peoples and ethnic minorities worldwide. The conference papers and subsequent discussions raised a number of difficult questions that call for multiple and overlapping levels of analysis capable of capturing the variety of processes and interconnections of cultural meaning, which cross spatial and temporal boundaries. Emphasizing the plight of indigenous peoples and the complex and contentious debates surrounding questions of ethnic identity, representation, and human rights, this collection sheds much-needed light on the local, national, and global dimensions of cultural pluralism. The authors of these essays draw on a wide spectrum of anthropological thought, social theory, and philosophical reflection in order to engage with formidable and deeply consequential issues about the substance and symbolism of indigenity, the processes of multicultural state building, the role of scholars and activists, and the need for an informed and critically engaged public.

Indigenous Peoples and the Creation of Indigenity

The negotiation of identity has long played a fundamental role in the resolution of a critical issue of modernity: how individuals, families, groups, and larger social networks can reconcile the strain between hierarchy and equality as fellow citizens in what Benedict Anderson (1983) has famously dubbed *imagined communities*. While it is fashionable in many academic quarters to address questions of identity (see, among others, Appiah and Gates 1995; Parker et al. 1992; Smith 1991; and Yaeger 1996), the term is often used quite loosely. Nevertheless, the concept of identity is of great utility, because it allows humans to perceive the existence of a *relation* among entities that would otherwise be seen as distinct—as Hume pointed out in his *Treatise of Human Nature* ([1739] 1978, 14).

The kind of relations that have been vital in determining and maintaining indigenous identity are ethnic relations. A group's ethnic identity "consists of its *subjective, symbolic* or *emblematic* use of any aspect of a culture, or a perceived separate origin and continuity in order to differentiate themselves from other groups" (DeVos 1995, 24). Indigenous identity, nonetheless, is not isomorphic with ethnic identity, for several reasons. Ethnic groups are not given naturally, as if they were species, but rather are products of structure and agency, forged in the crucibles of culture and history. An indigenous people *become* an ethnic group not simply by sharing such things as a group name (ethnonym), connection to a homeland, and beliefs in common ancestry, culture, language, or religion, but only when such traits are consciously recognized as emblems of connectivity and are mobilized at least in part to develop a sense of political solidarity. Typically, this occurs when such groups perceive their minority or submerged status within the polities where they reside. Although today almost all indigenous peoples are ethnic groups, the converse does not hold. In the United States, for example, African Americans constitute an ethnic group, but they are not indigenous, whereas Native Americans are both. In contrast, the Urarina of the Peruvian Amazon are an indigenous people, but they do not constitute an ethnic group per se, because they have not yet developed a pan-Urarina group consciousness or sense of solidarity that transcends local models of identity formation. Moreover, indigenous identities frequently become articulated in wider fields of symbolic and political relations of which ethnic relations are only a part. The most apparent examples of this are the emergent national and transnational indigenous rights movements.

In English, the term *indigenous* conveys the meaning of being native or belonging naturally to a place.[2] As a synonym for *native* (based on the idea of antecedence), *indigenous* has a long history of use in Europe (see, e.g., Maury et al. 1857). In contrast, the label *indigenous peoples* is a relatively novel one, appearing in treaties and conventions promulgated after the establishment of the UN in the wake of the Second World War (Brownlie 1992, 55).[3] Like the labels *tribal, native, aboriginal,* and *Indian,* the category *indigenous* is an artifact of colonial encounter (Carneiro da Cunha and Almeida 2000). The term became increasingly popular in general parlance in the postcolonial world after 1945. Of late, it has supplanted the labels *native* and *tribal,* which conjure up images of social hierarchy and intolerance associated with evolutionist thinking. More recently, the term *indigenous* has come to underscore a group's persistent vulnerability, "after decolonization had transferred power to the dominant group in the territory concerned" (Brownlie 1992, 56).

Notwithstanding UN estimates of 300 million indigenous people residing in more than seventy countries worldwide (Feiring 1998, 382), many analysts have highlighted the problematic nature of coupling the terms *indigenous* and *peoples*. It seems that just about everywhere, from Siberia to South Africa, the precise meaning of *indigenous peoples* is difficult to establish. As Benthall notes, "[i]n the New World certain dates such as 1492 mark sharp historical cut-offs," but in other areas the situation is different: for example, "in south-east Asia almost all groups except overseas Chinese and Malaysian Indians are in one sense indigenous" (Benthall 1998, 19; see also Bowen 2000, 13–14). From the perspective of historical precedence, indigenous peoples are the descendants of those who occupied an area prior to foreign invasion. Nevertheless, the distinction between indigenous and nonindigenous peoples is crosscut by so many confounding variables that the very definition of *indigenous* is frequently contested—particularly when residential precedence is blurred, as in many parts of Asia, Africa, and Europe.

Predicating indigenousness on historical continuity in precolonial territories is not without its problems, a point raised consistently throughout this volume. Béteille has recently asserted that the classification of a particular "population" in a given area as indigenous "acquires substance when there are other populations in the same region that can reasonably be described as settlers or aliens" (1998, 188). In settler societies such as those found in the Americas, Australia, New Zealand, and elsewhere, the boundary between indigenous and nonindigenous peoples is, at least in theory, relatively clear, though in practice it is fraught with complexities. The designation of indigenousness is associated with settler societies but cannot be restricted to them, as the case of New Guinea illustrates. If indigenousness is associated only with settler societies, people in "west" New Guinea (Irian Jaya, as it is known by the Indonesians) will be considered indigenous, whereas inhabitants of "eastern" New Guinea (Papua New Guinea) will not, because they are citizens of a formally independent nation-state. Clearly, limiting indigenousness to settler societies is not logically consistent.

Vulnerability, as Brownlie (1992) and others have suggested, is a criterion that is just as consequential as antecedence in designating "indigenous peoples." But the idea of indigenous peoples as it is advanced in international law—as a means to identify disadvantaged ethnic groups—does not apply to nationally dominant majority peoples such as the Malays. Although the ancestors of the Malays occupied the territory of modern Malaysia prior to British colonial rule, there are other groups, such as the Batek and Semai, whose historical, cultural, linguistic, and socioeconomic features distinguish these minority peoples from the Malays. These peoples' vulnerability, together with their prior occupation of the Malay Peninsula, identifies them, rather than the Malays, as indigenous. We therefore maintain that sociohistorical as well as political variables are involved in the designation of indigenous peoples.

In spite of its conceptual fuzziness, "indigenous peoples" is not a totally uncircumscribed category, nor one that is bereft of analytic power. Noteworthy here is Eriksen's assertion that *indigenous peoples*

> is a blanket term for aboriginal inhabitants of a territory, who are politically relatively powerless and who are only partly integrated into the dominant nation-state. Indigenous peoples are associated with a nonindustrial mode of production and a stateless political system. (1993, 13–14)

Rather than formulating an "accurate analytical" definition, Eriksen draws on "broad family resemblances and contemporary political issues" (14) to determine who is indigenous. He rightly isolates historical precedence in a region and subordination within colonial and postcolonial states as the two most salient features of indigenous peoples— a position accepted by many contemporary scholars, who often add that the marginalization of indigenous peoples is a result of conquest or colonization (see, e.g., Anaya 1996, 3; Maybury-Lewis 1997a, 7–8; and Perry 1996, 3–24). However, Eriksen's definition is not without a hitch. It excludes the Basques and the Welsh, even though they "are certainly as indigenous, technically speaking, as the Sami of northern Scandinavia or the Yanomami of the Amazon basin" (Eriksen 1993, 13–14).

The globe's hunting and gathering peoples, such as the Kalahari Bushmen, Inuit, Australian Aborigines, and Central African Pygmies, provide ample evidence for the continuing cultural survival of indigenous peoples (Lee and Daly 2000). Yet in contrast to Eriksen, we are reluctant to assert that a nonindustrial mode of production and stateless political system are definitive traits of indigenous peoples, for these criteria encourage us to arrest our views of indigenous peoples and see them as being outside the flow of history. One has only to think of the complexity of U.S. Indian "reservation economic developments" (Stull 1990), such as the casino and gaming industry, or the recent creation of the Territory of Nunavut in Canada's Eastern Arctic to question whether indigenousness is incompatible with modern industries and state structures. Advocacy groups such as Cultural Survival and IWGIA (International Work Group for Indigenous Affairs) have long pointed out that indigenous peoples and their cultures can and do survive in the modern, interconnected world.

Given that reference to indigenous peoples corresponds to overlapping empirical realities, how do we make sense of the various traits and contexts regularly associated with indigenousness? We believe that one would search in vain for the golden thread that links together all indigenous peoples, in all parts of the world, in all situations. Instead, with Gray (1997, 9) and Eriksen (1993, 13–14), we argue that *indigenous peoples* constitutes what Needham (1975) has called a "polythetic" category, or what Wittgenstein (1953) deemed a "family resemblance" or "family likeness" term.[4] We maintain that the concept of indigenous peoples can be used, not in spite of the concept's denotation of broad family resemblances, but *because* of it. Given the multiplicity of contexts in which the label *indigenous peoples* can be and is mobilized, a universally applicable definition of this category is neither plausible nor practical. Despite the difficulties in arriving at a precise definition of *indigenous,* it is clear that indigenity provides an idiom of social belonging for a wide range of peoples whose histories, habitats, and lifeways distinguish them from dominant "national" populations. Of equal or greater importance, indigenous identity provides people with a way to defend local cultural practices and worldviews through political mobilization.

This point underscores Brown Childs and Delgado-P's contention that "[t]he ways in which native peoples are giving form to the word 'indigenous' so that it can do good work in the world should be cause for celebration rather than condemnation" (1999, 212). Even though postcolonial states may assert that indigenous peoples are conquered and ipso facto inferior, such peoples may assume new identities in an effort to assert themselves in novel contexts. Subaltern groups regularly reclaim ethnonyms applied to them by outsiders, often redefining old colonial labels with newly empowered meanings of self-affirmation. Derogatory categories have been used by those forced to inhabit them as banners for political mobilization (Carneiro da Cunha and Almeida 2000).

The self-adoption of the term *indigenous* among diverse peoples itself constitutes a revaluation of identity, and one that has important historical precedents, particularly in the Americas. For example, North American indigenous leaders of the eighteenth and nineteenth centuries built on the assignation of *Indian* to mobilize multiethnic military alliances (Brown Childs and Delgado-P. 1999, 211). More recently, American Indian ethnic mobilization peaked in the 1960s and 1970s with the emergence of the Red Power movement, which regenerated cultural pride and revitalized interest in Native American ways of life (Nagel 1996). Similar processes have occurred elsewhere in the world, such as in the Philippines. Using the nomenclature of the expulsion of the Moors from Iberia, the Spanish imported labels for the victors and the vanquished in their colonization of the Philippines. The diverse Muslim peoples of the southern Philippines were designated negatively with the appellation *Moros,* meaning "Moors." Over time, these native peoples revaluated the meaning of *Moro,* which they now embrace as a pan-ethnic label for collective political action.

The emancipatory potential of indigenous movements is highlighted in a number of the essays in this volume. Across the planet, contemporary indigenous political mobilization presents examples of ethnogenesis, ethnic revitalization, and cultural survival, all in the face of tremendous demographic, ecological, and political challenges posed by the realignment of national and international power interests.

Indigenous Peoples' Rights and Postcolonial States

Persuading states and their citizens to hear and to take seriously the plight of indigenous peoples usually involves invoking powerful and politically volatile notions such as rights. This book, intended to complement the voluminous literature on the legal implications of indigenous peoples' rights,[5] explores the cultural and sociohistorical dimensions of political mobilization around indigenous-based rights claims. Like Wilson's recent volume (1997) on the comparative anthropology of human rights, this collection attempts to move beyond the absolutism of the universalist-relativist debate by evaluating the cultural elaboration of indigenous peoples' rights. This is not in any way to deny that both universalism and relativism have their advantages: universalism facilitates comparison, while relativism acknowledges context (Wilson 1997, 3; cf. Washburn 1987; Renteln 1988, 1990; and Turner 1997). Nor are these perspectives necessarily incompatible so long as one does not conflate prescriptive or normative relativism with descriptive relativism, as Renteln (1988, 1990) cogently demonstrates in her empirical defense of the latter. However, we do want to underline Wilson's measured contention that the "universality of human rights" is itself "a question of context, necessitating a situational analysis" (1997, 12; see also Dembour 1996). To this end, the contributors to this volume assess how indigenous peoples negotiate their positions in state and international power arenas by advancing "indigenous rights" as a special kind of cultural rights. In so doing, we analyze how well particular indigenous groups have been able to accommodate additional political concerns and human rights issues, such as feminism, which in some instances may be at odds with local notions of gendered authority, power, and personhood.

How rights are conceived is dependent on positionality, cultural context, and lived experience. The meaning and implementation of rights is always open to multiple interpretations. Indigenous peoples' rights are not predicated on abstract moral principles but rather are anchored in local moral worlds and entwined in translocal networks of power and identity formation shaped by the logic of postcolonial states. International human rights discourse, although tempered by calls from socialist and developing nations for socioeconomic solidarity, cultural tolerance, and environmental protection, reflects the individualism and universalism of the Western intellectual canon. Given the linguistic and cultural bias of rights discourse, it is not surprising that Westerners tend to cast rights in economic terms, whereby transactional metaphors of property, exchange, and money are privileged. A critical evaluation of human rights discourse reminds us that rights imply obligations and duties. Ethnography demonstrates that humanity is not merely individualistic, but always subject to multiple, cross-cutting social attachments.

Distinguishing between who is indigenous and who is not can have profound and far-reaching consequences for states, their citizens, and subjugated peoples. By considering rights as the language of national unity and as a barometer of the benefits and limitations of citizenship (Messer 1993), we face an old dilemma: in what way are collective cultural rights of enduring "nations" (in this case indigenous groups) consistent with individual, universal human rights? In some contexts, groups aspiring to self-determination may opt to emphasize national unity, rather than highlighting cultural distinctions that tend to reify separate indigenous identities in ways that give rise to ethnic competition. Claims for collective, indigenous rights, however, may be warranted in those instances where groups of people are unequivocally "disadvantaged with respect to a particular resource, whether land, language, or political representation, and where such a group-differentiated right . . . would rectify the inequality" (Bowen 2000, 14; see also Kingsbury 1998, 438). Efforts to rectify specific instances of inequality and ensure self-governance may indeed require the adoption and implementation of group-differentiated rights. Like the rights of children, women, and ethnic minorities, indigenous rights can fit comfortably under the canopy of human rights (Messer 1993; Nagengast 1997). They are not a new type of right but instead reflect the most recent category of persons requiring special consideration—indigenous peoples.

In exploring the dilemmas and opportunities that collective rights afford people belonging to culturally or ethnically distinct entities labeled *indigenous* (by self-assignment, ascription by others, or both), the contributors to this book illustrate that any unified theory of indigenous rights must consider particular sociocultural and historical circumstances. This calls for linking levels of analysis, from the local to the global.

Postcolonial States

The essays in this volume survey various aspects of the historical, cultural, and geographical specificity of indigenous identity and rights through the lens of postcolonialism. Indigenous peoples, often stigmatized as inferior, are, like other marginalized collectivities, usually situated within the frontier space of postcolonial states. States characterized as postcolonial may in fact still exercise neocolonial forms of control. To the extent that they do, they are by definition incapable of allowing indigenous peoples "to freely represent themselves as equal members of a political community" (Harvey 1998, 227). Under the guise of modernization, development, and national prosperity, political elites have auctioned off indigenous peoples' homelands to multinational corporations, irrespective of the detrimental impact on the environment and the well-being of local communities. Without a recognition of the historical impact of colonialism and the various forces of global modernity—including the conflation of spatial, temporal, and cultural boundaries—it is virtually impossible to comprehend the creation and conceptual import of indigenousness, whatever else the term conveys about rootedness and complex ties to land.

Some groups have special cultural rights in relation to their status as "indigenous people," a category that emerges from their articulation with postcolonial states and the global system.[6] In spite of the continued existence of a number of remaining "colonies,"[7] contemporary global politics are dominated by postcolonial states and transnational capitalism. The phrase *postcolonial state* implies enduring ties between imperial centers of power and colonized subjects. Like the modern European nation-states at their birth, postcolonial states have involved the partition or aggregation of territories occupied by a great variety of peoples from a multitude of cultural, linguistic, and religious traditions. From the outset of modern statecraft, there has been anxiety concerning the relation between the nation-state and the "foreign" nations (the proverbial "ethnic cysts") existing within it.

In postcolonial societies, state actors and their intellectual and political elites forge the nation, with crucial consequences for indigenous peoples circumscribed within the national territory (Stavenhagen 1996). The unifying discourses that postcolonial elites mobilize in their endeavors to hold these new social formations together are nationalist mythologies, which include elaborate symbols of civic participation (flags, parades, monuments, currency, etc.), national codes of citizenship (laws outlining rights and obligations), and foundational fictions responsible for narrating the nation into being.

Indigenous peoples and ethnic groups are clearly not immune to the ambiguities accompanying globalization and to the paradoxes of postcolonial national identity formation that can pit tropes of indigenousness against the foreign, sometimes with horrifically deadly consequences (Kingsbury 1998). In some regions of the world, such as Rwanda, essentialist constructions of identity have legitimized violence (Taylor 1999), in spite of the compelling evidence for crosscutting, multiple affiliations—such as patrilineal clan membership uniting the Hutu and Tutsi in a shared social universe (Janzen and Janzen 2000, 194).

Notwithstanding the potentially ruinous risks involved in tying indigenous rights claims to nationalist struggles for autonomy and self-determination, we emphasize the intellectual and political necessity for states to acknowledge forms of legal pluralism that can accommodate the heterogeneity of cultural identity (differences not only between groups, networks, and categories, but within them as well). Thus, the contributors to this volume recognize the need to strike a delicate balance between, on the one hand, homogenizing discourses that explain away differences—discourses that are explicit in nationalism, integrationist policies, and orthodox social movements—and, on the other hand, an emphasis on heterogeneity, which acknowledges pluralism but in the worst case could be misinterpreted as a postcolonial incarnation of the imperialist's military strategy of divide and conquer.

Achieving such a balance involves developing policies that preserve the liberty of individuals in ways that do not eradicate the autonomy of groups, social networks, or communities. The practical dilemmas remain ones that challenge us to reformulate rights claims so that they go beyond a facile dichotomy irrevocably separating liberal individualism from cultural or group-based rights. This calls for recognizing local notions of morality and personhood, as well as acknowledging regional or national ideas of citizenship in ways that do not exacerbate ethnic conflicts or facilitate socioeconomic marginalization. To this end, anthropology has provided an intellectual impetus for the elaboration of the "universal right to difference" (Turner 1997, 273). We need to broaden the universal concept of group-differentiated rights to include not just indigenous peoples, but also multiple, culturally dependent local ideas regarding personhood, place, citizenship, and state power (Bowen 2000, 12–14).

Political Mobilization and Strategic Essentialisms

Being heard involves political mobilization. Social movements animated by the trope of indigenous identity, or what Benedict Anderson refers to as "aggregated nativeness" (see chap. 5), are intimately bound up with colonial practices of census taking, mapmaking, and the establishment of the juridical machinery of state governance. To effectively mobilize as indigenous peoples, groups need allies, as this volume demonstrates. This is true among the Moros of the Philippines, for instance, who count on Islamic solidarity, and for Amazonian peoples who have benefited from a formidable international support network of ecologists and indigenous rights activists (a kind of support not without its pitfalls). As we have noted, although the term *indigenous* occludes the heterogeneity and divisions among the people it refers to, it remains a convenient conceptual construct for distilling and representing complex, and in many regards contradictory, social and historical processes—even when it refers to social and cultural relationships far less clearly defined than the single term *indigenous* would seem to imply. On the political terrain, this essentializing notion has been pivotal in the creation of a broad, transnational alliance, particularly between human rights lobbyists and environmentalists concerned with the fate of "Mother Earth." Alliances with environmental groups, political parties, human rights organizations, and social movements have permitted the instrumental use of indigenous ethnicity. At the same time, anthropologists as well as indigenous intellectuals and leaders have used essentialism in their efforts to define indigenous identity, secure recognition of indigenous peoples, and valorize their diverse and distinctive cultural traditions.

By *essentialism* we mean the attempt at "describing the ethnic identification of a particular group or people in terms of a set of essences, typically including language, modes of self-presentation . . . and ritual performances" (Field 1999, 194; see also Herzfeld 1992, 22).

Broadly speaking, essentialism refers to the conviction that groups or categories of persons or things have one or more defining traits particular to all members of that group or category. Some approaches to indigenousness assume the presence of essential characteristics distinguishing indigenous from nonindigenous identity. Essentialist portrayals of indigenousness differ from studies such as this collection, which emphasizes the cultural and historical specificity of identity formation. Paying close attention to both the representation and the negotiation of identity, the contributors here describe the process of identity formation in specific, nonprimordialist terms.

The metaphors of shared blood and soil are also often marshaled by essentialists in their definitions of ethnic identity. In contrast, a constructivist perspective sees cultural identities as "'imagined' in and over historical time." From this vantage point, "all identities are in effect fictive, their properties and origins traceable, mutable and vulnerable to deconstruction" (Field 1999, 195). Indigenous peoples, like other minority groups, have been encouraged "to reify particular practices in order to define and bound themselves as different from the wider society. Both the reifications and the demands which accompany them are products of legal systems" (Harris 1996, 1).

The conflict between essentialist and constructivist perspectives is often at the heart of legal debates on indigenous identity. The integrity of social relations and social organization are linked to indigenous rights because they are commonly considered vital to maintaining a group's identity over time. Indeed, the historical continuities of these social structures have in some instances been determinative factors in the adjudication of indigenous identity. The 1979 trial in Massachusetts *Mashpee Tribe v. The New Sudbury Corp.* is such a case (Clifford 1988, 277–346). Presented with five key dates stretching over a period of several hundred years, the jury found that the Mashpee existed as a "tribe" on some of these occasions but not on others. Consequently, the identity of the Mashpee as a recognizable tribe of American Indians was denied.

Implicit in this decision were tacit essentialist assumptions widely held by the dominant populations of postcolonial states about the nature of indigenous peoples. Perhaps most important, indigenous peoples are seen as being so dominated by the image of their past that they are denied a meaningful present. Indigenous peoples are trapped in a sort of "freeze-frame," their cultures regarded if not as static, then at least as not progressive. The Mashpee case also brought into sharp relief another issue impinging on the question of indigenous identity, namely whether indigenous identity is determined by the group itself or by other entities, such as external legislative bodies. While a group's claims to indigenous identity are complex and are mobilized through a number of cultural expressions (language, shared beliefs, myths of common origin, and symbolic ties to the land), visual emblems have been especially salient in the ritualized performance of indigenous autochthony.

Indigenous imagery attains national artistic recognition once indigenous peoples cease to threaten the political integrity of the singular nation-state, as in Australia, the United States, and South Africa. "Post-Indian" reversals of Western tropes of savagism and civilization continue to emphasize simulations of indigenous peoples in terms of romantic idealism, naturalism, survivance, and an obsessive interest in signs or markers of traditional authenticity (Vizenor and Lee 1999, 86). Nevertheless, visual symbols provide indigenous peoples and their advocates with a powerful medium for performing alterity and community, particularly for nonnative audiences located beyond the region.

In the absence of electoral clout, economic prowess, or military might, the "symbolic capital" accompanying authentically performed cultural identities represents one of the most influential political resources available to indigenous peoples (Conklin 1997). This is not to imply that indigenous peoples necessarily agree on what is their "authentic tradition," particularly when the process of cultural revalorization is itself animated by nationalist aspirations of political liberation (Hanson 1997). In some regions of the world, such as Amazonia and Melanesia, body imagery—with its feathers and paint, appealing to Western views of exoticism and primitivism—constitutes a significant means of cultural performance and political savoir faire (see Wright 1998, 14–15; and Benthall 1998, 19). Similar forces are at play in South Africa's Kagga Kamma theme park, where "authentic" Bushmen wear "traditional" clothing for throngs of tourists. But as Richard B. Lee notes in chapter 2, the Kagga Kamma people's attempt to refashion themselves as the legitimate carriers of timeless tradition is itself predicated on what he calls a "reverse orientalism that reveals the authenticating power that the West can exert over the colonized" subject. Dawid Kruiper, a Kagga Kamma leader, reiterates this irony by opining that the only way the Kagga Kammas' customary way of life can survive is "to live in the memory of those who see us." While acknowledging the benefits of employing exotic visual symbols to foster a politically effective transnational alliance of pro-indigenous and environmental activists, the use of such symbols raises questions about the inherent contradictions of cultural performances that uncritically traffic in strategic essentialisms.

Occidental notions have shaped indigenous modes of activism.[8] Confronted with the need to construct political subjects organized in terms of a perceived shared collective identity, indigenous activists have capitalized on the iconographic conventions accompanying the West's savage slot (as optically inscribed in *National Geographic* photography and in cinematographic representations such as *The Gods Must Be Crazy, Emerald Forest,* and *Dances with Wolves*). Yet, as Graham has argued, this strategy is not without its problems, for it may in fact restrict indigenous peoples' "political maneuverability in national and international arenas" (1998, 163–64). The value of indigenous peoples in the international arena has all too often been predicated on "symbols and images, and not real economic or political advantage" (165). In today's mediatic, or televisualist, global culture, attire is perhaps the most important measure by which indigenous heritage and cultural "authenticity" are valorized.[9] Putatively indigenous and traditional regalia are commonly used as a means of legitimating a group's right to speak and to control a territory.

While indigenous activists have strategically used Western fantasies to their own political advantage, they have themselves been susceptible to challenges questioning their authenticity and cultural purity (Graham 1998, 165; Conklin 1997; Jackson 1994, 1995; Conklin and Graham 1995; Ramos 1994; Maybury-Lewis 1991).[10] Essentialist definitions of indigenity do not allow for the recognition of "unified and inseparable" strands of multiple ancestral heritages and life experiences among distinctive groups such as "mixed bloods" in North America (Penn 1997), mestizos in Latin America, or the Coloured community in South Africa. Certainly, critiquing essentialist portrayals of identity runs the risk of undermining their strategic use in various local and regional movements aimed at the revalorization of indigenous cultural identities. But we feel a cautionary note should be offered here, particularly if we want to avoid simply transposing the labels "oppressed" and "oppressor" and thereby fail to call into question the political system and cultural logic responsible for generating divisive dualisms in the first place.

Self-Determination and the Rights of Indigenous Peoples

Discourse on indigenous rights brings into play the idea of self-determination and the concept of collective rights, two related concepts that are as crucial to the aspirations of indigenous peoples as they are troubling to the majorities in most nation-states. Under international human rights covenants, self-determination is a right of all peoples, and when it is claimed, the subjects are exercising a collective right. The West, however, has historically exhibited deeply ambivalent feelings about collective rights.[11] Many legal theorists in the United States appear to be genuinely perplexed by questions of group rights (Rosen 1997). Throughout the Western industrial world, rights issues are framed largely in terms of the interests of the individual, rather than the community or group. The United States supports a language of legal uniformity—one corpus of laws applied to all citizens in the same way—while simultaneously acknowledging that some groups (such as religious communities, cultural minorities, and Native Americans) are affected differently by the general enforcement of state and/or federal laws. People in the United States have long supported the "ideal of unitarian nationhood without relinquishing their romance of community" (Rosen 1997, 227).

In the international arena, a number of legal instruments have been formulated to guarantee the well-being of indigenous peoples. In 1989, the International Labor Organization (ILO) adopted the Indigenous and Tribal Peoples Convention (No. 169), a revision of the 1957 ILO Convention No. 107, which had been ratified by twenty-seven countries and was the first international treaty pertaining specifically to the rights of indigenous and tribal peoples.[12] These legal measures were undertaken not only to protect the designated peoples, but also to set standards that would influence similar documents, such as the Draft UN Declaration on the Rights of Indigenous Peoples and the draft of the Inter-American Declaration on the Rights of Indigenous Peoples (Swepston 1998, 17–19). Whereas ILO Convention No. 169 specifically mentions "indigenous" *and* "tribal" peoples, the UN draft declaration uses only "indigenous." While the word *indigenous* suffers from the problem of potentially excluding societies that should be covered under the UN draft declaration and similar instruments, the difficulty with the word *peoples* is that some states fear the degree of autonomy that may be claimed by the groups that are included, since in international legal agreements, self-determination is a basic right of all peoples.[13] The term *people* highlights the implicit Western bias in international human rights discourse. It accompanies a liberal definition of human rights based on individual persons, whereas the word *peoples* suggests an alternative conception of rights deriving from membership in a collectivity.

Many states support the general principles of the Draft UN Declaration on the Rights of Indigenous Peoples but reject the notion of self-determination as elaborated in the draft. Similarly, many governments endorse the concept of self-determination but retain their privileges as sovereigns and express concern regarding territorial integrity (Gray and Dahl 1998, 351). Simply put, many state actors fear that the inclusion of self-determination in the draft will advance the claims of ethnic separatists and undermine the state's authority (Scott 1996; cf. Corntassel and Primeau 1995).[14] The misgivings that current states have about indigenous rights that may create "nations within a nation," and particularly about concepts such as autonomy and self-determination, have important European precedents. Autonomy is an expression of self-determination, a right ostensibly guaranteed by international law to all peoples on the planet. Official recognition of cultural difference can jeopardize the unity of the state when calls for indigenous autonomy amount to secessionist demands or thinly veiled ethnic chauvinism. Nevertheless, it is important to recognize that indigenous rights are not in themselves contrary or threatening to the existence of states. We believe that indigenous rights may well serve as a sort of litmus test for postcolonial states championing democracy and cultural pluralism. In other words, a state that is more willing to acknowledge the rights of its indigenous peoples has more obviously transcended forms of neo-colonial governance.

Perspectives from the Crossroads: Identity and Indigenous Rights in the Context of Postcolonial States

To avoid the drawbacks of positing either an essentialized indigenous identity (celebrated for its resistance to colonial incursions or for its ability to authorize its own cultural productions) or the complete loss of local identity as a result of the forces of globalization and the assimilationist power grid of postcolonial states, we opt instead for a third perspective. This emphasizes how indigenous peoples' inescapable insertion into an interconnected world is infused by and intermittently unsettled by their self-conscious sense of coming from "distinctive" cultural spaces.

The ethnographic cases presented in this volume show that despite a diversity of scenarios in Africa, Asia, the Americas, and Oceania (map 1 indicates the chapter numbers corresponding to particular regions), the struggle for indigenous rights confronts a common core of critical issues around the world. The sociopolitical, cultural, and economic objectives of indigenous peoples everywhere are in many

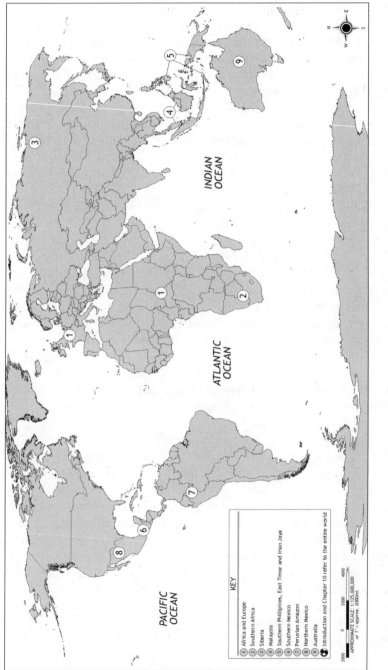

World map displaying the focus of the essays in this volume. Numbers correspond to chapters. (Cartography by Nate Greenberg, Talon Associates, 2001.)

respects similar. These peoples want a secure land base, control over their natural resources, a modicum of political autonomy, the right to speak their ancestral languages, and freedom of religious and cultural expression. The contributors to this volume demonstrate how state governments and their political and corporate allies have all too often pursued ethnocidal policies aimed at extinguishing indigenous peoples' cultural survival. In the name of "progress," economic "development," and "nation building," states have expropriated indigenous territories for mining and logging, forced peoples from their homelands, encouraged them to abandon their traditional languages and cultures, and turned them into folkloric national citizens and international tourist commodities.

In response to these pressures, indigenous peoples have not only relied on various "weapons of the weak" (Scott 1985), they have also begun organizing themselves, by forming political parties and advocacy groups. This political mobilization has occurred across the globe, from Mexico to Malaysia, from Peru to the Philippines. For their part, state governments and their allies have often tried to muzzle emergent indigenous movements by intimidating their leaders and supporters. The tendency of postcolonial states to silence calls for indigenous autonomy is illustrated in a number of the essays in this volume. The independence movement in East Timor, one of the three cases in Southeast Asia about which Benedict Anderson writes in chapter 5, represented just such a scenario: the Indonesian state relied until very recently on the barrels of guns to quash cries for self-governance.

Indonesia invaded East Timor in 1975, following the collapse of Portuguese colonial rule. Indonesian occupation of the eastern half of the island of Timor continued until the fall of the Suharto regime and the 1999 UN-sponsored referendum that granted provisional independence. Pro-Indonesian militia groups retaliated by slaughtering hundreds of people and destroying much of East Timor's infrastructure. A UN peacekeeping force intervened in September 1999, causing most of the pro-Jakarta militia to flee to West Timor, which remains under Indonesian rule. As part of the transition to self-governance, the UN sent about eight thousand peacekeeping troops to East Timor, and scheduled elections. As a result, pro-independence leader Xanana Gusmao met with leaders of the pro-Indonesian militia bands that devastated East Timor during the 1999 carnage.

While the contributors to this book reveal the brutal and violent consequences of attacking the nation-state at its core, they also draw attention to the ongoing erosion of the nation-state's absolutist claims to sovereignty—indigenous rights movements being one such challenge. Global interest in indigenous rights claims has accompanied the overall rise of the human rights movement internationally. This increased attention to indigenous rights has been associated with the growth in literacy rates and greater accessibility to the media—including the Internet, which has made the plight of subordinated peoples more apparent to the public. Discourse about the need to recognize the rights of indigenous peoples carries unprecedented prestige in the international community, as well as in some national contexts. The political rhetoric that indigenous spokespersons and their allies rely on to bolster indigenous peoples' claims and to voice their resistance to state-driven policies and practices has several distinctive features. It is a rhetoric of respect and empathy that unites views of indigenous peoples' special sociopolitical status "with a historical critique of the manner in which governments have denied them ordinary civil rights" (Dyck 1985, 15). Strategically speaking, it is discourse that attempts to stir disinclined governments into action by appealing to what Dyck calls the "politics of embarrassment" (15). Both analysts and activists are challenged not only to gauge whether human rights discourse amounts to more than paper promises, but also to unmask the hidden agendas of state actors deploying oppositional discourses to justify their continued pillage of indigenous lands, resources, and cultural traditions.

Before embarking on an exploration of the use and abuse of indigenous rights in various parts of the world, it is necessary to get one's intellectual bearings by reflecting critically on the notion of "rights" in general. What are rights? Who has them? And is everyone entitled to them equally? Parker Shipton's opening chapter in this volume addresses these questions by presenting an anthropology of rights. He considers both the possibilities and the limitations implicit in translating essentially European ideas about rights into non-Western cultural contexts. Drawing heavily on his perspective as an Africanist, Shipton demonstrates that rights are radically contingent on the culturally constructed worlds in which they are embedded. This does not mean that universal claims for human rights are impossible or misguided. It does, however, imply that everyone—development planners, anthropological advocates, and theorists—needs to look carefully at the unexamined bases of bias and commit themselves to the principle that a balanced treatment of such delicate matters is a basic right in itself.

If analyses of rights need to be contextualized, then discussions of indigenous rights hinge upon considerations of who is indigenous. It is precisely this issue that Richard Lee explores in his analysis of identity politics in post-apartheid southern Africa (chap. 2). The rediscovery, valorization, and reimagination of indigenous histories and ethnic identities are one of the most significant developments in the post-apartheid era. As Lee argues, the revival of Khoisan identity has entailed not only recapturing history, but also affirming new ethnic identities.

In Siberia, the tenacity of indigenous identity has accompanied religious revival and grassroots political mobilization (Balzer 1999). Analysis of the negotiation of supralocal ethnic identities in the face of state "transition" takes precedence in chapter 3, where Marjorie Mandelstam Balzer assesses the plight of indigenous peoples in northwest Siberia. Interethnic conflict in the far-flung empire of the Soviet Union resulted from localized conflicts that were exacerbated by disruptive economic and cultural policies emanating from the metropolis. The postcolonial legacy of this strife continues to shape the character of indigenous peoples' struggles for cultural survival. Despite a number of promising developments, such as the creation of the multiethnic Sakha Republic, Siberia's indigenous peoples are caught "between systems" in a plight Balzer appositely calls "dependency without sustenance." Saddled with difficult historical legacies, these peoples are now striving to refashion themselves to adapt to demographic decline and a changed political and economic order.

In chapter 4, Kirk Endicott examines the place of indigenous peoples in a so-called plural society—Malaysia, which comprises culturally distinctive and economically specialized ethnic groups (Malays, Chinese, Indians, and indigenous peoples) that coexist yet remain socially divided. While the recognition of ethnic difference is itself an important ingredient in the relative stability of Malaysia's political history, Endicott demonstrates how ethnically based interest politics have marginalized the country's numerically small and politically vulnerable indigenous peoples of Borneo (Iban, Bidayuh, Melanau, Bajau, Murut, Kadazan, Rungus, and Penan) and the Malay Peninsula (Orang Asli). For Malaysia's indigenous peoples, the state has failed to live up to the promise of cultural pluralism.

The consequences of nationalism for indigenous peoples are taken up in Benedict Anderson's essay (chap. 5). Anderson develops three primary levels of analysis: (1) the changing international climate that allows new states to join the UN; (2) the nature of postcolonial states' strategies for national incorporation; and (3) the emergence of separatist nationalisms among three politically marginalized "indigenous peoples": Moros in the Philippines; East Timorese; and Papuans in

Irian Jaya. A major predicament that he considers is to what extent these three emergent nationalisms obey the homogenizing tendency of all nationalisms. Anderson concludes by pondering the extent to which existing indigenous peoples are obliged to be subordinated—and hence radically transformed—in the name of cultural survival.

In chapter 6, Lynn Stephen assesses the prospects for nation formation from below. By exploring the various ways that indigenous peoples in southern Mexico are mobilizing claims to their past and their cultural heritage in reaction to economic restructuring aimed at facilitating "free trade," Stephen examines how local nationalisms—or what she aptly calls "imagined communities in the plural"—spawn distinct conceptions of the broader nation. Taking her lead from Florencia Mallon's influential work (1995), Stephen charts the development of the ideology of "indigenous autonomy" in Chiapas, follows its growth at the national level, and then underscores the challenges of creating a national network out of disparate local and regional experiences. These contradictions are particularly evident in indigenous women's challenges to "tradition" when it is deployed in ways that constrain their autonomy—a point also taken up by Bartholomew Dean in chapter 7.

Dean tackles the issue of gender inequality in indigenous Amazonian federations that are led only by men. This exclusion of women from leadership positions in supralocal political forums is often justified in Peruvian Amazonia by appeal to "tradition." Dean's discussion provokes larger considerations of the role of gender hierarchies, educational opportunities, and local politics in the struggle for indigenous representation, and he invites readers to pay closer attention to the ways in which "tradition" is strategically invoked to exclude certain groups while empowering others. Notwithstanding these limitations, the Amazonian indigenous movement continues to be identified with a discourse of equality, and it thus carries an enormous moral weight capable of mobilizing collective social action.

Questions of political agency are also explored in chapter 8, where Jerome Levi, moving from local to global levels of representation, illustrates how the Rarámuri (Tarahumara) of northern Mexico employ a wide range of responses to multiple problems affecting their environment and communities. These responses include conventional displays of silence, withdrawal, and passive resistance, as well as more recent assertions of their rights through public protest, participation in multiethnic coalitions, and running for political office in local and even national elections. This diversity, however, has frequently been obfuscated by homogenizing discourses and ethnographic orientations privileging descriptions of "tradition" over new and hybrid forms of social action. Rarámuri strategies of silence can and often do coexist with acts of speaking out, which shows the need for cultural analysis that is dynamic enough to describe social praxis that draws upon "convention" as well as "invention" (see Watanabe 1992; and Hanson 1989). In describing different parts of Mexico, the chapters by Stephen and Levi demonstrate that in countries with diverse indigenous peoples, it is important to remain sensitive to different cultural constructions of indigenous action.

The indigenous movement in Australia, as in Mexico, is socially heterogeneous and marked by an intense need to come to terms with a painful national history. In chapter 9, Ian McIntosh compares and contrasts the personal, pan-Aboriginal perspectives on reconciliation with the largely "impersonal" federal Australian approach to national reconciliation. Highlighting the challenges facing Australia's indigenous peoples, McIntosh's discussion of Aboriginal understandings of "unity in diversity" through the metaphor of the intermixing of saltwater and freshwater peoples urges us to take seriously the possibilities of reconciliation. Influenced by the twin notion of "membership and remembership," many Aborigines have begun considering their new roles and responsibilities in the worlds they inhabit beyond the "traditional" boundaries of their sacred homelands. McIntosh suggests that the multiple levels of communal membership activated by the Dreaming provide the various parties locked in conflict with a means to achieve reconciliation.

David Maybury-Lewis's summary chapter reiterates an issue of central concern in many of the essays: the relationship between indigenous autonomy, self-determination, and secession. Autonomy for indigenous peoples usually means the right to exercise local control over their affairs, but within the larger framework of the nation-state. As Maybury-Lewis argues, indigenous people's struggles for cultural autonomy do not necessarily subvert the state. Rather, their efforts become a threat when authoritarian and assimilationist national governments attempt to silence indigenous peoples by refusing to recognize the pluriethnic nature of the nation-state.

Through a review of the history of Cultural Survival, the human rights organization he cofounded, Maybury-Lewis chronicles the gradual change in world opinion, which has increasingly come to embrace, rather than reject, the necessity of pluriethnic states. In Maybury-Lewis's estimation, the international indigenous movement is now engaging with "interlocutors who understand what indigenous peoples want and who are willing to negotiate with them." Private and public organizations are now providing critically needed financial support and technical assistance for the creation and ongoing operation of indigenous advocacy organizations. Thanks in part to the vitality of this diverse and committed advocacy movement, the rights of indigenous peoples now figure as part of the world's official agenda. Anthropologists are in a special position to help take the initiative in demonstrating that marginalized indigenous peoples are not archaic (Levi 1998a; Dean 1999a, 2000) nor a threat to economic "development," once they are given an opportunity to participate in it and enjoy its fruits. Through education and outreach, pro-indigenous academics and advocates can help make the public aware of the plight and the prospects for indigenous peoples.

Each essay in this volume describes a specific set of circumstances at a specific point in time. Of course, there have been changes in the world, including indigenous affairs, since this project was begun in late 1997. Nonetheless, the broader structural relations, challenges, and opportunities facing indigenous peoples in the present era have remained largely unaltered. Indeed, the ability of our authors to situate recent events within the scope of culturally salient patterns and processes is what makes their essays ethnography rather than journalism. The recent developments in Mexico (discussed in chapters 6 and 8) and Southeast Asia (discussed in chapter 5) illustrate this point.

In July 2000, Mexico elected Vicente Fox of the center-right National Action Party (PAN) as its new president. This event signaled the nation's willingness to make the transition to democracy, after seventy-one years of single-party rule by the Institutional Revolutionary Party (PRI). One of the most pressing issues that Fox inherited from the former government was the unresolved national debate on indigenous rights and a virtual civil war in the southern state of Chiapas, an ongoing conflict that had begun when Maya rebels emerged there in January 1994 as the Zapatista Army of National Liberation (EZLN). At the heart of the controversy were the San Andrés Accords on Indigenous Rights and Culture, which outlined constitutional reforms in the areas of indigenous rights, cultural autonomy, land reform, and political participation. The accords were signed in February 1996 by representatives of the federal government and the EZLN and were endorsed by the recently formed National Indigenous Congress (CNI). Yet the government of that time consistently failed to implement the accords, even though its own representatives had signed them.

Vowing during his campaign that his first act as president would be to implement the accords, Fox seemed to make good on this promise four days after taking office on December 1, 2000, by sending a proposal for implementation to the Mexican Senate. During the first few months of his administration, there were indications that a new relationship between indigenous peoples and the Mexican state might be in the offing. Fox ordered the dismantling of military blockades in Chiapas, and in March 2001 he saw to it that representatives of the EZLN and the CNI addressed the Mexican Congress and that EZLN leader Subcomandante Marcos spoke safely in Mexico City's Zócalo, to the largest crowds that had gathered there since the Revolution. In late April 2001, the Senate claimed to have ratified the accords with the passage of a wide range of constitutional reforms on indigenous issues. But these reforms, which replaced the proposal sent by Fox, had been unilaterally drafted by the Senate, without consultation with the EZLN, CNI, or their representatives. In essence, these reforms violated both the letter and the spirit of the San Andrés Accords, and they have been rejected almost unanimously by Mexico's indigenous movement. As of this writing, the final outcome remains uncertain, but for the indigenous peoples of Mexico, their demands remain unfulfilled (Levi, 2002).[15]

Similarly, important developments have taken place in Southeast Asia. East Timor gained independence in May 2002. The United States is back in the Philippines hunting down "terrorists" in Moroland said to be backed by Al Qaeda. Moreover, Irianese/Paupan nationalism has made great strides. Their principal leader was recently assassinated by the military but some of the low-level murderers are going on trial (B. Anderson, personal communication).

Conclusion: Anthropology and the Cultural Survival of Indigenous Peoples

We maintain that contemporary indigenous struggles worldwide can be summed up in the form of a paradox. Over the past two and a half decades, the international community has witnessed a change in the political climate such that many nation-states have become more tolerant of difference. In order to avail themselves of new political openings, indigenous peoples face a double bind: they must become activists to protect their rights, yet by becoming activists they may jeopardize their special status as "indigenous," which is the basis of their claims. What is the solution to the risks of being heard?

First, as the contributors to this volume argue, it is only by building

on the emancipatory potential of postcolonial indigenity that indigenous peoples can extricate themselves from this apparent paradox.
Second, the public at large must jettison its "imperialist nostalgia"
(Rosaldo 1989, 68–87)–the idea that insists on linking indigenous
authenticity with exotic alterity, while absolving imperialism for its
own role in destroying the "traditional" cultures it now demands to see
and hear. By acknowledging that the cherished association between
indigenous legitimacy and representations of the Exotic Other is a conventional but not necessary connection, the international community
will realize the importance of seeing indigenous peoples representing
themselves for who they are, rather than permitting them to speak only
when they cater to the confused logic of our own colonial longings.
The central contention of this book, therefore, is that the category of
native, aboriginal, or indigenous peoples—although formerly an
instrument of oppression wielded by colonial powers—is emerging in
today's postcolonial environment as a platform for the mobilization of
identity and political action among diverse peoples, both within and
between existing countries.

The complexity of indigenous identity, its internal heterogeneity
and outward performance, and its utter dependence on multiple cultural, political, and historical contexts are all areas that have been
receiving more attention in recent years. Research has demonstrated
significant intragroup diversity in identity formation and transformation and has included analysis of the significant roles of numerous factors: media and information technology; national and international
frameworks; religious conversion, ritual healing, and the moral order;
violence; academic and participatory research agendas; state systems;
and indigenous peoples' personal perspectives.[16] Two significant areas
that our case studies do not address are the leading role taken by
Native Americans in articulating indigenous rights, and the relations
between indigenous peoples and biodiversity, conservation, and intellectual property rights.[17] We see this book as complementing these rich
bodies of literature. Our collection of case studies is significant not only
for recognizing that specific historical circumstances influence the politics of cultural identity, but also for reminding us of the critical need
to expand anthropology's gaze.

In the wake of its emergence from postmodernist concerns, the possibilities of practical action and advocacy are returning to the forefront
of a politically committed and morally engaged anthropology
(Scheper-Hughes 1995; D'Andrade 1995), one that is reclaiming its
"critically humanist sensibilities" (Knauft 1996). Moreover, the grow-

ing international acknowledgment of group rights, acceptance of the benefits of cultural pluralism, and recognition of the plight of subaltern peoples have provided the stimulus for the reimagination of how indigenous peoples are portrayed both in ethnographic and in popular accounts. Overall, these efforts are aimed not at creating a time warp and preserving indigenous "societies in aspic" (Geertz 1998); rather, they are being conceived to give indigenous peoples a real voice as formidable stakeholders in determining their own futures and the shape of their cultural survival.

Anthropology's support for the rights of indigenous peoples presupposes a rediscovery of our discipline's roots (such as Lewis Henry Morgan's defense of the Seneca in Washington, D.C., or Franz Boas's moral and empirical critique of racism), as well as a candid examination of the mass media, the global economy, and the various motivations underpinning exotic representations of indigenous peoples. The challenge remains how to translate the reimagined account of the Other in ways that promote the reconfiguration of regional, national, and international policies and beliefs that adversely affect the lives of the world's indigenous peoples and ethnic minorities (Dean 1999a).[18] For anthropology, this vital enterprise entails articulating the various components of cultural identity constitutive of social being in ways that promote multiple attachments and facilitate complex, and at times deeply contradictory, affiliations.

To this end, anthropological research has begun assessing the connections between micro and macro domains within the state and within the international arena. Likewise, the contributors to this volume explore ethnic and national identities in relation to power hierarchies in local, regional, and transnational arenas. This is an important corrective to the shortcomings of anthropology's traditional reliance on participant observation at the local level. By examining the collective representations of social, political, economic, and cultural boundaries as refractions of domination, struggle, negotiation, accommodation, reciprocity, and resistance, anthropology now plays an integral role in exploring the politics of cultural identity as a means for comprehending, reproducing, and transforming social relations.

In addition to publishing research findings that can provide support for indigenous peoples' legal and political battles to secure recognition of their rights (Appell 1985, xvii), anthropologists can aid the efforts of advocacy groups, by lending them technical assistance and advice based on the experience of listening to the voiced aspirations of indigenous peoples themselves. In the face of worldwide "language death"

(Crystal 2000), support for and understanding of the expressive genres of indigenous peoples has become vitally important to their cultural survival (see, among others, Watahomigie and Yamamoto 1992; Garzon et al. 1998; Watahomigie, McCarty, and Yamamoto 1999; and Dean 1999c, 2001).

Cultural survival is a relative concept; it is not about cultural stasis. It involves, as David Maybury-Lewis notes in chapter 10, a people's "cultural control and continuity" in the face of an ever-changing world dominated by global processes. In addition to a secure land base, it means freedom of religious, cultural, and linguistic expression—rights that members of dominant national groups all too often take for granted. Notwithstanding governments' historical disinclination to act in behalf of subalterns, the participation of indigenous peoples in national and international forums is an essential part of transforming abstract policy formulations into long-awaited results that make a real difference in peoples' lives (Quesenberry 1997).

Indigenous confederations and their political allies, including scholars, nongovernmental organizations, and environmentalists (see Johnston 1997), have joined forces to exert pressure on governments in an effort to "secure a place at the negotiating table" (Kolata 1998, 3). As demonstrated by a number of the essays in this volume, ethnic federations have assumed a new importance in voicing the supralocal political concerns of indigenous minorities, though for some it is their tactical silence, relative invisibility, and conspicuous underrepresentation that warrant understanding and merit closer analysis. Negotiation between center and periphery over what constitutes use or abuse of indigenous lands, particularly concerning natural resources and the conservation of protected or fragile environments, is a recurring theme in this book.

There can be no substitute for the practical lessons learned through advocacy and cooperation in projects meant to secure indigenous rights. Such experience cannot be separated, however, from understanding how different levels of identity mobilization place indigenous peoples at a decisive point, allowing them—sometimes for the first time in their history—not only to assess the stakes involved in the struggle for their own culture's survival, but also to voice their concerns. While not without risks, the articulation of indigenous peoples' rights-based claims is integral to sustaining a public realm that allows for critical reflection and the potential resolution of some of the most fundamental dilemmas confronting humanity. While postcolonial states must forge effective unity in their "national" projects, they must at the same time recognize heterogeneity and not expunge or silence the plurality of indigenous people's voices in their ongoing struggles for autonomy and cultural survival. Such a path calls for a sustained reconceptualization of the connections between social change and cultural continuity. The contributors to this volume demonstrate how peoples' attachments to their indigenous identity have been shaped by variable personal and group associations, which are part of the wider fabric of changing national circumstances, and by specific mediating international contexts, such as the organized indigenous rights movement.

In light of the humanitarian debacles in Chiapas and Dili—not to mention Mogadishu and Sarajevo—the prevalent orthodoxy suggesting that "the categorical imperative of human rights will provide the moral underpinnings of a better world" is, as Rieff argues, sadly misguided (1999, 14). Simply formulating more precise or encompassing legal doctrines when the world has no way of effectively implementing or guaranteeing international law is not an answer (Robinson 1999, 8; Rieff 1999, 14; Macdonald 1994). But if the plea for universal human rights is bereft of its moral efficacy, then what? Humanizing the plight of indigenous peoples is a constructive step toward wresting moral authority away from dominant groups who have all too often failed to protect the rights of indigenous peoples and ethnic minorities. Through critically examining the inevitably case-specific yet maddeningly complex contexts and circumstances of indigenous peoples in postcolonial states, the authors of the essays presented here describe emergent fields of social action that can be undertaken in ways that enhance moral accountability and facilitate greater human solidarity. Such action involves sensitivity to the contingencies and contexts of social practice in which indigenous peoples choose to engage.

Acknowledging contemporary anthropology's reticence to generalize, its calls for "ethnographies of the particular" (Abu-Lughod 1991, 149), and its assertions that individuals too must be understood as sites of multiple subjectivities, the contributors to this volume recognize a need to theorize heterogeneity among indigenous peoples, without reproducing an intellectual corollary to the imperialist's military strategy of divide and conquer. They do so whether the peoples about whom they write are located in former empires, whole continents or parts of them, single countries, or individual "localized" cultures. Some groups have been able to revalorize reviled histories as a proto-nationalism or otherwise refashion their cultural genealogies as celebratory vindications of their cultural survival and legitimate place in the world, often building on the emancipatory potential encoded in their self-description as "indigenous peoples." This is by no means true for all marginalized collectivities. Clearly, the answer for indigenous peoples is not to reject their past, but instead to fully embrace the predicament that their past often presents for them. By acknowledging the pragmatic urgency of generating discourses and practices capable of transcending former boundaries and creating venues for new alliances, plural rights, and collective action, indigenous peoples and their allies will be better equipped to straddle or sidestep crises in their attempts to realize unity through diversity.

Notes

1. On the political and practical implications of "life stories," see McKinley 1997; and Fisher 1998.

2. The *Oxford English Dictionary* (1986) tells us that *indigenous* comes from the Latin term *indigena,* which literally means "inborn person." The word appeared in English as early as 1646, when Sir Thomas Browne distinguished the Africans serving under the Spaniards from the native, or indigenous, inhabitants of the Americas. In spite of its linguistic longevity, there is a general sense that the label fails to distinguish adequately among the immense variety of peoples who are heaped together under it. A number of competing terms are in currency, such as First Nations, Aboriginal Peoples, and Native Americans, to name but a few.

3. Brownlie notes that before the Second World War, the term *indigenous peoples* was not in vogue, except for its appearance in certain legal conventions approved by the International Labor Organization between 1930 and 1939. In these "early" instances of its use, the term referred to indigenous workers (Brownlie 1992, 56).

4. For instance, one can speak intelligibly about "games," a favorite example of Wittgenstein's, even though there is no single criterion or finite set of traits common to all games. Neither balls, cards, teams, competitiveness, winning, skill, entertainment, nor even rule-guidedness are a feature of all phenomena classed as games. Still, there is a "family resemblance" among games due to the existence of a number of overlapping and complex relations. Hence, games exist as a logically permissible and conceptually sensible category of things, notwithstanding the lack of a definitive set of common attributes.

5. See, among others, Amnesty International 1992a, 1992b; Anaya 1996; Barsh 1996; Brownlie 1992; Burger 1998; Greaves 1994; Heinz 1988; Hitchcock 1994; ILO 1953; Price Cohen 1998; Pritchard 1998; Rosen 1997; Sanders 1989; Stamatopoulou 1994; Swepston 1989; Tennant 1994; and Ismaelillo and Wright 1982.

6. This is not to deny that ethnic distinctions predate colonialism, as Kirk Endicott notes in chapter 4 for the case of Malaysia. Like other contributors, Endicott argues that the idea of indigenous peoples makes sense only in terms

of the politics accompanying nation-states. He maintains that indigenous peoples are disadvantaged ethnic groups that have been denied the benefits of full citizenship conferred by the state and enjoyed by those who control national government.

7. Many of the true "last colonies" are found in places such as the Balkans, Tibet, and Kurdistan. Most of the remnants of colonialism are geographically tiny, except Greenland, and sparsely populated—although Puerto Rico, for example, boasts a population of more than three million and is larger than many sovereign nations (see Aldrich and Connell 1998).

8. Admittedly, *occidental* and *Western* are terms that suffer from the same homogenizing tendencies that are, we argue, implicit in the phrase *indigenous peoples*.

9. Many see the adoption of "Western" clothing styles as tantamount to the abandonment of indigenous cultural heritage (cf. Braun 1995, 13). Yet the "ethnic badge" of indigenous heritage is marked by modes of dress that are themselves paradoxically dependent on and historically intermeshed with occidental technologies (Roe 1995, 38–39) and "hybridized" aesthetic sensibilities (García Canclini 1995). Recent scholarship has persuasively highlighted the creative potential signaled by the colonial encounter, particularly as it represented increased access to "alluring" imported goods (see, e.g., Orlove 1997).

10. The visual performance of identity—in this case, indigenous peoples' imitations of the dominant society's way of representing indigenous authenticity—appears to be an important political strategy that subaltern groups can follow to assert their difference. Nevertheless, this situation gives rise to the postmodern paradox that some have called the "dereferentialization imparted by the simulacrum" (Caiuby Novaes 1997, 24). This occurs when people dress up and paint themselves in ways that coincide remarkably with our popular imagery of what indigenous people should look like. In some cases, this has meant authenticating "indigenous" identities by embracing modes of dress and body attire that do not correspond with local realities. Conversely, indigenous peoples who have appropriated Western clothing and social conventions are seen—both by the dominant society and by the transnational indigenous movement—as subscribing to false, nonindigenous rhetorics, whose perceived inauthenticity subverts their political claims and ultimately serves to silence their voice.

11. By *ambivalent* we mean to signal the complex mix of appeal, intrigue, repulsion, and aversion characteristic of the relationship between the dominant national society and indigenous peoples. Seldom are indigenous peoples completely opposed to the dominant national societies in which they find themselves embedded. More commonly, their actions vis-à-vis the national society inhabit a space marked by complicity and resistance, subordination and defiance. Ambivalence also characterizes the postcolonial state and the relationship of its actors toward indigenous peoples. State policies formulated for indigenous communities are often a mix of paternalistic nurturing and hos-

tile negation of indigenous identity and rights claims. By bringing into question the simple equation of master-servant or colonizer-colonized, ambivalence, like hybridity, tends to destabilize the authority of colonial discourse, and thus it is an important site for critical inquiry (see Bhabha 1994; Young 1995; and Dean 1999b).

12. Although ILO 169 is largely regarded as the best international legal instrument supporting indigenous rights, it may also imply certain limitations regarding self-determination, as appositely noted by Díaz Polanco and Sánchez (2000). This is because ILO 169 states that when the word *peoples* appears in the document in reference to "indigenous and tribal peoples," it should not be inferred that it has the same meaning as does the word *peoples* when it appears in international law. This caveat effectively takes the teeth out of the document, because in international legal agreements, self-determination is a basic right of all peoples. Thus, governments may be signing ILO 169, appeasing their indigenous peoples, and apparently demonstrating to the international community how tolerant they are when in actuality the convention they have ratified accords to "indigenous and tribal peoples" only vague cultural rights, and not even the first principle of political rights of peoples— the right to self-determination. Consequently, in uncritically supporting ILO 169 and similar legal documents, indigenous peoples throughout the world may not be advancing their rights, but rather limiting them, by unwittingly amplifying the power of the states in which they live.

13. Inconsistencies and complexities abound in the Draft United Nations Declaration on the Rights of Indigenous Peoples, which uses the word *peoples* even in its title. Of the forty-five articles in the draft declaration, Article 3 "is considered by indigenous organizations as fundamental to the entire text"; it reads: "Indigenous peoples have the right to self-determination. By virtue of that right they freely determine their political status and freely pursue their economic, social, and cultural development" (Burger 1998, 7). But the document, finished in 1993, was completed by a subcommission that the UN persists in calling the Working Group on Indigenous *Populations.* Desiring to use the word *peoples* without implying that self-determination means secession from existing states, the ILO Conference on Convention 169 "therefore was forced to insert the following provision as paragraph three of Article one: 'The use of the term "peoples" in this Convention shall not be construed as having any implications as regards the rights which may attach to the term under international law'" (Swepston 1998, 22). Recently, however, even the word *population* has become unacceptable to the governments of many sovereign states. The connection of the word *peoples* with the concept of self-determination is the greatest, but not the only, concern with the word's use.

14. Many questions have yet to be resolved in the Draft UN Declaration on the Rights of Indigenous Peoples. Though many in the UN have applauded the overall human rights principles developed in the draft, the practicalities of implementation remain problematic (Barsh 1996).

15. Many thanks to Joshua Paulson for his astute assessment of recent developments in indigenous affairs in Mexico.

16. For a review of the impact of media and information technology on identity formation and transformation, see Escobar 1994; Fair in press; Ginsburg 1997; Smith and Ward 2000; Dean 2001; Leuthold 1998; Nash 1997; and Ronfeldt et al. 1998. National and international frameworks are addressed in Anaya 1996; Collier and Quaratiello 1994; Fisher 1998; Harvey 1998; Pritchard 1998; Price Cohen 1998; Ramos 1998; Warren 1998; and Macdonald 1999. On religious conversion, ritual healing, and indigenous moral orders, see Bucko 1999; Csordas 1999; George 1996; Gossen 1999; Levi 1999a; and Molinari 1998. The subject of violence and indigenous peoples is taken up in Nagel 1999; Dean 1999b, 2002; Schirmer 2000; and Stephen 1999. Academic and participatory research agendas are discussed in Hess 1997; Salas and Tillmann 1998; Smith 1999; and Reed 1997. State systems and indigenous peoples are the focus of Collins 1998; Gelles 2000; Levi 1998b, 1998c, 2000; and Perry 1996. Finally, indigenous peoples' personal perspectives are addressed in Battiste 2000; and Burgete Cal y Mayor 2000.

17. On the role played by Native Americans and their advocates in articulating indigenous rights, see, among others, Benedek 1992; Champagne 1999; LaDuke 1999; and Johnson 1999. On the relations between indigenous peoples and biodiversity, conservation, and intellectual property rights, see Brush and Stabinsky 1996; Greaves 1994; Herlihy 1997; Johnston 1997; and Dean 1995.

18. Clearly, this also entails the productive interrogation of the tensions implied by "indigenous" critical scholarship or "native" anthropology—a topic beyond the scope of this essay (see, among others, Ohnuki-Tierney 1984; Narayan 1993; Kanaaneh 1997; and Knauft 1999).

References

Abu-Lughod, Lila. 1991. Writing against Culture. In *Recapturing Anthropology: Working in the Present,* edited by R. G. Fox, 137–62. Santa Fe: School of American Research Press.

Aldrich, Robert, and John Connell. 1998. *The Last Colonies.* Cambridge: Cambridge University Press.

Amnesty International. 1992a. *Human Rights Violations against the Indigenous Peoples of the Americas.* New York: Amnesty International.

———. 1992b. *United States of America: Human Rights and American Indians.* New York: Amnesty International.

Anaya, James. 1996. *Indigenous Peoples in International Law.* New York: Oxford University Press.

Anderson, Benedict. 1983. *Imagined Communities: Reflections on the Origin and Spread of Nationalism.* London: Verso.

———. 1998. *The Spectre of Comparisons: Nationalism, Southeast Asia, and the World.* London: Verso.

Appell, George, ed. 1985. Preface to *Modernization and the Emergence of a*

Landless Peasantry: Essays on the Integration of Peripheries to Socioeconomic Centers. Studies in Third World Societies Publication No. 33. Williamsburg, Va.: Studies in Third World Societies.

Appiah, Kwame Anthony, and Henry Louis Gates, Jr. 1995. *Identities.* Chicago: University of Chicago Press.

Balzer, Marjorie Mandelstam. 1999. *The Tenacity of Ethnicity.* Princeton: Princeton University Press.

Barsh, Russel Lawrence. 1996. Indigenous Peoples and the UN Commission on Human Rights: A Case of the Immovable Object and the Irresistible Force. *Human Rights Quarterly* 18 (4): 782–816.

Battiste, Marie, ed. 2000. *Reclaiming Indigenous Voice and Vision.* Vancouver: University of British Columbia Press.

Benedek, Emily. 1992. *The Wind Won't Know Me: A History of the Navajo-Hopi Land Dispute.* New York: Knopf.

Benthall, Jonathan. 1998. Indigenes' Rights, Anthropologists' Roots? *Anthropology Today* 14 (2): 18–19.

Béteille, André. 1998. The Idea of Indigenous People. *Current Anthropology* 39 (2): 187–91.

Bhabha, H. K. 1994. *The Location of Culture.* London: Routledge.

Bowen, John. 2000. Should We Have a Universal Concept of "Indigenous Peoples' Rights"? *Anthropology Today* 16 (4): 12–16.

Braun, Barbara. 1995. The Amazon Today. In *Arts of the Amazon,* edited by B. Braun, 13–16. London: Thames and Hudson.

Brown Childs, John, and Guillermo Delgado-P. 1999. On the Idea of the Indigenous. *Current Anthropology* 40 (2): 211–12.

Brownlie, Ian. 1992. *Treaties and Indigenous Peoples.* Edited by F. M. Brookfield. Oxford: Clarendon Press.

Brush, Stephen, and Doreen Stabinsky. 1996. *Valuing Local Knowledge: Indigenous People and Intellectual Property Rights.* Washington, D.C.: Island Press.

Bucko, Raymond. 1999. *The Lakota Ritual of the Sweat Lodge: History and Contemporary Practice.* Lincoln: University of Nebraska Press.

Burger, Julian. 1998. Indigenous Peoples and the United Nations. In *The Human Rights of Indigenous Peoples,* edited by C. Price Cohen, 3–16. Ardsley, N.Y.: Transnational Publishers.

Burgete Cal y Mayor, Aracely, ed. 2000. *Indigenous Autonomy in Mexico.* Copenhagen: International Work Group for Indigenous Affairs.

Caiuby Novaes, Sylvia. 1997. *The Play of Mirrors: The Representation of Self Mirrored in the Other.* Translated by I. M. Burbridge. Austin: University of Texas Press.

Canby, Peter. 1999. The Truth about Rigoberta Menchú. *New York Review of Books* 46 (6): 28–38.

Carneiro da Cunha, Manuela, and Mauro de Almeida. 2000. Indigenous People, Traditional People, and Conservation in the Amazon. *Daedalus* 129 (2): 315.

Champagne, Duane. 1999. *Contemporary Native American Cultural Issues.* Walnut Creek, Calif.: AltaMira Press.

Clifford, James. 1988. *The Predicament of Culture: Twentieth-Century Ethnography, Literature, and Art.* Cambridge, Mass.: Harvard University Press.

Collier, George, and Elizabeth Quaratiello. 1994. *Basta! Land and the Zapatista Rebellion in Chiapas.* Oakland, Calif.: Food First Book.

Collins, James. 1998. *Understanding Tolowa Histories: Western Hegemonies and Native American Responses.* New York: Routledge.

Conklin, Beth. 1997. Body Paint, Feathers, and VCRs: Aesthetics and Authenticity in Amazonian Activism. *American Ethnologist* 24 (4): 711–37.

Conklin, Beth A., and Laura R. Graham. 1995. The Shifting Middle Ground: Amazonian Indians and Eco-politics. *American Anthropologist* 97 (4): 695–721.

Corntassel, Jeff J., and Tomas Hopkins Primeau. 1995. Indigenous "Sovereignty" and International Law: Revised Strategies for Pursuing "Self-Determination." *Human Rights Quarterly* 17 (2): 343–65.

Crystal, David. 2000. *Language Death.* Cambridge: Cambridge University Press.

Csordas, Thomas. 1999. Ritual Healing and the Politics of Identity in Contemporary Navajo Society. *American Ethnologist* 26 (1): 3–23.

D'Andrade, Roy. 1995. Moral Models in Anthropology. *Current Anthropology* 36 (3): 399–408.

Dean, Bartholomew. 1995. Towards a Political-Ecology of Amazonia. Review of *Indigenous Peoples and the Future of Amazonia: An Ecological Anthropology of an Endangered World,* edited by Leslie Sponsel. *Cultural Survival Quarterly* 19 (2): 9.

———. 1999a. Critical Re-vision: Clastres' *Chronicle* and the Optic of Primitivism. *Anthropology Today* 15 (2): 9–11.

———. 1999b. Intercambios ambivalentes en la amazonía: Formación discursiva y la violencia del patronazgo. *Anthropologica,* no. 17: 85–115.

———. 1999c. Language, Culture, and Power: Intercultural Bilingual Education among the Urarina of Peruvian Amazonia. *Practicing Anthropology,* special issue, Reversing Language Shift in Indigenous America: Collaborations and Views from the Field, edited by L. Watahomigie, T. McCarty, and A. Yamamoto, 20 (2): 39–43.

———. 2000. Respeto a los derechos de los pueblos indígenas. *El Comercio* (Lima), August 4, p. A20.

———. 2001. Digitizing Indigenous Sounds: Cultural Activists and Local Music in the Age of Memorex. *Cultural Survival Quarterly* 24 (4): 41–46.

———. 2002. State Power and Indigenous Peoples in Peruvian Amazonia: A Lost Decade, 1990–2000. In *The Politics of Ethnicity: Indigenous Peoples in Latin American States,* edited by D. Maybury-Lewis, 199–238. Cambridge, Mass.: Harvard University Press.

Dembour, Marie-Bénédicte. 1996. Human Rights Talk and Anthropological

Ambivalence: The Particular Contexts of Universal Claims. In *Inside and Outside the Law: Anthropological Studies of Authority and Ambiguity,* edited by O. Harris, 19–40. London: Routledge.

DeVos, George A. 1995. Ethnic Pluralism: Conflict and Accommodation. In *Ethnic Identity: Creation, Conflict, and Accommodation,* edited by L. Romanucci-Ross and G. DeVos, 15–47. Walnut Creek, Calif.: AltaMira Press.

Díaz Polanco, Héctor, and Consuelo Sánchez. 2000. Self-Determination and Autonomy: Achievements and Uncertainty. In *Indigenous Autonomy in Mexico,* edited by A. Burgete Cal y Mayor, 83–96. Copenhagen: International Work Group for Indigenous Affairs.

Dyck, Noel. 1985. Aboriginal Peoples and Nation-States: An Introduction to the Analytical Issues. In *Indigenous Peoples and the Nation-State: Fourth World Politics in Canada, Australia, and Norway,* edited by N. Dyck, 1–26. Social and Economic Papers No. 14. St. Johns: Memorial University of Newfoundland.

Eriksen, Thomas Hylland. 1993. *Ethnicity and Nationalism: Anthropological Perspectives.* London: Pluto Press.

Escobar, Arturo. 1994. Welcome to Cyberia: Notes on the Anthropology of Cyberculture. *Current Anthropology* 35 (3): 211–31.

Fair, Rhonda. 2000. Becoming the White Man's Indian: An Examination of Native American Web Sites. *Plains Anthropologist* 45 (172): 203–110.

Feiring, Birgitte. 1998. Towards a European Policy on Indigenous Peoples and Development Cooperation. In *The Indigenous World, 1997–1998,* edited by C. Erni, 379–82. Copenhagen: International Work Group for Indigenous Affairs.

Field, Les. 1999. Complicities and Collaborations: Anthropologists and the "Unacknowledged Tribes" of California. *Current Anthropology* 40 (2): 193–209.

Fisher, James F. 1998. *Living Martyrs: Individuals and Revolution in Nepal.* Delhi: Oxford University Press.

García Canclini, Néstor. 1995. *Hybrid Cultures: Strategies for Entering and Leaving Modernity.* Foreword by Renato Rosaldo. Translated by C. Chiappati and S. López. Minneapolis: University of Minnesota Press.

Garzon, Susan, R. McKenna Brown, Julia Becker Richards, and Wupu' Ajpub' (Arnulfo Simón). 1998. *The Life of Our Language: Kaqchikel Maya Maintenance, Shift, and Revitalization.* Austin: University of Texas Press.

Geertz, Clifford. 1998. Deep Hanging Out. *New York Review of Books* 45 (16): 69–73.

Gelles, Paul. 2000. *Water and Power in Highland Peru: The Cultural Politics of Irrigation and Development.* New Brunswick, N.J.: Rutgers University Press.

George, Kenneth. 1996. *Showing Signs of Violence: The Cultural Politics of a Twentieth-Century Headhunting Ritual.* Berkeley: University of California Press.

Ginsburg, Faye. 1997. "From Little Things, Big Things Grow": Indigenous Media and Cultural Activism. In *Between Resistance and Revolution: Cultural Politics and Social Protest,* edited by R. Fox and O. Starn, 118–44. New Brunswick, N.J.: Rutgers University Press.

Gossen, Gary. 1999. *Telling Maya Tales: Tzotzil Identities in Modern Mexico.* New York: Routledge.

Graham, Laura. 1998. Eye on the Amazon: Brazilian Indians, the State, and Global Culture. *American Anthropologist* 100 (1): 163–69.

Gray, Andrew. 1997. *Indigenous Rights and Development: Self-Determination in an Amazonian Community.* Providence: Berghahn Books.

Gray, Andrew, and Jens Dahl. 1998. UN Declaration Enters a Third Year at the UN Commission on Human Rights. In *The Indigenous World, 1997–1998,* edited by C. Erni. Copenhagen: International Work Group for Indigenous Affairs.

Greaves, Tom, ed. 1994. *Intellectual Property Rights for Indigenous Peoples: A Sourcebook.* Oklahoma City, Okla.: Society for Applied Anthropology.

Hanson, F. Allan. 1989. The Making of the Maori: Culture Invention and Its Logic. *American Anthropologist* 91: 890–902.

———. 1997. Empirical Anthropology, Postmodernism, and the Invention of Tradition. In *Present Is Past: Some Uses of Tradition in Native Societies,* edited by M. Mauzé, 195–214. New York: University Press of America.

Harris, Olivia. 1996. Introduction: Inside and Outside the Law. In *Inside and Outside the Law: Anthropological Studies of Authority and Ambiguity,* edited by O. Harris, 1–15. London: Routledge.

Harvey, Neil. 1998. *The Chiapas Rebellion: The Struggle for Land and Democracy.* Durham, N.C.: Duke University Press.

Heinz, Wolfgang. 1988. *Indigenous Populations, Ethnic Minorities, and Human Rights.* Berlin: Quorum Verlag.

Herlihy, Peter. 1997. Central American Indian Peoples and Lands Today. In *Central America: A Natural and Cultural History,* edited by A. Coates, 215–40. New Haven: Yale University Press.

Herzfeld, Michael. 1992. *The Social Production of Indifference: Exploring the Symbolic Roots of Western Bureaucracy.* New York: Berg.

Hess, Carmen. 1997. *Hungry for Hope: On the Cultural and Communicative Dimensions of Development in Highland Ecuador.* London: Intermediate Technology Publications.

Hitchcock, Robert. 1994. International Human Rights, the Environment, and Indigenous Peoples. *Colorado Journal of International Environmental Law and Policy* 5 (1): 1–22.

Hume, David. [1739] 1978. *A Treatise of Human Nature.* Edited by L. A. Selby-Bigge. 2d ed., P. H. Nidditch. Oxford: Clarendon Press.

International Labour Office (ILO). 1953. *Indigenous Peoples: Living and Working Conditions of Aboriginal Populations in Independent Countries.* Geneva: International Labour Office.

Ismaelillo, and Robin Wright, eds. 1982. *Native Peoples in Struggle: Cases from the Fourth Russell Tribunal.* Bombay, N.Y.: Anthropology Resource Center (ARC) and Emergency Response International Network (E.R.I.N.).

Jackson, Jean. 1994. Becoming Indians: The Politics of Tukanoan Ethnicity. In *Amazonian Indians: From Prehistory to the Present,* edited by A. Roosevelt, 383–406. Tucson: University of Arizona Press.

———. 1995. Culture, Genuine and Spurious: The Politics of Indianness in the Vaupes, Colombia. *American Ethnologist* 22 (1): 3–28.

Janzen, John, and Reinhild Kauenhoven Janzen. 2000. *Do I Still Have a Life? Voices from the Aftermath of War in Rwanda and Burundi.* Publications in Anthropology 20. Lawrence: University of Kansas.

Johnson, Troy. 1999. *Contemporary Native American Political Issues.* Walnut Creek, Calif.: AltaMira Press.

Johnston, Barbara Rose. 1997. Conclusion: Crisis, Chaos, Conflict, and Change. In *Life and Death Matters: Human Rights and the Environment at the End of the Millennium,* edited by B. R. Johnston, 330–39. Walnut Creek, Calif.: AltaMira Press.

Kanaaneh, Moslih. 1997. The "Anthropologicality" of Indigenous Anthropology. *Dialectical Anthropology* 22:1–21.

Kingsbury, B. 1998. "Indigenous Peoples" in International Law. *American Journal of International Law* 92:414–57.

Knauft, Bruce. 1996. *Genealogies for the Present in Cultural Anthropology.* New York: Routledge.

———. 1999. *From Primitive to Postcolonial in Melanesia and Anthropology.* Ann Arbor: University of Michigan Press.

Kolata, Alan L. 1998. Introduction to *Regional Worlds: Cultural Environments and Development Debates—Latin America.* Edited by A. L. Kolata, K. Taylor Berardo, E. Corral, J. Scott Jerome, J. Johnson, 1–5. Annotated Bibliographies, Bibliographic Essays, and Course Curriculum. Chicago: University of Chicago Globalization Project.

LaDuke, Winona. 1999. *All Our Relations: Native Struggles for Land and Life.* Cambridge, Mass.: South End Press.

Lee, Richard B., and Richard Heywood Daly. 2000. *The Cambridge Encyclopedia of Hunters and Gatherers.* Cambridge: Cambridge University Press.

Leuthold, Steven. 1998. *Indigenous Aesthetics: Native Art, Media, and Identity.* Austin: University of Texas Press.

Levi, Jerome. 1998a. The Bow and the Blanket: Religion, Identity, and Resistance in Rarámuri Material Culture. *Journal of Anthropological Research* 54 (3): 299–324.

———. 1998b. Review of *Indians into Mexicans: History and Identity in a Mexican Town,* by David Frye. *American Ethnologist* 25 (1): 51–52.

———. 1998c. Review of *México Profundo: Reclaiming a Civilization,* by Guillermo Bonbil Batalla. *American Ethnologist* 25 (3): 42–43.

———. 1999a. The Embodiment of a Working Identity: Power and Process in Rarámuri Ritual Healing. *American Indian Culture and Research Journal* 23 (3): 13–46.

———. 1999b. Hidden Transcripts among the Rarámuri: Culture, Resistance, and Interethnic Relations in Northern Mexico. *American Ethnologist* 26 (1): 1–24.

———. 2000. Review of *The Chiapas Rebellion: The Struggle for Land and Democracy,* by Neil Harvey. *Journal of Interamerican Studies and World Affairs* 42 (4): 151–57.

———. 2002. A New Dawn or a Cycle Restored? Regional Dynamics and Cultural Politics in Indigenous Mexico, 1978–2001. In *The Politics of Ethnicity: Indigenous Peoples in Latin American States,* edited by D. Maybury-Lewis, 3–49. Cambridge, Mass.: Harvard University Press.

Macdonald, Theodore. 1994. Some Essential, Not Simply "New" Approaches to Human Rights. *Cultural Survival Quarterly* 18 (1): 1.

———. 1999. *Ethnicity and Culture amidst New "Neighbors": The Runa of Ecuador's Amazon Region.* Boston: Allyn and Bacon.

Mallon, Florencia. 1995. *Peasant and Nation: The Making of Postcolonial Mexico and Peru.* Berkeley: University of California Press.

Maury, Alfred Francis Pulszky, J. Aitken Meigs, J. C. Nott, and G. R. Gliddon. 1857. *Indigenous Races of the Earth; or, New Chapters of Ethnological Inquiry; Including Monographs on Special Departments of Philology, Iconography, Cranioscopy, Palaeontology, Pathology, Archaeology, Comparative Geography, and Natural History.* Philadelphia: J. B. Lippincott and Co.

Maybury-Lewis, David. 1991. Becoming Indian in Lowland South America. In *Nation-States and Indians in Latin America,* edited by G. Urban and J. Sherzer, 207–35. Austin: University of Texas Press.

———. 1997a. *Indigenous Peoples, Ethnic Groups, and the State.* The Cultural Survival Studies in Ethnicity and Change. Boston: Allyn and Bacon.

———. 1997b. World System, Local Peoples. *Cultural Survival Quarterly* 21 (3): 27–29.

McKinley, Michelle. 1997. Life Stories, Disclosure, and the Law. *POLAR: Political and Legal Anthropology Review* 20 (2): 70–82.

Menchú, Rigoberta. 1984. *I, Rigoberta Menchú: An Indian Woman in Guatemala.* Translated by Ann Wright, edited by E. Burgos-Debray. London: Verso.

Messer, Ellen. 1993. Anthropology and Human Rights. *Annual Review of Anthropology* 22:221–49.

Minow, Martha. 1995. Rights and Cultural Difference. In *Identities, Politics, and Rights,* edited by A. Sarat and T. Kearns, 347–65. Ann Arbor: University of Michigan Press.

Molinari M., Claudia. 1998. Protestantismo y cambio religioso en la Tarahumara: Apuntes para una teoría de la conversión. In *Sectas o iglesias: Viejos o nuevos movimientos religiosos.* Edited by E. Masferrer Kan. Mexico City: Plaza y Valdés.

Nagel, Beverly. 1999. "Unleashing the Fury": The Cultural Discourse of Rural Violence and Land Rights in Paraguay. *Comparative Studies in Society and History* 41 (1): 148–81.

Nagel, Joane. 1996. *American Indian Ethnic Renewal: Red Power and the Resurgence of Indian Identity and Culture.* New York: Oxford University Press.

Nagengast, Carole. 1997. Women, Minorities, and Indigenous Peoples: Universalism and Cultural Relativity. *Journal of Anthropological Research* 53 (3): 349–69.

Narayan, Kirin. 1993. How Native Is a "Native" Anthropologist? *American Anthropologist* 95 (3): 671–86.

Nash, June. 1997. Press Reports on the Chiapas Uprising: Towards a Transnational Communication. *Journal of Latin American Anthropology* 2 (2): 42–75.

Needham, Rodney. 1975. Polythetic Classification: Convergence and Consequences. *Man,* n.s., 10:349–69.

Nelson, Diane. 1999. *A Finger in the Wound: Body Politics in Quincentennial Guatemala.* Berkeley: University of California Press.

Ohnuki-Tierney, Emiko. 1984. Native Anthropologist. *American Ethnologist* 11:584–86.

Orlove, Benjamin, ed. 1997. *The Allure of the Foreign: Imported Goods in Postcolonial Latin America.* Ann Arbor: University of Michigan Press.

Parker, Andrew, Mary Russo, Doris Sommer, and Patricia Yaeger, eds. 1992. *Nationalisms and Sexualities.* New York: Routledge.

Penn, William S., ed. 1997. *As We Are Now: Mixblood Essays on Race and Identity.* Berkeley: University of California Press.

Perry, Richard. 1996. *From Time Immemorial: Indigenous Peoples and State Systems.* Austin: University of Texas Press.

Price Cohen, Cynthia, ed. 1998. *The Human Rights of Indigenous Peoples.* Ardsley, N.Y.: Transnational Publishers.

Pritchard, Sarah, ed. 1998. *Indigenous Peoples, the United Nations, and Human Rights.* New York: St. Martin's Press.

Quesenberry, Stephen. 1997. Recent United Nations Initiatives concerning the Rights of Indigenous Peoples. *American Indian Culture and Research Journal* 27 (3): 231–60.

Ramos, Alcida. 1994. The Hyperreal Indian. *Critique of Anthropology* 14 (2): 153–71.

———. 1998. *Indigenism: Ethnic Politics in Brazil.* Madison: University of Wisconsin Press.

Reed, Richard. 1997. *Forest Dwellers, Forest Protectors: Indigenous Models for International Development.* Boston: Allyn and Bacon.

Renteln, A. D. 1988. Relativism and the Search for Human Rights. *American Anthropologist* 90:56–72.

————. 1990. *International Human Rights: Universalism versus Relativism.* Newbury Park, Calif.: Sage.

Rieff, David. 1999. Concealing the Bad News: The Failure of Practical Means to Match Our Moral Ambitions. *The Times Literary Supplement,* May 7, no. 5014, p. 14.

Robinson, Mary. 1999. Respect Human Rights in Fact, Not Just in Theory. *International Herald Tribune,* May 30, p. 8.

Roe, Peter. 1995. Arts of the Amazon. In *Arts of the Amazon,* edited by B. Braun, 17–23. London: Thames and Hudson.

Ronfeldt, David, John Arquilla, Graham Fuller, and Melissa Fuller. 1998. *The Zapatista Social Netwar in Mexico.* Santa Monica, Calif.: Rand Arroyo Center.

Rosaldo, Renato. 1989. *Culture and Truth: The Remaking of Social Analysis.* Boston: Beacon Press.

Rosen, Lawrence. 1997. Indigenous Peoples in International Law. *Yale Law Journal* 107 (1): 227–59.

Salas, Maruja, and Timmi Tillmann. 1998. About People's Dreams and Visions and How to Retune Our Perceptions: Convergence of PAR and PRA in Latin America. *Studies in Cultures, Organizations, and Societies* 4 (2): 169–86.

Sanders, Douglas. 1989. The UN Working Group on Indigenous Populations. *Human Rights Quarterly* 11 (3): 406–33.

Scheper-Hughes, Nancy. 1995. The Primacy of the Ethical Propositions for a Militant Anthropology. *Current Anthropology* 36 (3): 409–20.

Schirmer, Jennifer. 2000. *The Guatemalan Military Project: A Violence Called Democracy.* Philadelphia: University of Pennsylvania Press.

Scott, Craig. 1996. Indigenous Self-Determination and Decolonization of the International Imagination: A Plea. *Human Rights Quarterly* 18 (4): 821.

Scott, James. 1985. *Weapons of the Weak: Everyday Forms of Peasant Resistance.* New Haven: Yale University Press.

Smith, Anthony D. 1991. *National Identity.* Reno: University of Nevada Press.

Smith, Linda Tuhiwai. 1999. *Decolonizing Methodologies: Research and Indigenous Peoples.* London: Zed Books.

Smith, Claire, and Graeme Ward, eds. 2000. *Indigenous Cultures in an Interconnected World.* Vancouver: University of British Columbia Press.

Stamatopoulou, Elsa. 1994. Indigenous Peoples and the United Nations: Human Rights as a Developing Dynamic. *Human Rights Quarterly* 16 (1): 58–81.

Stavans, Ilan. 1999. The Humanizing of Rigoberta Menchú. *The Times Literary Supplement,* April 23, p. 10.

Stavenhagen, Rodolfo. 1996. Indigenous Rights: Some Conceptual Problems. In *Constructing Democracy: Human Rights, Citizenship, and Society in Latin America,* edited by E. Jelin and E. Herschberg, 141–59. Boulder, Colo.: Westview Press.

———. 2000. Towards the Right to Autonomy in Mexico. In *Indigenous Autonomy in Mexico,* edited by A. Burgete Cal y Mayor, 10–21. Copenhagen: International Work Group for Indigenous Affairs.

Stephen, Lynn. 1999. The Construction of Indigenous Suspects: Militarization and the Gendered and Ethnic Dynamics of Human Rights Abuses in Southern Mexico. *American Ethnologist* 26 (4): 822–42.

Stoll, David. 1998. *Rigoberta Menchú and the Story of All Poor Guatemalans.* Boulder, Colo.: Westview Press.

Stull, Donald. 1990. Reservation Economic Development in the Era of Self-Determination. *American Anthropologist* 92 (1): 206–11.

Swepston, Lee. 1989. Indigenous and Tribal Peoples and International Law: Recent Developments. *Current Anthropology* 30 (2): 259–64.

———. 1998. The Indigenous and Tribal Peoples Convention (No. 169): Eight Years after Adoption. In *The Human Rights of Indigenous Peoples,* edited by C. Price Cohen, 16–36. Ardsley, N.Y.: Transnational Publishers.

Taylor, Christopher. 1999. *Sacrifice as Terror: The Rwanda Genocide of 1994.* Oxford: Berg Publishers.

Tennant, Chris. 1994. Indigenous Peoples, International Institutions, and the International Legal Literature from 1945–1993. *Human Rights Quarterly* 16 (1): 1–57.

Trouillot, Michel-Ralph. 1991. Anthropology and the Savage Slot: The Poetics and Politics of Otherness. In *Recapturing Anthropology: Working in the Present,* edited by R. G. Fox, 17–44. Santa Fe: School of American Research Press.

Turner, Terence. 1997. Human Rights, Human Difference: Anthropology's Contribution to an Emancipatory Cultural Politics. *Journal of Anthropological Research* 53 (3): 273–91.

Vizenor, Gerald, and A. Robert Lee. 1999. *Postindian Conversations.* Lincoln: University of Nebraska Press.

Warren, Kay. 1998. *Indigenous Movements and Their Critics: Pan-Maya Activism in Guatemala.* Princeton: Princeton University Press.

Washburn, W. 1987. Cultural Relativism, Human Rights, and the AAA. *American Anthropologist* 89:939–43.

Watahomigie, Lucille, Teresa McCarty, and Akira Yamamoto, eds. 1999. Reversing Language Shift in Indigenous America: Collaborations and Views from the Field. Special issue of *Practicing Anthropology,* 20 (2).

Watahomigie, Lucille, and Akira Yamamoto. 1992. Local Reactions to Perceived Language Decline. *Language* 68 (1): 10–18.

Watanabe, John M. 1992. *Maya Saints and Souls in a Changing World.* Austin: University of Texas Press.

Wilson, Richard A., ed. 1997. *Human Rights, Culture and Context: Anthropological Perspectives.* London: Pluto Press.

Wittgenstein, Ludwig. 1953. *Philosophical Investigations.* Translated by G. E. M. Anscombe. New York: Macmillan.

Wright, Susan. 1998. The Politicization of "Culture." *Anthropology Today* 14
    (1): 7–15.
Yaeger, Patricia, ed. 1996. *The Geography of Identity.* Ann Arbor: University
    of Michigan Press.
Young, R. J. C. 1995. *Colonial Desire: Hybridity in Theory, Culture, and Race.*
    London: Routledge.

1 Legalism and Loyalism: European, African, and Human "Rights"

Parker Shipton

Jurists and moral philosophers sometimes turn to anthropologists for perspectives on rights. They ask whether all peoples or cultures have concepts of rights, and whether everyone thinks about these things the same way. An answer to this question, some hope, will help them with another one, less relativist and more absolutist in aim: do all people actually have rights?

These questions are hotly debated. Some, both inside and outside the academy, feel that all humans have basic or natural rights and that it therefore becomes the duty of others everywhere to guarantee them against, for instance, ethnic persecution, genital mutilation, or toxic waste dumping. Others feel that to pitch social, economic, or political discourse in terms of "rights" is to impose one people's ideas on another and to place rights in the province of lawyers and state actors who have too much power already.

Rights are an idea, or a family of ideas, with a long intellectual pedigree. One of the problems in examining this idea's origins and distribution is that it was written about in some parts of the world before it was in others—and by only certain kinds of people. This makes it tempting, but maybe misleading, to infer that it was *thought* about in some parts of the world before others, or that some people or peoples have a superior claim on it. A more basic problem is that to ask whether all people think in terms of rights, one needs to use the word in English or some other language, and doing so itself is likely to bias the discussion in favor of one people's tradition or another's from the word go.[1]

Who, then, calls what a "right?" If rights may be a culture-specific idea, then who is included in that culture? If the idea has spread, then can one call the spread an imposition of one culture or civilization on another, or perhaps a sign of a growing need for the idea among those turning to it? Alternatively, are rights a tool that some borrow from others only when it's handy—for instance, to defend themselves against precisely the kinds of people (lawyers, missionaries, humanitarian activists) who propound them?

With questions like these in mind, this brief essay offers a few preliminary remarks on the concept of "rights" as understood in western European intellectual tradition and in parts of Africa south of the Sahara where some have attempted to apply it. This is done from the position of one who is neither European nor African (but who has had the good fortune to live and study in more than one part of each continent) and might thus hope to offer a perspective more neutral than some.

A canonical European tradition of thought on rights focuses most closely on the individual and on universals, as in the notion of human rights and the duties these imply. I trace the use of these notions since the seventeenth century by a few social and political philosophers who represent some of the most influential ways of thinking about rights and duties in Europe and overseas. Individualism and universalism, I suggest, reinforce each other in an idealized cultural self-image, really a self-caricature. Seventeenth- and eighteenth-century ideas about the solitary "natural man" and the "social contract" undergird the concept of human rights, and this concept has been turned and applied in ways that tend to legitimize nation-states (and bodies composed of their representatives) and laws as the natural or proper defenders of those rights. The ethnographic and historical foundations of the "natural man" and "social contract" ideas are shaky, I shall argue, and ideas of human rights should no longer rest upon them. No less important, if "rights" are needed, is to recognize a premise and a human right of connectedness, which may form a basis of other rights or interests.

While the idea of individual and universal human rights is well understood and accepted by many African people, it does not translate well into, or accurately reflect, the most common African understandings of morality. It can appear unnatural to minds more accustomed to considering moral issues by reference to intimacy, position, or actual circumstance, and more oriented toward particular loyalties. Individual freedoms may mean less than connectedness—to both the living and the dead—which may be construed as a right in itself; indeed, individuals may not even be recognized without connection to others. Nation-states as defenders of universal rights may also appear suspect where they were imposed under foreign power in the first place, have earned little loyalty, and remain subject to sudden takeovers and policy shifts. People in control of national and multinational agencies in Africa, sometimes acting in the name of aid or development, have co-participated in varied human rights abuses, sometimes unwittingly or with benign intentions. If the two-edged ideal of individual and universal human rights is to be invoked as a versatile tool in Africa's culturally diverse settings—for the defense of others or for African people's own self-defense—it may need some culturally sensitive rethinking.

Anthropology's Engagement with Rights

Edward Evans-Pritchard is said once to have quipped about anthropology that "the comparative method is all we have, and that is impossible." Any comparison worth making yields both similarities and differences, and where translating is involved, some ambiguity too. Seldom is it clear just what "a culture" is, or where one culture or language ends and another picks up. Comparing cultures can produce extreme conclusions—that people are all alike or all different. Most anthropologists would say that how people think about rights, or whether they do at all, depends on context, translation, or interpretation. Many would seek to divide human societies up somehow: by time or place, by ethnic group, by age or sex, by class or caste. Some would sort ideal from real, thought from deed, and norm from habit. Many of the world's real people identify with more than one culture. It becomes easy thus to hide behind seemingly safe conclusions like "it's complex." However, debates about whether to lump or split never end, and what seems like a safe conclusion for an intellectual purpose may be riskier for a practical one.

Anthropology's recent emergence from a period of self-examination and self-criticism has prompted questions both new and old at once. Whereas in the 1980s and early 1990s the emphasis was on comparing "the self" and "the other," it seems lately to have re-occurred to anthropologists that it might be worthwhile also to compare the other with the *other* other. The delicate work of comparing regions (and of comparing periods within them) begins to pick up the threads where it left off, but with heightened sensitivity to issues of position and power, the dynamics of transcultural contact, and the intricacy of cultural mixture and overlay.

Moving back to the forefront of anthropology's concerns are possibilities of practical action and political advocacy. There seems to have been a sea change. An earnest idealism about the usefulness of social research to influence lives—an attitude that seemed to wash away in the aftermath of the Euro-American social upheavals of the 1960s and early 1970s—was likely, in the 1980s and early 1990s, to bring smiles and eye-rolling among anthropologists, as though the notion of committed engagement were naive beyond the pale. By the turn of the millennium all this had changed. In an era of state collapses, ethnic purges, and racially charged conflicts over migration, anthropologists were forced to think again about their own usefulness. Relevance was coming back in.

To those wishing to take on theoretical challenges but also put their cultural insights to use, no idea has been more central than rights. If people have rights, then others have duties to see that they are realized and respected—scholars included.[2] Action and advocacy, for anthropologists, have usually meant trying to work in behalf of the more neglected, misunderstood, or threatened people(s): traditionally, the people in "the field." Indigenous ethnic minorities, together with refugees and other migrants, are the people most vulnerable to forced resettlement, land dispossession, and so on. Since few with power over them speak their tongues, these peoples have had few allies besides anthropologists, missionaries, and humanitarian aid workers (three sets of people with more in common than they sometimes let on). Convincing others to listen may take strong words like "rights."[3] So who, among the peoples who seem so wronged in such varied ways, has rights to begin with? Who gets to define them? And why should anyone care?

Rights (. . . and Duties?)

Rights, in English, take their place at the upper end of a continuum something like this:

right
    entitlement
        claim
            aspiration
                pretension

Rights carry not only legal but also ethical or religious connotations: the word implies something ultimate—something sacred. To defend rights is something like engaging in a crusade, carrying both the connotation of deadly seriousness and the risk of dismissal as fanaticism.

Clearly, in conventional usage the word *rights* has ambiguity, or polyvalence, like most sacred signs and symbols. Therefore, we look it

up. In the *Oxford English Dictionary,* without the *Supplement,* the term
fills eight pages—more than any other word but one. For our purposes,
the definition most relevant is this one (no. II): "Justifiable claim, on
legal or moral grounds, to have or obtain something, or to act in a certain way."[4] Rights are assumed to be about getting and keeping, it
seems, rather than about sharing or giving. As such, they describe only
a piece of human interaction, always begging the question of what
duties or obligations are attached. If rights imply duties, these may be
perceived as duties of the right holder, to compensate for or justify the
right; or as duties of others to respect the right, perhaps in return for
enjoying rights of their own.

Anglophones, like all people, think and communicate with
metaphors. Contemporary English terminology surrounding rights
and duties has a way of inclining a speaker into economic idiom. Owning, owing, possessing, paying and repaying, compensating . . . it is
hard to think long about rights and duties in English without eventually alluding to property, exchange, or money. Debts and duties, property and liberty . . . where not etymologically related, the ideas can sub-
tly slide together as if by magnetism.

Rights and Social Contract Theory

Terms such as *rights* or *entitlements* on the one hand and *duties* or
obligations on the other smuggle their own freight into discourse. In the
most revered texts in Anglo-American political and legal theory, they
are usually found in discussions of the individual and of the body
politic as a whole: a small social unit projected onto a large one. It is
largely to English and French social contract theorists of the seventeenth and eighteenth centuries—among others, Thomas Hobbes,
John Locke, Jean-Jacques Rousseau, and their followers—that contemporary thinkers owe much of their received wisdom about individual rights.

Singling out just a few "dead white European men" for naming and
comment requires a disclaimer or two. Here they are chosen only
because of their universally acknowledged influence over philosophical
and juro-political history. These three thinkers, so different in the com-
pass of their interests but overlapping on the topic of individual and
universal human rights and on the social contract, did not, of course,
invent those ideas. Variants of these notions extend millennia earlier
into history and literature (and not just to the Greeks or Romans or to
the Judeo-Christians) and cannot be pinned to particular names.[5] Nor
were the ideas of these men altogether unique in their times: others who

aren't read today, and still others who didn't or couldn't write, surely shared many of them. Individual and universal rights are *not* an exclusively European or "Western" idea. Nevertheless, they are typically so, and they have become part of a cultural self-image of those who deem themselves Western.

Hobbes, Locke, and Rousseau were undeniably instrumental in raising individual rights to the semisacred position they have recently occupied in public political, legal, and religious culture, and no longer just in Europe and North America. When these authors wrote of rights and duties, they wrote of subjects and sovereigns: of individual enfranchised subjects and often-unnamed individual rulers. Their phrases continue to be penned into constitutions and law texts, served up in speeches, and pondered by pundits.

The theories of these men derived not just from their particular cultural backgrounds—something that has been widely noted—but also from unusual and identifiable personal experiences in their own lives and readings. A brief, simplified sketch of the relevant contributions of Hobbes, Locke, and Rousseau—to take them in the chronological order of their most influential writings on rights and duties—suggests how the notion of individual rights became so salient a feature of the juro-political philosophies influenced by their works. To each, there was a particular image of the "natural man" or savage in the background, a fragmentary image based largely, and perforce, on imagination.

We can learn something, I suggest, about the nature of society and about ideas of rights and duties by comparing these influential old notions of the "natural man" with what anthropologists now know (or at least think they know) about some of the world's more peripheral peoples. By this I mean people far from the biggest centers of wealth, power, and technological prestige: not necessarily the better or worse for it—not noble or ignoble savages—just people in what the rest of the world deems the backwaters.[6] These are the kinds of people the social contract theorists seem to have had in mind when they wrote of the natural man.

Individuals, Sovereigns, and the Hobbesian Vision of Chaos

Thomas Hobbes was a product of turbulent times. Born in 1588, as England was struggling against Spain's Armada, he grew up with the constant threat and anxiety of a protracted war. He matured in an era in which churchmen and secular monarchs vied for political sovereignty and in which the English monarchy (to which he was exposed as a tutor to the aristocratic Cavendish family and to the future Charles II as Prince of Wales) was engaging in a struggle that would amount to a governmental and social revolution. Hobbes lived through the English civil war, observing it from the safe distance of self-exile across the Channel, and his *Leviathan* appeared in 1651, just two years after Charles I was executed, the House of Lords abolished, and England declared a commonwealth. Hobbes scorned what some deemed the divine right of kings, but he was also terrified of anarchy and its threat to what he deemed the personal rights of subjects.

A key formative experience for Hobbes had been translating Thucydides' unique account of the Peloponnesian War. From this remarkable historian, whose whereabouts during the war remain unknown (apart from briefly noted episodes of plague, military duty, and exile), Hobbes had learned of the horrors of social collapse; it seems to have been the descriptions of violent anarchy in the Athenian plague and the Corcyrean civil war that affected him most. Here the most frightening facet of human nature—to Hobbes the most central—was revealed.

> So that in the first place, I put for a generall inclination of all mankind, a perpetuall and restlesse desire of Power after power, that ceaseth onely in Death. . . .
> Competition of Riches, Honor, Command, or other power enclineth to Contention, Enmity, and War: Because the way of one Competitor, to the attaining of his desire, is to kill, subdue, supplant, or repell the other. (Hobbes [1651] 1950, pt. 1, chap. 11, pp. 79, 80)

A timid man with a dark, rather cynical outlook and a keen interest in mathematics, Hobbes seems to have valued tranquillity and order above all else. He was willing to suggest a permanent collective sacrifice of individual liberties to a chosen secular sovereign in order to guarantee these. "[W]ithout a common Power to keep them all in awe," he wrote in another oft-quoted passage, men "are in that condition which is called Warre, and such a warre, as is of every man against every man" (chap. 13, p. 103), a phrase he repeats and repeats with only slight alteration (e.g., on pp. 104–5, 107, 113, and 210).[7] In such a condition, wrote Hobbes,

> there is no place for Industry, because the fruit thereof is uncertain: and consequently no Culture of the Earth, no Navigation, nor use of the commodities that may be imported by Sea; no commodious Building; no Instruments of moving, and removing such things as require much force; no Knowledge of the face of the

> Earth; no account of Time; no Arts; no Letters; no Society; and
> which is worst of all, continuall feare, and danger of violent
> death; And the life of man, solitary, poore, nasty, brutish, and
> short. (Chap. 13, p. 104)

This savage, anarchic, atomized condition was one that Hobbes
deemed typical of human prehistory and of many parts of the earth in
his time (he mentioned parts of America). Humans should submit to
almost anything to avoid it, and they have therefore properly
appointed their sovereigns by "contract" or (if the delivery of what is
promised is to be delayed) by "covenant."

In so doing, they surrendered basic rights or liberties. They gave up,
for example, free access to all land and material goods. Whereas in the
state of nature there is "no Propriety, no Dominion, no *Mine* and
Thine distinct, but onely that to be every mans, that he can get; and for
so long, as he can keep it" (chap. 13, p. 106), the organized body politic
under a sovereign power and civil law guarantees men separate rights
to "propriety" (property), among them rights of exclusion (chap. 24,
pp. 209–11).[8] Moreover, the sovereign does the dividing up of property
and sets the rules of exchange. Hobbes supposes that this is done in the
interest of "Equity, and the Common Good" and says that men should
not have the right to protest against such actions of their sovereign,
"because they have authorised all his actions, and in bestowing the
Soveraign power, made them their own" (212). And sovereign rights
extend to conqueror's rights (211).

However, Hobbes did not go so far as to suggest that anyone should
sacrifice to the sovereign his or her right to life. This was to Hobbes,
and probably to many of his English contemporaries, more sacred still
than political solidarity.

> THE RIGHT OF NATURE, which writers commonly call *Jus Natu-*
> *rale,* is the Liberty each man hath, to use his own power, as he will
> himselfe, for the preservation of his own Nature, that is to say, of
> his own Life. (Chap. 14, p. 106)[9]

For Hobbes's natural man was ultimately alone. It is the solitude of the
natural, stateless man that anthropological knowledge from Africa
and elsewhere leads us to question—a point to which we will return.

John Locke's Twist

Strongly influenced by *Leviathan* several decades after its publication,
John Locke carried on Hobbes's dual tradition of individualism and

statism and gave each a new form, with a curious blend of economic conservatism and political radicalism.

Locke, a lawyer's son and land heir from a devout Anglican Somerset family, had all the advantages of Westminster and Oxford training, and he served as medic, adviser, and confidant to the Chancellor of the Exchequer. He was (either because of or despite all this) a man of lively imagination. Having served in the early 1670s as secretary to the council for trade and plantations, Locke had an interest in England's colonies and in their native peoples long before he wrote his *Second Treatise of Government* around 1689.

From these dealings at a distance with the colonies, among other things, Locke had derived a passing acquaintance with travelers' reports on the native peoples of North America—the people that he, like Hobbes, seems to have deemed most representative of man's natural condition. Now, most of these reports came from persons who had no real knowledge of the languages or cultures they were studying. Some were based on little more than casually observing an individual hunter, gatherer, or farmer walking through a forest; others were based on haphazard encounters in trade or war. Like the people any seasoned ethnographer remembers as his or her first informants, many were marginal to their own communities. The reports from these encounters left much to fill in. They were a canvas with large blanks, onto which social theorists of all kinds could paint their own images.

And this John Locke was willing to do. From Hobbes and others he borrowed the concepts of natural rights (like self-preservation), natural law, and the solitary savage or natural man. But Locke invented his own story about the natural man, with a God-given right to his body, annexing to it (at first by labor) the land he worked and the fruits of his labor, and finally his money. The individual was the starting point. Wrote Locke,

> The state of nature has a Law of Nature to govern it, which obliges every *one:* And Reason, which is that Law, teaches all Mankind . . . that being all equal and independent, no *one* ought to harm another in *his* life, health, liberty, or possessions. (Locke [1689] 1976, sec. 6, ll. 6–10, emphasis added)

Locke's belief in individual rights bore directly on his views of state sovereignty. By the time he wrote the *Second Treatise,* Locke had come to reject the divine right of monarchs, as Hobbes had done. But unlike Hobbes, Locke opined that if the subjects didn't find their rulers or system of government ("constitution") to their liking after fair experience, they had the right to replace them—even replacing their government with one differently constituted. For they together, not the ruler(s), were the real sovereign.

This is, of course, the work from which Thomas Jefferson cribbed most directly in penning the Declaration of Independence, adjusting phrases as he went, to come up with formulations like "life, liberty, and the pursuit of happiness." (A further mutation would appear in the UN's Universal Declaration of Human Rights in 1948, as "life, liberty, and security of persons," along with property and a standard of living adequate for health and well-being, among other specified rights.) The liberty phrase, for both men, concealed a wrinkle. Jefferson, like Locke, was tolerant of slavery in practice if not altogether happy with it in theory; to them both (as to so many of their intellectual forebears—notably including Aristotle), the sacredness of private property extended to property in persons. That the right of property could vie with the right to one's own body may have been a private concern, but not one expressed in print. On this particular issue, at least, it was clearly the authors' own social position and the happenstance of their birth that determined which of these competing ideas they would inscribe into their tradition.

John Locke's philosophy of rights, and of property rights in particular, may not find ready support in parts of the world where it is not so clear that one's body is one's own to begin with. In the kinds of African settings where a person may be born into servitude for another and may be taught, growing up, that it is normal and natural to be so (as among some Mauritanian Tukulor), where one person may be pledged in marriage to pay the famine debts of another (as in Kenyan Luoland), or where an individual's will or testament about body disposal may be overridden by the superior claims of senior kin (as might happen in many places in between), a superstructure of ideas based on bodily self-possession may not seem to follow as naturally as night follows day.

Rousseau and Rights Inside Out

The third European political theorist most in vogue during the American and French revolutions and the American constitution-writing period, when rights were so much in the air, was Jean-Jacques Rousseau. Rousseau was, in some respects, more of a maverick than either Hobbes or Locke. Rejecting the "Enlightenment's" celebration of reason and rationality and focusing instead on passion and morality (which he deemed the root of reason), Rousseau opposed and ridiculed

John Locke's notion of natural individual property rights acquired through a God-given right to the body, then through labor, and later through monetary exchange and investment. Rousseau's early "Discours sur l'origine et les fondements de l'inégalité parmi les hommes" (Discourse on the Origin and Foundations of Inequality among Men), traced the moral corruption of society back to an imagined time when, in the very beginnings of human society, a man, becoming aware of differences between himself and his neighbor, said of the land around him, "this is mine" (Rousseau [1755] 1967, pt. 2, p. 211). This was, to Rousseau, a kind of original sin that gradually led to the fall into what he saw as all the social ills of his time: general moral turpitude, competition, elitism, and hypocrisy.

Humanity started out without any of that, wrote Rousseau:

> Let us conclude that savage man, wandering about in the forests, without industry, without speech, without any fixed residence, and equal stranger to war and every social tie, without any need of his fellows, as well as without any desire of hurting them, and perhaps even without ever distinguishing them individually one from the other, subject to few passions, and finding in himself all he wants, let us, I say, conclude that savage man had no knowledge or feelings but such as were proper to that situation. (Pt. 1, pp. 207–8)

Rousseau seems to have concocted his beguiling model of presocial man from several sources. He apparently took it from western Swiss mountain canton communities remembered from his childhood, compounded with secondhand reports from authors like Tacitus (whom he partially translated), who wrote about a Germany that, for all we know today, the latter had never visited.[10] He took it from Defoe's *Robinson Crusoe,* a favorite novel of his youth. And he took it from travelers in the Americas and the Caribbean, many of whom, as noted earlier, wrote tall tales home, and few of whom spoke the tongues of their subjects. Most importantly, it seems, he cooked it up out of projections from his own peripatetic, socially confused, and lonely life. Whatever the quality of his sources—and ethnographically speaking, Tacitus, writing in about A.D. 98, was probably the best of them—by the time Rousseau finished with the picture, it was mostly made up.

On property rights, Rousseau's expressed sentiments were more egalitarian than Locke's. (His critique of private property later inspired Karl Marx and his followers, whereas Locke's *Second Treatise* has more often inspired free marketeers.)[11] But Rousseau shared an important idea with Locke: they both started out their discussions of property rights by focusing on individuals, not aggregations. Both, like Hobbes before them, envisaged the social contract as something arising from the voluntary agreement of originally autonomous, free-willed persons. The natural man, the foil for the civilized man, was all alone.

By the time he wrote *The Social Contract* in about 1762, Rousseau had decided that such a contract, if reformed along moral lines, was a good idea, not least to level men out. Here Rousseau turns upside down Hobbes's notion that humans are created basically equal in physical and mental ability:

> [I]nstead of destroying natural inequality, the fundamental pact, on the contrary, substitutes a moral and lawful equality for the physical inequality which nature imposed on men, so that, though unequal in strength or intellect, they all become equal by convention and legal right. (Rousseau [1762] 1967, bk. 1, chap. 9, p. 26)

And again,

> By whatever path we return to our principle we always arrive at the same conclusion, viz., that the social compact establishes among the citizens such an equality that they all pledge themselves under the same conditions and ought all to enjoy the same rights. (Bk. 2, chap. 4, p. 34)

The right of the strongest is a false right, replaced by a more genuine right—a social right, an equal right.

Rousseau's fervent individualism, turned inside out yet left intact, reappears as his fervent hope for a strong social contract and a strong sovereign. To him, in his later writings like *The Social Contract,* the ideal is to fuse the wills of the many into one collective will—the *volonté générale*—which restrains the individual and by so doing also liberates the individual for self-fulfillment.[12] The social contract depends on individual free will, and this depends in turn on the contract. Because of their ambiguities and seeming contradictions, Rousseau's ideas can be used by just about anyone for just about any cause: libertarian, totalitarian, populist, elitist . . . Rousseau has been accused, at some time or another, of being the father of just about every ideology. (And—self-absorbed loner that he was—he would have loved the attention.) Together, his earlier and later work lends itself readily to both individualism and statism.

By now it should be clear that the leading proponents of social contract theory relied on scanty secondhand reports and their own imaginations in concocting their image of the solitary natural man and natural law that served as their foil for civilization. In devising their origin stories for the rights and duties of the contract or covenant—stories that would become popular origin myths in their societies and others—these men relied largely on imagery that they had happened to come across, in whatever way and for whatever reason, early in their intellectual lives. Hobbes had come up with his image of the natural man by translating Thucydides' war stories (themselves possibly secondhand) and by hearing stories about the English civil war from across the Channel. Locke had come up with his image by clerking in a bureau in charge of colonial plantations and by reading travelers' tales from the Americas. Rousseau had cooked up his images by recalling childhood vacations in Swiss mountain villages, by translating Tacitus's secondhand reports on tribal Germany, and perhaps by projecting his own solitary wanderings onto humanity as a whole. All of them filled in large gaps in the canvas with their own brushes. And, of course, they learned in succession from each other.

"Rights" in Relief: A Skeptical Voice

The social contract theorists themselves had a foil, a skeptical thinker who, by solely voicing disbelief in the social contract, showed just how conventional this idea was in his generation. This was David Hume. A sometime friend and host of Rousseau's whom the latter finally alienated (as he did nearly everyone in his life), Hume put political loyalty down not to an original covenant, but to coercion and to blind habit. Political power, in Hume's eyes, usually began as conquest or usurpation, and what men took to be sovereign "rights" was merely a process whereby people lulled themselves, over time (even if it took generations), into acquiescing to their rulers and taking them for granted. The nation-state and its leaders and borders were not as sacred to Hume as to other contemporaries. Hume refused to accept that individuals had ever consented to hand over their rights to a sovereign (or to the collectivity that he, she, or it represented) in any social contract. But Hume's political philosophy seems to have enjoyed less influence in world affairs than the philosophies of the social contract theorists. In its sobering portrait of human coercion and the resignation of many conquered people over time, it revealed facets of human life that it is more comforting to forget. It was perhaps too realistic.

Of all the thinkers mentioned so far, it is Hume whose understanding of rights and duties might resonate best with the experience of African people in postcolonial states, where despotic rulers have ruthlessly pursued a winner-take-all politics (or might have resonated had not Hume himself, like many others of his time and place, written various passages scornful of African "races").[13] To Hume the skeptic, usurpation of power and tyrannical behavior in African settings at the turn of the millennium might look like the normal, familiar course of human affairs—no breach of any original contract.

Rights and Evolution

While evolutionist notions of right were clearly evident in the work of the social contract theorists such as Hobbes, Locke, and Rousseau, they were nowhere plainer than in the moral philosophy of Adam Smith, and here the notions of right, individual property, and states to guarantee them are woven together from the outset. Smith's opening lecture on jurisprudence was transcribed as follows:

> The first and chief design of all civill governments, is . . . to preserve justice amongst the members of the state and prevent encroachments on the individuals in it, from others in the same society. [That is, to maintain each individual in his perfect rights.] (Smith [1762] 1982, Lec. 1, p. 7 [ms p. 9]; the bracketed explanation is a verso note.)

Rights are violated by injury to a person (body), his reputation, or his estate. Smith divided rights into two types: "real rights" (to things) and "personall rights" (to one's person). Humans have rights as men and as members of families and communities (or societies or states). The first real right, to Smith, is dominium, or the full right of property. "By this a man has the sole claim to a subject, exclusive of all others, but can use it himself as he thinks fit, and if he pleases abuse or destroy it" (Lec. 1, p. 10 [ms pp. 16–17]). Smith illustrated most of his writing on rights by reference to individuals. He placed these in each of four ages: the age of hunters, the age of shepherds, the age of agriculture, and the age of commerce. He does sometimes lecture about the "age of the hunter" (e.g., among "savage nations of America") as an age of "independent families, no otherwise connected than as they live together in the same town or village and speak the same language" (Lec. 4, p. 201 [ms p. 4]). But even in these discussions, he keeps returning most often to individuals, and he says that the community interferes in family matters only "to preserve the public quiet and the safety of the individualls" (Lec. 4, p. 201 [ms pp. 4–5]).

Hence, Smith's rights, and disputes about them, began with an individual: an apple picker, a hunter, a herder, and so on. Rights and disputes multiplied at each stage with increasing interdependency, division of labor, and productive efficiency.[14] In this evolution, the "age of shepherds" was the beginning of property, disputes, wealth inequalities, and government (Lec. 4, pp. 202–3 [ms pp. 7–10])—all causes or effects of rights. "And it is at this time too that men become in any considerable degree dependent on others." So here, too, as with the social contract theorists, the natural, primitive man is a solitary man, a family man at most.

Adam Smith might be surprised to see how many people in Africa today live in the "age of shepherds"—or, more to the point, how practical and adaptive this way of life has proved in landlocked countries with poor soils and unreliable rains. When trade and specialized labor fail African people (as they have done so often in the past half century as a result of integration into commodity markets whose pricing lies beyond their control), farming, herding, and even hunting have often been the only ways to survive. And these are most often cooperative, not solitary, ventures.

Spencer, Rights, and Empire

By about 1850, when Herbert Spencer in England began writing his all-embracing evolutionist philosophy just ahead of Darwin, most of these same themes surrounding rights—will, freedom, rationality, property, contract, state, individualism, universal law—would be enshrined in English philosophy too as accepted hallmarks of a highly evolved civilization. Spencer's "natural" human being was an individual whose supreme rights were individual rights. Like Adam Smith before him, Spencer divided the rise of civilization into stages, beginning with hunting, herding, and farming (and in Spencer's mind, moving from the military to the industrial), and traced the rise of property rights through the stages (1876–96). The value of private property as an aspect of socially guaranteed individual rights was a central part of Spencer's vision. As Spencer (along with Darwin) became a leading proponent of evolutionism in the social studies and philosophy, individualism became almost synonymous with human advancement.

It was a feature of German philosophy too; the tradition most influentially expressed by Immanuel Kant in the late eighteenth century and Georg Hegel in the early nineteenth tended to package together all these things: right, duty, reason, free will, individualism, universalism, property, and contract.[15] Like Kant and Hegel, Spencer saw the individual and society as mutually dependent, but whereas Kant had emphasized the constraints on the individual, Hegel and Spencer both emphasized the freedoms.

Spencer had his political misgivings about state government and his moral misgivings about British and European imperial expansion. But at the time of the European powers' scramble for Africa in the latter half of the 1800s, a teleology of state-guaranteed private property and individual liberty as evolved civilization was already a vision for export.

A Continuing Legacy

The natural, solitary man and the social contract are not dead. People who believe in them, or say they do, are still in power in parts of western Europe and a number of its former colonies. To be sure, not everything that Hobbes, Locke, Rousseau, and other social contract theorists prescribed about the mutual rights and duties of rulers and subjects has made it into British common law, or into the Napoleonic *Code civile,* or into the many other state blueprints onto which these have been copied in colonial and former colonial territories. But new variants of the social contract keep appearing in the political and legal philosophies of postcolonial states.[16] Rights and duties remain the twin pillars of legal and jurisprudential discourse.[17] And up until our times, the heavy emphasis on the individual and the nation as units of social aggregation, mutually supporting each other, has remained a salient feature of western European and North American juro-political tradition.[18] But what in African traditions corresponds to rights? And how well have European variants of the concept transplanted to that continent?

A Real "Natural Man"? An Ethnographic Corrective

The solitary natural man—so central a part of the formation of seventeenth- and eighteenth-century social contract theory, of eighteenth- and nineteenth-century evolutionism, and of twentieth-century statism and doctrines of universal human rights—was, I have suggested, largely a result of secondhand tales from travelers and imaginative embellishments. Now let us place the natural man in the cold light of anthropological knowledge at the turn of the millennium and ask who, in the world we live in, corresponds to that long-familiar image.

In probably no known era, and in no known region of the world, have most humans lived as individuals on their own in the wilderness. There is little evidence—ethnographic, archaeological, or paleontological—for what Jean-Jacques Rousseau, say, imagined as the "natural man." There is little to support the image of the atomized, each-on-his-own, Robinson Crusoesque existence that Rousseau's writing so influentially spread to his countless readers as the picture of the origins of human society.[19] Not among the native Americans and Caribbeans, from whom the social contract theorists drew so much of their inspiration. Not in highland New Guinea. Not among the San (or Sarwa or "Bushmen") of the Kalahari; not among the Hadza of the East African wooded savannah, nor the Efe "Pygmies" in the Ituri Forest, nor the Twareg in the Sahara, nor the Dinka near the upper-middle Nile.

The nearest conditions we find, in many of the smaller societies or more sparsely settled areas, are periods of ostracism for persons who have violated important norms. Persons who would in some larger or denser societies be incarcerated are sent out to live on their own for a while or for good (if they are not executed in either place). We also find individuals or very small groups isolated temporarily in rites of passage: in Amazonian or New Guinean initiation huts, in Australian walkabouts, in American Indian shamanic spirit quests, and so on. Rather than being evidence of some original condition of isolated individuals, these internal or external seclusions are instead *the exceptions that prove the rule* of normal social life. They are the isolations that emphasize and dramatize, in relief, the intense sociability of everyday existence. Rites of passage are the periods of reflection and intense celebration that allow kin, neighbors, and acquaintances to readjust to changed social roles, with respect to the parties directly undergoing the rites and to each other as well. The ritual liminals, like mythical man-monsters, put into perspective the norms of interdependent living that the intense emotions surrounding rituals can themselves help transmit and embed (even while leading some to question or flout those norms).

We can scarcely even become Robinson Crusoes when we try. When Americans or Europeans have attempted to go off and live on their own, they seem almost as likely to make news headlines as to vanish from public awareness. Henry David Thoreau shacked at Walden for less than two years (in fact keeping occasional contact with town merchants for food, nails, etc.) yet made world news for it and ensured that his journal would be pored over by puzzled students ever after. Persons who withdraw into backwoods Montana cabins, with a gun or two to keep out society, seem less likely to end up surrounded by peace and quiet than by flashbulbs and police dogs.

No. The natural human is a social being. This is what Aristotle called a political animal, one fit in its fullest development for the polis or city-state. The idea of the human as a basically social animal is not new in Africa either: it can be found, for instance, in ibn Khaldûn's *Muqaddimah,* written in about 1377.[20] But if the human is a social animal, do all humans recognize human rights?

Rights in Translation

Ideas about rights don't necessarily translate across languages. Many lexicons of African tongues simply list no word corresponding to *right* in the *Oxford English Dictionary* definition noted above (or corresponding meanings for terms like the French *droit* or German *Recht*). Others translate the term with a distinctive twist. Take, for instance, an example from Pulaar (or Fulfulde, the language of Fulbe or Fulani in West Africa). Some bilingual dictionaries list under *right* words such as the Pulaar term *baawal* (or *baawɗe*), which itself translates into "power of the chief, authority," as if to imply that might—not some abstract ethic—makes right.[21]

In English usage, the concept of rights has both a moral and a jural element, but some African languages split the jural and moral elements into separate words. In Kiswahili, for instance, jural right is *haki* (as in *haki za binadamu,* "human rights"), whereas moral right (in the sense of correctness) translates as *adabu* (as in *adabu njema,* "good correctness" or "propriety").[22] The normative aspect of the English word lends itself readily to political rhetoric and polemic: as often as not, the term *rights* is a loaded one in English. Sometimes, even when the basic idea translates, the overtones don't. Not everyone tends to think of rights as involving or alluding to property or money. These are some of the reasons why the concepts of rights and duties are so hard to define and why they translate so poorly.

Human Rights, Positive and Negative

Candidates for universal human rights aren't hard to dream up: life, health, food, water, shelter, and sleep, for example. Or something just as cherished but less easily demonstrable: dignity.[23] Again, though, some of these rights are hard to translate across languages. For example, in the Nilotic Luo tongue spoken in the Lake Victoria Basin of Africa, life and death are not spoken of as only an either-or proposition; one commonly speaks of a fat or healthy person as being more alive than a thin or sickly person. Or take the concept of family. A Luo term translated as "family"—*dhoot,* which means "doorway" (literally, "mouth of house")—can mean one woman and her offspring; or, in a telescoping way, it can signify a descent group as big as a clan of thousands. Rights to religious freedom are hard to translate into Luo, a language that does not have special terms for religion, since religion is not deemed something separate from the rest of life. Clearly, then, as soon as we begin to specify positive rights and try to translate them, we encounter major lexical and classificatory snags.

It may be easier to accept rights in the negative. If it is hard to agree on a positive universal human right, it may be easier to agree on a condition under which no human should have to live, at least not for long: war, terror, torture, nausea . . . But to spell these out too precisely begs the question of the ones unnamed or unnameable. Adverse conditions not always easy to specify include different kinds of subtle persecution, spatiotemporal disorientation, disconnectedness from kin or nurturing surrogates—any of which may contribute to trauma or post-traumatic depression, existential angst, hauntedness, or anomie (a normless, structureless condition unnameable by its very etymology and definition). The more thorough and precise the list of unacceptable living conditions, the easier it becomes to build a case allowing the one left unmentioned. A little vagueness isn't always a bad thing.

If there is a universal positive human right, perhaps it contains an irony. The American Anthropological Association's Task Force on Human Rights has lately agreed on a seemingly paradoxical idea: a *universal* human right to *difference*.[24] This formula is clever, and probably wise. But it isn't perfect: one can imagine plenty of ways of being miserable and different.

African Universalism?

Rights are born of hardship. The most fervent believers in universal human rights in Africa are mostly either in jail or just out.[25] But this isn't the only way to become a believer or knower. Some do it by growing up in, or converting to, Islam or Christianity.[26] Some do it by emulating Europeans or North Americans.[27] Rights were a rhetorical lever that Africans used most skillfully to pry their countries free from Europe in the decade and a half after the UN's Universal Declaration of Human Rights in 1948, in something like the way that the American colonies had used rights to pry themselves away from England in the late eighteenth century.

There are, to be sure, indigenous universalist traditions, too; it would be surprising if there were none in a continent of Africa's size. Some are traceable to visionaries and have been at the foundation of nativistic, messianic, or other revitalization movements.[28] Some derive from independent churches that spring partly out of European or American roots—sometimes as revitalization movements themselves. But whether internal or external in their origins, these movements have something of the flavor of radicalism in Africa. They challenge a more widespread premise that humans are not fundamentally equal.[29]

African States as Guarantors?

The question of who should guarantee human rights, if they exist, seems particularly apt in the world today. Whereas the European intellectual traditions of the social contract theorists, the German legalist philosophers, and the imperial evolutionists tend to look to the nation-state as a potential guarantor of human rights and liberties, evidence from many parts of Africa south of the Sahara suggests that national entities are often among the ones denying them.[30] Ogoni-speaking people in Nigeria, Dinka in southern Sudan, and Jola (Diola) of Casamance in Senegal, for instance, have all, with their different grievances, lately claimed to be victims of the nations to which they have belonged. More broadly, mobile people (transhumant and nomadic herders, migrant share contractors, refugees, et al.), people who live dispersed or far from capital cities, people with simple technology, and people with social structures deemed egalitarian or "acephalous" have historically been victims of state-sponsored discrimination and violence in Africa. Even among more densely settled agrarian and industrial populations, people representing groups out of power have argued that their people have been systematically denied basic services, political representation, or access to jobs and school places while being taxed, conscripted, or edged off their lands.[31] It is little coincidence, then, that a number of the African nation-states have proved brittle in civil wars or, where remaining intact, have changed regimes regularly in coups d'état.

African Test Cases for the "Warre of Every Man against Every Man"

When a national government dissolves, as happened in Somalia, Rwanda, and Sierra Leone as the turn of the millennium approached, what follows is *not* an atomized society, a "warre of every man against every man" such as Hobbes imagined from his reading of Thucydides. It is a different sort of chaos instead. It is a war not just of individuals, but also shifting combinations of friendships of convenience, kin groups such as clans or pseudo-clans, ethnic groups (or what are hastily constituted or reconstituted as such), cliques, gangs, factions, sodalities, and ad hoc coalitions. Some male youths band together in violent groups, while other people—younger, older, female—variously serve, subvert, hide from, or endure them. In Somalia, as the national government melted down in the early 1990s, people pressed their interests not just (or even mainly) as individuals, but rather as clans, classes, ethnic groups, and gangs (Simons 1995; Besteman and Cassanelli 1996). Research conducted in Rwandan refugee camps since that country dissolved into genocide in 1994 has shown that children cut off from their families hastily formed their own new ones there, a process that lowered the marriage age of both sexes (not just women) into the mid-teens (Smedt 1998). A study of Sierra Leonean youth combatants—a category lately both visible and powerful—sums up their attachments this way: "The combat group substitutes for lost family and friends" (Peters and Richards 1998, 187).

If African ethnography shows anything, it is that humankind—in peace and war, with or without states—is *not* at base just individualistic, even in extreme conditions. We are individuals, *and* we are members of bigger groupings that shift and vary in kind and size.

Rounding Out Rights

Rights need not refer to individuals, and this is something that recent scholarship has increasingly pointed out. Giving the ideas of rights and duties more leeway so that they can refer to social units other than individuals and sovereign states may make them more palatable to partisans of a wider range of political ideologies. This shift in thinking is increasingly reflected in policy documents of the UN (statist as it is by name and constitution) and of academic bodies such as the American Anthropological Association.

So what besides individuals may rights and duties refer to? Humans belong, I suggest, to three kinds of real or imputed sets:

Groups, such as nations, chiefdoms, clans, lineages, clubs, and households.

Networks, such as patron-client webs, affinal kin chains, and friends of friends.

Open Categories, such as genders, "races," age-grades, castes, classes, and occupations or modes of livelihood.

These tags—groups, networks, and open categories—are not mutually exclusive; a set of people such as a trade guild or union can be both a category and a group, while its members partake of their own networks inside and outside of it. Humans are not more basically "individual" than any of these other units of aggregation, including indigenous peoples. Any of these can have rights and duties if individuals can.

Some African Perspectives on Relative Rights

That rights and duties, as moral-jural absolutes, do not easily translate into many African tongues is a clue that Africans south of the Sahara may have other ways of thinking about them than the ways that western Europeans have favored in the past. Some of these African ways of thinking emphasize practical action and particular people more than abstract or universal principles. Some emphasize not so much the polarity of individual and society as the groups, networks, and categories in between—intermediaries that in Africa take myriad forms, many unnamed in English.[32] Some combine elements of law, politics, and religion in ways that do not fit western European ideals of compartmentalized institutions. So axioms like the following, which I have sometimes heard suggested or implied in local discourse in settings as far apart as inland western Kenya and upriver Gambia, may sometimes strike outsiders as alien, puzzling, or frightening.[33]

> What your rights are depends on who you are in the first place. Who you are may depend on your ascribed or achieved social roles—positions entered by birth or by agreement.
>
> Individuals do not have rights independently of kin groups or other enduring entities. One could phrase it this way: rights are relative, and relatives have rights. The enduring social entities may also be constituted according to principles other than kinship, such as age grading, territory or voluntary association.
>
> Some people are more human than others. Humanity has to do with socialization and with moral achievement, not just with biological speciation.
>
> Individuals are accountable for the actions of other members of their kin groups or wider communities.
>
> Autochthons may naturally enjoy more rights or privileges than immigrants.
>
> Elders have more rights than juniors. Their status, prestige, and power rest on experience, wisdom, wealth, or reproductive success, or on their nearness to ancestors and ancestorhood.
>
> Rich have more rights than poor—for instance, to speak out in public meetings. *Rich* may mean wealthy not just in money, but in people, animals, or other things.
>
> Rights are realized only in practice, and with the inclusion and support of other people.

It is the positional, personalized, and relative nature of rights, not their distance or abstraction, that is most striking in indigenous African cultures south of the Sahara. Whereas rights in European understandings seem based most often on *legalism,* African rights seem more often based on *loyalism.*

Particularly hard for some non-Africans to grasp is the concept that one may not be recognized as a real person without being demonstrably connected to other people. Among the Fulbe (Fulani) of western Africa, one is not deemed properly Fula—properly human—without having acquired from others a diverse package of social and moral qualities called *pulaaku* (see Riesman 1977). Maasai in Kenya and Tanzania sometimes express a comparable idea: one isn't born a Maasai but rather grows into (and is initiated into) Maasaihood, which is proper, socialized personhood. Among Akan peoples in Ghana, as Kwame Gyekye notes in a discussion of the term *onipa* (socialized person), "an individual can be a human being without being a person" (1997, 49). Many comparable findings are reported elsewhere on the continent (Dieterlen 1973, Karp 1997). Participation makes the person. This much a Europeanist might find familiar: in English, too, one speaks of cruel or antisocial individuals as being "beastly" or "inhuman." But a characteristically African understanding extends the idea by requiring specific personal contacts. Cohen and Atieno Odhiambo (1989, 27) put it this way: "In Siaya the individual is synonymous with the stranger, an alien, possibly an enemy . . . you do not in an important sense exist until you reveal your networks and, more importantly, until this network can be verified by your interrogators."[34]

It would be quite wrong, of course, to generalize that people in Africa south of the Sahara recognize no rights but positional or personalized ones, or that principles like kinship and seniority wholly govern African moral thought. It would be equally wrong to say that North Americans recognize only individualistic or universalistic principles of ethics, or that they manage to live out these ideals in daily life.[35] Instead, these are merely themes that recur often enough to be seen as being among the prevailing currents in these peoples' respective traditions and images of themselves. In lived experience, legalism and loyalism more often twist, turn, and trade places.

A Human Right of Connectedness?

The ideal of reproducing and leaving a living legacy is one that some people in Africa deem second to none in importance.[36] It can be interpreted as a right to be part of something bigger and longer-lasting than oneself, or as a claim to a kind of immortality. And all of this might be subsumed under a right of connectedness. This may mean a right to be part of a network of persons obligated to each other through marriage, marriage payments, and alliances. Or it can mean the right to partake of connections between the living and the dead, ties that are maintained by invocation, prayer, or sacrifice. Sometimes it means both. In the Luo country, for instance, one who dies without being properly married because of lack of access to bridewealth is deemed likely to return as a *jachien,* a troublesome spirit, to haunt the kin who denied the person the means to marry. This assumption is based on something like a right of connectedness among the living and a duty to appease the wronged after their death.

A right to connectedness may be taken to imply a duty of connectedness, too. In the Luo country, as in many other parts of Africa south of the Sahara, family members are held partly responsible for the deeds and misdeeds of other members. Debts are heritable, and at a Luo funeral, creditors will come forth to pronounce their judgments about whether standing obligations are to be forgiven or will carry through to the next generation.

Indigenous, African conceptions of rights and duties of connectedness contrast with the heavy emphasis on personal freedoms in European doctrines of rights. It is not that individual freedoms and rights are categorically absent from African minds,[37] but rather that they are not necessarily sacred, and they are not the beginning or the end.

Persons and Property

These seemingly abstract issues of personhood become quite concrete in contests over space, place, and property rights. As people in varied African settings under colonialism and in independent, postcolonial states have attempted to resist confinement into labor reserves, forced terracing, or resettlement caused by dam projects and the like, the question of who has what rights or access to land by virtue of what memberships, and who has the authority to guarantee these rights, has become paramount. Similarly, when bodies outside Africa attempt to transform land tenure to systems of individual ownership under state title, it matters who has the authority to set the rules, and whom they bind.

Observers from outside (and inside) Africa have often stereotyped traditional African modes of landholding as collective tenure, in order to trace an evolution toward individual tenure and justify such a reform. The truth is, however, that most African ways of relating to land have never been one or the other but are characterized by seasonal and local variation.[38] But attachments to land are nonetheless reckoned as, and through, attachments to people, both living and dead. Where kin groups are identified with particular spots on the landscape, and where graves justify the bonds of living descendants to the land (as among the Luo, Luhya, and Gusii in Kenya, the Chagga in Tanzania, and the Tiv in Nigeria), rights to land can be tantamount to rights to live in a place, or among a people, with a certain standing: that is, tantamount to a social right to be. In Luo tradition, for instance, people living on the land of their own lineage may speak up prominently at public meetings or erect an *osuri,* a sharpened vertical pinnacle pole (a proud symbol of maleness and dominion) atop their houses. But people living on borrowed land may not.

Conflict over land in such places—for instance, in the "ethnic cleansing" campaigns between "Kalenjins" and intersettled groups in Kenya in the 1990s and into the new century—is more than just a struggle for resources. It is a struggle for sovereignty, and for a symbolic spatial anchor for kin groups and ethnic groups that help give personal lives their justification and meaning. When a ruling regime sanctions or actively foments such ethnic violence within its borders, as Kenya's government has been accused of doing (Nowrojee 1993), it jeopardizes its own claim to legitimacy—whether by European or African understanding. In such a context, individuals can hardly justify rights to land by reference to titles provided by the state. They usually have, as Moore (1998, see also 1986) notes, no neutral forum for redress of any "rights." If they are to defend their interests, they need their own groups and networks, just as they have always known.

Units of Aggregation: The Possibility of Shared Sovereignty

Students of Africa everywhere have wondered about the artificial nature of nations and nationalism south of the Sahara; they have asked whether the territories and boundaries so arbitrarily imposed by Europeans in the 1884–85 Berlin Conference can make sense as bases for contemporary civil governments that purport to guarantee rights. Skeptics argue that the unit of the nation-state never fit Africa south of the Sahara in the first place (most of the boundaries followed no preexisting ethnic, linguistic, or religious divisions) and that few will ever respect the nation very deeply.

While this question cannot be resolved here, it is worth remembering three things. First, it would be incorrect to say that African people south of the Sahara generally think of themselves as members (whether citizens or subjects) of nations first and foremost.[39] Instead, national allegiances compete with loyalties to other entities smaller or larger in scale, from individual to global; as noted, these include not only transnational ethnolinguistic groups and "races," but also ostensibly global communities of worship in Christianity and Islam. Second, if Europeans have imposed states on Africans, they have done so on other Europeans, too. Welsh people in Great Britain, Bretons and Corsicans in France, Basques and Catalonians in Spain, and Venetians and Calabrians in Italy sometimes voice sentiments reminiscent of those of Luo in Kenya or Jola in Senegal about their marginal, subjectlike status in the nations that claim them within their borders, and their partisans have sometimes expressed their claims in terms of basic rights. Finally, some of the supranational entities that purport to defend human rights against national actions (such as the UN or the World Bank Group) are, of course, made up explicitly of and by nations themselves. In policing the acts of their member states, these organizations may only reinforce the power and authority of nation-states in general.

The hard question here is what, if anything, ought to replace the nation-states—or, more basically, whether *any* single sort of human aggregation ought to claim sovereignty, including the right to commit or regulate violence. If nation-states and their governments were somehow to wither away and their borders melt, would whatever filled the power vacuum be any more benign than what it replaced?

Possibly, but not likely. The danger, it would seem, lies in attempts by any one kind of entity to monopolize control of human allegiances and in public overdependence on any one unit for order, so that when that entity weakens or dissolves (as in Somalia, Rwanda, and Sierra Leone toward the turn of the millennium), genocidal chaos ensues, and no one seems to have any place whatsoever to claim rights. This is a plea for a kind of pluralism and for the spirit of tolerance that can come with it. Kin groups, nations, and religions are three kinds of human aggregations unlikely to go away. The second and third, which are sometimes explicitly modeled on the first, have long vied for ascendancy in Africa, sometimes cooperating and sometimes competing. All three will continue to hold their own claims to sovereignty in decisions about human rights.

Rights without the Old Baggage

The western European intellectual and juristic tradition of "rights" sometimes seems like an express train that runs from the individual to the universal—its two grand terminals—making only a few stops in between and skipping many others. It stops regularly for family, community, and nation. But it doesn't often stop for clan or age-set, for neighborhood or subchiefdom, for gang, club, or network. So there are parts of the world where people usually seek their livelihood, peace, and dignity by their own means, or by other terms; and many of these parts are in Africa.

That nations are so often metaphorically spoken of as projections of human bodies or families would seem to suggest widespread recurring tendencies of imagination. Humans need multiple affiliations, and we sometimes spin one kind out of another. We need stories and histories to dignify our social creations, and we have sometimes done this with origin myths about the "natural man," whom we make up if need be. This dummy serves as a foil for whatever we fancy we have become, and for the social contracts by which we may think we live.

But the figments of the natural man and the social contract may not be so necessary if we remember that all humans need crisscrossing social ties to fulfill their sense of belonging: ties of group, network, and open category. All humans need a mix of freedom and connectedness, but one people can scarcely prescribe the precise mix for another. By considering African understandings of rights (and duties) together with European ones—and remembering that many related ideas do not easily translate—we can round out an important humanitarian tradition that seems sometimes too individualist, sometimes too statist to fit the contexts where it may be most in need.

Notes

I thank Bartholomew Dean and Jerome Levi for their invitation to the symposium on which this volume is based, and for their comments on an earlier draft of this essay. My anthropology and core-curriculum students at Boston University have also offered valuable insights.

1. Philosophers sometimes divide themselves into the camps of "realists" (in the Aristotelian tradition, for instance) and "nominalists" (as in the Wittgensteinian tradition). Basically, a realist would hold that rights (or truth or justice) exist in nature, or as real principles or things, independently of what they are called; a nominalist would hold that a right is real only insofar as something is *called* a right. Where translation between languages is concerned, the difference in perspectives becomes crucial.

2. See Merry 1992; Messer 1993; and Wilson 1997 for summaries of anthropological literature on human rights.

3. Bibliographic searches on "human rights" turn up far more sources by people who assume or argue that such rights exist than by people who do not.

4. One might add to this list a claim to "be." A right to be may imply a duty or obligation on someone else's part to *let* be.

5. For a discussion of the history of the notion of human rights in Judeo-Christian tradition, see Stackhouse 1984, esp. chap. 2. Stackhouse considers that "the deepest roots of human rights are found in the biblical conception of life" (31), though this conception is not formed in such terms. He points to the concept of a divine, righteous reality outside and above the human, a concept that eventually incorporated some Greek ideas about universal moral law. Two key turning points in the establishment of universal rights, in his opinion, were the rise of Islam with its ostensibly universal law, and the religious reforms under Hildebrand's papacy as Gregory VII (1073–85), which established a "right of resistance" to unjust feudal rule by appeal to a centralized ecclesiastical government (43).

6. While the notion of the "noble savage" is often attributed to Rousseau, and while some of his work strongly hints at it, no such phrase is to be found in his writings.

7. For Hobbes, the state of war included the periods of tension and uncertainty between actual fighting.

8. Hobbes is not as specific on property rights, however, as he is on rights to life or to peace.

9. To Hobbes, rights and laws are distinct in kind. A right is a liberty to act or not to act, whereas a law is an obligation to do so (Hobbes [1651] 1950, chap. 14, p. 107).

10. Tacitus [c. A.D. 98] 1942. In Tacitus's time, "Germania" included part of present-day Switzerland.

11. Rousseau was a social and pedagogic revolutionary—not an economic revolutionary. He did not believe a permanent return to the state of nature possible. But he did express hope for a general reform of society and the implementation of a social contract along moral lines.

12. This idea, expressed in *The Social Contract,* is perhaps Rousseau's hardest nut to crack, the deepest and most influential of the writer's many ironies, contradictions, and enigmas. He never clearly explained just what he meant, but volumes of exegesis have since been written by people who have thought they knew. Note the influence of Rousseau's individualist-collectivist way of thinking (the group makes the man) on the work of Karl Marx, Emile Durkheim, and, somewhat less directly, Claude Lévi-Strauss and structuralists.

13. Some, perhaps most, African philosophers trained in the European canon find the social contract theorists, as well as Hume, Kant, Hegel, and others who carried on some of their traditions, to be objectionably racist and ethnocentric. (See, for instance, the essays in Eze 1997.) While the criticism of these thinkers is well founded by latter-day standards of politics and scholarship (if it is fair to judge them for living in their times), it is their views of humanity in general and of Europeans in particular, rather than of Africans, that are the subject here.

14. The proper arbiter of rights, to Smith, was another individual: the "impartial spectator" who witnessed a theft, dispute, etc., as a silent third party. The impartial spectator, like the invisible hand, is a quasi-religious image in Smith's work. Smith deemed that third party necessary because, like Aristotle before him, he considered it normal and natural for humans to favor disproportionally their own near and dear (Smith [1759] 1984, part 3, ch. 3).

15. Particularly in Kant's *Critique of Practical Reason,* where he sets out his moral-legal "categorical imperative" ("So act that the maxim of your will could always hold at the same time as a principle establishing universal law") (Kant [1788] 1956, pt. 1, bk. 1, chap. 1, sec. 7), and in his earlier essays (e.g., Kant [1795] 1983, 119); and in Hegel's *Philosophy of Right,* where he posits, among other things, that freedom embodies itself in the right of property ownership and that "in the state duty and right are united in one and the same relation" (Hegel [1821] 1967, pt. 3, chap. 3, para. 261).

16. Prominent among late-twentieth-century variants is John Rawls's idea of the "original position," elaborated in *A Theory of Justice* (1972). This involves a hypothetical collection of ordinary, rational, self-interested individuals (though ones ignorant of their own characters) who come together to form a social contract and must inevitably decide on mutually assured liberty and on limitations to inequality. See Dworkin 1977, chap. 6, for a critique; see also Donnelly 1990.

17. Dworkin (1977, 169–73) proposes a tripartite taxonomy of political theories of law as goal-based, right-based, and duty-based. He supposes that the social contract makes the most sense in a theory that assumes natural rights.

18. The only other units of aggregation that come close to the sanctity of "individual" and "country" (nation) in North American juro-political ideology—taken here as a kind of lowest common denominator, as in election-campaign rhetoric—are "family" and, lower on the scale, "community." Note how much more legitimacy these concepts are publicly accorded than, say, lineage, clan, or age-set (let alone network or gang, or even indigenous tribe or nation).

19. Rousseau [1755] 1967. My remarks are not meant to suggest that Rousseau's essay does not have its own original brilliance of narrative, polemic, and style, or that anthropologists aren't still profoundly influenced by it. On the contrary, see the conclusion of Lévi-Strauss's *Totemism* (1963) for one resounding endorsement of the essay.

20. Ibn Khaldûn, the Tunisian-born sage who so admired Saharan nomads for their valor and toughness, considered this idea important enough to place on the first page of his multivolume introduction to world history. Ibn Khaldûn was familiar with and admired at least some of Aristotle's work.

21. Eguchi 1986; Eldridge 1970. Of course, the moral or jural concepts of the translators may sometimes color translations, too.

22. I am grateful to the lexicographer Chege wa Githioru for consultation on this point.

23. Some anglophone African writers have argued for human rights to political self-determination and socioeconomic development. Both of these

figure prominently in Shepherd and Anikpo (1990, passim). See also Welch 1995 for discussions of nongovernmental organizations' activities in support of these principles.

24. See also Eriksen 1997, 51–52, on Mauritius; and other essays in Wilson 1997.

25. The scholarly literature on human rights in Africa and other concepts that translate roughly thereto is still sparse, though see An-Na'im and Deng 1990; Cohen, Hyden, and Nagan 1993; Eriksen 1997; Messer 1993; Moore 1998; Shepherd and Anikpo 1990; Wilson 1997; and other sources they cite.

26. Tibi (1990, 119–20) summarizes the twenty-three Principles of the Universal Islamic Declaration of Human Rights (*al-bayan al-'alami 'an huquq al-insan fi al-islam*) as follows: the right to live in dignity; the right to freedom, equality, and justice; the right to lawful and just treatment in courts; the right to protection from the arbitrariness of political rule; the right to protection from torture; the right of the individual to protect his honor and his reputation; the right to political asylum; the rights of minorities; the right of participation; the freedom of thought, of conviction, and of speech; the right to freedom of religious thought; the right to campaign for and disseminate one's own beliefs; economic rights; the right of private property; the right of labor; the right to satisfy basic human needs; the right to build a family; the rights of wives (e.g., to ask for divorce); the right to education; the right to privacy; and the right to travel (freedom of movement) and choice of residence. As Tibi notes, these principles are heavily influenced by non-Muslim culture and law, and some are not deeply grounded in Islamic history or tradition.

27. An example of an African rights agreement heavily influenced by Euro-American tradition (through the UN's 1948 Universal Declaration of Human Rights and the two 1966 covenants that became the International Bill of Human Rights) is the International African Charter on Human and Peoples' Rights (Banjul Charter), adopted by African states in 1981.

28. Kenya presents several striking examples of revitalization movements, including the Mumbo "cult" among Gusii and Luo of the early 1910s, the Dini ya Msambwa movement among Bukusu (Luhya) and Pokot (Kalenjin) of Kenya in the early 1940s, and the Mau Mau movement among Gikuyu in the early 1950s.

29. See Maquet 1961 on human inequality as a "given" in precolonial and colonial Rwanda. This "premise" has been a focal point of debates about the causes of genocidal war between Hutu and Tutsi—episodic violence traceable in part to Belgian colonial favoritism based on similar presumptions of natural ethnic hierarchy.

30. Dictators sometimes raise objections about universal human rights: that rights of collectivities supersede the rights of individuals; that rulers have the duty to uplift their subjects, no matter what these wish or say; and that majority groups are *as indigenous as minorities* and should enjoy at least as much of whatever is to be called a right (on East Asian variants of these views,

see Kirk Endicott's essay in this volume). Such arguments on the part of leaders underline the point that one's philosophy about who has rights, or ought to have them, is sometimes heavily conditioned by who one is in society to begin with. They also suggest once again that individualism and universalism tend to appear together: in the case of these arguments, they are both just about absent.

31. Periodic surveys of such cases may be found in *Cultural Survival Quarterly*. It isn't that national governments in Africa cannot defend human rights (however defined), but rather that they have not done so consistently and have in fact often been among the prime human rights offenders. Scott (1998) discusses the role of what he calls "high modernist" ideology and aesthetics behind state bureaucratic coersion, for instance in resettlement schemes in Tanzania and Ethiopia.

32. Take, for instance, the Gambian Mandinko *kafoo,* a multipurpose, village-level men's, women's, or youth association and quasi-government; *sinkiro* and *dabada,* two family units that do not precisely correspond to the concept of a household; or *daara,* a tight hearthside circle consisting of a Qur'anic master and his disciples that grows into a widespread network later in life.

33. The following impressions—which are no more than that—are drawn mainly from my own experiences in western Kenya between 1980 and 1983 and on briefer visits since that time; in the Gambia in 1986, 1987, and 1991 (about eight months); and in a few other parts of Africa.

34. Cohen and Atieno Odhiambo take care to point out that the Luo social universe is not confined to Luoland; for many, it stretches internationally and intercontinentally. See also Deng 1990 and Hutchinson 1996 on related Dinka and Nuer in Sudan. Shack and Skinner (1979) discuss the role of the stranger in Africa. On the importance of crisscrossing social ties (or, seen another way, crisscrossing schisms) in holding societies together, see Dyson-Hudson 1966, McIntosh 1998.

35. See Carrier's discussion (1995) of "occidentalism," the counterpart to Edward Said's influential idea of "orientalism." Occidentalism means stereotyping "the West" as individualistic, materialistic, rational, market-oriented, and so on, and thus as fundamentally different from "the rest," who are presumed to operate by different principles.

36. Deng (1990, 264–66) notes that immortality through procreation and through respect by one's progeny is an ideal and "overriding goal" of Dinka in Sudan; on this point he could almost be writing on Africa south of the Sahara in general.

37. Indeed, one Ghanaian philosopher, Kwame Gyekye, faults both African and European communitarian philosophers for the "short shrift given to individual rights" (Gyekye 1997, 62). He argues that regard for human dignity should give rise to regard for personal rights in a community. For Gyekye, "rights belong primarily and irreducibly to the individual" (67), although indi-

vidual rights must be matched by social duties, and the common good can trump individual rights (66). This view is not so different from Rousseau's later writings or Kant's writings on the subject.

38. Anthropological literature on landholding in Africa is reviewed in Goheen and Shipton 1992; and Shipton 1994.

39. Mamdani (1996) provocatively distinguishes between citizen and subject in Africa, arguing that colonialism treated people on that continent as one or the other in a way that profoundly affected their self-image.

References

An-Na'im, Abdullahi Ahmed, and Francis M. Deng, eds. 1990. *Human Rights in Africa: Cross-Cultural Perspectives.* Washington, D.C.: Brookings Institution.

Aristotle. 1962. *The Politics.* Harmondsworth: Penguin.

Aristotle. 1980. *Nicomachean Ethics.* Oxford: Oxford University Press.

Besteman, Catherine, and Lee Cassanelli. 1996. *The Struggle for Land in Southern Somalia: The War behind the War.* Boulder, Colo.: Westview Press.

Carrier, James. 1995. *Occidentalism: Images of the West.* Oxford: Clarendon Press.

Cohen, David William, and E. S. Atieno Odhiambo. 1989. *Siaya: The Historical Anthropology of an African Landscape.* London, Athens, and Nairobi: James Currey, Ohio University Press, and Heinemann Kenya.

Cohen, Ronald, Goran Hyden, and Winston P. Nagan, eds. 1993. *Human Rights and Governance in Africa.* Gainesville: University Press of Florida.

Deng, Francis. 1990. A Cultural Approach to Human Rights among the Dinka. In *Human Rights in Africa: Cross-Cultural Perspectives,* edited by Abdullahi Ahmed An-Na'im and Francis M. Deng, 261–89. Washington, D.C.: Brookings Institution.

Dieterlen, Germaine, ed. 1973. *La notion de personne en Afrique noire.* Paris: Editions du Centre National de la Recherche Scientifique.

Donnelly, Jack. 1990. Human Rights and Western Liberalism. In *Human Rights in Africa: Cross-Cultural Perspectives,* edited by Abdullahi Ahmed An-Na'im and Francis M. Deng, 31–55. Washington, D.C.: Brookings Institution.

Dworkin, Ronald. 1977. *Taking Rights Seriously.* Cambridge, Mass.: Harvard University Press.

Dyson-Hudson, Neville. 1966. *Karimojong Politics.* Oxford: Clarendon Press.

Eguchi, Paul Kazuhisa. 1986. *An English-Fulfulde Dictionary.* African Languages and Ethnography 21. Tokyo: Institute for the Study of Languages and Cultures, Tokyo University of Foreign Studies.

Eldridge, Mohammadou. 1970. *Lexique Fulfulde comparé.* Yaoundé, Cameroon: Centre Fédéral Linguistique et Culturel, Ministère de l'Education et de la Culture.

Eriksen, Thomas Hylland. 1997. Multiculturalism, Individualism, and Human
Rights: Romanticism, the Enlightenment, and Lessons from Mauritius. In
Human Rights, Culture and Context: Anthropological Perspectives, edited
by Richard A. Wilson, 49–69. London: Pluto Press.

Eze, Emmanuel Chukwudi, ed. 1997. *Postcolonial African Philosophy: A Critical Reader.* Oxford: Blackwell.

Goheen, Mitzi, and Parker Shipton, eds. 1992. *Rights over Land: Categories
and Controversies.* Special issue of *Africa: Journal of the International
African Institute.*

Gyekye, Kwame. 1997. *Tradition and Modernity: Philosophical Reflections on
the African Experience.* New York: Oxford University Press.

Hegel, Georg Wilhelm Friedrich. [1821] 1967. *Philosophy of Right.* Translated
by T. M. Knox. Oxford: Oxford University Press.

Hobbes, Thomas. [1651] 1950. *Leviathan.* New York: E. P. Dutton.

Hutchinson, Sharon. 1996. *Nuer Dilemmas: Coping with Money, War, and the
State.* Berkeley: University of California Press.

Ibn Khaldûn. [c. 1377] 1967. *The Muqaddimah: An Introduction to History.*
Translated by Franz Rosenthal, edited and abridged by N. J. Dawood.
Princeton: Princeton University Press.

Kant, Immanuel. [1788] 1956. *Critique of Practical Reason.* Translated by
Lewis White Beck. Indianapolis: Bobbs-Merrill.

———. [1795] 1983. *Perpetual Peace and Other Essays.* Translated by Ted
Humphrey. Indianapolis: Hackett.

Karp, Ivan. 1997. Person, Notions of. In *Encyclopedia of Africa South of the
Sahara,* vol. 3, edited by John Middleton, 392–96. New York: Charles
Scribner's Sons.

Lévi-Strauss, Claude. 1963. *Totemism* (Le Totémisme aujourd'hui). Boston:
Beacon.

Locke, John. [1689] 1976. *The Second Treatise of Government.* Oxford: Blackwell.

Mamdani, Mahmood. 1996. *Citizen and Subject: Contemporary Africa and the
Dilemma of Late Colonialism.* Princeton: Princeton University Press.

Maquet, Jacques. 1961. *The Premise of Inequality in Rwanda.* London: Oxford
University Press for International African Institute.

McIntosh, Roderick. 1998. *Peoples of the Middle Niger: The Island of Gold.*
Oxford: Blackwell.

Merry, Sally. 1992. Anthropology, Law, and Transnational Processes. *Annual
Review of Anthropology* 21:357–79.

Messer, Ellen. 1993. Anthropology and Human Rights. *Annual Review of
Anthropology* 22:221–49.

Moore, Sally Falk. 1986. *Social Facts and Fabrications: "Customary" Law on
Kilimanjaro, 1880–1980.* Cambridge: Cambridge University Press.

———. 1998. Changing African Land Tenure: Reflections on the Incapacities
of the State. *European Journal of Development Research* 10 (2): 33–49.

Nowrojee, Binaifer. 1993. *Divide and Rule: State Sponsored Ethnic Violence in Kenya.* New York: Africa Watch.

Peters, Krijn, and Paul Richards. 1998. Why We Fight: Voices of Youth Combatants in Sierra Leone. *Africa: Journal of the International African Institute,* 68 (2): 183–210.

Rawls, John. 1972. *A Theory of Justice.* Cambridge, Mass.: Belknap Press of Harvard University Press.

Riesman, Paul. 1977. *Freedom in Fulani Social Life: An Introspective Ethnography.* Chicago: University of Chicago Press.

———. 1986. The Person and the Life Cycle in African Social Life and Thought. *Africa Studies Review* 29 (2): 71–198.

Rousseau, Jean-Jacques. [1755] 1967. Discourse on the Origin and Foundation of Inequality among Mankind (Discours sur l'origine et les fondements de l'inégalité parmi les hommes). In *The Social Contract and Discourse on the Origin of Inequality,* anonymous translation, edited by Lester G. Crocker. New York: Simon and Schuster.

———. [1762] 1967. The Social Contract (du Contrat Social). In *The Social Contract and Discourse on the Origin of Inequality,* anonymous translation, edited by Lester G. Crocker. New York: Simon and Schuster.

Scott, James C. 1998. *Seeing Like a State: How Some Projects to Improve the Human Condition Have Failed.* New Haven: Yale University Press.

Shack, William A., and Elliott P. Skinner, eds. 1979. *Strangers in African Societies.* Berkeley: University of California Press.

Shepherd, George W., Jr., and Mark O. C. Anikpo. 1990. *Emerging Human Rights: The African Political Economy Context.* Westport, Conn.: Greenwood Press.

Shipton, Parker. 1994. Land and Culture in Tropical Africa: Soils, Symbols, and the Metaphysics of the Mundane. *Annual Review of Anthropology* 23:347–77.

Simons, Anna. 1995. *Networks of Dissolution: Somalia Undone.* Boulder, Colo.: Westview Press.

Smedt, Johan de. 1998. Child Marriages in Rwandan Refugee Camps. *Africa: Journal of the International African Institute,* 68 (2): 211–37.

Smith, Adam. [1762–66] 1982. *Lectures on Jurisprudence.* Indianapolis: Liberty Press.

———. [1759, last rev. 1790] 1984. *The Theory of Moral Sentiments.* Indianapolis: Liberty Press.

Spencer, Herbert. 1876–96. *Principles of Sociology.* 3 vols. New York: Appleton.

Stackhouse, Max L. 1984. *Creeds, Society, and Human Rights: A Study in Three Cultures.* Grand Rapids, Mich.: W. B. Eerdmans.

Tacitus. [c. A.D. 98] 1942. Germany and Its Tribes. In *The Complete Works of Tacitus,* translated by Alfred John Church and William Jackson Brodribb, edited by Moses Hadas, 709–34. New York: Modern Library.

Tibi, Bassam. 1990. The European Tradition of Human Rights and the Culture of Islam. In *Human Rights in Africa: Cross-Cultural Perspectives,* edited by Abdullahi Ahmed An-Na'im and Francis M. Deng, 104–32. Washington, D.C.: Brookings Institution.

Welch, Claude. 1995. *Protecting Human Rights in Africa: Roles and Strategies of Non-governmental Organizations.* Philadelphia: University of Pennsylvania Press.

Wilson, Richard A., ed. 1997. *Human Rights, Culture and Context: Anthropological Perspectives.* London: Pluto Press.

2 Indigenous Rights and the Politics of Identity in Post-Apartheid Southern Africa

Richard B. Lee

The terms *indigenous rights* and *post-apartheid* raise a number of questions in the context of southern Africa. The situation with rights is straightforward enough: we know that South Africa has been grossly deficient in upholding those (at least until 1994); but what about indigenous rights? What exactly does *indigenous* mean in the South African context? And how do we gloss *post-Apartheid* in South Africa, since the laws are no longer on the books but the structural violence instituted by apartheid still affects the lives of millions of people?

To start untangling the conundrums, I will begin from the premise that a complex terrain of struggle exists today at many levels in South Africa and its former satellites. The primary contradiction is, of course, the three-hundred-year struggle of African peoples against expropriation, racism, oppression, and underdevelopment under the European colonialists. But within that broad canvas are woven the strands of many smaller struggles by local groupings in specific historical circumstances.

One of the most interesting of these strands is the issue of Khoisan history and identity: how these have been constructed by Khoi and San themselves and by others in colonial and modern South Africa, and how the present government and emerging civil society of South Africa is searching for new approaches to a very old issue. So this is a story— actually, several stories—about the politics of identity in the era of apartheid and about the reconstruction of identities and the realignment of forces in the post-apartheid period.

If we draw a line north to south from the Zambezi River to the Indian Ocean, bisecting the subcontinent into two equal portions (see map 2.1), we find that—both precolonially and today—90 percent of the population lives in the eastern half of the subcontinent and only 10 per-

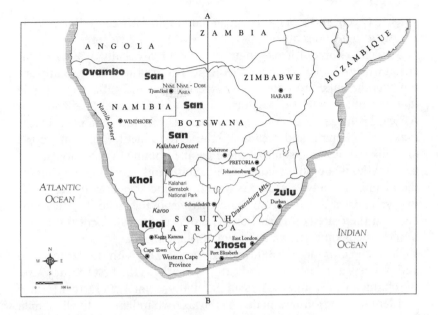

Map 2.1.   Map locating major ethnic groups, geographical features, and case studies mentioned in the text. North-south line A–B illustrates the subcontinent's division between the densely populated east and the sparsely populated west.

cent in the west. With the exception of Cape Town and its surrounding districts, the western half of southern Africa consists largely of the Karoo and the Kalahari, two vast, starkly beautiful, and sparsely populated semideserts. Precolonially, this north-south line marked a major ethnocultural division: between the Bantu-speaking peoples in the eastern half and the far less numerous Khoisan peoples in the west. The term *Khoisan* is a neologism, coined in the twentieth century and used to describe two related peoples: the pastoral Khoi, or "Hottentots," and the hunting and gathering San, or "Bushmen."

There is a series of complex links between San and Khoi, but the focus here is on the links between the historic Khoisan and their twentieth-century descendants, the deracinated and proletarianized people called Coloureds in South Africa's racialized terminology. The Khoi and especially the San are known to us largely through an ethnographic discourse, while the Coloured appear primarily in the sociological and political treatises on Apartheid. This chapter explores these links between ancestors and descendants and between ethnographic and sociological discourses.

Khoisan peoples form a linguistically and physically distinct population within Africa. Their archaeological associations have significant time depths linked to Later Stone Age hunting and gathering cultures that are millennia old. They formerly occupied the whole of southern Africa, both east and west. Their legacy can be found in magnificent rock art the length and breadth of the subcontinent. Sometime in the first millennium B.C., some of these people obtained sheep, goats, and later cattle, while others continued to hunt and gather—the origin of the distinction between the pastoral Khoi and the foraging San. The two categories are far from watertight, and the historical relations between them are complex. For the moment, we will focus our attention on the people known as San or Bushmen.

With the entrance of Bantu-speaking peoples with domestic sheep and pottery, and later iron and cattle, as early as the first century A.D., the character of southern African populations changed further (Nurse and Jenkins 1977). But even during the last two millennia, the Bushmen have been the exclusive occupants of significant portions of southern Africa, living as autonomous hunter-gatherers in parts of the Karoo, Kalahari, and Namib deserts (Solway and Lee 1990). For much of this period there is evidence of trade relations between the San peoples and their non-San neighbors (Phillipson 1985; Wilmsen 1989; Wilmsen and Denbow 1990). To the southwest they interacted with the related Khoi (Hottentot) pastoralists, from whom they differentiated linguistically sometime before the first millennium A.D.; in fact, well over half of all the San today speak Khoi languages (Silberbauer 1981; Tanaka 1989). In the east and southeast, Khoisan peoples coexisted with, inter-married with, and were eventually assimilated to the powerful Bantu-speaking chiefdoms that now form the bulk of South Africa's population. The standard explanation for the numerous click sounds found in modern Zulu, Swazi, and Xhosa is the linguistic influence of click speakers, assumed to be female, intermarrying with Bantu speakers and passing on the clicks to their offspring.[1]

The colonial period—initiated in 1652 with the arrival of Jan van Riebeeck at the Cape of Good Hope—placed enormous pressures on Khoisan inside the Cape Colony and the later Boer republics. Bush-man peoples played a major role in the colonial history of South Africa. They met the early explorers at the Cape, guided them into the interior, and later fought tenaciously to preserve their land in the face of European expansion (Wright 1971; Marks 1972; Elphick 1977).

As graphically described in a famous article by Shula Marks (1972), the San of the western Cape were hounded by waves of white settlers and were driven further and further north into the desert. In retaliation, they raided the invaders' cattle, provoking further armed assaults by the notorious Boer "Commandos" of the eighteenth and nineteenth centuries. By the twentieth century, the living, breathing San people had become largely a matter of memory overlaid with a thickening accretion of myth.

Ironically, it was only after the San ceased to be a military threat that San art, myth, and folklore became part of the cultural imagination of the region's peoples, both black and white. Bushman themes are inscribed in the South African historical and literary canon, in the works of such writers as W. H. I. Bleek and Lucy Lloyd (1911), Eugène Marais (1969), J. M. Stow (1905), George McCall Theal (1888–93, 1915–26), and Laurens van der Post (1958, 1961). And today Bushman themes provide a seemingly inexhaustible source of inspiration for South African artists, poets, and writers ranging from the internationally known Pippa Skotnes to anonymous black artists peddling their wares on the streets of Cape Town.[2]

Beyond South Africa's borders, leather-clad hunter-gatherers identifying themselves as Bushmen persisted into the twentieth century; many had a very different and far less traumatic experience at the hands of the imperialists. But within South Africa, what happened to the San people themselves, as distinguished from their mythologized legacy? The conventional wisdom is that as a result of the horrors of the Commando period, the Bushman people were exterminated in South Africa proper. But this is not strictly true. The South African historian Nigel Penn (1999) and the Swiss-Hungarian anthropologist Miklos Szalay (1995) have documented what we have long known to be the case: that many of the Coloured of today must have had Bushman ancestors. Szalay notes that while thousands of San *were* exterminated,

[t]he documentary evidence suggests that a much higher percentage of San . . . have been incorporated into colonial society. "Bushmen" who had lived on the farm for an extended period were . . . no longer called such. They were considered "Hottentots," and appear, as do their descendants, in the documents as "Hottentots." The "Bushmen" after their incorporation into the colony as "Hottentots" and later "Coloureds," were no longer visible to the casual observer. (109)

Where are all these people, and can any of the present-day Coloureds trace their heritage? The historical transitions from San to Hottentot and from Hottentot to Coloured represent one of the most intriguing examples of ethnic transformation and the emergence of new identities in southern Africa. Yet the issue of San and Khoi historical memory has barely been addressed. We shall return to this point later on.

To the question of the changing San identities can be added the equally intriguing question of exactly who is indigenous in the South African context. Examination of the South African example highlights some of the ambiguities inherent in the concept of "indigenous." In settler societies such as Canada, the United States, and Australia, the question of "indigenism" is relatively straightforward, because the line between indigenous and nonindigenous is clear. Since virtually all the nonaboriginal peoples of North America are post-1492 immigrants from Europe, Africa, and elsewhere, it is possible (in theory) to draw sharp conceptual boundaries around who can be considered indigenous.[3] Latin America has a long scholarly and political tradition of *indigenismo,* but African discourse is quite different again. As Murumbi (1994) has pointed out, the black peoples of Africa, whether hunter-gatherers, herders, farmers, or city dwellers, can all claim great antiquity on the continent. Thus, any distinctions between indigenous and nonindigenous must necessarily be invidious ones. The government of Botswana, for example, home to over half of all the Bushman peoples of Africa, refused to participate in the UN-declared Year of the Indigenous People (1993), on the grounds that in their country, *everyone* was indigenous.

The Botswana government's objections reveal a hidden subtext in the use of the term *indigenous* by Western media and intellectuals. In this usage, it refers not just to people who have lived in place for a long time, but specifically to encapsulated minorities, who are ethnically (and often linguistically) distinct from the surrounding population and who carry on an economic adaptation—invariably based on simpler technology— that further marginalizes them (cf. Perry 1996). What indigenous people do have is what migrants and the children of migrants (i.e., most of the rest of us) feel they lack: a sense of belonging, a sense of rootedness in place. It is this longing to belong that has become one of the most valued ideological commodities in the era of late capitalism. This perspective enables us to explore the fate and fortunes of some of the people in the region, such as the San/Bushmen, who might lay claim to a more specialized and restricted sense of indigenicity.

The changing nomenclature over the last thirty years reflects some of these issues. In the late 1960s, the term *Bushmen,* long considered pejorative, was replaced in scholarly circles by the seemingly more neutral indigenous term *San,* introduced by Monica Wilson and Leonard Thompson in their *Oxford History of South Africa* (1968). But *San* was not without its detractors. Meaning "aborigines or settlers proper" in the Khoi language (Hahn 1881), it also had the connotation of "worthless vagabond"—a view of San people that is, incidentally, still prevalent among contemporary rural Coloureds (Robin Oakley, personal communication, 1995). In 1989 a group of literate "San" (Namibian Ju/'hoansi) expressed a preference for the term *Bushmen* over *San,* and scholars and activists reintroduced *Bushmen* in solidarity (Biesele 1990; Hitchcock 1996). In 1996, however, the same Ju/'hoansi decided, upon reflection, that *Bushmen* carried too great a historical burden; they opted for rehabilitating *San,* a move welcomed by many scholars who had continued to use that word. Other terms have regional usage. For instance, in Botswana, the various groups of San—elegantly analyzed by Pnina Motzafi-Haller (1994)—refer to themselves collectively as Basarwa, the Setswana term for San. The late John Hardbattle, part Nharo and founder of the advocacy group Kgeikani Kweni (First People of the Kalahari), introduced the Nharo term *Nǀoakwe* (*Washington Post,* January 16, 1996). For an excellent general discussion of the political uses of ethnic labels, see Isaacs 1989.

Khoisan Peoples as Discourse

In writing about Khoisan peoples today, one has to deal with a century of discourses, some rooted in European and African notions of "difference" and race, others springing from European ideas of the "natural man," and all of these closely bound up with discourses to rationalize European colonialism and imperialism (Wolf 1982; Gordon 1992; Skotnes 1996). These ideologically saturated discourses form an implicit background of unstated assumptions, predispositions, and prejudices. European settlers of the seventeenth to nineteenth centuries in the main regarded the Khoisan with thinly veiled contempt, as incorrigible bandits speaking scarcely intelligible tongues. The South African Bushmen, along with the "Hottentots," were positioned on the bottom rung of the *scala natura* of humanity, serving as a text for ruminations on who may or may not be part of the human family (Moodie 1976; Thompson 1985; Gordon 1992). A more nuanced view of the hunter-gatherers was expressed by their agricultural and pastoral neighbors, who, while according them an inferior social position, nevertheless intermarried with them and regarded them with a mixture of paternalism and respect (the latter in deference to their poisoned arrows).[4]

White South African attitudes in this century have undergone an almost complete reversal, from fear and loathing to uncritical admiration; witness the idealization of "the Bushman" as the embodiment of noble virtues in the writings of Laurens van der Post (1958, 1961). Conservationists, indigenous rights advocates, and ethnographers have written about them in largely positive ways (Miller 1993; Kent 1996). The gods may have been crazy, but the producers knew exactly what they were doing when the late Jamie Uys brought N!au, the Bushman, iconic status in two enormously successful commercial films, casting him in the role of "Urmensch" in a vision of pristine Africa.[5] The Euro–South African public continues to see in the Bushmen images of the good and simple life lived close to nature.

Ironically, however, the African elite of Botswana now have come to see the "Basarwa" as quite the opposite: a social problem, a feckless underclass standing in the way of progress. In a striking and curious inversion, these contemporary African elite views mirror closely the condescension of the white settlers of the ninteenth century.

Contemporary anthropological scholarship has, of course, interrogated and discarded much of the racist baggage that burdened nineteenth-century discourse, but new debates over competing orthodoxies invariably echo older controversies. Archaeologists and historians have focused on the encounter between resident hunter-gatherers and incoming farmers and herders during the last two millennia. This has been one of the key themes in African history and oral traditions (Kopytoff 1987; Smith 1992). Some have read the evidence as showing that the foragers were subordinated, as early as 800 A.D., to powerful Iron Age newcomers (Schrire 1984; Wilmsen 1989; Wilmsen and Denbow 1990). Others, myself included, have argued that the evidence supports a far more pluralistic view of San prehistory: the early subordination of some and the autonomous persistence of others, with still others lying in between (Solway and Lee 1990; Yellen and Brooks 1990; Lee and Guenther 1991, 1993, 1995).

The San/Bushmen Today: Nations within Nations?

Whatever the historical facts, the situation for San peoples early in the third millennium is not encouraging. Since San people have been invoked in so many anthropological discussions over the years, a brief survey may be useful in order to give a sense of their current status and to introduce the players in the arena of identity politics (Biesele et al. 1989).

Namibia's thirty-eight thousand San are found on white farms, in urban areas, in former government-sponsored settlements such as the famous Tjum!kui located in Bushmanland, and in small communities where people make their living through a mixture of foraging, herding, and rural industries (Marshall 1976; Marshall and Ritchie 1984; Biesele 1990; Gordon 1992; Hitchcock 1992, 1996). The Nyae Nyae Farmers Cooperative is a successful grassroots organization that has grown up around the communities that were subjects of the Marshall family's famous ethnographic and film studies (Marshall 1976, 1999).

The !Kung San populations in Angola and Namibia were heavily affected by the protracted warfare waged first by the Portuguese and later the South Africans against the Popular Movement for the Liberation of Angola (MPLA) and the South West Africa People's Organization (SWAPO). Moreover, a number of San in Namibia, Zimbabwe, and Botswana were dispossessed as a result of the establishment of game reserves and national parks (Gordon 1992; Hitchcock 1987, 1993, 1996). Ranching, agriculture, dams, and road projects have also had significant impacts on the well-being of San populations (Wily 1979, 1994; Gordon 1992; Hitchcock 1996; Hitchcock and Holm 1993). Many have become dependent on the state for support via welfare payments and drought-relief programs (Mogwe 1992; Hitchcock and Holm 1993).

The Republic of Botswana is unusual in Africa in that it has had a program aimed directly at assisting its Bushman, or Basarwa, minority (Hitchcock and Holm 1993). In spite of the government's Remote Area Development Program, the socioeconomic status of the fifty thousand Bushmen and other rural people has declined considerably in recent years. They are regarded by other Africans as ethnically distinct and socially inferior, and their current underclass position is compounded by disabilities of race. Thus, the internal politics of the Botswana Basarwa have come to resemble very much a politics of the oppressed (Hitchcock and Holm 1993; Hitchcock 1996).

The Botswana government is pursuing a policy of assimilation ("villagization") (Wily 1979; Hitchcock and Holm 1993). As one government official said, "We must absorb all of 'these people' into the body politic of the nation of Botswana" (Robert Hitchcock, personal communication, 1994). But many, if not most, of the Basarwa of Botswana are resisting assimilationist pressures, seeking at least a degree of cultural and political autonomy. As one member of the northeastern San group, the Kua, told the anthropologist Robert Hitchcock, "We are different from the Tswana majority, and we have the right to be different." They would like land of their own and, as another put it, "to be left alone so that we can live the way we wish." John Hardbattle's group First People of the Kalahari is but one of a dozen advocacy groups and nongovernmental organizations working on behalf of Botswana Basarwa and Namibian San (Lee, Hitchcock, and Biesele 2002).

Khoisan Marginality: Historical Perspectives

Despite encouraging signs of political mobilization, most observers would agree that the social and economic situation of the contemporary San is desperate. But what of the past? Is their present plight a recent phenomenon preceded by a longer history of autonomous foraging? Or were the Bushmen, as some argue, long subordinated to more powerful outsiders?[6]

In other words, do those San now seeking to throw off the burden of ethnic discrimination have to overcome merely some decades of domination, or is there a far deeper history of oppression? This is an issue debated in the pages of *Current Anthropology* and known as the Great Kalahari Debate (Wilmsen 1989; Barnard 1992b; Lee 1992b; Kuper 1992).

In *Land Filled with Flies* (1989), Edwin Wilmsen presented a twofold thesis: first, that the Dobe-area Ju/'hoansi had experienced a millennium of subordination at the hands of Iron Age outsiders and incorporation into an Iron Age pastoral economy; and second, that this subordination was followed by their early and devastating collapse under the pressure of merchant capital. This now-famous "revisionist" argument has had a lot of appeal among Western scholars trying to come to grips with globalization in the new world order, but it came as a complete surprise to the Ju/'hoansi themselves.

Letting the subaltern speak is one of the prime directives of the postcolonial and post-structuralist agenda espoused by the Kalahari revisionists. Had they bothered to listen to Ju voices, they would have found an interesting story: in area after area, Ju/'hoan oral traditions tell of a long history of autonomous hunting and gathering without agriculture or domesticated animals, and they insist that neither blacks nor whites appeared in the interior until the latter part of the nineteenth century.

In oral historical accounts, from both Namibia and Botswana, the Ju/'hoansi articulated a strong sense of their own history as hunter-

Fig. 2.1.   Listening to the subaltern. Author recording oral histories with Ju/'hoan elders, N//oma, northern Namibia, 1997.

gatherers who, though by no means isolated, lived largely independently on their wild food resources and carried on long-distance trade with farming peoples on their periphery. By themselves, these Ju/'hoan accounts can be considered only as an interesting cultural construction. However, archaeological research by Alison Brooks and John Yellen (1988, 1990), Andrew Smith and myself (1997), and Karim Sadr (1997) confirms the Ju story. We failed to turn up any evidence of domesticated animals or non-Bushman occupation of the Dobe–Nyae Nyae areas before the twentieth century.

The Ju/'hoan view of their own autonomy is also strongly corroborated by the accounts of Western explorers in the late nineteenth and early twentieth centuries—observers such as Schinz (1891), Passarge (1904, 1907), and Müller (1912). The German geographer Siegfried Passarge, for example, was emphatic on both San autonomy and their noninvolvement in the pastoral economy. Of the powerful and well-organized "Buschmanreich" of the mid-nineteenth-century Ghanzi San, he wrote:

They were a hunting people par excellence. All social and political relations, all rights and laws, their entire political organization was based on the hunt. (1907, 119)[7]

Elsewhere he noted:

The honour of the chief was hereditary in those days and the
Bushmen were totally independent. The Batuana did not dare set
foot into their region and the Hottentots only entered it on raids.
(1907, 115)

The oral histories mentioned above, never previously published, and
the corresponding explorers' accounts are set out in Smith and Lee
1997 and Lee 2002. The larger historical issues are addressed in a growing critical literature (Barnard 1992b; Lee and Guenther 1993, 1995; Lee
1992a; Guenther 1993–94; Kent 1996). What the revisionists do is seriously underestimate the sheer diversity of historical circumstances of
the Khoisan peoples in the precolonial period.

San autonomy is *not* a figment of the romantic imagination. While
there were wretched San peoples in the nineteenth century living in
abject poverty, there were also independent cattleholding San and a
number of very successful groups who lived by the hunt and maintained a proud independence (Kent 1996). For example, the Namibian
historian Frieda-Nela Williams (1991) describes the relations between
the eighteenth- and nineteenth-century Ovambo kingdoms of northern
Namibia and the Bushmen—whom they called the Khwankala—as
equitable and friendly. They traded on the basis of equality, not as
masters and servants. In at least two kingdoms, traditions have it that
the royal line was founded upon marriages between Ovambo men and
hunter-gatherer women.

But what of the San in South Africa itself? Does historiography
offer support for the revisionist thesis of long subordination and early
collapse? Certainly, in colonial South Africa the pressure on foraging
peoples was vastly greater than in the Kalahari, as thousands of Boer
trekkers and Khoi freebooters moved into the interior. Shula Marks's
classic article "Khoisan Resistance to the Dutch in the Seventeenth
and Eighteenth Centuries" (1972) documented the military resistance
by the San peoples to Boer expansion. And then there is John Wright's
famous study "Bushman Raiders of the Drakensberg" (1971), which
shows how resilient the San people had been in the face of increasing
pressure by both European and other African forces on the Natal frontier from the 1840s to the 1870s.

Khoisan Marginality: Three Stories

That was then. This is now. Despite the heroic stands of the nineteenth century, San/Bushman peoples were ruthlessly hounded in colonial South Africa, and those who did survive merged imperceptibly into the generalized mass of rural Coloured. By 1950, the dawn of the apartheid era, San people were virtually extinct inside South Africa except for a few isolated remnants. *Or so we thought.*

The fall of Apartheid and the coming to power of Nelson Mandela and the African National Congress (ANC) triggered a remarkable phenomenon: people claiming the Khoisan mantle appeared suddenly and proliferated rapidly, each claiming to be the authentic voice of one or another indigenous Khoisan people. I would like to relate three stories that together illustrate the state of indigenicity in contemporary South Africa.

Khoisan Histories I: ≠Khomani Bushmen

The first story concerns a band of fifty to sixty ≠Khomani, or N/huki, Bushmen who up until the 1970s lived around the gates of the Kalahari Gemsbok National Park in the extreme north of the Cape Province. In periodic surveys of Bushman peoples through the 1950s and 1960s, they were usually trotted out as the only surviving representatives within South Africa proper (with the possible exception of an even smaller group at Lake Chrissie in the eastern Transvaal). The Gemsbok Park San are famous in another way. A *Life* magazine photographer did a photo shoot there in 1948, and several of these photos—including a famous over-the-shoulder shot of a Bushman showing his son how to spear a gemsbok—found their way into the 1950s best-selling photo book *The Family of Man*.

However, the ≠Khomani had an "unfortunate" custom: they liked to actually hunt and eat the animals they lived with, not just pose with them for photographs! This earned them the ire of the powers that be. In 1976, the South African game department chased the last of the ≠Khomani away from Gemsbok Park. The ≠Khomani became simply one of the hundreds of displaced peoples cast adrift in South Africa by the workings of apartheid-era statutes. For years they lived dispersed on white farms in the northern Cape, eking out a living doing odd jobs, raising a few goats, and making use of veld foods. In this respect, they were no different from millions of other rural black South Africans.

The truly postmodern history of the ≠Khomani begins in 1991, and here I draw on the recent study by Hylton White *In the Tradition of the*

Forefathers: Bushman Traditionality at Kagga Kamma (1995), which chronicles the saga of Dawid Kruiper and his group. When the ≠Khomani were evicted as squatters from yet another farm in 1991, their plight came to the attention of the local press. The South African public's appetite for things Bushman was fed by the account of the sorry state of these, the "last surviving," etc., etc., within the Republic.

A farmer and entrepreneur named Pieter de Waal then opened a theme park and resort at Kagga Kamma, in the beautiful Cedarberg Mountains north of Cape Town. He gathered Kruiper's people together and brought them to Kagga Kamma, where they became the centerpiece attractions at the "Bushman theme park" (White 1995). Its pamphlet conveys the flavor of the place:

> Imagine yourself . . . in the company of . . . unbelievably, several families of stone-age Bushmen. . . . A unique experience for visitors is the privilege to step into the world of the authentic Bushmen. Here they let you share in their age-old skills of hunting and firelighting, and in the beauty of their handicrafts, dancing and story-telling. (White 1995, 11)

The world of the "authentic Bushmen" in the Kagga Kamma camp today consists of San dressing in "traditional" clothing and presenting themselves before a daily stream of tourists. They make and sell crafts and perform dances, for which they receive modest wages and rations.[8]

Far from being a cynical sellout, the leader of the group, Dawid Kruiper, is a thoughtful and reflective man, trying to come to grips with the world turned upside down. Reflecting on his present circumstances, Kruiper is quoted by White as saying:

> I am a child of nature. I want people to see me and know who I am. The only way our tradition and way of life can survive is to live in the memory of those who see us. (17)

And elsewhere, he is at pains to set himself apart from the corruptions of "civilization":

> Today I have to wear deodorant, but I do not know it. I can find plants that smell nicer. . . . Here I have to put on clothes because there are dangerous things here. But in the Kalahari I can throw away my clothes and wear the /ai [loincloth]. (19)

The Kagga Kamma people are attempting to reinvent themselves as "authentic" carriers of an age-old tradition. Living on the white farms of the northern Cape, the ≠Khomani were long known as Bastars, the endearing local term for Coloured people, but Dawid Kruiper resists inclusion in the Bastar category:

> The largest difference between a Bushman and a Bastar is that a Bushman wants to keep his Bushman tradition, but not a Bastar. He just wants to be a white man. I am a person of nature, who bears the knowledge: I do not want to westernize. . . . I have my own language, an Englishman has his own language, but where is the Bastar language? He speaks Jan van Riebeeck's language. (19)

Dawid Kruiper emerges from Hylton White's sensitive account as a tragic figure, almost a character in a Fugard play. One is struck by his convoluted argument that his people can survive only by being visible to the Western gaze, a kind of self-imposed or reverse orientalism that reveals the authenticating power that the West can exert over the colonized.[9] White (1995) also addresses the white South African public's appetite for "authentic Africa," and how the two imaginaries came together in the incongruous circumstances of Kagga Kamma.

The Kagga Kamma story continues to unfold. Legislation passed by the ANC government attempted to redress Apartheid wrongs by restoring to Africans land lost during the period from 1913 to 1990. In August 1995, Roger Chennells, a Stellenbosch lawyer, filed a land claim with the Minister of Land Affairs on behalf of the Kagga Kamma people and other Bushman farm laborers of the northern Cape, in the name of an entity called the Land Claim Committee of the Southern Kalahari Bushmen. The committee is claiming large sections of the Kalahari Gemsbok National Park, but the move is being challenged in court by the National Parks Board on various grounds.

On October 9, 1995, it was reported by the South African Broadcasting Corporation that Derek Hanekom, the Minister of Lands of South Africa, and Anthony Hall-Martin of the Parks Board met with thirty of the two hundred ≠Khomani Bushmen who live in the vicinity of the Kalahari Gemsbok National Park. The point was made by Minister Hanekom that there was a possibility that the Bushmen could be given the right to co-manage the park with the Parks Board. The rights of the Bushmen were thus seen as important by government officials, which in itself is a tacit recognition of the Bushmen's significance in the contemporary politics of South Africa. In 1997 the Southern Kalahari Bushmen Committee were awarded two abandoned farms in the Gemsbok Park area (Chennells 2002).[10] In March 1999, Thabo Mbehi was photographed embracing Dawid Kruiper at the handing-over ceremony. Negotiations have continued through early 2002 to grant San further ecotourism concessions in and near what is now called "The Kgalagadi Transfrontier Park."

Khoisan Histories II: Schmidtsdrift

The second of our stories has an even more postmodern twist. One of modern South Africa's most tragic chapters is the Apartheid regime's ultimately unsuccessful attempt to preserve Namibia as a neocolony. In the course of the conflict, from 1966 to 1989, thousands of Namibian peasant farmers, herders, and hunters were recruited into the South African Defence Forces (SADF). Arguably the most heavily militarized of Namibia's ethnic groups were the San people of Nyae Nyae and the Angolan border areas. In its efforts to fight SWAPO, the South African war machine had absorbed, at its peak, up to eight thousand of the estimated thirty-eight thousand Namibian San, making them one of the most heavily militarized peoples in Africa. The propaganda images of the savage and cunning fighters of Bushman commando units purveyed by the psywar branch of the SADF were very popular with the "guns and ammo" crowd in the United States and were featured regularly through the 1980s in *Soldier of Fortune* magazine.

But after the UN-brokered peace process and the independence of Namibia in 1989 under SWAPO, South Africa was faced with the problem of what to do with these thousands of Bushman soldiers and their dependents. In a memorable and chilling scene from John Marshall's classic 1980 film *N!ai: The Story of a !Kung Woman,* the South African commander of 31 Battalion, "the Bushman Battalion," is asked how long he was planning to stay in Namibia. He pauses and then replies, "The rest of my life." And when he is gently asked what would happen to the Bushmen if South Africa should lose the war, he replies, "I hadn't thought of that. I suppose if we go, the Bushmen will go with us" (Marshall 1980; Volkman 1985).

When the South Africans did leave in 1990, most of the Nyae Nyae people portrayed in the film were repatriated to their home territories. Others were settled elsewhere in Namibia. However, many soldiers had spent the last thirty years first in Portuguese units, then in South African ones, and they had nowhere to "go home" to. The commanding officer's prophecy was fulfilled when many of these Vasekela and !Kung people elected to travel south with the departing South Africans. Until recently, more than forty-five hundred former soldiers and their families had resided at Schmidtsdrift, an army base near Kimberley (Uys 1994; Steyn 1994). Even under the Apartheid regime their status was ambiguous, but with the coming to power of the Man-

Fig. 2.2.   !Xuu and Khwe men from Angola, former soldiers in the South African Defence Forces, building a new life in postwar, post-Apartheid Namibia.

dela government in April 1994, it has become even more problematic. Because they had fought against the allies of the present government, their continued presence in post-Apartheid South Africa is an unpleasant reminder of the evils of Apartheid, and because of their cultural and linguistic distinctiveness, neither the black nor the white communities have been willing to absorb them. They remained housed on the Schmidtsdrift base in a temporary military bivouac years after their arrival.

A twist on the Kagga Kamma story is the land claim suit that has been launched in connection with Schmidtsdrift. However, here the roles are reversed. It is the Batlaping, a Tswana-speaking group, who are suing and the Bushmen who are threatened with removal. After generations of residence, the Batlaping were evicted from the area in 1968 when the original Schmidtsdrift army base was set up as a staging point for troops heading to the front in Namibia. The Batlaping claim on the area is thus much stronger than that of former mercenaries and their families who were caught up in the South African war machine, and in early 1997, their claim to Schmidtsdrift was accepted by the courts.

Like Bushmen elsewhere, the Schmidtsdrift people have mobilized; in the mid-1990s they formed the !Xuu and Khwe Trust, with over half of the trust board made up of Bushmen drawn from the Schmidtsdrift population. The trust's activities consist of advocacy efforts and community development projects, including a craftmakers' cooperative, an arts project, an art center, and a living museum. Working in acrylics and oils, some of the artists are achieving international recognition for their powerful depictions of "traditional" scenes and the horrors of war. By 2002 the Schmidtsdrift colony had been relocated to abandoned farms elsewhere in the Northern Cape.

Khoisan Histories III: Neo-Khoisan Identities

The third story about Khoisan identities begins not in South Africa, but at a conference on Khoisan studies that was convened near Munich, Germany, in July 1994. Present were the usual assortment of linguists, historians, and anthropologists, and the tone of the meeting was suitably scholarly. The issue of Bushmen in South Africa and the broader question of Khoisan identities gained immediate relevancy when the atmosphere of probity and gravity was jarred on the opening day. Prof. Henry Bredekamp, a historian from the former Coloured University of the Western Cape (UWC), rose to address the meeting, with deep conviction. The gist of his speech was as follows:

> This meeting has a great deal of significance for me because I am a person of Khoisan heritage. There are millions of South Africans like me who trace their ancestry back to the Khoi and the San peoples. These are *our* histories, *our* languages you are discussing. Under Apartheid we lost much of our culture. Now we want to work closely with you in recovering our past and our traditions.[11]

Bredekamp's intervention energized the meeting, and before it dispersed, the participants agreed to hold the next Khoisan studies meeting at the UWC in 1997 (discussed later in this essay). The speech gave a new lease on life to the field of Khoisan studies and the study of African hunter-gatherers; an entire new constituency was awakening to the importance of recording the traditions and ways of life of the small cultures of Africa, against the day when they might be rediscovered.

Thirty years ago, the great African philosopher-revolutionary Amilcar Cabral wrote that the task before the African people was not only achieving independence but also recapturing history, a history taken from the African peoples by the colonialists (Cabral 1974). These views were echoed in the writings of Steve Biko, the founder of the Black Consciousness movement in South Africa. A year after the Munich meeting, I was invited to the UWC, by Henry Bredekamp, where I noted in an address that recovering history appeared to be one of the most important cultural processes underway in post-Apartheid South Africa. In fact, it is one of the most significant social movements world-wide in the early twenty-first century. Everywhere, it seems, minority peoples are rediscovering aspects of themselves that had long been sup-pressed. Recapturing history has become a major movement in litera-ture, history, and anthropology: the study of colonial discourse, post-coloniality, and the attempts by subaltern peoples to liberate their consciousness from colonialism and its legacies (for the South African context, see, e.g., Smith 1988).

It goes without saying that the history of the so-called nonwhites of South Africa is not a unitary one; diverse historical streams are repre-sented within it. Thus, recapturing histories is not simply a question of reviving old ethnicities. It is also about acknowledging the birth of new ones—ethnicities like those of the people in the UWC Coloured stu-dent body, whose roots could be traced to not only Khoi and San, but also Dutch, Malay, Xhosa, British, and other sources drawn from three continents (du Plessis 1972; Mayson [1861] 1963; Marais 1937; for a relevant discussion, see García Canclini 1995).

Nonetheless, links to Khoi and San are among the most salient, although most neglected, components of these personal and family his-tories. Up to 2.5 million Coloured South Africans would identify themselves as Khoi or San, but until recently the opportunity for these peoples to explore their roots has been compromised and thwarted by the distortions of Apartheid (Ross 1976, 1993; Schapera 1930).

As Robert Gordon in *The Bushman Myth* (1992) has noted, previous representations of the Khoisan peoples had been saturated with racist colonial discourse. Khoi and San were presented as the castoffs of cre-ation, a doctrine tailor-made to justify oppression and dispossession. For centuries, the masses of South African people labeled "Coloured" have struggled with the problem of identity, situated halfway between the white oppressors, with whom they shared language and religion, and the black majority, toward whom they felt a mixture of fear and ambivalence (Moodie 1976; Thompson 1985). The term *Coloured* itself is an example of a Foucauldian "dividing practice," only coming into prominence as recently as the beginning of the twentieth century as the Cape's small middle class of nonwhite/non-Africans sought to carve out a bureaucratic and legal space by emphasizing their degree of "difference" from the category "native" (Goldin 1992).

With the heightening of the struggle against Apartheid, a new era opened in Coloured identity politics. One can trace the Khoisan revival ultimately to the Black Consciousness movement of the 1970s, led by the charismatic Steve Biko (1978, 1979). Black Consciousness had part of its genesis among Coloured students and intellectuals in the Cape Town area. And the anthropological world, in developing an anthropology of liberation, has been intensely interested in what was and is happening in South Africa. It is of particular interest how people of Khoisan heritage have espoused this powerful set of ideas and reidentified themselves with their ancestors and with the millions of their countrywomen and countrymen who were fighting oppression (Pityana et al. 1992).

Of course, wherever we turn in exploring ethnicity and identity politics, new complexities emerge. In the first post-Apartheid election characterized by full suffrage (1994), the Western Cape, dominated by Coloured voters, was the only province that voted the National Party back into power, with the ANC a distant second. Coloured politics in South Africa now has many diverse currents, including right as well as left tendencies. In addition to support for the "reformed" National Party and the ANC, there are, in no particular order, the left-separatist Pan-Africanist Congress, the fascist Kleurling Weerstandbeweging (Coloured Resistance Movement)—which is closely modeled after Ernest Terreblanche's far-right Afrikaner Weerstandbeweging (Afrikaner Resistance Movement)—Islamic fundamentalists, and various cultural nationalist tendencies. There is also the "workerist" left grouping centered around the Coloured intellectual and former Robben Island inmate Neville Alexander. Another prominent Coloured political figure of Trotskyist persuasion recently had his name legally changed from Benny Alexander to Khoisan X. The fact remains, however, that the "Khoisan roots" question is only one of a number of different crosscurrents affecting Coloured identity politics today.

For those who do wish to identify with the Khoisan past, there is no lack of examples to choose from. The works of Frieda-Nela Williams (1991), John Wright (1971), and Shula Marks (1972) offer historical examples of the resilience and pragmatism, the ability to project power, and the desire of the Khoisan peoples to survive in the face of overwhelming odds. These stories could form the bases of a popular history of the Khoisan peoples, and in fact such projects are already underway at the UWC.

The existence of this hidden history, hitherto suppressed by colonial discourse and Apartheid ideology, suggests a number of new directions for anthropologists in South Africa and abroad. An expanded anthropology, by celebrating the birth of new ethnicities and not just mourning the passing of the old, embraces new possibilities for research on the politics of identity. The southern African cases offer parallels to what is happening in other parts of the world (cf. Durning 1992; Lee 1992a; and Hitchcock 1993, 1994). At the UWC, analysts of identity politics are attempting to understand how a nonwhite, nonblack proletarianized community juggles ethnicity, traditionality, race, class, and internal divisions in an ongoing attempt to find their place in a racialized society. One can observe similarities here to the dilemmas of, for example, Native Americans in the U.S. South, caught between black, white, and native identities.[12]

Indigenism is emerging as a significant political discourse in the postcolonial world. In Australia and North America, perhaps the most significant development of the last two decades has been the indigenous peoples' speaking to the rest of us in their own voices. In Canada the Innu, the Lubicon, the Teme-Augama, and others (as shown in Richardson 1989) speak to the Canadian public through the medium of plays, novels, documentary films, and pop music. Rock performers such as Yothu Yindi from Australia's Arnhem Land, Kashtin from the Labrador Innu, and the Inuit pop star Susan Aglukark have had enormous appeal through their music. Increasingly, indigenous peoples are making political alliances with environmentalists, feminists, youth groups, and peoples of color (Burger 1990; Durning 1992; Hitchcock 1993, 1994; Miller 1993). Clearly, the cultural renaissance underway in a number of indigenous communities has generated considerable interest in a "traditional" ethos and worldview, governance, subsistence, arts, crafts, ethnobotany, and healing; for these and other spheres of knowledge, the elders and the extant anthropological texts are the main sources of information. So if it is happening in Australia and Canada, why not in southern Africa, too?

If we can situate the problem within the intellectual currents of the present, Coloured identity in South Africa could be seen as an artifact of "modernity," a product of the great processes by which commodity capitalism dissolved all previous human ties: in Marx's memorable phrase, "all that is solid melts into air" (Berman 1983). A major point of distinction made by blacks in South Africa is that whatever they have lost, they still have their Xhosa, Tswana, or Zulu traditions. The Coloureds, however, are a people who have lost theirs (a sentiment we saw echoed by Dawid Kruiper). Thus, black South Africans, despite their inferior social and legal position under Apartheid, could still feel a sense of superiority over the Coloured, given the latter's truncated and deracinated heritage.

So if Apartheid is a particular product of modernity, what is signified by the ethnic revival following Apartheid's collapse? I would liken it to the breaking of a dam, the unleashing of long-suppressed yearnings of a deeply emotional nature: the need for a sense of belonging to the land. Others may see this revival in more instrumental terms, as a use of authenticity to gain purchase for staking claims on the political landscape. Whatever one's conclusion on this score, the final fall of the political structures of Apartheid (though not its economic inequities) has opened up significant political and intellectual space.

A Khoisan Renaissance?

On the cultural front, there are intriguing signs that a Khoisan renaissance of a sort is already underway. In April 1996 the artist and art historian Pippa Skotnes opened the controversial exhibit "Miscast: Negotiating the Presence of the Bushmen" at the National Gallery in Cape Town, covering the horrors of genocide against the nineteenth-century Bushmen (Skotnes 1996). A parallel exhibit at the South African Museum brought together for the first time examples of Bushman rock art in museum collections with the work of contemporary Bushman artists from Schmidtsdrift, the Kuru artist group in Botswana, and other artists. At the opening of "Miscast," a remarkable forum was held bringing together leaders of Bushman groups from Namibia and Botswana with representatives of half a dozen Khoisan/Coloured political groupings within South Africa that had sprung up since 1994—groups with names such as the Khoisan Representative Council, the Griqua National Conference, the Working Group for Indigenous Minorities in Southern Africa (WIMSA), and the South African San Institute (SASI).

Kiewiet /Angn!ao, chairman of the Nyae Nyae Farmers Cooperative of Namibia—the group working with John Marshall and Megan Biesele—gave the keynote address. He spoke eloquently (in Ju/'hoansi with simultaneous translation) of his people's aspirations to make their way in the world while preserving their culture and values. According to Dr. Megan Biesele, who was present, members of the largely urban audience were visibly moved, some to tears. One blond, blue-eyed Afrikaner member of the audience told the meeting that "we have all been impoverished by the ignorance and denial of the Khoisan," while

another, also white, arose to publicly acknowledge her long-suppressed Khoisan heritage—an announcement followed by more tears
from audience members (Biesele, personal communication April 1996).
The event was an epiphany for more than one Coloured academic; for
these scholars, the core curriculum of Franz Fanon, Steve Biko, Amilcar Cabral, Paulo Freire, and Joe Slovo took on a deeper and more
personal meaning.

The organizing committee for the 1997 Khoisan studies conference
at the UWC continued the process begun at the 1996 forum by inviting
San and Khoi political activists from South Africa, Botswana, and
Namibia to meet with student and civic groups in the Cape Town area
for more extended discussions and the planning of collaborative
research. In July 1997, the long-awaited conference "Khoisan Identities
and Cultural Heritage" convened in Cape Town. Unlike at previous
conferences on Khoisan issues, here the academics and policymakers
were outnumbered by members of the existing Khoisan communities
and many representatives of the Cape Town "nonwhite" intelligentsia.
Present were Griquas from the eastern Cape, Damaras from central
Namibia, Basarwa students from the University of Botswana, and representatives of a dozen remote Kalahari communities brought together
by WIMSA (which is based in Windhoek).[13]

The opening ceremonies (conducted largely in Afrikaans) featured a
succession of choirs from Griqua, Nama, and other Khoisan congregations from around the Cape Province. Then, eleven members of
Coloured communities in the western Cape were introduced to a
packed auditorium as the present chiefs of eleven of the original Khoi
clans encountered by Jan van Riebeeck at the Cape in the 1650s. Some
of these clans had been virtually wiped out by the early eighteenth century. The chiefs' appearance in imaginative regalia based loosely on
seventeenth- and eighteenth-century accounts, accompanied by impassioned speeches about "reclaiming our heritage," was enthusiastically
received by the partisan audience. Culture heroes were celebrated, such
as the seventeenth-century Khoi chief Achimoa—the "King of Robben
Island," who became the island's first political prisoner when he was
exiled there after an abortive rebellion. And poetry written for the
occasion was recited, such as this offering from the Plakkekamp
(Squatters' Camp) Poetry Collective:

Khoisan, rise from the vast valleys of Africa,
Khoisan, this was once in your hand,
This could be, once more, your promised land.

Fig. 2.3. Khoi, Neo-Khoi, and San activists address the "Khoisan Identities and Cultural Heritage" conference, a key moment in the Khoisan renaissance in post-Apartheid South Africa, Cape Town, July 1997.

By contrast, the San presence at the conference was less visible. Not having had the educational opportunities or the sense of their own histories enjoyed by the Khoi delegates, the San people from Botswana and Namibia gave less polished presentations. Their subject matter was not focused on heritage and identity but instead emphasized land, hunting and grazing rights, and the ongoing discrimination they experience at the hands of their fellow citizens in Botswana and Namibia. By the end of the conference, it was clear that there were two quite different kinds of stakeholders represented. One group, largely San with some Khoi, had claims to cultural legitimacy that were impeccable, but their political leverage and media savvy were weak. The other group, largely Khoi (and Neo-Khoi), had political and media clout but, by reason of land and language loss, had claims to legitimacy that were far more tenuous.

Each of these two constituencies has, in effect, what the other lacks. However, hopes that they will combine their strengths and make common cause may be premature at this point, given the vast differences in the historical experiences between, say, Khoi communities in the post-Apartheid northern Cape and San peoples scattered though northern Namibia and Botswana, who have been integrated into the regional political economy far more recently.

Nevertheless, *within* their respective constituencies, much can be done. In the Coloured community, there are exciting possibilities for collecting the oral traditions of the old people. Constituting the living history of the nation is an extremely well established branch of research in, for example, Aboriginal Australia, but it has barely begun in the Khoisan areas of South Africa. There is a need for scholars to walk over the land with rural elders, a need for studies of place-names; accounts of sacred sites, battles, and other historical events need to be memorialized. Studies are needed of Khoi and San words that have remained in the language, of their meanings and significance. And there is still much to be mined from existing archival sources, such as the Bleek and Lloyd collection (1911; cf. Deacon and Dowson 1996). The San people of South Africa, Namibia, and Botswana continue to expand their political actions on a number of fronts: land and language rights, health issues, and governmentality. A recent guest-edited issue of *Cultural Survival Quarterly* contains over twenty-five articles about the current political situation of the San (Lee, Hitchcock, and Biesele 2002).

The San people and their supporters see in the educated Capetonians a legion of potential allies. Urban educated people—the students at the UWC, for example—who feel a sense of kinship with their Khoisan roots could make connections with the living representatives of that tradition, people like the Ju/'hoansi of Namibia and Botswana. Urban students from the Cape Town area might seek them out to find a sense of *communitas* with those of similar cultural background, but the northern Ju/'hoansi need the strengths of the Cape Town students—literacy, technical, and business skills—at least as much as the Capetonians need them. Initiatives in this direction have already been taken in Botswana by the Basarwa Research Committee (BRC), a group of faculty and students (including some who are themselves Basarwa) at the University of Botswana. The BRC, aided by overseas support from Norway and elsewhere, has been instrumental in placing Basarwa human rights and land issues squarely on the national agenda (Saugestad 2002).

In South Africa, recent developments indicate the degree to which Khoisan issues have been foregrounded on the political and cultural agenda. On the national political front, the ANC government formed a ministerial committee in 1998 to study the "Bushman problem" and to make recommendations. Consisting of bureaucrats and academics reviewing pending land claims, this ministerial committee flies in academic "experts" as well as bringing local-level leaders to Pretoria for major meetings. Cynics may say that all this is a political game that the government is playing to capture the Khoisan agenda and woo the Coloured vote. To this I would answer: more power to them! Would it be preferable to see the Khoisan agenda captured by the National Party and the far-right KWB and turned into the kind of right-wing nativism that now dominates the politics of the Zulu-based Inkatha Freedom Party?

The Khoisan peoples of southern Africa are numerically small, but in terms of African history and civilization, they loom large. Today, Khoisan in urban, rural, and remote areas are struggling on diverse fronts to retain, revive, or reinvent distinct identities while grappling with the still-virulent legacy of Apartheid and colonialism.

Where sheer survival is not an issue, encapsulated and marginalized peoples are turning their attention to the reestablishment of their historical roots, joining the worldwide social movement of indigenous minorities not only in South Africa, but also in Canada, the United States, Australia, New Zealand, Russia, and elsewhere (Burger 1990; Durning 1992). And such a revival is not just an issue for one people or one nation: the cultural diversity, both old and new, that is represented by the former hunting and herding Khoisan peoples of southern Africa is part of the heritage of all humanity. It is important that members of these societies themselves be drawn into the task of valorizing and preserving their own cultural heritage. Ultimately, it is they who will carry forward this work.

Notes

The research on which this essay is based was carried out on brief field trips between 1993 and 2001. I wish to thank the University of Toronto travel fund for financial support. Part of this essay was written while I was a Visiting Scholar at Australian National University in 1995. Earlier versions have been read at the Massachusetts Institute of Technology, Northeastern University, Hunter College, and the City University of New York Graduate Center. The following were extremely helpful in aspects of the research: in Namibia and South Africa, /Ontah Boo, Henry Bredekamp, Janette Deacon,, N!ai Kumsa, Kxau Royal /O/oo, /Ui Keyter /Oma, John Sharp, Andrew Smith, and Denny Smith; and in Australia, Graham Connah, Nic Peterson, and Joanna Casey. S. Nombuso Dlamini read the entire manuscript and offered detailed suggestions. Special thanks to Yo-Yo Ma, who made possible the 1993 trip to Namibia; and to Megan Biesele, Mathias Guenther, and Robert Hitchcock, who, as always, were indispensable sources of materials and ideas.

1. S. Nombuso Dlamini has collected Zulu oral traditions in the Drakensberg area relating how Bushmen were involved in the Shakan wars of conquest and incorporated into the Zulu kingdom as cattle keepers. Some San men even married Zulu women. These oral traditions have it that the San boys imparted the click sounds to Zulu boys during the long days they spent herding together (personal communication, April 1996).

2. The image of the San in South African literature, culture, and art is explored in a special issue of *Critical Arts: A Journal of Cultural Studies,* entitled "Recuperating the San" and published by the University of Natal, Durban (Tomaselli 1995).

3. Of course, "indigenous" can be a highly contested category even in the United States and Canada. In the case of the Lumbee Indians of North Carolina (and many similar examples), the question of who is and is not an "Indian" is often the subject of vigorous debate.

4. Some Ovambo kingdoms record their dynasties as being founded on the marriage of Ovambo men and hunter-gatherer women. On Zulu intermarriage, see n. 1.

5. *The Gods Must Be Crazy* and *The Gods Must Be Crazy II* have been the highest-grossing non-Hollywood films in history. For a revealing account of the background to the films, see Davis 1996, 81–94. See also Peter Davis and Daniel Riesenfeld's documentary film *In Darkest Hollywood* (1996) for a refreshing critique of Uys and of the cinema's South Africa.

6. Before that question can be addressed, we have to consider a prior one: what is the relationship between historic "Khoi" pastoralists and "San" hunter-gatherers? Were they even separate peoples, or were the San in the Cape merely impoverished Khoi who had lost their cattle and sheep? Similarly, could San people adopt cattle husbandry and immediately "raise themselves up"? Richard Elphick (1977) made the argument for the fluidity and interchangeability between Khoi and San in the Cape area, and it has been influential (Schrire 1984). Whatever the situation in the Cape—and the archaeological evidence is complex—there were certainly many Bushman groups outside the Cape without a history of herding (Lee 1965, 1979; Smith 1992).

7. The translations of this quotation and the following one are by Mathias Guenther.

8. The *New York Times* ran a feature story on them on January 18, 1996. As a result of this publicity, it became known that the Bushmen's wages were subpar even by South African standards. The group was able to agitate successfully for a doubling of wages and an improvement in working conditions (Daley 1996).

9. I am grateful to Jerome Levi and Bartholomew Dean for drawing this line of analysis to my attention (personal communication, 1997).

10. An indication of the degree to which the Western media have grabbed

on to the Kalahari Bushman story is the fact that the obituary of Dawid Kruiper's ninety-six-year-old father, Regopstan, ran in the "Passages" section of *Time* on March 13, 1996 (International Edition).

11. These remarks are taken from the author's notes.

12. In certain respects, the ambiguities of their situation resembled that of the Lumbee Indians of North Carolina, so it seemed appropriate to present my hosts at UWC with a copy of Gerald Sider's *Lumbee Indian Histories* (1993).

13. The WIMSA delegations' attendance and participation was made possible by a grant from the Wenner-Gren Foundation of New York, with support from Axel Toma and other WIMSA staff, to overcome the complex logistical problems of bringing the WIMSA delegates together.

References

Barnard, Alan. 1992a. *Hunters and Herders of Southern Africa: A Comparative Ethnography of the Khoisan Peoples.* Cambridge: Cambridge University Press.

―――. 1992b. *The Kalahari Debate: A Bibliographical Essay.* Centre of African Studies Occasional Paper 35. Edinburgh: University of Edinburgh.

Berman, Marshall. 1983. *All that Is Solid Melts into Air.* New York: Simon and Shuster.

Biesele, Megan. 1990. *Shaken Roots: The Bushmen of Namibia.* Marshalltown, South Africa: EDA Publications.

Biesele, Megan, Mathias Guenther, Robert Hitchcock, Richard Lee, and Jean MacGregor. 1989. Hunters, Clients, and Squatters: The Contemporary Socioeconomic Status of Botswana Basarwa. *African Study Monographs* 9 (3): 109–51.

Biko, Steve. 1978. *Black Consciousness in South Africa.* New York: Random House.

―――. 1979. *I Write What I Like.* London: Heinemann.

Bleek, W. H. I., and Lucy Lloyd. 1911. *Specimens of Bushman Folklore.* London: G. Allen.

Burger, Julian. 1990. *Gala Atlas of First Peoples: A Future for the Indigenous World.* New York: Anchor Books.

Cabral, Amilcar. 1974. *Return to the Source: Selected Speeches.* New York: Monthly Review Press.

Chennells, Roger. 2002. The ≠Khomani San Land Claim. In *The Kalahari San: Self-Determination in the Desert.* Richard B. Lee, Robert Hitchcock, and Megan Biesele, guest editors. *Cultural Survival Quarterly* 26 (1): 51–52.

Crawhall, Nigel. 2002. Reclaiming Language and Identity. In *The Kalahari San: Self-Determination in the Desert.* Richard B. Lee, Robert Hitchcock, and Megan Biesele, guest editors. *Cultural Survival Quarterly* 26 (1): 49–51.

Daley, S. 1996. Kagga Kamma Journal: Endangered Bushmen Find Hope in a Game Park. *New York Times,* January 16, International section.

Davis, Peter. 1996. *In Darkest Hollywood: Exploring the Jungles of Cinema's South Africa.* Johannesburg: Ravan Press; Athens: Ohio University Press.

Deacon, Janette, and Thomas Dowson, eds. 1996. *Voices from the Past: /Xam Bushmen and the Bleek and Lloyd Collection.* Johannesburg: Witwatersrand University Press.

Durning, Alan B. (1989) 1992. Guardians of the Land: Indigenous Peoples and the Health of the Earth. *Worldwatch Paper* 112. Washington, D.C.: Worldwatch Institute.

du Plessis, I. D. 1972. *The Cape Malays: History, Religion, Traditions, Folk Tales, the Malay Quarter.* Cape Town: A. A. Balkema.

Elphick, Richard. 1977. *Kraal and Castle: The Birth of South African Society.* New Haven: Yale University Press.

García Canclini, Néstor. 1995. *Hybrid Cultures: Strategies for Entering and Leaving Modernity.* Minneapolis: University of Minnesota Press.

Goldin, Ian. 1992. Coloured Identity and Coloured Politics in the Western Cape Region of South Africa. *Journal of Southern African Studies* 20: 241–54.

Gordon, Robert. 1992. *The Bushman Myth: The Making of a Namibian Underclass.* Boulder, Colo.: Westview Press.

Guenther, Mathias. 1993–94. "Independent, Fearless, and Rather Bold:" A Historical Narrative on the Ghanzi Bushmen of Botswana. *Journal of the Namibia Scientific Society* 44:25–40.

Hahn, T. 1881. *Tsuni-//Goam, the Supreme Being of the Khoi-Khoi.* London: Trubner.

Hitchcock, Robert K. 1987. Socioeconomic Change among the Basarwa in Botswana: An Ethnohistorical Analysis. *Ethnohistory* 34 (3): 219–55.

———. 1992. *Communities and Consensus: An Evaluation of the Activities of the Nyae Nyae Development Foundation and the Nyae Nyae Farmers Cooperative in Northeastern Namibia.* Windhoek: Nyae Nyae Development Foundation; New York: Ford Foundation.

———. 1993. Africa and Discovery: Human Rights, Environment, and Development. *American Indian Culture and Research Journal* 17 (1): 129–52.

———. 1994. International Human Rights, the Environment, and Indigenous Peoples. *Colorado Journal of International Environmental Law and Policy* 5 (1): 1–22.

———. 1996. *Kalahari Communities: Indigenous Peoples, Politics, and the Environment in Southern Africa.* Copenhagen: International Work Group for Indigenous Affairs.

Hitchcock, Robert K., and John D. Holm. 1993. Grassroots Political Organizing among Kalahari Bushmen. *Indigenous Affairs* 3 (95): 4–10.

Isaacs, Harold. 1989. *Idols of the Tribe: Group Identity and Political Change.* Cambridge, Mass.: Harvard University Press.

Kent, Susan, ed. 1996. *Cultural Diversity among Twentieth Century Foragers: An African Perspective.* Cambridge: Cambridge University Press.

Kopytoff, Igor, ed. 1987. *The African Frontier: The Reproduction of Traditional African Societies.* Bloomington: Indiana University Press.

Kuper, Adam. 1992. Postmodernism, Cambridge, and the Great Kalahari Debate. *Social Anthropology* 1:57–71.

Lee, Richard B. 1965. Subsistence Ecology of !Kung Bushmen. Ph.D. diss., Department of Anthropology, University of California, Berkeley.

———. 1979. *The !Kung San: Men, Women, and Work in a Foraging Society.* Cambridge: Cambridge University Press.

———. 1992a. Art, Science, or Politics: The Crisis in Hunter-Gatherer Studies. *American Anthropologist* 90:14–34.

———. 1992b. The !Kung in Question: Evidence and Context in the Kalahari Debate. *Michigan Discussions in Anthropology* 10:9–16.

———. 2002. Solitude or Servitude? Ju/'hoan Images of the Colonial Encounter. In *Ethnicity and Hunter-Gatherers: Association or Assimilation,* edited by Susan Kent, 176–98. Washington, D.C.: Smithsonian Institution Press.

Lee, R., and M. Guenther. 1991. Oxen or Onions? The Search for Trade (and Truth) in the Kalahari. *Current Anthropology* 32:592–601.

———. 1993. Problems in Kalahari Historical Ethnography and the Tolerance of Error. *History in Africa* 20:185–235.

———. 1995. Errors Corrected or Compounded? A Reply to Wilmsen. *Current Anthropology* 36:298–305.

Lee, Richard B., Robert Hitchcock, and Megan Biesele, guest editors. 2002. The Kalahari San: Self-Determination in the Desert. *Cultural Survival Quarterly* 26 (1): 8–61.

Marais, E. 1969. *The Soul of the Ape.* New York: Atheneum.

Marais, J. S. 1937. *The Cape Coloured People: 1652–1937.* Johannesburg: Witwatersrand University Press.

Marks, Shula. 1972. Khoisan Resistance to the Dutch in the Seventeenth and Eighteenth Centuries. *Journal of African History* 8:55–80.

Marshall, John, and Clare Ritchie. 1984. *Where Are the Ju/wasi of Nyae Nyae? Changes in a Bushman Society, 1958–1981.* Centre for African Studies Communication No. 9. Capetown: University of Cape Town.

Marshall, John. 1980. *N!ai: The Story of a !Kung Woman.* (Film). Watertown, Mass.: Documentary Educational Resources.

Marshall, Lorna. 1976. *The !Kung of Nyae Nyae.* Cambridge, Mass.: Harvard University Press.

———. 1999. *Nyae Nyae !Kung Beliefs and Rites.* Cambridge, Mass: Peabody Museum.

Mayson, John Schofield. [1861] 1963. *The Malays of Capetown.* Cape Town: Africana Connoisseurs Press.

Miller, M., with the staff of Cultural Survival. 1993. *State of the Peoples: A Global Human Rights Report on Societies in Danger.* Boston: Beacon Press.

Mogwe, Alice. 1992. *Who Was (T)here First? An Assessment of the Human Rights Situation of Basarwa in Selected Communities in the Gantsi District.*

Occasional Paper No. 10. Gaborone, Botswana: Botswana Christian Council.

Moodie, T. Dunbar. 1976. *The Afrikaner Civil Religion.* Berkeley: University of California Press.

Motzafi-Haller, Pnina. 1994. When Bushmen Are Known as Basarwa: Gender, Ethnicity, and Differentiation in Rural Botswana. *American Ethnologist* 21 (3): 539–63.

Müller, H. 1912. Ein Erkundungsritt in das Kaukau-veld. *Deutsches Kolonialblatt* 23:530–41.

Murumbi, D. 1994. The Concept of Indigenous Peoples in Africa. *Indigenous Affairs* 1 (94): 51–57.

Nurse, G. T., and T. Jenkins. 1977. *Health and the Hunter-Gatherer: Biomedical Studies on the Hunting and Gathering Populations of Southern Africa.* Basel: S. Karger.

Passarge, S. 1904. *Die Kalahari.* Berlin: Dietrich Reimer Verlag.

———. 1907. *Die Buschmänner der Kalahari.* Berlin: Dietrich Reimer Verlag.

Penn, Nigel. 1999. *Rogues, Rebels, and Runaways: Eighteenth-Century Cape Characters.* Cape Town: D. Philip Publishers.

Perry, Richard. 1996. *From Time Immemorial: Indigenous Peoples and State Systems.* Austin: University of Texas Press.

Phillipson, David W. 1985. *African Archaeology.* Cambridge: Cambridge University Press.

Pityana, Barney, Mamphela Ramphele, Malusi Mpumlwana, and Lindy Wilson, eds. 1992. *Bounds of Possibility: The Legacy of Steve Biko and Black Consciousness.* London: Zed Books.

Richardson, Boyce, ed. 1989. *Drumbeat: Anger and Renewal in the Indian Country.* Toronto: Summerhill Press/Assembly of First Nations.

Ross, Robert. 1976. *Adam Kok's Griquas: A Study in the Development of Stratification in South Africa.* Cambridge: Cambridge University Press.

———. 1993. *Beyond the Pale: Essays on the History of Colonial South Africa.* Hanover, N.H.: Wesleyan University Press.

Sadr, Karim. 1997. Kalahari archaeology and the Bushman debate. *Current Anthropology* 38: 104–12.

Saugestad, Sidsel. 2002. San/Basarwa Studies at the University of Botswana. In *The Kalahari San: Self-Determination in the Desert.* Richard B. Lee, Robert Hitchcock, and Megan Biesele, guest editors. *Cultural Survival Quarterly* 26 (1): 53–54.

Schapera, I. 1930. *The Khoisan Peoples of South Africa: Bushmen and Hottentots.* London: Routledge and Kegan Paul.

Schinz, H. 1891. *Deutsch-Südwest Afrika: Forschungreisen durch die deutschen Schutzgebiete, Gross-Nama-und Hereroland, nach dem Kunene, dem Ngami-See und der Kalahari, 1884–1887.* Oldenburg: Schulzescher Hof.

Schrire, Carmel, ed. 1984. *Past and Present in Hunter-Gatherer Studies.* Orlando: Academic Press.

Sider, Gerald M. 1993. *Lumbee Indian Histories.* Cambridge: Cambridge University Press.

Silberbauer, George B. 1981. *Hunter and Habitat in the Central Kalahari Desert.* Cambridge: Cambridge University Press.

Skotnes, Pippa, ed. 1996. *Miscast: Negotiating the Presence of the Bushmen.* Cape Town: University of Cape Town Press.

Smith, Andrew. 1992. *Pastoralism in Africa: Origins and Development Ecology.* London: C. Hurst and Co.

Smith, Andrew, and Richard B. Lee. 1997. Cho/ana: Archaeological and Ethnohistorical Evidence for Recent Hunger-Gatherer/Agro-pastoralist Contact in Northern Bushmanland. *South African Archaeological Bulletin* 52:52–58.

Smith, Ken. 1988. *The Changing Past: Trends in South African Historical Writing.* Athens: Ohio University Press.

Solway, J., and R. Lee. 1990. Foragers Genuine or Spurious? Situating the Kalahari San in History. *Current Anthropology* 31 (2): 109–46.

Steyn, H. P. 1994. Role and Position of Elderly !Xu in the Schmidtsdrift Bushman Community. *South African Journal of Ethnology* 17 (2): 31–37.

Stow, J. M. 1905. *The Native Races of South Africa.* London: Swan and Sonnenschein.

Szalay, M. 1995. *The San and the Colonization of the Cape, 1770–1879.* Research in Khoisan Studies, vol. 11. Cologne: Rüdiger Köppe Verlag.

Tanaka, Jiro. 1989. *The San, Hunter-Gatherers of the Kalahari: A Study in Human Ecology.* Tokyo: University of Tokyo Press.

Theal, George McCall. *A History of South Africa.* Vols. 6–9. London: Allen and Unwin.

Thompson, Leonard. 1985. *The Political Mythology of Apartheid.* New Haven: Yale University Press.

Tomaselli, K., ed. 1995. Recuperating the San. Theme issue of *Critical Arts: A Journal of Cultural Studies.*

Uys, Cheryl. 1994. Schmidtsdrift: Where Next? Diploma in African Studies, University of Cape Town.

van der Post, Laurens. 1958. *The Lost World of the Kalahari.* Harmondsworth: Penguin.

———. 1961. *The Heart of the Hunter.* Harmondsworth: Penguin.

Volkman, Toby Alice. 1985. *Study Guide: N!ai: The Story of a !Kung Woman.* Watertown, Mass.: Documentary Educational Resources.

White, Hylton. 1995. *In the Tradition of the Forefathers: Bushman Traditionality at Kagga Kamma.* Centre for African Studies. Cape Town: University of Cape Town.

Williams, Frieda-Nela. 1991. *Precolonial Communities of Southwestern Africa: A History of the Owambo Kingdoms, 1600–1920.* Windhoek: National Archives of Namibia.

Wilmsen, Edwin A. 1989. *Land Filled with Flies: A Political Economy of the Kalahari.* Chicago: University of Chicago Press.

Wilmsen, E., and J. Denbow. 1990. Paradigmatic History of San-Speaking Peoples and Current Attempts at Revision. *Current Anthropology* 31 (5): 489–524.

Wilson, Monica, and Leonard Thompson, eds. 1968. *The Oxford History of South Africa.* Vol. 1. Oxford: Oxford University Press.

Wily, Elizabeth A. 1979. *Official Policy towards San (Bushmen) Hunter-Gatherers in Modern Botswana, 1966–1978.* Gaborone, Botswana: National Institute of Development and Cultural Research.

———. 1994. Hunter-Gatherers and the Land Issue in Botswana. *Indigenous Affairs* 2 (94): 6–19.

Wolf, Eric. 1982. *Europe and the People without History.* Berkeley: University of California Press.

Wright, J. 1971. *Bushman Raiders of the Drakensberg, 1840–1870.* Pietermaritzburg: University of Natal Press.

In press. Rethinking the History of Bushmen in the Southern Drakensberg in the Mid-nineteenth Century. In *Language, History, and Identity: Papers from the Tutzing Conference on Khoisan Studies.* R. Vossen, et al., eds. Hamburg: Helmut Buske Verlag.

Yellen, John E., and Alison S. Brooks. 1988. The Late Stone Age Archaeology of the !Kangwa–/Xai/Xai Valleys, Ngamiland. *Botswana Notes and Records* 20:5–28.

———. 1990. The Late Stone Age Archaeology in the /Xai /Xai Region: A Response to Wilmsen. *Botswana Notes and Records* 22:17–19.

3 Hot and Cold: Interethnic Relations in Siberia

Marjorie Mandelstam Balzer

In a cafe in Paris in 1997, I noticed some "New Russians" (slang for newly rich Russian businessmen) enjoying themselves. As the evening progressed with internationally customary libations and table-hopping, I landed next to their leader, an energy executive from West Siberia, Khanty territory. The executive was adamant: "All Khanty are alcoholics and die by age thirty, far too young to absorb any wisdom from any elders, who do not exist anyway. . . . No land exploration deal can be negotiated without a bottle, for the Khanty want and expect it that way. Khanty like to shoot at energy prospectors, and it has gotten quite dangerous to venture into the woods of the Eastern Khanty Surgut region." He concluded: "Let the few pitiful Khanty who are left on this earth live in town. Russian villages are dying too. The world needs gas. You need all we can pump."

The executive's logic and prejudice were sobering. He refused to believe that any Siberians were leaders, could be in an intelligentsia, or were capable of writing books and producing films. Sadly, his views cannot be dismissed, for they are characteristic of many in his industry—not as dark as the portrayals in Conrad's *Heart of Darkness* or Taussig's *Shamanism, Colonialism, and the Wild Man* (1987), but particularly disturbing in a post-Soviet, post-socialist country that presents itself as handling indigenous rights through affirmative action and federalism. The executive's chilling words "Whose homeland is it, anyway?" pointed to the crux of the tension as Khanty writers, hunters, and reindeer breeders compete with newcomers for a home they thought was theirs.

The post-Soviet age, chaotically combining "wild east" marketization with lingering paternalism and mingling regionalization with left-over administrative control by Moscow, leaves indigenous Siberian groups in precarious positions. In conditions of uncertainty, political movements of cultural survival are emerging with varying measures of heat and resonance in their own communities.

Since the collapse of the Soviet Union (XSSR), various degrees of federalism have evolved in Russia (Rossiia) through center-periphery negotiation and the interethnic politics of power and pressure. In areas such as West Siberia, energy development lobbies have galvanized, co-opted, and splintered an indigenous rights movement that began in the Gorbachev period. In areas such as the Sakha Republic (Yakutia) of the Far East, indigenous leaders negotiating bilateral treaties with Moscow authorities have had relatively more leverage and control over rich resources. But treaties are being abrogated, and even within the multiethnic Sakha Republic, indigenous groups have varying degrees of linguistic, spiritual, and political vitality. Interethnic polarization stems from local conflicts, plus economic and psychological disruptions caused by Moscow's central policies, not least the Chechnya war.

In this chapter, I explore interethnic politics in West Siberia, focusing on the Ob-Ugrian Khanty (Ostiak), with whom I did fieldwork in 1976 and 1991 and with whom I have since had reunions. I also assess interethnic relations in the Far East, featuring the Sakha Republic (Yakutia), where I lived in 1986 and part of nearly each year of the 1990s. Within the Sakha Republic, I discuss two groups with contrasting political experiences—the "titular" Sakha and the dispersed Yukagir. The resulting three-case comparison reveals three very different strategies and contexts for cultural survival.

Soviet Legacies: Mixed Signals and Mixed Marriages

One of the tragedies of Native Siberian histories viewed over multiple generations is that each time indigenous peoples have responded to outsider encroachment with adaptation, escape, or other strategies, new challenges have emerged. In particular, the inflow of settlers has changed the demographic and power balances, which over time have evolved uneasily but creatively.

When coercive, Soviet policy led to considerable ethnic polarization. Ethnic self-awareness was also stimulated more positively, by establishing such bounded territories as the Yakut Autonomous Socialist Republic (Yakutia) and the Khanty-Mansi and Yamal-Nenets Districts. Eventually, some officials, especially those who were themselves Native Siberians or part Native, learned to wait for outlying villages to be abandoned, young people to be educated, and shamanic cures to fail. Such interactive learning meant that the pace of forced change slowed, and intermarriage, leading to the formation of Siberiaki, increased.[1] The pace of change accelerated with the arrival of greedy energy companies, who began stealing communal land, displacing local people, and ignoring the weak pleas of poorly mobilized indigenous groups. In a market-oriented socialist version of colonialism, "development" campaigns began in the region in the 1960s and intensified in the 1980s.

Native Siberians are quite aware of differences in their experiences of Sovietization, despite propaganda stressing homogenized "nationalities policies" and affirmative action for minorities of the North. Some of these differences stemmed from demographics and geography, reinforced by Soviet structures, definitions, and mythology. Literacy campaigns created small intelligentsias, though some literate Sakha (Yakut) went from prerevolutionary "print capitalism" to "print socialism" (cf. Anderson 1991; and Chatterjee 1993).

The ultimate symbolic Native group was the Chukchi, about whom ethnic jokes were generated, for they were the farthest east and the most exoticized as the "primitive" other. Outsiders linked them with the peoples of the Amur and Sakhalin, such as the Nivkh, described by Bruce Grant (1995). In particularly dire straits were the Yukagir of Yakutia and Chukotka, tiny in number, devastated by disease in pre-Soviet times and then by Soviet-style assimilation (Balzer 1995).[2]

Members of most Siberian indigenous groups fell into a legal protection category termed the "twenty-six small peoples of the North"—later amended to the "small-numbered peoples." Many affirmative-action-style privileges (*l'goty*), while progressive on paper, were in practice not uniformly applied or not observed at all. Literacy programs, however, became building blocks for the expression of discontent.

By the late 1980s, fury over the forced moving of villages and over energy and mining development combined with shifting political conditions to allow a few members of the Siberian intelligentsia to form the Association of the Minority Peoples of the North. Regional meetings led to a full Congress of the Minority Peoples of the North in Moscow's Kremlin in March 1990, with the explicit goal of empowering indigenous Siberians to have a greater voice in the distribution of resources, power, and authority in their own territories and to monitor government programs ostensibly designed to improve their lives.[3] Within the association, later called the Association of the Peoples of the North, Siberia, and the Far East, smaller regional activist groups formed, among them the Association for the Salvation of the Ugra, to defend Khanty and Mansi cultural, political, and economic rights; and the similar Association of the Minorities of the Sakha Republic. Attempts to control or co-opt these groups "from above" failed, as indigenous leaders found their voices.

The Association of the Minority Peoples of the North was a response to increased opportunities for local peoples throughout the Soviet Union to participate in the political and cultural processes that were changing the country and fostering newly revitalized identities. These opportunities were illustrated by the famed catchwords of the Gorbachev era, *glasnost'* (frankness) and *perestroika* (restructuring). But the cultural and political ferment did not begin in a vacuum. Rather, people's participation in new political forms had roots in their historical experiences, in their nurturing of ethnic identities they defined on the basis of cultural differences.

Larger groups—the Sakha (Yakuts), Tyvans (Tuvans), and Buryats—had earlier gained so-called autonomous republics within the Soviet system and thus fared relatively better. Indeed, sometimes members of non-"titular" groups viewed the Sakha, Tyvans, and Buryats with jealousy because of their perceived dominance and better access within the Communist Party system (Balzer 1994a; Humphrey 1998). Yukagir, Even, and Evenk complain that they experienced Yakutization almost as sharply as Russification.

In retrospect, the Soviet experience teaches that some interethnic milieus were more conducive than others to enabling personal and indigenous group strategies for survival. In the Khanty-Mansi District (*okrug*), where the Khanty were long a tiny minority in their own lands, bi- or multiculturalism and multilingualism became for many Khanty (not for most Russians) an expected and necessary way of life. Political access was primarily at the village-council level. In "Yakutia," the "Yakut," as the Sakha were called, also became Sovietized, but they were able to develop a larger and stronger political, economic, and cultural elite. By the Gorbachev period, their intelligentsia was using a history of prerevolutionary ethnonationalism to bolster an evolving pride and self-definition as an indigenous group determined to actualize federal promises of sovereignty within the Russian Federation.

The Sakha (Yakut) of the Sakha Republic: Rich and Pivotal

Injurious republic politics, oriented only to short-term economic benefits, not to long-term survival, result not only in the weak-

ening of the economic basis of republic sovereignty, but also in
the acceleration of interethnic polarization.
                                            —Uliana Vinokurova, Sakha
                        ethnosociologist and member of parliament, 1994

The Sakha Republic, while one of the poorest per capita in Russia, has
nonetheless been in a position of strength with central authorities
because of its vast and underexploited wealth in minerals (gold, diamonds, copper) and energy (oil, gas, coal). Its leaders declared sovereignty within Russia in 1990 but signaled moderation by hyphenating
the republic name as "Yakut-Sakha Republic." By 1992, they were
signing official documents as the Sakha Republic (Yakutia). Multiethnic voters in the republic elected a Sakha president, Mikhail Nikolaev,
and in 1992 a majority Sakha parliament (optimistically called Il
Tumen, "meeting for agreement") passed a constitution, before Russia
managed to ratify its own constitution in December 1993. The Sakha
constitution was written after a diverse, multiethnic commission
appointed by the president studied and adapted constitutions from all
over the world.[4]

Yakut is an outsider's corruption of one early ethnonym for the people who today call themselves, when speaking among themselves, the
Sakha. Many Sakha are aware of their Turkic linguistic and cultural
roots; they are the farthest northeast of Turkic-language speakers.
Members of the Sakha intelligentsia, urban and rural, are fascinated by
ethnographic and archeological evidence of a mixed ethnic background that includes local northern peoples (Evenk, Even, Yukagir)
plus ancestors who may have come from the area around Lake Baikal,
driven north by kin of the Mongolic Buryat (Gogolev 1986, 1995).

Sakha religion has evolved into a complex blend of Russian Orthodoxy, Turkic cosmology, soul beliefs, and shamanic practice, with a
focus on sacred sites and trees associated with once carefully defined
patrilineal clan territories. Though shamanic ritual was, as elsewhere,
driven underground in the Soviet period, it was not entirely destroyed.
Adapted shamanic belief and practice, symbolized by the founding of
the Association of Folk Medicine, has become an important aspect of
Sakha cultural revival. Another group, Kut-Siur (glossed as Heart-
Soul-Mind-Life Force), leads a campaign for more general awareness
of Sakha ritual and philosophical traditions of "folk wisdom."[5]

The Sakha cultural and spiritual revival began before the Gorbachev era but intensified in the late 1980s, leading to a campaign for
rebirth of the Sakha language and literature. While only 5 percent of

the Sakha listed their primary language as Russian in 1989, fear of linguistic Russification, especially in the capital, Yakutsk, has led to close monitoring of politicians' language abilities, legislation mandating more Sakha training in the schools, and "state language" status for Sakha and Russian.[6]

The recovery of historical memory has been stimulated by a revision of the Soviet propaganda that stressed the peaceful incorporation of Yakutia into the Russian Empire in the sixteenth century and belittled the degree of economic efficiency and literacy among prerevolutionary Sakha. The most passionate revisions have focused on twentieth-century figures such as Platon Sleptsov, pseudonym Oiunsky (from the Sakha word for shaman)—revolutionary, folklorist, and founder of the Institute of Languages, Literature, and History—who died in Stalin's jails in 1939. Other revered members of the Sakha intelligentsia of the period spanning the revolution include the writer and ethnographer A. E. Kulakovsky (1979), the ethnographer and activist P. V. Ksenofontov ([1927] 1991), the dramatist and reformist A. I. Sofronov, the writer N. D. Neustroev, and the jurist, dramatist, and politician V. V. Nikiforov—all of whom were punished for nationalism in the Stalin era.[7] Ravaging of the small national elite continued in the Soviet period. By the 1990s, conferences and rituals memorializing the work of Oiunsky, Kulakovsky, and Ksenofontov became popular symbols of cultural revival and pride.

The Sakha Republic encompasses territory four times the size of Texas, but in 1989 the Sakha numbered only 381,922 and made up only 33 percent of their republic's population, while Russians made up 50 percent. Today the Sakha number around 400,000 and represent about 40 percent of the population—still a minority in a very multiethnic republic. In 1926, before massive influxes of Russian settlers, the Sakha constituted 82 percent of the population. They could claim land reaching to the Sea of Okhotsk, land taken from them under Stalin, but this has not been the focus of their ethnic politics.[8]

In the early 1990s, a group called Sakha Omuk (the Sakha People) sponsored campaigns for cultural, ecological, political, and economic rights. Led by Andrei Borisov, a theater director who became Minister of Culture, Sakha Omuk at first functioned like a popular front, bringing diverse groups together. Members were active in the election of reformist deputies to various levels of legislatures, in the passing of sovereignty legislation, and in the election of the moderate and popular Sakha president Mikhail Nikolaev. More-radical political groups have been less effective in a republic with a majority Slavic population and a rate of interethnic marriage greater than the federation average.

Many reform leaders have stressed unifying, not polarizing, the republic's population.[9] Sakha Omuk foundered after some of its leaders became deputies in the parliament or members of President Nikolaev's government. A more multiethnic group called Myi Yakutiany (We Yakutians) emerged in 1996, competing with Novaia Yakutia (New Yakutia) by 1997. They are all trying to appeal to a fledgling sense of republicwide citizenship.

Both political and economic concerns led some of the Slavic population to leave the republic during the 1990s, although not in enormous numbers, and often for purposes of claiming citizenship in one of the countries of the new Commonwealth of Independent States or in a Baltic state. As in many areas of Siberia, most of these people had come north as temporary workers, to earn a "long ruble" (generous Northern hardship salaries) and then return to their homelands. Siberians of both Slavic and indigenous backgrounds often blame such workers for a psychology of immediate gratification that has led to ecological destruction in mining and lumbering areas and to ethnic friction.

Tensions between Sakha university students and Russian toughs erupted in spring 1986, while I was living in a Yakutsk University dorm. Police mishandling of the fighting led to a street demonstration three days later by several hundred Sakha students, the first of a series of such demonstrations in the Gorbachev era. While this incident was particularly famous, categorized as "nationalist" in the Russian press, other cases of interethnic conflict were also locally known, going back to the late 1970s and even the 1960s.[10] Local residents attributed street fights in the late 1990s to interethnic tension, widespread alcoholism, and crime gangs in Yakutsk.

The issue of interethnic tension is intertwined with that of economic viability, for the Slavic newcomer population has dominated the energy and mining industries, while Sakha Communist Party leaders dominated traditional Soviet political positions. Some of these groups have formed an uneasy conservative alliance slowing reforms, but most politicians, including former Communists, favor some economic and political reforms in the republic, hammered out through dialogue between the president and the parliament. As demands for economic rights in certain areas within the republic reached strike proportions, Sakha president Nikolaev had to balance the political pressures of minority national rights on the one side with ultimatums by economic interests on the other. His compelling argument in trying to stave off strikes was that all will benefit if both Russian and Sakha leaders in the republic can negotiate with the center for a greater share of the republic's phenomenal wealth while still maintaining the ties that provide food subsidies to the North (Nikolaev 1994, 1995).

Negotiations led to a 1992 agreement that the republic could get a cut of gem diamond profits by dealing directly with foreign bidders such as De Beers. By 1997, the Russian-Sakha coalition company Almaz Sakha-Rossiia (Alrosa) had negotiated with Moscow and De Beers for a contract less lucrative than earlier deals.[11] Before this, most people in the republic (regardless of ethnicity) were not paid for months while funds from Moscow were held hostage to diamond negotiations. The South Korean firm Khende signed another controversial deal involving the Elgin coal deposits and a branch line off the Baikal-Amur railway. Japanese firms are interested in the republic's lumber and other possible investments. As Moscow has loosened but not relinquished its grip on natural resources, the Sakha have been able to turn toward direct, profitable international contacts, especially in the Far East and the circumpolar North, through leadership in the Northern Forum. President Nikolaev, representing Russia and the republic, traveled to South Korea, Japan, Mongolia, and Europe on "state" visits. Back home, Sakha—uneasily collectivized yet hesitant about privatization—express fear that old economic and ecological exploitation by Moscow authorities will be mixed with new exploitation by foreigners.

The central government and the Russian parliament have been sensitive to the political implications of the Sakha Republic's wealth. Officials acknowledge that workers in diamond mines should not have to live in wooden barracks. Central authorities acceded to some Sakha demands during negotiations over the 1992 Federal Treaty, and by 1994, after a tax-withholding protest, the republic gained temporary guarantees from Moscow that federal taxes could be used within the republic for federal expenditures. But a Russian backlash followed the tax deal and the 1995 Bilateral Treaty that gives the republic access to specific percentages of its resource profits and greater control over its social and cultural policies.[12]

President Nikolaev had a personal friendship with Russian president Boris Yeltsin, but strains developed, especially after the outbreak of the war in Chechnya. Both Nikolaev and the Il Tumen protested the invasion. Equally serious, Moscow officials stopped observing the Bilateral Treaty, halted humanitarian food and supply subsidies to the North, and threatened to take the Sakha constitution to the Russian Federation Supreme Court. Russian President Vladimir Putin has criticized the Sakha constitution, including its provision for the "right to leave the Russian Federation." Many Sakha say they would prefer not to exercise that right, unless a major upheaval in the center pushes them into it. By 2002, republic voters elected a new president, the Sakha-speaking Russian Vyacheslav Shtyrov, former director of Alrosa.

The Yukagir: Poor and Dispersed

> If you wait too much longer to pass the law guaranteeing us a homeland (Suktul), there will not be any Yukagir left, and then you will not have any Yukagir problem anymore.
> —Gavril Kurilov, Yukagir leader and linguist, addressing the Sakha Republic parliament, 1996

At the opposite end of a continuum of political-cultural vitality from the Sakha are the Yukagir, a small minority within the Sakha Republic without an official, land-based "homeland." The tiny Yukagir intelligentsia has, however, become quite vocal in the republic, agitating for the creation of a small, community-led homeland for the Yukagir of Upper and Lower Kolyma. Legislation for this homeland, called Suktul, many times failed to pass the Sakha Republic parliament, leading Gavril Kurilov, head of the Yukagir Council of Elders, to make the statement above before he stormed out of the Sakha parliament in 1996.[13] In spring 1998, on the ninth try, a newly elected parliament finally passed a watered-down version of the law, one that gives all ethnic groups living within the proposed homeland equal rights.[14] The victory was only theoretical, given subsequent economic crisis. By 1998, the republic issued a worldwide appeal to pay for emergency flood relief along the Lena River. The homeland was established in principle, not in practice.

The significance of the Yukagir is not in their numbers. They numbered only 1,142 in the 1989 census, with some of these outside the boundaries of the Sakha Republic. They are less numerous than they were in the 1920s, when S. A. Buterlin recorded 1,500 Yukagir of Northern Yakutia and Chukotka (with 450 Chuvantsy listed separately).[15] Their primary significance is also not in the moral authority of being next in line to "die out" among Siberian peoples, although this certainly should weigh on the conscience of politicians. Rather, the importance of the Suktul project lies in its legal potential to be a precedent-setting ethnic-based land agreement, crucial in the history of the post-Soviet Russian Federation.[16]

Creating legal precedent worries Sakha deputies in the Il Tumen. They are concerned that Even, Evenk, and, most threatening, Russian workers in more southern or central areas will demand federative subdivisions within the republic. Thus, the larger question becomes "How far will federalism go?" The Yukagir homeland has been caught in the crossfire of interethnic politics, as ethnic groups compete in an unstable economy. Arguments that salvaged the law went two ways: (1) the Yukagir are in such crisis and so numerically unthreatening that they deserve to be the exception to a rule banning further ethnic-based subdivisions; and (2) in principle, creating various levels of autonomous territories is valid, as long as these are carefully negotiated, with their parameters understood by all sides. More deputies made the first argument than the second. The current but as yet unrealized goal is to foster economic and cultural recovery through enlightened self-rule, not dependencies within a state or republic.

The Yukagir homeland law can be summarized as follows:

◆ Yukagir land—Suktul—is set aside "for self-rule on questions of social-economic, cultural, and ethnic development."
◆ The territory is based on two existing clan-tribal *obshchiny* (communities), Teki Odulok and Chaila, where Yukagir live relatively compactly.
◆ Delineation of borders is to be guided by the Il Tumen on the basis of local history and "opinions of the local population."
◆ *Obshchiny* members are to follow Sakha Republic and Russian Federation laws, including respect for the "language, culture, and traditions of other peoples living in the territory." All residents have equal rights.
◆ Suktul's main governance is through a council of citizens (*shakhdzhiba*), with a two-thirds vote needed for passage of a given issue. While the full council meets once or twice a year, a smaller "elders council" meets more frequently. A leader, called the *anidzha,* is elected in a secret ballot and authorized to represent the community to local and republic authorities.
◆ Suktul's economic basis is its "natural resources (land, mineral wealth, water, forest, flora and fauna)." *Obshchiny* members, together with other local authorities, control land and forest use, including who hunts, fishes, and has rights to mineral and energy wealth. The population living within Suktul has free use; others have licensed use. Although financing and credit arrangements with the Sakha Republic are planned, including access to foreign currency funds, it is as yet unrealistic to

expect support for "socioeconomic and cultural development from the republic budget."

◆ Conflict resolution is handled by a multiethnic commission.

Debate over Suktul includes concerns regarding the formation of a special-interest, ethnic-based group of dependents draining republic government resources. One Sakha scientist returning from the village of Andrushkino (in Upper Kolyma) in 1996 suggested that the Yukagir would do better economically if only they could follow a Sakha home-steading way of life, keeping cattle and horses and feeding them with grasses collected in summer and stored in winter. "They want an [Indian] reservation and dependency from cradle to grave," he complained. However, cattle raising has not been the Yukagir pattern, and it is unclear how well such a lifestyle could be sustained so far north for each family.

A more telling concern is whether the two Yukagir groups have compact enough settlement. In Andrushkino, the base of the Chaila *obshchina,* where Yukagir were herded like deer in the 1960s to create the local *sovkhoz* (collective), ethnic proportions are about 35–40 percent Yukagir, 30 percent Even, 26 percent Sakha, and the rest Slavic.[17] Provisions for legal rights regardless of ethnicity are contained in the law, and local traditions of interethnic marriage, multilingualism, and intercommunity communication make ethnic discrimination no more likely within Suktul than outside it.

Yukagir leadership stems mostly from a few revered families of hunters and shamans, some of whom have become intelligentsia in recent generations, such as the Kurilovs (Okorokova 1995). A young man of mixed Yukagir-Sakha-Russian heritage, Viacheslav Shadrin, has emerged as chairperson of one of the two indigenous communities. Each family has had more than its share of tragedy. Alcoholism plagues these communities even more than in most of the North, as well as the identity crises that accompany rapid change.

Gavril Kurilov, today a well-respected linguist, remembers that in his childhood, when there were no matches in their nomadic tundra camps, his family used fire-drills. His training in childhood not to look people straight in the eyes, for fear of spirit reprisals, still lingers in his interpersonal relations and causes occasional awkwardness. His anguish for his people means that he is rarely able to put aside his sense of responsibility for them and his sense of representing them. Lately, moments of community solidarity have been bittersweet, since they mostly revolve around funerals and memorials for some of the last elders speaking fluent Yukagir on territory still not officially confirmed as Suktul.

Nikolaev's government began with well-publicized good intentions toward Northern minorities, supporting efforts toward their special development through the Ministry of the Peoples of the North. This closed after a corruption scandal, and the Ministry of the Peoples of Sakha was established. The newer ministry did not push as hard for special legislation defending indigenous minorities. Current leaders argue that economic improvement for all citizens of northern Sakha is crucial. The Academy of Sciences Institute for the Problems of Minority Peoples, headed by the Even linguist Vasily Robbek, continues to be an important forum for activist and research projects, despite funding struggles. The ethnically splintered Association of the Minorities of the Sakha Republic is less official, less well supported, and less effective.

An alternative or supplement to the Yukagir homeland plan came from the federal bureaucracy in Moscow, but the relevant department was abolished and budgets for northern reform have shrunk. The Moscow proposal suggested that the ethnic minorities of Kolyma, especially the Yukagir and the Even, be incorporated into an experimental "preserve" (*zapovednik*) receiving direct federal government funding.[18] This "preserve" approach is a return to concepts backed by some Communists of the 1920s, and it could stimulate further dependencies. Creating controversy by bypassing the republic's jurisdiction is a last and probably unrealistic resort for those who wish to mitigate the current crisis of poverty and spirit among the Yukagir and the Even.

The Khanty of Khanty-Mansi District: Mired in Oil

The main questions that concern the Yugan Khanty are self-rule, preservation of our territory, and how to survive under conditions of economic reform. Without adequately addressing these questions, nothing else matters.
—Vladimir Kogonchin, head of the Yugan Khanty National Obshchina (Community), May 1996

The Khanty (known as Ostiak in historical accounts) are a Ugrian people, with hunting, fishing, and reindeer-breeding adaptations to the harsh Siberian North. They have a complex kinship organization and a rich ritual life influenced, but not eclipsed, by Russian settlement. Like the Yukagir, they are significant as a post-tribal people with a difficult historical legacy who are trying to remake themselves into a mobilized political and cultural group. Nomadic-camp and lineage identities continue to be important as other levels of identity (regional, national, international) are added.

By the 1989 census, the Khanty were 22,500; their neighbors, the related Mansi, were 9,000. In 1999, they numbered approximately 25,000 and 10,000, respectively. While not all Khanty live within the bounds of their *okrug* (district), most live within the larger Tyumen Oblast (region) of Siberia. The Khanty-Mansi District gives them a token level of administrative recognition, better than for groups without any land base, but with far fewer benefits than currently afforded by republic status. Since 1991, the nesting, "matrioshka doll" governmental structure of the former Soviet Union has changed to allow for declarations of greater status and sovereignty for the regions (*oblasti*), but a basic hierarchy is maintained. Groups at the level of Khanty communities have had less, not more, security since Yeltsin abolished local councils in 1993. Khanty have minimal influence in the district parliament, though an affiliated, advisory indigenous "assembly" of Khanty leaders has been established.

While many Khanty are aware that their language is distantly related to Hungarian and that their kin in Hungarian and Estonian activist groups support their cultural-revival efforts, they are far more concerned about internal dialectal and political differences.[19] The most significant cultural distinctions are among Northern, Eastern, and Southern Khanty, on the basis of language, environment, and ethnic interaction. In southern areas of the Ob region, the Khanty historically were associated with Russians more than in the north, where interconnections with the Samodeic Nentsy [formerly called Samoyeds] were crucial. By the early 1990s, about 60 percent of the Khanty spoke their Native language (Vakhtin 1994, 42–49).

Siberian Khanty rarely agitate at the level of pan-Khanty political identity; they more often speak for a particular part, such as the Eastern Khanty of the Yugan River, who are fighting for their rights to land against oil companies. When some Khanty leaders formed a political movement in the late 1980s, they chose, together with Mansi, to call themselves Ugra, stressing their common roots rather than what drew them apart. Their activism is one variation in a broad range of potential kinds of nationalisms. More accurately, it is a form of non-chauvinist ethnonationalism, a politicized yet usually liberal ethnic consciousness born of the need to defend their culture and lands. Khanty activism fits with the wider community of Native rights agitation represented by the Association of the Minority Peoples of the North, Siberia, and the Far East, led first by the Nivkh writer Vladimir Sangi, followed by the Khanty writer Eremei Aipin and the Nentsy politician Sergei Kharyutchi. This association is in turn in communication with other indigenous rights groups, such as the Inuit Circumpolar Conference and the Saami Nordic Council.

Tatiana Gogoleva, one of the founders of the Association for the Salvation of the Ugra and its long-term president, described their goals in a 1991 interview with me:

> It was the wish of our intelligentsia to join together to reclaim our culture and our rights. . . . We were inspired by the activism of the Inuit Circumpolar Conference, which was begun in Denmark back in 1977. But we in the Soviet Union have had no political experience. . . . We had to begin somewhere. We are trying to develop ties and create an organization. Our main issues are the culture . . . and land, the most important of all. Even now many of our people are living scattered in small communities as they have traditionally. . . . We have to protect them. . . . Because of the gas and development, people are kicked out of their homes.

Khanty outrage at the forced moving of numerous villages and the destruction of their environment by the energy industry was expressed during the 1990s, beyond their tentative cries of anguish in 1986–89. In an atypical, extreme incident in 1992, a group of armed Khanty hunters encircled a camp of Russian geologist-prospectors and demanded that they leave within twenty-four hours. The hunters, fearing that their tiny settlements would be moved once again, were trying to curtail yet another influx of outsiders into their territories. Frightened and surprised, the Russian geologists packed up, though they vowed to return.

A more organized, multiethnic protest occurred around the same time when Khanty, Mansi, Nentsy, and Nganasan activists used a large conical tent to block the planned site of a railroad spur into the Yamal peninsula. They also occupied the main supply road north into the Yamal, attracting the attention of local authorities, who had been giving indigenous rights only lip service. In 1995, the Nenets-Khanty poet Yuri Vella protested threats to his family territories by placing a tent at the parliament of the Khanty-Mansi District in its capital, Khanty-Mansiisk.[20]

Public, organized protests have been rare, however. Far more common is a seething anger voiced within local communities and to a few outside supporters. A Khanty museum activist, for example, emerging from a trip near Kazym, where the roadside is littered with debris for kilometers, exclaimed, "How can anyone hate themselves so much as to spoil their own environment like this? They must not think of it as theirs, even though they have taken it from us."

Using demonstrations for political results is not a long-term solution to Native concerns, as indigenous leaders acknowledge. It has drawn dangerous attention to specific local leaders, who are targeted by non-Native regional administrators for threats and even beatings by local police. Violence erupted in 1993 at Russkinskie after an unusually public Khanty ceremony sacrificing seven reindeer in a culmination of the Fourth International Finno-Ugric Peoples' Folklore Festival. The shamanic ceremony was significant for the Khanty as an assertion of their right to practice their traditional religion and as a symbol of regenerating spiritual-cultural meaning. The Estonian Society of Ugrians reported:

> Violence of the militia toward the native people of the area continues. On June 25, a sacrifice ceremony took place at the Fourth International Finno-Ugric Peoples' Folklore Festival in the village of Russkinskiye. The following night militia sergeant Aleksandr Ludvigovich Dyagilev, with a car from the Fedorovskoe Militia Department, along with another unknown man, destroyed the sacrifice structure. The same night, Leonid Sopochin and Evgeni Multanov, the shamans who had conducted the ceremony, as well as natives Daniel Devlin and Ivan Vylla, were savagely beaten by the militia. The two others who had assisted with the ceremony were not found, although they were hunted.[21]

Olga Balalaeva, a folklorist and activist fieldworker, provided insights into this high-profile event (personal communication, 1994): "The sacrifice was more open this time because it was for the festival. The destruction of the sacrifice structure was a threat, a symbolic way to show the locals they must give up land to Surgutneft-gaz [oil and gas company]." Energy and district administrators claimed that the leaders of the sacrifice were the same people who had been telling Natives not to sign over their land for energy exploration, so they decided to teach them a lesson. No one was arrested for the beatings, although it was widely known who was involved. Because the violence occurred as people were preparing for a follow-up ceremony, witnesses were numerous, but they were later intimidated. In Nizhnevartovsk, where oil development has been especially extensive, energy workers and geologists who were temporarily expelled from their camps returned and systematically hunted the Khanty's deer.

To save at least one major remaining ecologically clean Eastern Khanty territory from energy development, a coalition of activists advocated the expansion of an already existing "ecology preserve" (*zapovednik*) in the Yugan region. This is the homeland of Vladimir Kogonchin's *obshchina,* Yaon Yakh; his community of eight hundred members is fully behind their elected leader's efforts. The envisioned indigenous-ruled homeland, modeled after UNESCO's biosphere reserve concept and supported by Goskomsevera, stretched definitions of "ecology preserve" in current Russian Federation law. It would give local Khanty full access to land that was already legally theirs, for the continuation of their "traditional means of livelihood." Since 1996, activists have lobbied local and energy officials to accept a special status for this territory.[22]

Local officials, including the district governor Alexander Filipenko, accepted the biosphere concept in principle but have blocked it in practice. Serious international lobbying efforts, including at the highest levels of Russian–United States contact, are needed to expose illegality in land transfers. Extensive land parcels in the region have been auctioned. As Andrew Wiget and Olga Balalaeva explain (1997c, 25), "Tracts of the Yugan, which the Khanty use to feed their families, are still being sold out from under them without their knowledge or consent." One of the parcels even cuts into the supposedly inviolate Russian Federation *zapovednik.*[23]

In late 1997, under increased pressure, Governor Filipenko appointed a commission to review the possibility of creating a biosphere for the Yugan Khanty. In a business-bolstering public appearance in Washington, D.C., he seconded the confident gloss of his fellow district governor Yuri Neelov of Yamal-Nenets: "We support the traditional way of life of the numerically small peoples. We should not disturb their way of life. They are not us. One must be especially careful with them."[24]

Russian officials of the Khanty-Mansi District also backed political maneuvers to change local administrative boundaries in the 1990s. Their tactics point to patterns of using indigenous peoples to gain access to resources and splitting indigenous territories so that Native activists will be less able to influence local development in mixed ethnic communities. Such manipulations fit into larger political games of wresting power (and tax revenues) from Moscow. Many of these boundary-change attempts have failed, but a few, at the most local levels, have succeeded.

The local district administration has given Khanty activists some token cultural support, most publicly for the Fourth International Finno-Ugric Peoples' Folklore Festival, as well as for the Association for the Salvation of the Ugra and the Institute for Ob-Ugrian Revival, both based in Khanty-Mansiisk. The association's accepting of energy money, even indirectly, has created controversy, with moralists arguing that its leaders cannot effectively fight development if they are in the pay of administrators, who are in turn too cozy with energy company officials. Others argue that precisely energy money, in negotiated fixed percentages, should go toward cultural programs and infrastructure such as schools, housing, and clinics.[25]

One of the most important aspects of Khanty identity is their sense of themselves as a besieged minority. Why they feel this way is clear from narratives of intimidation by oil companies, desecration of sacred groves, and reindeer poaching. Often, Khanty have turned their anger against themselves, with family tragedies and suicide compounding the difficulty of already impoverished lives. But they have also taken organized political actions to recover their own sense of cultural dignity, through the Association for the Salvation of the Ugra and through the *obshchiny*. Such actions need support, monetary and moral, in order to be sustained.

A sense of being besieged helps people maintain ethnic boundaries in remote camps and forces them into creative resistance and adaptation in villages and towns.[26] Khanty have developed diverse strategies in response to the various crises and encounters of post-Soviet development. Their leaders are astonished when they are called "nationalist," in part because of the pejorative way this word is used in Russia and in part because they feel justified in their strategies.

At a Kazym dinner table in 1991, a Khanty leader, having been called a "nationalist" by a local Ukrainian, asked, "What is wrong with being proud of your own people?" Another added, "How can Khanty be chauvinist when we never went against anyone violently?" This provoked a debate about history, in which someone admitted that in the past, Khanty had been in wars with Nentsy as well as with Russians, but "not as aggressors." Theories that stress "defensive nationalism" need to take into account the situational nature of defense and aggression and the varied ways that multiple sides in ethnic conflicts perceive themselves as "nonaggressive" through their constructions of history.[27]

Tensions between Khanty and Nentsy in Salekhard and between Khanty and Mansi in Khanty-Mansiisk were acknowledged to me privately during the 1990s, usually with expressions of sorrow. The tensions that remain most dominant, however, are those between the indigenous peoples of West Siberia and the usually Slavic newcomers.[28] Power and resources are today being redistributed in Siberia, with no guarantee that Khanty will be in any position to share in them.

Some Khanty explain that a key to their strength in engaging questions of cultural survival is their spirituality. In 1993 a young, talented Northern Khanty artist, Nadezhda Taligina, astounded attendees at a suburban Moscow conference, "Traditional Cultures and Their Environment," by asserting that most of the Khanty she knew had been given reincarnation soul names—*liaksum.* She assured me privately that the tradition of naming according to soul beliefs was alive and well in the Khanty North but that it had been kept secret in the Soviet period. The lesson was humbling, for even I, who had been proclaiming that shamanic beliefs lasted far into the Soviet period, was not fully prepared for the implications that Khanty, especially women, had done so well counteracting Soviet ideology in this crucial, identity-reproducing realm.

Khanty soul beliefs constitute the core of their confidence in their continuity as a people, but that confidence has been badly shaken. Their religion, broadly defined, is integral to their ethnic identity because it is crucial to what Khanty intellectuals say sets them apart from others (cf. Fox 1995). Khanty still living in their family territories or near their sacred places also have a worldview and spiritual intuition that transcend appeals to specific shamans and reinforce their sense of themselves.[29]

After Soviet repression, shamans ceased being major political leaders, but shamanic spiritual revival is part of a desperate and uneven Khanty ethnic revival. Aspects of shamanic belief live on in Khanty approaches to life crises, and many Khanty stress both positive and negative aspects of shamanic practice. Shamanic values include not only patriarchalism (for order), but also the potential for female power; not only sorcery, but also compassionate group therapy; not only animal sacrifice (for virility), but also ecological prudence. These values are being resurrected in new ways, in new contexts.

Naming ceremonies, animal sacrifices, and bear-festival revitalization, sponsored by the Association for the Salvation of the Ugra and other groups, are at once symbols and mechanisms to communicate ethnic pride. But it is no coincidence that some of the worst extremes of local Russian violence against the Khanty occurred following the unusually public mass reindeer sacrifice performed in connection with the International Finno-Ugric Congress. Perceived primitive "otherness" led to violence in a polarization process.

Conclusion

A friend in the Sakha Republic once confided to me that he had had a nightmare about the geographically distant but psychologically close war in Chechnya. It was 1995, at a height of the fighting, and my friend dreamed that he had been drafted to kill for the Russian side, to his horror. In the dream, modern dress gave way to the war regalia of helmeted Sakha (Yakut) epic heroes. Time, place, and sides became confused. The dream, he agreed, reflected the anger of many Sakha and other indigenous minorities over the war and its politics of pressure against a non-Russian people. Sakha also say that, as a minority people struggling to maintain their own republic, they can ill afford to lose any of their own sons.

The history of ethnic interaction across Siberia reveals examples of ethnic group formation, cultural survival, and persistence against considerable ecological, demographic, and political odds. The process has been painful, uneven, and unstable. Even groups closest to being "nations," with the most advantageous demographic situations and governmental structures (i.e., their own republic), are in peril. Other Native Siberian groups, ones who have been especially marginalized by state policies and politics, share with many indigenous peoples of the world a dangerous spiral of sickness, dispiritedness, and population decline.

Reviewing diverse Siberian cases, I find my old working distinctions between an "ethnic group" (with members having a mildly politicized sense of cultural difference) and a "nation" (with members agitating for some degree of self-determination) to be often artificial, a problem avoided by the term *ethnonational group* as used by Walker Connor (1994). Ethnonational groups are indigenous to various degrees and politicized to various degrees. Siberians have been forced by circumstances to think of themselves as fighting for cultural survival at multiple levels of politically and ethnonationally salient hierarchies.

Ethnonational interrelations change over time and differ from place to place, particularly in a post-socialist, transition society whose members are at least debating ideals of federation and civic political culture.[30] For the Sakha, having their own elected president and parliament in a resource-rich republic named for them has meant greater sovereignty in a contested center-regional dynamic. For the Yukagir, the lack of a homeland and their tiny numbers have meant despair and last-gasp political action, thwarted as much by Sakha as by Russians. For the Khanty, who lived through a harshly suppressed rebellion in the 1930s, regional energy politics have led to further violence.

In the post-Soviet period, at least thirty-two Siberian groups (up from the twenty-six of Soviet law, not including those with republics) are recognized in Russian Federation statutes, though they are often lumped with other minorities—for example, of the North Caucasus. *L'goty* (privileges, especially in tax and education matters) for Northern minorities have dwindled, as indicated by an appeal to President Yeltsin in 1996 signed by most leaders of the indigenous groups. Their current plight of being caught between systems can be termed dependency without sustenance.

No society or people, not even the most remote Siberian Nentsy reindeer breeders in the Yamal peninsula—who were falsely rumored to have escaped Sovietization—should be romantically described in the late twentieth century as untouched by the technology and pressures of "outsiders." But people deserve more and better choices concerning how much interpenetration they want, how the dialectic of interaction evolves. Native Siberians can flee the "noise" of Russian civilization no further. In an all too familiar colonial and postcolonial story, they have been pushed to the limits of their territories and their health. To survive, many have decided that they must learn, with multiethnic help and through multilevel political action, better routes to self-defense, self-determination, and self-guided development. Silence, as Jerome Levi stresses in chapter 8 of this volume, has become a luxury.

The role of an anthropologist, with the inspiration of Cultural Survival in mind, is to be a tactful facilitator when asked, whether as an "outside expert" in legal cases or, in my case, as a middleperson (a variation on the old-fashioned "culture broker") helping to bring representatives of indigenous peoples together across borders. Not until the post-Soviet period, when I have had the privilege to be part of meetings with indigenous leaders from across the North, have I understood ways that they can offer each other not only dialogue and advice, but also adaptable pieces of their own models, constructed and reconstructed from interactive histories with Russian/Slavic or American/Anglo others. On both sides of the Bering Sea, multiple identities on multiple levels, activated situationally with flexible styles, have become normal for indigenous leaders, if not for all their peoples.

For all the problems with Native American reservations, Bureau of

Indian Affairs legacies, and debates about degrees of sovereignty in Canada, Alaska, and the other U.S. states, Native North Americans clearly have a head start over Siberians in dealing with development, self-determination, and legal self-defense. While I have mixed feelings about wishing on any group the means to become more litigious, one of the most significant improvements in Native Americans' ability to defend themselves against further land thefts has come from the increased proportion of liberally educated Native American leaders— especially but not only lawyers—who have rejected full assimilation while still accommodating themselves to living in the Anglo world with dignity. All too predictably, Tatiana Gogoleva of the Association for the Salvation of the Ugra explained in 1997 her need to find a good lawyer well versed in Russian Federation and international indigenous rights legislation.

A further way that anthropologists can help is to use our range of cross-cultural knowledge, built in part through Cultural Survival projects, in order to have dialogues with indigenous intellectual friends that facilitate a mutual opening up of worlds. Such dialogues, or multilogues, enable us to better understand nationalism in theory and practice—including the dangers when its fires rage out of control. While avoiding taking models whole, I have searched the anthropological and historical literatures for cases of moderate, nonchauvinist ethnonationalism. It is urgent to understand the dynamics of how mildly politicized ethnonationalism oriented toward positive goals can be maintained by the minorities of the Russian Federation, without turning into the polarized, embittered nationalisms of Chechnya or the former Yugoslavia. Polarization stems far more often from center-based policies than from dependent, periphery peoples, but their radicalized responses can create a storm of mutually self-defeating hatred (Balzer 1994a, 1995; Drobizheva et al. 1996).

Theories by non-Western scholars, many of whom were trained in the West, such as Yael Tamir (1993) and Partha Chatterjee (1993), are particularly salient. Tamir's "liberal nationalism" reopens Mazzini's creative approach to nationalism in the context of the Middle East. Chatterjee's "the nation and its fragments" helps us understand how a Bengali intelligentsia seared by British colonialism in India can get beyond having its "imagination" forever shaped by others (cf. Anderson 1991; Gellner 1983). These case-oriented theorists teach the inescapability of interrelations and interpenetrations of multiethnic societies in global contexts, as does Arjun Appadurai (1996), using a broader brush. But globalization need not mean homogenization. And attention to transnational trends in history, and at various levels, has come from many sources with many styles.[31]

"Global" and "traditional" mean something different to each generation of a people. International energy corporations, cross-state trade agreements, collapsing collectives, and interpenetrated mafia-government alliances represent contemporary versions of much earlier multilevel, multiethnic, shifting relationships of trade, war, and nomad-settler interaction. The shaping of group politics is an ancient art. To acknowledge this is not an invitation to project a specific group's identity backward in time using some analytical shopping list of frozen ethnic characteristics, such as language, lifestyle, religion, worldview, or "tradition." The time for indulging in an imagined primordialism has long passed in anthropology. Rather, it is an invitation to empathize with indigenous peoples through their changing self-definitions. Traditions and symbols are selected and manipulated not only by rote but through diverse forms of social and political community negotiation.[32]

Analysis of multiple levels of political identity formation in an increasingly interconnected and multiethnic world can help transcend seeming contradictions between the specificity of cultural values and the commonality of human rights, including group rights. Anthropologists, together with indigenous leaders and intellectuals, become cultural translators as well as theorists, advocates, and activists.

Notes

I am indebted to the International Research and Exchanges Board (IREX), the Social Science Research Council (SSRC), Yakutsk University, the Academy of Sciences Institute for the Problems of Northern Minorities, the Academy of Sciences Institute of Languages, Literature, and History in Yakutsk (AN IIaLI, now the Humanities Institute), and the Sakha Republic Ministry of Culture; and to the Kennan Institute of the Smithsonian's Wilson Center for fieldwork and/or research support. Fieldwork relevant to this paper was begun on official exchanges in 1975–76 and 1985–86 and continued periodically from 1991 to 2000. I am deeply thankful to my Sakha-language teacher, Klara Belkin, and to Khanty, Yukagir, and Sakha friends and colleagues, especially to Zinaida and the late Vladimir Ivanov for sharing their home.

Unless otherwise noted, all translations of quotations from foreign-language sources are mine.

1. Mixed marriages throughout Siberia helped to create the Siberiaki, an ethnic group formed especially in backwoods areas where newcomers were dependent on Native expertise and goodwill. More similar to Canada's Métis than to South Africa's Coloureds, Siberiaki are mildly politicized, self-consciously differentiating themselves from "mainland" rural Russians and

appropriating the term *Siberiak* from more derogatory usage. See also Balzer 1994b.

2. See also the Yukagir writer Semen Kurilov (1983) and the Chukchi writer Yuri Rytkheu (1983, 215–16). For current Siberian perspectives, see the website of the Russian Association of Indigenous Peoples of the North (RAIPON): www.raipon.org.

3. The full transcript of this congress was given to me by Aleksei Tomtosov, to whom I am very grateful. See Tomtosov 1990; Chichlo 1990; and Fondahl 1997.

4. My friend and colleague Uliana Vinokurova, who became a deputy in the Sakha parliament, was on the Constitutional Commission. See Deklaratsiia 1990; Konstitutsiia 1992; and Balzer and Vinokurova 1996.

5. See Afanas'ev 1993; and Balzer 1996. My interviews with Kut-Siur leaders Lazar Afanas'ev and Aleksei Romanov in the 1990s have been particularly illuminating.

6. See Konstitutsiia 1992; Argunova 1994; and Muchin 1992. Sakha-language newspapers have blossomed—for example, *Késkil, Sakha siré,* and *Sakhaada,* with *Kyym,* the old Communist Party paper, adapting somewhat.

7. See documents in Nikolaev and Ushnitskii 1990; see also Alekseev 1991; Diachkovsky 1992; and Antonov 1993–94, all three from the "archive" section of the journal *Ilin,* sponsored by the activist group Sakha Omuk. Sakha historians estimate that in the "Ksenofontovshchina" purge alone, at least 261 people were arrested.

8. Indigenous "titular" groups are a minority in their own homelands in more than half the republics of the Russian Federation. This sociopolitical phenomenon is characteristic of many indigenous demographic contexts beyond Russia, as Bartholomew Dean and Jerome Levi point out (personal communication, August 1998).

9. Andrei Borisov, for example, explained: "Sakha Omuk was formed in response to Gorbachev's call for new ideas. It is not a Party" (personal communication, Yakutsk, June 1991). Their bylaws ("Ustav Sakha Omuk," August 10, 1990, ms.) are in the author's files. The group was accepted by the UN as a Nongovernmental Organization but did not last long enough to take advantage of this international opportunity. See also Maksimov 1990; Vinokurova 1994; and Zykov 1994.

10. Unlike many analysts of Russia, I see "nationalism" and "ethnonationalism" as having many interrelated, not necessarily chauvinist, forms. I was falsely accused of being an outside agitator of the demonstrations and narrowly avoided being deported. Many Sakha saw the incident as an effort to introduce perestroika into their republic. Communist Party leader Yurii N. Prokop'ev made matters worse by accusing the students of having had an improper, nationalist upbringing (see, e.g., Prokop'ev 1986). A university quota system was introduced to recruit greater numbers of Slavic students. Several Sakha student leaders were arrested, but the Russian instigators were not punished. Students were exonerated only in 1990.

11. Almaz Sakha-Rossiia (Alrosa) has both Sakha and Russian leadership. The Sakha head was beaten on the street in Moscow in 1996, in circumstances many attribute to intimidation. The De Beers diamond deal was portrayed in the Russian media as too beneficial to the republic. In contrast, see President Nikolaev (e.g., 1995) on economic negotiations. The Udachnyi mine alone accounts for 80 percent of Russia's diamond output; overall, the republic produces more than 95 percent of Russian diamonds.

12. A high-ranking Moscow official, ominously expressing often-heard "unofficial" Russian sentiments, said he regrets that the bilateral treaty process was ever begun and that he does not expect all points to be honored by the central government (personal communication, March 1997). Cf. Il Tumen head Afanasii Illarionov (1995) on "sovereignty" and Vinokurova (1994, 1995). For what was published of the treaty, see Dogovor 1995. Under President Putin, the treaties are all being reevaluated.

13. Gavril Nikolaevich Kurilov, personal communication, March 1996. See also Kurilov 1996.

14. My analysis of the law is based on a version entitled "O Suktule Iuka-girskogo Naroda," December 21, 1995, with updates from interviews I conducted in summers 1998 and 2000. Data on the Yukagir come from interviews with Yukagir; from perceptive non-Yukagir, including Klara Belkin, Boris Chichlo, Vladimir Ivanov, Andrei Krivoshapkin, and Uliana Vinokurova; and from ethnohistorical research. For historical perspective, see Jochelson 1910; and Gogolev et al. 1975.

15. Smidovich, Buterlin, and Leonov 1929, 8. The 1989 census figure is slightly more than the 1,112 given in a letter signed by N. Zakharov that accompanied the 1995 draft law. Zakharov notes that only 697 Yukagir were listed as living in the republic in 1989.

16. Another possible precedent is the Evenk District established in Northern Buryatia. However, like Eveno-Bytantaisk, the Evenk District has not been as conducive to self-rule as Evenk activists had originally hoped (Gail Fondahl, personal communication, May 1996). Yukagir leaders claim they are "next in line to die out," citing the history of the Kamasinets, Kerek, Omok, Vod, Yug, and other peoples of Siberia.

17. These approximate 1996 figures derive from a "genofond" project being researched in the area. According to Gavril Kurilov (personal communication, March 1996), about 400 Yukagir (Tundra Yukagir of Lower Kolyma) were in Andrushkino in 1993, and fewer than 200 Forest Yukagir were in the Upper Kolyma area, with a total of only 712 in the Sakha Republic. The Suktul project creators envision some Yukagir moving into its territory.

18. Three such experimental preserves were considered at the federal level: in Kolyma, Turukhan Krai, and the Yugan Khanty "biosphere project," discussed ahead. Vice Minister Anatoly Volgin announced support for this *zapovednik* at a 1996 "Working Seminar on Problems of Northern Peoples" in Canada, but Volgin's job and department were later abolished.

19. The Khanty language is divided into three major dialect groups: North-

ern (including Kazym, Obdorsk, Berezovo, and Sherkaly Khanty), Southern (Irtysh-Konda, Altym, and Leusha Khanty), and Eastern (Surgut, Salym, and Vakh-Vasyugan Khanty). These divisions also reflect cultural distinctions that many Khanty themselves make. See also Comrie 1981, 105–7; and the Khanty writer Eremei Aipin (1990).

20. I am grateful to the Khanty leaders Vladimir Kogonchin, the late Joseph Sapochin and to Yuri Vella for information they provided (in 1995, 1996, and 1997, respectively) on the organized protests. Yuri Vella and his Khanty wife have been active, along with members of the Association for the Salvation of the Ugra, in several protests. Information on the Yamal protest also comes from the Nivkh ethnographer-politician Evdokiia Gayer, a former Supreme Soviet deputy, who was there to lend her support.

21. The quotation is from an Internet alert put out by the Estonian Society of Ugrians in 1993, titled "Eestilas—Sapmelas Oktavuonta." For an upbeat report on the public events, see Osherenko 1993.

22. Credit for this concept goes to Andrew Wiget of New Mexico State University and to Olga Balalaeva, codirectors of the Khanty Atlas Project, funded by the MacArthur Foundation. See Wiget and Balalaeva 1997a, 1997b, 1997c.

23. The parcels Achimovsk, Multanovsk, and Tailokhovsk were coveted by the energy company Rosinvestneft. Though it is illegal to auction land without the signatures of indigenous occupants, the auctions were only temporarily halted. The Association for the Salvation of the Ugra and the Yuoan Yakh *obshchina* have worked with the Moscow-based ecology-oriented activist law firm Ecojuris to try to stop such illegal land grabs. Together with Olga Balalaeva and Andrew Wiget, I was among those trying to bring the threatened biosphere project to the attention of authorities during the Gore-Chernomyrdin summits.

24. Governor Filipenko (who spoke at a seminar at the Woodrow Wilson International Center for Scholars, Kennan Institute for Advanced Russian Studies, on October 23, 1997) added that he was particularly concerned about welfare fraud in the Khanty-Mansi District, since a full 20 percent of the population of the region is on welfare. Filipenko's commission, headed by himself and composed mostly of Russians associated with the energy industry, included Vladimir Kogonchin, one biosphere advocate from the Yugan ecology preserve, and a Goskomsevera representative.

25. In Yamal-Nenets, according to its governor, Yuri Neelov (speaking at the Woodrow Wilson Center, Kennan Institute seminar, October 23, 1997), 0.5 percent of the profits of the government energy company Gazprom go to indigenous communities. Debates about the use of energy profits to benefit local communities are typical throughout the North, as Native Americans explained to Native Siberians in seminars in the 1990s. Contracts for subsurface use of indigenous lands in the United States usually include specific percentages of profits designated for community infrastructure. But indigenous communities in Siberia have no subsurface rights. The perils of co-option and

intimidation were evident at a 1998 Khanty-Mansiisk conference sponsored by the Association for the Salvation of the Ugra and the Khanty-Mansi District to discuss land and energy development.

26. Sherry Ortner (1995, 191) stresses that "resistance can be more than opposition, it can be truly creative and transformative." Cf. Barth 1969; Comaroff 1985; Marcus 1993; Maybury-Lewis 1997.

27. Cf. Moscow researchers Victor Shnirelman (1996) and Valery Tishkov (1997) of the Institute of Ethnology and Anthropology.

28. Khanty resentment is expressed in various modes. One of the most poignant was a 1991 story about the Kazym graveyard, disturbed by the laying of a gas line with a tractor: "The graves that were disturbed were the Khanty ones, not the Russian ones, as if specially." Khanty were sure that energy workers had robbed the graves of grave goods, a complaint that eerily echoed reports I had read from the nineteenth century.

29. Khanty perceptions of difference do not refute ethnographic evidence of interpenetrating beliefs, especially cosmologies, among the Khanty, Mansi, and especially Nentsy. See Golovnev 1995; and Kulemzin and Lukina 1992. Joseph Sapochin (personal communication, March 1995), a hunter from a renowned shamanic family, stressed a special Khanty intuition: "Sometimes in the woods maybe you are hunting and something feels not right. You can just sense it, something out of place or too much in place. But if you are drunk, you do not catch the feeling. Drunks die, because they do not feel the danger signals."

30. Cf. Humphrey 1991; Verdery 1996; Hann and Dunn 1996; and Smith and McCarter 1997.

31. To sample a range, see Wolf 1982; Mintz 1986; Herzfeld 1987; Eley and Suny 1996; Friedman 1994; and Balzer 1999.

32. Cf. Williams 1994, 600; and Lynn Stephen's essay in this volume (chap. 6). While acknowledging the role of manipulative ethnic entrepreneurs in some ethnic-conflict situations, my formulation avoids the trap of neo-Marxist overgeneralization about culture in relation to tradition, hegemony, class, and globalization of economies.

References

Afanas'ev, Lazar [Téris]. 1993. *Aiyy yorehe* (Teachings of the spirit) (in Sakha). Yakutsk: Ministerstvo Kul'tura.

Aipin, Eremei. 1990. *Khanty.* Moscow: Molodaia Gvardiia.

Alekseev, Egor. 1991. O tak nazyvaemoi Ksenofontovshchine. *Ilin* 1 (2): 27–29.

Antonov, Egor. 1993–94. Sakha Omuk: 1925–1928. *Ilin* 3–4:73–76.

Anderson, Benedict. 1991. *Imagined Communities: Reflections on the Origins and Spread of Nationalism.* 2d ed. London: Verso. Original edition, 1983.

Appadurai, Arjun. 1996. *Modernity at Large: Cultural Dynamics of Globalization.* Minneapolis: University of Minnesota Press.

Argunova, Tatiana. 1994. The Interaction of Languages in the Sakha Republic. *Anthropology and Archeology of Eurasia* 32 (4): 85–90.

Balzer, Marjorie Mandelstam. 1994a. From Ethnicity to Nationalism: Turmoil in the Russian Mini-empire. In *The Social Legacy of Communism,* edited by James Millar and Sharon Wolchik, 56–88. Cambridge: Cambridge University Press.

———. 1994b. Siberiaki. In *Encyclopedia of World Cultures,* edited by Paul Friedrich and Norma Diamond. Vol. 6. 331–35. Boston: G. K. Hall.

———. 1995. Homelands, Leadership, and Self Rule: Interethnic Relations in the Russian Federation North. *Polar Geography* 19 (4): 284–305.

———. 1996. Flights of the Sacred: Symbolism and Theory in Siberian Shamanism. *American Anthropologist* 98 (2): 305–18.

———. 1999. *The Tenacity of Ethnicity: A Siberian Saga in Global Perspective.* Princeton: Princeton University Press.

Balzer, Marjorie Mandelstam, and Uliana A. Vinokurova. 1996. Nationalism, Interethnic Relations, and Federalism: The Case of the Sakha Republic (Yakutia). *Europe-Asia Studies* 48 (1): 101–20.

Barth, Fredrik, ed. 1969. *Ethnic Groups and Boundaries.* Boston: Little, Brown.

Chatterjee, Partha. 1993. *The Nation and Its Fragments: Colonial and Postcolonial Histories.* Princeton: Princeton University Press.

Chichlo, Boris. 1990. Pervaia pobeda 'malykh narodov.' *Strana i mir* 5 (September–October): 108–12.

Comaroff, Jean. 1985. *Body of Power, Spirit of Resistance: The Culture and History of a South African People.* Chicago: University of Chicago Press.

Comrie, Bernard. 1981. *The Languages of the Soviet Union.* Cambridge: Cambridge University Press.

Connor, Walker. 1994. *Ethnonationalism: The Quest for Understanding.* Princeton: Princeton University Press.

Deklaratsiia (Declaration). 1990. *Sotsialisticheskaia Yakutia,* September 28, p. 1.

Diachkovsky, I. 1992. Eshe raz o "Ksenofontovshchine." *Ilin* 2:30–34.

Dogovor (Treaty). 1995. *Respublika Sakha* 5 (June): 3.

Drobizheva, L. M., A. P. Aklaev, V. V. Koroteeva, and G. U. Soldatova. 1996. *Demokratizatsiia i obrazy natsionalizma v Rossiiskoi Federatsii 90-kh godov.* Moscow: Mysl'.

Eley, Geoff, and Ronald Grigor Suny, eds. 1996. *Becoming National.* Oxford: Oxford University Press.

Fondahl, Gail. 1997. Siberia: Assimilation and Its Discontents. In *New States, New Politics: Building the Post-Soviet Nations,* edited by I. Bremmer and Ray Taras, 190–232. Cambridge: Cambridge University Press.

Fox, Richard. 1995. Editorial: The Breakdown of Culture. *Current Anthropology* 36 (1): [i–ii].

Friedman, Jonathan. 1994. *Cultural Identity and Global Process.* London: Sage.

Gellner, Ernest. 1983. *Nations and Nationalism.* Oxford: Basil Blackwell.

Gogolev, Anatoly I. 1986. *Istoricheskaia etnografiia yakutov.* Yakutsk: Yakutskogo Gosudarstvenogo Universiteta.

———. 1995. Yakuty kak etnos. *Mezhdunarodnaia zhizn'*. Theme issue, pp. 109–11.

Gogolev, Z., I. Gurvich, I. Zolotareva, and M. Zhornitskaia. 1975. *Iukagiry (Istoriko-etnograficheskii ocherk)*. Novosibirsk: Nauka.

Golovnev, Andrei V. 1995. *Govoriashchie kul'tury: Traditsii samodiitsev i ugrov*. Ekaterinburg: Ural Otdelenie Akademii Nauk.

Grant, Bruce. 1995. *In the Soviet House of Culture: A Century of Perestroikas*. Princeton: Princeton University Press.

Hann, C. M., and Elizabeth Dunn, eds. 1996. *Civil Society: Challenging Western Models*. London: Routledge.

Herzfeld, Michael. 1987. *Anthropology through the Looking Glass: Critical Ethnography in the Margins of Europe*. Cambridge: Cambridge University Press.

Humphrey, Caroline. 1991. "Icebergs," Barter, and the Mafia in Provincial Russia. *Anthropology Today* 7:8–13.

———. 1998. *Marx Went Away—But Karl Stayed Behind*. Updated Edition of *Karl Marx Collective: Economy, Society and Religion in a Siberian Collective Farm*. Ann Arbor: University of Michigan Press. Original ed., 1983.

Illarionov, Afanasii P. 1995. Pervye shagi k suverenitetu. *Mezhdunarodnaia zhizn'*. Theme issue, pp. 7–9.

Jochelson, Waldemar. 1910–26. *The Yukaghir and the Yukaghirized Tungus*. Memoirs of the American Museum of Natural History 13, pts. 1–3; Publications of the Jesup North Pacific Expedition 9, pts. 1–3.

Konstitutsiia (Constitution). 1992. *Yakutskie vedomosti*, February 27, pp. 1–8.

Ksenofontov, P. V. 1991 [1927]. Rassekrechennye dokumenty. *Ilin* 1:18–20.

Kulakovsky, Aleksei E. 1979. *Nauchnye trudy*. Yakutsk: Institut Iazyka, Literatury i Istorii.

Kulemzin, V. M., and N. V. Lukina. 1992. *Znakom'tes': Khanty*. Novosibirsk: Nauka.

Kurilov, Gavril N. 1996. The Origins and Mystery of the Yukagir People. *Surviving Together* 14 (summer): 35–39; adapted from "Mit omo, Koil, oghoniik!" (God save our people!), parts 1–3, *Respublika Sakha*, March 1995.

Kurilov, Semen. 1983. *Khanido i Khalerkha*. Moscow: Sovremmenik.

Maksimov, Petr S., ed. 1990. *Mezhnatsional'nye otnosheniia v regione (po materialam Iakutskoi ASSR)*. Yakutsk: Institut Iazyka, Literatury i Istorii.

Marcus, George, ed. 1993. *Perilous States: Conversations on Culture, Politics, and Nation*. Chicago: University of Chicago Press.

Maybury-Lewis, David. 1997. *Indigenous Peoples, Ethnic Groups and the State*. Boston: Allyn and Bacon.

Mintz, Sidney. 1986. *Sweetness and Power: The Place of Sugar in Modern History*. New York: Penguin.

Muchin, M. 1992. Nuzhen li zakon o iazykakh? *Sovety Yakutii*, March 18, p. 6.

Nikolaev, I. I., and I. P. Ushnitskii. 1990. *Tsentral'noe delo: Khronika Stalin-*

skikh repressii v Yakutii. Yakutsk: Yakutskoe Izdat for Sakha Omuk, Memorial.

Nikolaev, Mikhail E. 1994. *The Arctic: Despair and Hope of Russia.* Yakutsk: Sakha-Centre.

———. 1995. Respublika Sakha (Yakutia): Suverenitet sostoialsia. *Chelovek i trud* no. 1: 4–12.

Okorokova, V. B., ed. 1995. *Semen Kurilov v vospominaniiakh sovremennikov.* Yakutsk: Yakutskii Nauchnyi Tsentr.

Ortner, Sherry. 1995. Resistance and the Problem of Ethnographic Refusal. *Comparative Studies in Society and History* 37 (1): 173–93.

Osherenko, Gail. 1993. Northwest Siberian Festival Celebrates Revival of Indigenous Culture. *Surviving Together* 11 (4): 53–55.

Prokop'ev, Iurii N. 1986. Internatsional'noe vospitanie—delo vsei oblastnoi partiinoi organizatsii. *Sotsialisticheskaia Iakutiia,* May 18, pp. 2–4.

Rytkheu, Yuri. 1983. People of the Long Spring. *National Geographic* 163 (2): 206–23.

Shnirelman, Victor. 1996. *Who Gets the Past? Competition for Ancestors among Non-Russian Intellectuals in Russia.* Washington, D.C.: Woodrow Wilson Center, with Johns Hopkins University Press.

Smidovich, P. G., S. A. Buterlin, and N. I. Ivanov, eds. 1929. *Sovetskii sever: Pervyi sborniki statei.* Moscow: Komitet Sodeistviia Narodnostiam Severnykh Okrain pre Presidiume VTsIK.

Smith, Eric Alden, and Joan McCarter, eds. 1997. *Contested Arctic: Indigenous Peoples, Industrial States, and the Circumpolar Environment.* Seattle: University of Washington Press.

Tamir, Yael. 1993. *Liberal Nationalism.* Princeton: Princeton University Press.

Taussig, Michael. 1987. *Shamanism, Colonialism, and the Wild Man: A Study in Terror and Healing.* Chicago: University of Chicago Press.

Tishkov, Valery A. 1997. *Ethnicity, Nationalism, and Conflict in and after the Soviet Union: The Mind Aflame.* London: Sage for PRIO, UNRISD.

Tomtosov, Aleksei. 1990. Net malykh narodov. *Soiuz* 13 (March): 2.

Vakhtin, Nikolai. 1994. *Native Peoples of the Russian Far North.* London: Minority Rights Group International.

Verdery, Katherine. 1996. *What Was Socialism and What Comes Next?* Princeton: Princeton University Press.

Vinokurova, Uliana A. 1994. Etnopoliticheskaia situatsiia v respublike Sakha. In *Natsional'noe samosoznanie i natsionalizm v rossiiskoi federatsii nachala 1990kh godov,* edited by L. M. Drobizheva, 135–52. Moscow: RAN, Institut Etnologii i Antropologii.

———. 1995. The Road to Hell Is Paved with Good Intentions: Reflections of a Native. *Polar Geography* 19 (4): 306–11.

Wiget, Andrew, and Olga Balalaeva. 1997a. Black Snow: Oil and the Khanty of Western Siberia. *Cultural Survival Quarterly* 20 (4): 17–19.

———. 1997b. National Communities, Native Land Tenure, and Self-Determination. *Polar Geography* 21 (1): 10–33.

————. 1997c. Saving Siberia's Khanty from Oil Development. *Surviving Together* 15 (1): 22–25.

Williams, Raymond. 1994. Selections from Marxism and Literature. In *Culture/Power/History,* edited by Nicholas B. Dirks, Geoff Eley, and Sherry Ortner, 585–609. Princeton: Princeton University Press.

Wolf, Eric R. 1982. *Europe and the People without History.* Berkeley: University of California Press.

Zykov, Fedor M. 1994. *Etnopoliticheskaia situatsiia v respublike Sakha do i posle vyborov 12 dekabria, 1993.* Applied, Urgent Ethnology series, document 71. Moscow: Institut Etnologii i Antropologii.

4 Indigenous Rights Issues in Malaysia

Kirk Endicott

Malaysia, which includes Peninsular Malaysia and the states of Sabah and Sarawak in Borneo (see map 4.1), is a classic "plural society," a society made up of several culturally distinct and economically specialized ethnic groups that interact but remain socially separate (Furnival 1948). Though the emphasis on ethnicity may have increased during the colonial period due to British policies (Anderson 1987, 9–10), people made ethnic distinctions long before Europeans arrived, and ethnicity is still the preeminent basis of self-identity and social divisions in Malaysian society today. The Federal Constitution, laws, and government policies treat different ethnic groups differently. Most political parties are based on particular "races" or "communities" (Malay *bangsa*), and their first priority is to promote the interests of their group members.

Social stability in Malaysia is not achieved by downplaying ethnic differences. Instead, political parties compete to advance the interests of the ethnic groups they represent, but their competition is restrained by their mutual desire to avoid violent conflict, like the bloody fighting that broke out between Malays and Chinese in May 1969. In Malaysia's parliamentary system of government, the political power of the different ethnic groups is closely connected with their size. Government policies have come to reflect the interests of the ethnic groups roughly in proportion to their size and political influence. Significantly, Malaysia's indigenous peoples are the smallest and weakest ethnic groups, so it is no accident that government policies work against their interests.

In this essay, I discuss who Malaysia's indigenous peoples are and how they fit into the nation's ethnic politics. I show that their problems are mostly due to government policies and programs intended to benefit other segments of the national population.

Map 4.1. Malaysia and adjacent countries

Who Are Malaysia's Indigenous Peoples?

Malays form the largest ethnic group in the country, numbering 8,918,000 in 1991, about 51 percent of the total population (Leete 1996, 15, 18, 124). According to the Malaysian Federal Constitution, a Malay is anyone who habitually speaks the Malay language, follows Malay customs, and is Muslim (Malaysian Government 1982, Article 160). The Malay population has a mixed and highly varied ancestry. Some ancestors were Austronesian-speaking "sea people" who began settling the shores of Borneo and the peninsula after about 2000 B.C. (Bellwood 1997, 224–67). Some were Arab and Indian Muslim traders who came in the second millennium A.D. And others were immigrants from various parts of modern-day Indonesia. "Malay" immigrants are arriving from Indonesia and the southern Philippines even today. Traditionally, Malays have been predominantly rural farmers and coastal fishermen. Before the colonial period, Malays in the peninsula were organized in small feudal kingdoms (sultanates), which later became states in independent Malaysia. The British colonial rulers incorporated royalty and aristocrats into the colonial government as figurehead rulers and bureaucrats. In the "Bargain" that formed the basis of the independence constitution, British negotiators endorsed the Malay leaders' demands for political dominance and special rights, which were justified by their supposedly being indigenous peoples. Since independence in 1957, the dominant political party in the governing coalition (Barisan Nasional) has been a Malay-based party, the United Malays National Organization (UMNO).

Chinese form the next largest group, numbering 5,215,000 in 1991, or about 30 percent of the total population (Leete 1996, 15, 18, 124). Most Chinese Malaysians are descendants of immigrants from the southern provinces of China who came in the nineteenth and early twentieth centuries to work in the tin mining industry. Those who stayed gravitated into business and commercial farming. Today most Chinese live in cities or towns. Malays long distrusted the Chinese, suspecting them of having loyalties split between Malaysia and their own ethnic group. Indeed, Chinese formed the core of the Communist group that tried unsuccessfully to take control of the country following the Second World War, through a protracted guerrilla insurgency ("the Emergency"). The "Bargain" ensured that Chinese would be free to pursue their business interests if they did not challenge the Malays for political power.

Indians, numbering 1,613,300 in 1991, or about 9 percent of the total population, are the country's third major group (Leete 1996, 15, 18, 124). Most Malaysian Indians are Hindu Tamils from South India, brought by the British in the late nineteenth and early twentieth centuries to work in the newly established rubber plantations. Many Indians still live and work on plantations. Others work for government agencies (e.g., the national railroads), run businesses, and practice professions (e.g., law). The Bargain basically ignored the Indians, and they are still relatively neglected in Malaysian ethnic politics (Robertson 1984, 241).

The native peoples of Sabah and Sarawak states on the island of Borneo numbered 1,728,500 in 1991, roughly 10 percent of the total national population (Leete 1996, 15, 18, 124). They comprise many different ethnic groups, including Iban, Bidayuh, Melanau, Bajau, Murut, Kadazan, Rungus, and Penan. Traditionally they were hunter-gatherers (e.g., Penan), swidden farmers (e.g., Iban), and coastal fishermen (e.g., Bajau). Most Bornean natives are now rural farmers, growing a mixture of subsistence and cash crops. When Sabah and Sarawak joined the Malaysian federation in 1963, one of the conditions was that the region's native peoples would get the same rights as Malays. Consequently, the constitution was amended to include the native peoples of Sabah and Sarawak wherever the special rights of Malays were mentioned.

The Orang Asli ("Original People") of the Malay Peninsula, with a population of about 93,000 in 1995 (less than half a percent of the total population) (Nicholas 1996b, 158), form the smallest ethnic category. They comprise nineteen or more culturally distinct groups, the numerically largest being the Semai, Temiar, Jakun (Orang Hulu), and Temuan peoples. The Orang Asli are the aboriginal inhabitants of the Malay Peninsula.[1] Until recently, Orang Asli groups lived by various combinations of hunting, fishing, gathering, swidden farming, arboriculture, and trading forest products. They were once thinly dispersed throughout the peninsula, but most were forced back into the interior forests and mountains as the Malay population expanded in size along the coastal plains and in the major river valleys. The majority of Orang Asli still live in rural and remote areas of the Malay Peninsula.

According to official government ideology, the Malays, natives of Malaysian Borneo, and Orang Asli—in contrast with the immigrant Chinese and Indians—are the country's "indigenous people" (*bumiputera*). For this reason, the Federal Constitution (Malaysian Government 1982, Article 153) gives Malays and natives of Sabah and Sarawak special rights and privileges, including favored access to government jobs, places in institutions of higher education, and business licenses. In practice, however, the non-Muslim natives of Sabah and Sarawak do not receive the same treatment as Malays. As King notes,

> In constitutional terms . . . the natives of Sarawak have shared the special rights and privileges enjoyed by the Malays. Yet their general political and economic position in the Federation remains subordinate to that of the Peninsular Malays overall, so much so that it is no exaggeration to refer to the Dayaks [natives] of Sarawak collectively as "second-class *bumiputra*." (1995, 294)

The Orang Asli, who are acknowledged even by the government to be descendants of the earliest occupants of the Malay Peninsula, are not included in the constitutional category of peoples guaranteed special rights and privileges. In fact, the Aboriginal Peoples Act (Malaysian Government 1994) severely restricts their rights and freedoms compared to those of other citizens (see below). In practice, both the government and ordinary Malaysians equate the term *bumiputera*, "indigenous people," with Malays, and they alone are the ones who receive favored treatment. In contrast, the natives of Malaysian Borneo and the Orang Asli of the peninsula are treated as anomalous afterthoughts.

Clearly, the concept of "indigenous peoples" as it has developed in international agreements (International Labor Organization, United Nations, World Bank, etc.) does not include nationally dominant majority peoples like the Malays. The fact that some of their ancestors occupied the territory of present-day Malaysia before its colonization by Britain is not sufficient in itself to make them indigenous. Numerous definitions of indigenous peoples have been proposed, and the discussion is continuing (see, e.g., Kingsbury 1995; Gray 1995; Barnes 1995; and Howitt, Connell, and Hirsch 1996), but it is clear that the concept is meant to identify ethnic groups that are disadvantaged in the modern nation-states they find themselves occupying. The widely quoted definition from Jose R. Martinez Cobo's 1986 report to the United Nations (*Study of the Problem of Discrimination against Indigenous Populations*) illustrates the point.

> Indigenous communities, peoples and nations are those which, having a historical continuity with pre-invasion and pre-colonial societies that developed on their territories, consider themselves distinct from other sectors of the societies now prevailing in those territories, or parts of them. They form at present non-dominant sectors of society and are determined to preserve, develop and transmit to future generations their ancestral territories, and their ethnic identity, as the basis of their continued existence as peoples, in accordance with their own cultural patterns, social institutions and legal systems. (Cobo 1986, para. 378)

According to this and similar definitions, the indigenous peoples of Malaysia are not the Malays, but the Bornean natives and the Orang Asli. Indeed, their politically marginal status in the nation and their problems have much in common with those of peoples termed *indigenous* in other parts of the world.

The Nature and Priorities of the Malaysian Government

The concept of indigenous peoples only has meaning within the context of states. Indigenous peoples are ethnic groups that are excluded to some extent from the benefits bestowed by the state, and they are disadvantaged compared to the group or groups that dominate the national government. To understand the position of indigenous peoples in Malaysia, then, it is necessary to understand the nature and priorities of the federal and state governments.

The Federation of Malaysia originated through the welding together of a number of separate states and territories that were British colonies of various sorts before independence. Most of the states of Peninsular Malaysia were independent sultanates before the British extended their control over them in the nineteenth century. Sabah (formerly North Borneo) and Sarawak were separate colonies that joined the peninsular states (and briefly Singapore) to form the Federation of Malaysia in 1963. The individual states now have their own state governments, some with sultans, and they retain control over such matters as religion, agriculture, local government, some public works functions, and, significantly, land ownership and use (Beaglehole 1976, 78). The two Borneo states insisted upon retaining greater sovereignty, such as control over immigration even by Malaysians from the peninsula, as a condition for joining the federation (Milne and Ratnam 1974).

Nevertheless, the federal government has overall control over the national agenda, and its policies are generally superordinate to those of the states. Important governmental functions like defense, police, and education are organized on a national basis. Accordingly, the federal government maintains control over the expenditure of most public funds (Robertson 1984, 245).

In Peninsular Malaysia, the federal government's Department of Aboriginal Affairs—the Jabatan Hal Ehwal Orang Asli (JHEOA)—handles all matters concerning Orang Asli, sometimes drawing on the assistance of other federal and state government agencies.[2] One major priority of the federal government is nation building, which involves, among other things, integrating the national and state governments into a coherent political unit and creating a sense of unity among the various ethnic groups. Political integration has taken the form of the federal government's increasing its power relative to other parts of the polity (Crouch 1996). The trend since the formation of the Malaysian federation has been for the federal government—and the dominant political party, UMNO—to acquire more and more control over state governments. This is achieved by, for example, withholding development funds from states ruled by opposition parties. Recent prime ministers have also increased the power of the executive branch relative to other institutions and branches of the government (Khoo 1992, 61). Dr. Mahathir Mohamad, who has been prime minister since 1981, has been especially adept at this. Among other achievements, he has broken the power of the sultans, undermined the independence of the judiciary and police, gained control over all news media, and imposed severe restrictions on opposition parties and nongovernmental organizations (Crouch 1996, 144–47, 244–45).

The government has also attempted to unify the country by creating a national culture, which subsumes the diverse cultural traditions of Malaysia's ethnic groups. The national culture is based on Malay culture (Robertson 1984, 259; Crouch 1996, 152–76, 239). Similarly, the national language and medium of education is Malay. The Malay religion, Islam, is the state religion. The ceremonial government of sultans and king is based on the traditional Malay political system. The symbols of national identity are strongly Malay and Muslim. But the government also guarantees the right of the other major ethnic groups, the Chinese and Indians, to maintain their distinctive cultures. They have the right, among other things, to practice their religions, celebrate their holidays, and use their own languages.

The government's other major priority is economic development. Its goal is to make Malaysia a fully industrialized country with a standard of living similar to that of the countries of Europe by the year 2020 (Mahathir and Ishihara 1995, 18–20). The federal government has encouraged multinational companies to invest in factories in Malaysia by providing various facilities (roads, land, etc.), giving tax incentives, and instituting controls over labor unions designed to prevent strikes and to keep the cost of labor low (Crouch 1996, 224–33, 239). In addition, both federal and state governments have become deeply involved in economic planning and even in owning business enterprises.[3] Political parties, especially the dominant Malay party UMNO, also own or partially own numerous businesses (Gomes 1990; Crouch 1996, 214–16).

Since 1971, economic development has been carried out within the framework of the New Economic Policy (NEP). This program was established in response to race riots that broke out in Kuala Lumpur in 1969 between Malays and Chinese who were celebrating their election successes. Government leaders blamed the rioting on Malays' resentment of the relative affluence of the Chinese and on Malay fear of rising Chinese political power (Robertson 1984, 251–60; Crouch 1996, 23–25). The NEP was designed to eradicate poverty among all ethnic groups—but especially among rural Malays—and to eliminate the identification of ethnic affiliation with economic function and income, with the particular aim of bringing Malays into the modern sector of the economy and ensuring them a higher proportion of the national wealth. One specific goal was for Malays and other "indigenous peoples" to own 30 percent of the country's productive wealth by 1990 (Crouch 1996, 24–27). "In implementation, [the NEP] was geared towards the utilization of state resources to sponsor a Malay capitalist class. In realization, it assumed in large part the form of public corporations acquiring assets for and on behalf of Malays, and run by political appointees and bureaucrats" (Khoo 1992, 50; see also Crouch 1996, 200; and Robertson 1984, 261–62). In addition,

> the government pressured major companies to make special issues of shares to Malays at discounted prices through the Ministry of Trade and Industry. . . . Unfortunately, however, virtually all the shares acquired cheaply by individuals and private companies were resold almost immediately to non-bumiputeras at the market rate, thereby bringing about increased wealth for a tiny minority of politically well connected bumiputeras but little addition to bumiputera share ownership. (Crouch 1996, 213)

The NEP has substantially improved the economic position of Malays. Despite their nominal status as *bumiputeras,* however, the Orang Asli of the peninsula and the natives of Sabah and Sarawak have received few if any benefits from the New Economic Policy.

Although the government is strongly promoting manufacturing and information-based industries as the means to future prosperity, it is also continuing to develop primary industries that exploit the country's land and natural resources. Malaysia is one of the world's leading producers of tin, rubber, palm oil, and tropical timber, and it also produces some petroleum. State governments are especially fond of logging because much of the income from it goes to them, rather than to the federal government. In Malaysia, both state and federal agencies are involved in establishing plantations in the logged areas. Since its founding in 1956, the Federal Land Development Authority (FELDA) has converted millions of acres of former forestland in Peninsular Malaysia into rubber and oil palm estates. This program began as a way of providing parcels of land and thus livelihood opportunities to poor Malay settlers, yet the government began running some FELDA plantations as commercial enterprises (Robertson 1984, 232–92).

General Problems of Malaysian Indigenes

Indigenous peoples in Malaysia, like those elsewhere, want above all to have ownership of their land and resources, some degree of self-government, and the right to practice their own religions and customs (POASM 1991; Colchester 1995, 61; Gray 1995, 35; Lasimbang 1996,

Fig. 4.1.   This land, in Kelantan state in Peninsular Malaysia, was formerly covered with lowland tropical rain forest and was home to Batek hunter-gatherers. Here, in 1990, it has been logged and will soon be planted with oil palms. (Photo by Kirk Endicott.)

195; Nicholas 1996a). They also want the same rights and services as other citizens. These are among the fundamental rights emphasized in the 1994 Draft United Nations Declaration on the Rights of Indigenous Peoples and the International Labor Organization's 1989 Indigenous and Tribal Peoples Convention (C169) (Bodley 1999, 213–41). However, in Malaysia these desires clash with the goals of the federal and state governments. Most of the problems facing Malaysia's indigenous peoples arise from their unequal competition with the government and other ethnic groups.

Loss of Land and Resources

Most of the land targeted for development in Malaysia is that of the indigenous peoples. They usually live in remote areas where raw materials (timber, minerals, etc.) have not yet been exploited. They often employ nonintensive methods of land use (e.g., hunting and gathering, swiddening), giving the illusion that the land is underutilized. From the point of view of economic planners, the land and resources are available for development.

In addition, indigenes do not have secure legal rights to their ancestral territories. Traditional Orang Asli concepts of land and resource rights vary from group to group. Foragers like the Batek are mobile, but people have an undisputed right to live in valleys where they, their family members, or their spouses were born; they do not claim exclusive rights over those areas, however. Among swiddeners like the Temiar and east Semai, villages are associated with territories, usually sections of river valleys, where village members have the right to clear swiddens on any unused land. Families own all produce of the fields they clear, but the land itself becomes available for others to use after it has been abandoned and allowed to regenerate. Only valuable trees are durable property; they are owned by the person who discovered or planted them and are passed on to descendants by inheritance (Benjamin 1966, 18–21; 1968, 26–27; Dentan et al. 1997, 34, 39–40). Since coming into contact with government officials and other outsiders, some Orang Asli farmers have adopted the idea of bounded, individually owned plots of land (Juli 1998). However, none of these notions have force in Malaysian land law except for limited recognition of individual ownership of fruit trees (Hooker 1991; Williams-Hunt 1995; Dentan et al. 1997, 73–76).

Peninsular Malaysian land law is based on the British-introduced Torrens system (Means 1985–86, 639; Colchester 1995, 65). This states that all land not owned by title deeds belongs to the individual states. Thus, most Orang Asli are legally "squatters" on state land. State governments can use the land in any way without even consulting the Orang Asli living on it; the states are only required to pay minimal compensation for fruit trees destroyed by development. Even land that is officially recognized (gazetted) as "Aboriginal Reserves" or "Aboriginal Areas" can be repossessed by the state without compensation to the Orang Asli (Dentan et al. 1997, 73–76).

Natives of Borneo also have their own concepts of land and resource rights. Foragers like the Penan have ties with areas in which they individually claim resources (e.g., sago trees) that they nurture and where their ancestors are buried (Brosius 1986, 1993, 1997; Davis 1993, 25). Farmers follow a variety of land tenure systems (Appell 1985, 115–16; 1997; Hong 1987, 14–15, 37–38; Lasimbang 1996, 184; Phoa 1996, 202).[4]

In Sabah and Sarawak, unlike on the Malay Peninsula, state governments recognize what is termed Native Customary Land. This is not, as the name implies, a straightforward recognition of native concepts of land tenure, however. Native Customary Land is actually a concept created and imposed by the state governments (Hong 1987, 37–58). In Sabah, Native Customary Land refers to fifteen-acre allotments of land given to natives for individual tenure. The government charges holders a reduced annual payment on them. Natives can obtain more land, but they have to pay as much as anyone else (George Appell, personal communication, 1998). Sarawak has two categories of land associated with native groups. One is Native Area Land, where "only indigenes may exercise rights under title" (King 1995, 298; see also Hong 1987, 47–48; and Phoa 1996, 202). The other is Native Customary Land, where land is untitled but held individually or communally by natives (King 1995, 298; Hong 1987, 48–49; Phoa 1996, 202).

State recognition of Native Customary Land does not mean that rights over that land are secure, however. In practice, state governments can extinguish those rights at will (Phoa 1996, 203; King 1995, 298–99). "Native customary rights have little force in law. The overriding legal right . . . is that which is exercised by the state. . . . Native rights are held subject to the will and pleasure of the state since any land not covered by a formal document or title is considered in law to be state land" (King 1995, 299). For instance, politicians can convert Native Customary Land to Reserved Land, and grant logging concessions on it, merely by "gazetting" the change. Gazetting means that the government publishes a notice in the government gazette and gives those likely to be harmed sixty days to object, but in fact the people affected are seldom notified (Lasimbang 1996, 191–94; Human Rights Watch 1992, 48; King 1995, 299; Colchester 1995, 65; The Borneo Project 1998a, 1, 3). As Lasimbang notes, "[v]ery often, native communities are not aware that their customary land has been included in a reserve until the logging companies come to log the area" (1996, 191).

Political leaders have a strong incentive to convert Native Customary Land into Reserved Land, which is then parceled out in logging concessions, because they themselves are among the largest holders of logging concessions. In 1987, the Chief Minister of Sarawak, Abdul Taib Mahmud, directly controlled 10 percent of the state's logging concessions, and his relatives and political allies held roughly one-third of the logging concessions in the state (Human Rights Watch 1992, 51; Davis 1993, 26). In a blatant conflict of interest, James Wong, the Minister for the Environment and Tourism, owned three hundred thousand hectares of forest concessions and one of the country's largest logging companies (Human Rights Watch 1992, 51). Politicians in

Sarawak and Sabah routinely reward political supporters with timber concessions, which is one reason politicians on the losing side in elections often switch over to the winning party afterward (Human Rights Watch 1992, 52; Crouch 1996, 54).

The result of these laws and practices is that in both the peninsula and Borneo, state and local governments can and do seize land from indigenes at will and either displace the people or destroy the resources on which they depend for survival. The indigenous occupants of the land are not consulted. There are numerous examples of Orang Asli being displaced for logging, plantations, mining, dams, golf courses, resorts, airports, and so forth (Endicott 1982; Dentan et al. 1997, 94–116; Nicholas 1991, 1993).

Logging and dams have been the main culprits in Sarawak and Sabah (Hong 1987; World Rainforest Movement and Sahabat Alam Malaysia 1989; INSAN 1989). For example, the hydroelectric dam across the Batang Ai River in Sarawak uprooted some three thousand Iban from twenty-six longhouses (Hong 1987, 170–79; Masing 1988, 65; Phoa 1996, 210–11). These Iban were forced to move to an eight-thousand-acre resettlement area a few miles below the dam. The government paid them compensation for the loss of their longhouses, swiddens, and fruit trees. At the resettlement site, each family was allotted an apartment in a new longhouse and given title to eleven acres of land (designated as five acres for rubber trees, three acres for cocoa trees, two acres for wet rice fields, and one acre for fruit trees). But the displaced Iban found that most of their land had not even been cleared, much less planted (as promised), so there was no hope of getting income from their cash crops for at least three to eight years. The Sarawak Land Consolidation and Rehabilitation Authority expected the displaced Iban to obtain work with companies building the dam until their cash crops were mature, but many people were unable to get jobs. In addition, the Iban discovered that they were expected to pay nearly three times as much for their new longhouse apartments as they were paid for those they lost. Moreover, they were charged M$2,000 per acre for the development of their new land. The result was that many of the displaced Iban were forced to live off their compensation money, as they had no way of paying off their debts or returning to a life of subsistence agriculture. Needless to say, the Iban's "traditional" way of life was destroyed. When journalists went to the resettlement area for the funeral of a prominent Iban man, "they were shocked by the deplorable living conditions the resettled families were living in" (Hong 1987, 174). Nevertheless, until the economic crisis in 1997, the federal government was intent on building the even bigger Bakun dam, which was slated to "displace more than 5,000 people living in 52 long-houses belonging to 16 communities" (Hong 1987, 180; see also Masing 1988, 65–66; and Arnold 1995).

The experience of the Batang Ai Iban is typical of resettlement in Malaysia. Usually the government resettles displaced people in small, planned settlements located in logged-off wastelands (Endicott 1979; Masing 1988; Colchester 1995, 63; Dentan et al. 1997, 117–41; Nicholas 1994). This removes people from land slated for development and permits the government to more effectively control and manipulate the indigenous population. The government expects them to support themselves by means of cash cropping (rubber, oil palm, peppers, etc.) and small kitchen gardens, but generally the amount of land in the resettlement area is insufficient for the people's needs. The Orang Asli in the peninsula are not granted secure titles to the land, so they cannot obtain loans or assistance from banks or government agencies to develop and improve it. Infrastructure facilities promised before the people are resettled (roads, houses, electricity, running water, etc.) often prove inadequate or nonexistent. The result is poverty and dependence on government assistance (Nicholas 1994; 1996b, 168). With few skills and no resources, many people are forced to become menial laborers, cutting weeds on plantations, for example. Some drift into towns, where they live in squatter settlements and eke out a living as unskilled laborers, factory workers, servants, and even prostitutes (Hong 1987, 177–78, 209–10). In short, resettlement leads to the breakdown of indigenous cultures (Hong 1987, 182), which is one result the government wants to achieve.

Loss of Self-Government

Unlike such peoples as the Moros of the southern Philippines, who want full independence (see Anderson, chap. 5 in this volume), Malaysian indigenes merely want some control over their own affairs and matters affecting them (Nicholas 1996a; POASM 1991). What they have gotten, however, is almost complete loss of self-government and lack of influence over programs and activities that affect them.

The Orang Asli are totally governed by a federal government department, the JHEOA. The Aboriginal Peoples Act (Malaysian Government 1994) gives the JHEOA control over almost every aspect of their lives.[5] This law was intended to enable the government to remove the Orang Asli from the influence of Communists during the Emergency, which ended in 1960, but it has been continued to the present so that the government can control the Orang Asli and impose its wishes on them. The JHEOA instituted a system of headmen, selected by department officers, which has replaced traditional political systems except in minor internal matters. All government programs affecting the Orang Asli are planned by the department and imposed with minimal input from the people affected.

The JHEOA's responsibility is to carry out the policies of the government regarding Orang Asli, not to help the Orang Asli to influence government policy. All the senior officers and the majority of the other employees of the department are Malays and, perhaps not surprisingly, tend to see things from the Malay point of view. The JHEOA consistently sides with government agencies and Malays in disputes between Orang Asli and others (Dentan et al. 1997, 76–79). One of the demands of Orang Asli leaders in the last few years has been that the JHEOA should be either abolished or turned over to Orang Asli.

Natives of Borneo have retained control over some local political functions, but most major decisions affecting them are made by state governments or the federal government without consulting them (Lasimbang 1996, 182). Iban in Sarawak and Kadazan in Sabah have formed political parties, but they have proved unable to compete with the federally supported Malay-based parties. In legal disputes, they, like the Orang Asli, are at a disadvantage because they do not have the education, connections, or money needed to effectively use the legal system, which is stacked against them anyway.

Loss of Cultural Identity

Orang Asli and Borneo natives both wish to maintain at least some of their distinctive cultural values, customary practices, languages, and religions. This does not mean that Malaysia's indigenous peoples are opposed to all change; they oppose only those changes that harm them. Typically, they want some of the benefits of development and modern social services—like education, health care, roads, running water, and electricity (Appell 1985, 137–43; Zawawi 1996)—but they do not want to have to give up their cultures and ethnic identities to get them.

However, they are under strong pressure to assimilate, to adopt the Malay-based national culture (Lasimbang 1996, 188–90; Dentan et al. 1997). As noted, education is in the Malay language, and hence it conveys Malay values, academic knowledge, and popular wisdom, including the Malays' low opinion of indigenous ways of life. Outsiders ridicule indigenous peoples and pressure them to abandon "uncivilized" practices, like tattooing, immodest dress, and eating "unclean" foods such as pork and monkeys. In Sabah, for instance, "Rungus students were actively discouraged from using their own language in schools, from wearing their traditional clothing, or using their traditional baskets" (George Appell, personal communication, 1998).

In the case of the Orang Asli of the peninsula, the Malaysian government is going further; it is actively pressuring them to "become Malays" by adopting the Malay language, customs, and religion—Islam (Karim 1995; Nicholas 1996b; Dentan et al. 1997, 142–50). Despite the constitutional guarantee of freedom of religion (Malaysian Government 1982, Articles 3 and 11), the JHEOA works with other government agencies and missionary organizations to proselytize Orang Asli and to keep missionaries of other religions away from them; it uses "positive discrimination" to reward converts and discourage those who refuse to convert. By 1993 the government had built 265 community halls with Muslim chapels in Orang Asli villages and provided them with social workers trained as missionaries, often before the villages had basic services like running water (Dentan et al. 1997, 146–47). In 1981 a high-ranking official in the JHEOA told anthropologist Barbara Nowak that once the Orang Asli are culturally indistinguishable from Malays, the department can self-destruct (Nowak 1985, 89).

In Sabah and Sarawak also, government officials and missionary groups pressure pagan and Christian natives to become Muslims. They use bribes, threats, and discriminatory policies to achieve their ends. For example, choice government positions are often reserved for Muslims. To avoid being subject to Muslim rules and restrictions in government dormitories in Sabah, schoolchildren who are not Muslims must pay extra to live in dormitories run by Christian groups (George Appell, personal communication, 1998).

To increase the political strength of the Malay community, the government wants to "absorb" the Orang Asli and Bornean natives into the Malay population. In the case of the Orang Asli, another, perhaps more important reason is that the very existence of a category of people who are arguably "more indigenous" than Malays undermines the official ideology that the Malays are the indigenous people of Malaysia—the claim that is their basis for the special rights and privileges of the Malays.

Indigenes' Responses

Malaysia's indigenous peoples learned long ago that armed resistance to outsiders and government agents was useless. However, indigenous peoples have used various "weapons of the weak" (Scott 1985) and other nonviolent methods to resist the disruptions of their lives and the pressures to change. Some Orang Asli have adopted Christianity and Bahaism, and some Bornean natives have become Christians in order to resist having to become Muslims (Appell 1985, 131, 149; Dentan et al. 1997, 149–50; Juli 1998). Over the past decade or so, some indigenous groups have publicized their plight by appealing to government agencies and to sympathetic nongovernmental organizations (NGOs). For example, in June 1987 a group of native leaders from Sarawak went to Kuala Lumpur and made the rounds of a number of government ministries, protesting the logging that was destroying their homelands and the loss of their customary land rights (see news reports in World Rainforest Movement and Sahabat Alam Malaysia 1989). They were supported by Sahabat Alam Malaysia (Malaysian Friends of the Earth) and the Malaysian Bar Council's Human Rights Sub-Committee. They received tremendous amounts of local publicity as they traipsed around Kuala Lumpur in their native costumes. The inspector general of police and the acting prime minister promised to discuss their grievances with state authorities but warned that they could not interfere in matters that were under the jurisdiction of the state government, such as land use. State government representatives offered the predictable excuses and obfuscations, and, after the native leaders returned to Sarawak, the matter disappeared from the news.

Since then, federal and state governments have taken measures to muzzle and intimidate indigenous activists from the Bornean states. In October 1987, the federal government arrested a large number of critics and political opponents under the Internal Security Act (ISA), which allows those people deemed to be threats to the security of the nation to be detained indefinitely without charges or trial. One of those arrested was Harrison Ngau Laing, a Kayan activist and the Sahabat Alam Malaysia representative in Sarawak. He was released after sixty days but was prohibited from leaving his hometown of Marudi without a police permit (Human Rights Watch 1992, 56; Much done 1995). Anderson Mutang Urud, a Kelabit activist, was arrested in 1992 under a similar Sarawak state law (Human Rights Watch 1992, 53–54; Phoa 1996, 207). In 1993 customs officials confiscated the passport of Jok Jau Evong, a native activist and winner of the 1998 *Condé Nast Traveler* Environmental Award, "without explanation when he was *en route* to an indigenous peoples conference in Peru"; although he filed suit to get his passport back, it had not been returned five years later (The Borneo Project 1998b, 1).

Some indigenous groups have attempted to peacefully obstruct the "development" of their land by outsiders. The best-known example is the Penan and other indigenous groups of Sarawak who blockaded logging roads through their land in the late 1980s and early 1990s (Davis 1993; Sesser 1994, 239–94; Human Rights Watch 1992; Phoa 1996). The international media reported the spectacle of indigenous people putting up barriers of tree limbs and rattan and camping in the logging roads in a desperate attempt to stop their traditional home-lands from being logged. Armed police and soldiers broke up the blockades and arrested and jailed many of the participants. The state Legislative Assembly responded by passing a law making it an offense to obstruct logging activities, blockade logging roads, or prevent authorities from removing blockades; offenders "will be jailed for two years and fined M$6,000 for the first offence and M$50 each day that the offence continues" (Phoa 1996, 203). The state also created regula-tions preventing foreign journalists, film crews, and environmentalists from entering the state and reporting the news about the blockades to the outside world (Phoa 1996, 207–8). This example shows clearly how government officials use all the powers of the state to control and exploit the indigenous peoples.

Some indigenous groups have organized political parties and partic-ipated in the political system for many years (Crouch 1996, 50–54). In Sarawak, Iban, the largest indigenous group, formed the core of sev-eral multiethnic political parties, including the Sarawak National Party (SNAP) and the Sarawak Dayak Party (PBDS). The largest indigenous group in Sabah, the Kadazan, have played a similar role in Sabah state politics. However, native-based parties have generally been outmaneuvered by Malay-based parties and the federal govern-ment in the bare-knuckle politics of Malaysia. For example, when the Kadazan-based United Sabah Party (PBS) had the temerity to with-draw from the national coalition shortly before an election in 1990, the federal government undermined the PBS state government, "by depriving it of development funds, charging Chief Minister Joseph Pairin Kitingan with corruption and arresting several of his close asso-ciates, including his brother Jeffrey, under the ISA" (Crouch 1996, 52). King argues (1995, 304–5) that the natives must form "cohesive and unifying political organizations" if they are to gain control over their destinies, but they have not managed to do that so far. The Orang Asli, on the other hand, are not numerous enough to become a political force on their own, either in federal or state politics.

Some Orang Asli and Borneo natives have recently formed indige-nous peoples' organizations to promote their interests. For example, the Orang Asli Association of Peninsular Malaysia (Persatuan Orang Asli Semenanjung Malaysia, or POASM), founded in 1977, has become an important voice for Orang Asli concerns (Dentan et al. 1997, 153–54; POASM 1991). In Borneo, various indigenous groups have formed their own associations, like the Penan Association of Sarawak. The Indigenous Peoples Network of Malaysia (Jaringan Orang Asal SeMalaysia, or JOAS) strives to unite indigenes from the peninsula and the Bornean states. Indigenous organizations have had to tread carefully, however, because the government uses its powers to suppress organizations that oppose government policies.[6] This can be seen in the case of the Kelabit leader Mutang Urud, who was arrested in 1992 for allegedly running an unregistered society, the Sarawak Indigenous People's Alliance (SIPA) (Human Rights Watch 1992, 53).

Conclusion

Malaysia's poor treatment of its indigenous peoples is due in large part to the indigenous peoples' "standing in the way" of the government's goals of nation building and development. This is especially true when those goals benefit powerful politicians and members of dominant ethnic groups. Unlike the Chinese and Indians, indigenous peoples are politically weak and have thus far been unable to effectively resist the power of the Malaysian state.

Federal and state governments justify their heavy-handed treatment of indigenes by claiming that programs and development actually benefit indigenes, whether they realize it or not. Government officials consider practices like nomadism and subsistence farming to be "backward." Many bureaucrats claim, therefore, that it is inherently better for indigenes to be wage earners or cash-croppers in the market economy. In this regard, Sarawak officials contend that logging is good for the local native peoples because it forces them to enter the "modern" world. In response to the criticisms by environmentalists and human rights activists of the logging of the nomadic Penan people's homelands, Minister for the Environment and Tourism James Wong stated, "No one has the ethical right to deprive the Penan of their right to socio-economic development and assimilation into the mainstream of Malaysian society" (quoted in Davis 1993, 31). Government programs (particularly in the areas of health and education) are supposedly designed to prepare the country's indigenous peoples to enter the "mainstream" of society, by giving them new opportunities and appropriate training. But, as we have seen, the standard of living and health of indigenes typically has suffered because of "development" initiatives and government-sponsored "aid" programs. They are provided with minimal and inferior services, and they lose the resources needed to remain self-sufficient. Often they become dependent on government welfare and subsidies. At best, government-sponsored programs are designed only to turn indigenes into rural cash-croppers, one of the poorest segments of the national population.

Throughout the world, the rich and powerful take advantage of the poor and weak. Malaysia, sadly, is no exception. Most development projects in Malaysia shift wealth from the poor (including indigenes) to the wealthy (including politicians). In Sarawak, influential politicians bestow valuable logging concessions on relatives and political allies, making them "instant millionaires" (Colchester 1995, 68). Powerful individuals, both officials and private citizens, are benefiting by destroying the livelihoods, cultures, and sometimes the lives of indigenous peoples. Far from protecting Malaysia's indigenous peoples from such exploitation and impoverishment, the Malaysian government, at federal and state levels, is actively participating in the process.

Notes

I thank George Appell, Bartholomew Dean, and Jerome Levi for their valuable information and suggestions. Of course, I bear the responsibility for any errors of fact or interpretation.

1. They are descended from the earliest well-documented human population of the peninsula, the pebble-tool-using "Hoabinhians," who began arriving about thirteen thousand years ago (Bellwood 1997, 155–71).

2. The JHEOA has no jurisdiction over the natives of Sabah and Sarawak, and those states do not have similar all-purpose agencies for dealing with their indigenes. However, Sarawak has the Sarawak Land Consolidation and Rehabilitation Authority (SALCRA), which is charged with inducing the natives to give up subsistence farming and adopt cash crops (Hong 1987, 64–65).

3. According to Robertson, "[b]y 1981 there were 657 federally controlled corporations" (1984, 260–61).

4. But there are two basic types of land tenure in the region (Appell 1997). In one, which Appell calls "circulating usufruct," people who clear swiddens gain temporary rights over the land, but the land reverts to the community and is available for others to use once the last crops have been harvested and the land left to regenerate. In the other, which Appell calls "devolvable usufruct," those who clear swiddens acquire enduring use rights over that land. They can pass those rights on to their heirs by various systems of inheritance.

5. For instance, "there are provisions in the Act which empower the Minister concerned to prohibit any non–Orang Asli from entering an Orang Asli area, or to prohibit the entry of any written or printed material (or anything

capable of conveying a message). Even in the appointment of headmen, the Minister has the final say" (Nicholas 1996b, 164).

6. To be legal, "all organizations must be registered with the Registrar of Societies under the Societies Act. Registration can take as little as a month for [organizations] that promote the official 'party line' and more than three years for groups that go against it" (Human Rights Watch 1992, 53).

References

Anderson, Benedict R. O'G. 1987. Introduction to *Southeast Asian Tribal Groups and Ethnic Minorities: Prospects for the Eighties and Beyond,* edited by Ruth Taswell, 1–15. Cultural Survival Report 22. Cambridge, Mass.: Cultural Survival.

Appell, G. N. 1985. Land Tenure and Development among the Rungus of Sabah, Malaysia. In *Modernization and the Emergence of a Landless Peasantry: Essays on the Integration of Peripheries to Socioeconomic Centers,* edited by G. N. Appell, 111–55. Williamsburg, Va.: Department of Anthropology, College of William and Mary.

———. 1997. The History of Research on Traditional Land Tenure and Tree Ownership in Borneo. *Borneo Research Bulletin* 28:82–97.

Arnold, Wayne. 1995. Bakun. *Asiaweek,* November 10, pp. 46–50.

Barnes, R. H. 1995. Being Indigenous in Eastern Indonesia. In *Indigenous Peoples of Asia,* edited by R. H. Barnes, Andrew Gray, and Benedict Kingsbury, 307–22. Ann Arbor, Mich.: Association for Asian Studies.

Beaglehole, J. H. 1976. *The District: A Study of Decentralization in West Malaysia.* London: Oxford University Press for the University of Hull.

Bellwood, Peter. 1997. *Prehistory of the Indo-Malaysian Archipelago.* Rev. ed. Honolulu: University of Hawai'i Press.

Benjamin, Geoffrey. 1966. Temiar Social Groupings. *Federation Museums Journal,* n.s., 11:1–25.

———. 1968. Headmanship and Leadership in Temiar Society. *Federation Museums Journal,* n.s., 13:1–43.

Bodley, John H. 1999. *Victims of Progress.* 4th ed. Mountain View, Calif.: Mayfield Publishing Co.

Borneo Project, The. 1998a. Customary Land Claims in the Balance. *Borneo Wire,* autumn 1998, 1, 3.

———. 1998b. Jok Jau Evong: *Condé Nast Traveler* Environmentalist of the Year! *Borneo Wire,* autumn 1998, 1.

Brosius, J. Peter. 1986. River, Forest, and Mountain: The Penan Gang Landscape. *Sarawak Museum Journal,* n.s., 57:173–84.

———. 1993. Penan of Sarawak. In *State of the Peoples: A Global Human Rights Report on Societies in Danger,* edited by Marc S. Miller, 142–43. Boston: Beacon Press.

———. 1997. Endangered Forest, Endangered People: Environmentalist Representations of Indigenous Knowledge. *Human Ecology* 25 (1): 47–69.

Cobo, Jose R. Martinez. 1986. *Study of the Problem of Discrimination against Indigenous Populations.* United Nations Document E/CN.4/Sub.2/1986/7.

Colchester, Marcus. 1995. Indigenous Peoples' Rights and Sustainable Resource Use in South and Southeast Asia. In *Indigenous Peoples of Asia,* edited by R. H. Barnes, Andrew Gray, and Benedict Kingsbury, 59–76. Ann Arbor, Mich.: Association for Asian Studies.

Crouch, Harold. 1996. *Government and Society in Malaysia.* Ithaca: Cornell University Press.

Davis, Wade. 1993. Death of a People: Logging in the Penan Homeland. In *State of the Peoples: A Global Human Rights Report on Societies in Danger,* edited by Marc S. Miller, 23–32. Boston: Beacon Press.

Dentan, Robert Knox, Kirk Endicott, Alberto G. Gomes, and M. B. Hooker. 1997. *Malaysia and the "Original People": A Case Study of the Impact of Development on Indigenous Peoples.* Boston: Allyn and Bacon.

Endicott, Kirk. 1979. The Impact of Economic Modernization on the *Orang Asli* (Aborigines) of Northern Peninsular Malaysia. In *Issues in Malaysian Development,* edited by M. Rudner and J. C. Jackson, 167–204. Singapore: Heinemann Educational Books (Asia).

———. 1982. The Effects of Logging on the Batek of Malaysia. *Cultural Survival Quarterly* 6:19–20.

Furnival, J. S. 1948. *Colonial Policy and Practice: A Comparative Study of Burma and Netherlands India.* Cambridge: Cambridge University Press.

Gomes, Edmund. 1990. *Politics in Business: UMNO's Corporate Investments.* Kuala Lumpur: Forum.

Gray, Andrew. 1995. The Indigenous Movement in Asia. In *Indigenous Peoples of Asia,* edited by R. H. Barnes, Andrew Gray, and Benedict Kingsbury, 35–58. Ann Arbor, Mich.: Association for Asian Studies.

Hong, Evelyne. 1987. *Natives of Sarawak: Survival in Borneo's Vanishing Forest.* Penang: Institut Masyarakat.

Hooker, M. B. 1991. The Orang Asli and the Laws of Malaysia with Special Reference to Land. *Ilmu Masyarakat* 18:51–79.

Howitt, Richard, John Connell, and Philip Hirsch. 1996. Resources, Nations and Indigenous Peoples. In *Resources, Nations and Indigenous Peoples: Case Studies from Australia, Melanesia and Southeast Asia,* edited by Richard Howitt, John Connell, and Philip Hirsch, 1–30. Melbourne: Oxford University Press.

Human Rights Watch. 1992. *Defending the Earth: Abuses of Human Rights and the Environment.* New York: Human Rights Watch, Natural Resources Defense Council.

INSAN (Institute of Social Analysis). 1989. *Logging against the Natives of Sarawak.* Petaling Jaya, Malaysia: Institute of Social Analysis.

Juli, Edo. 1998. Claiming Our Ancestors' Land: An Ethnohistorical Study of *Seng-oi* Land Rights in Perak, Malaysia. Ph.D. diss., Research School of Pacific and Asian Studies, The Australian National University.

Karim, Wazir Jahan. 1995. Malaysia's Indigenous Minorities: Discrepancies between Nation-Building and Ethnic Consciousness. In *Indigenous Minorities of Peninsular Malaysia: Selected Issues and Ethnographies,* edited by Razha Rashid, 18–35. Kuala Lumpur: Intersocietal and Scientific Sdn. Bhd.

Khoo Kay Jin. 1992. The Grand Vision: Mahathir and Modernization. In *Fragmented Vision: Culture and Politics in Contemporary Malaysia,* edited by Joel S. Kahn and Francis Loh Kok Wah, 44–76. Honolulu: University of Hawaii Press.

King, Victor T. 1995. Indigenous Peoples and Land Rights in Sarawak, Malaysia: To Be or Not to Be a Bumiputra. In *Indigenous Peoples of Asia,* edited by R. H. Barnes, Andrew Gray, and Benedict Kingsbury, 289–305. Ann Arbor, Mich.: Association for Asian Studies.

Kingsbury, Benedict. 1995. "Indigenous Peoples" as an International Legal Concept. In *Indigenous Peoples of Asia,* edited by R. H. Barnes, Andrew Gray, and Benedict Kingsbury, 13–34. Ann Arbor, Mich.: Association for Asian Studies.

Lasimbang, Jannie. 1996. The Indigenous Peoples of Sabah. In *Indigenous Peoples of Asia: Many Peoples, One Struggle,* edited by Colin Nicholas and Raajen Singh, 177–95. Bangkok: Asia Indigenous Peoples Pact.

Leete, Richard. 1996. *Malaysia's Demographic Transition: Rapid Development, Culture, and Politics.* Kuala Lumpur: Oxford University Press.

Mahathir Mohamad and Shintaro Ishihara. 1995. *The Voice of Asia: Two Leaders Discuss the Coming Century.* Tokyo: Kodansha International.

Malaysian Government. 1982. *Malaysia: Federal Constitution.* Kuala Lumpur: Malaysian Government.

———. 1994. *Akta Orang Asli: 1954/Aboriginal Peoples Act 1954* (with all amendments up to June 1994). Kuala Lumpur: Malaysian Government.

Masing, James. 1988. The Role of Resettlement in Rural Development. In *Development in Sarawak: Historical and Contemporary Perspectives,* edited by R. A. Cramb and R. H. W. Reece, 57–68. Clayton, Victoria: Centre of Southeast Asian Studies, Monash University.

Means, Gordon P. 1985–86. The Orang Asli: Aboriginal Policies in Malaysia. *Pacific Affairs* 58:637–52.

Milne, R. S., and K. J. Ratnam. 1974. *Malaysia—New States in a New Nation: Political Development of Sarawak and Sabah in Malaysia.* London: Frank Cass.

Much Done and More to Do: A Malaysian Activist Prepares His Next Move. 1995. *Asiaweek,* November 3, p. 9.

Nicholas, Colin. 1991. Orang Asli and Development: Chased Away by a Runway. *Pernloi Gah* 3 (October): 5–6.

———. 1993. Mysteries and Miseries: The Jakuns of Tasik Cini. *Pernloi Gah* 5 (March): 14–16.

———. 1994. *Pathway to Dependence: Commodity Relations and the Dissolu-*

tion of Semai Society. Clayton, Victoria: Centre of Southeast Asian Studies, Monash University.

————. 1996a. A Common Struggle: Regaining Control. In *Indigenous Peoples of Asia: Many Peoples, One Struggle,* edited by Colin Nicholas and Raajen Singh, 1–10. Bangkok: Asia Indigenous Peoples Pact.

————. 1996b. The Orang Asli of Peninsular Malaysia. In *Indigenous Peoples of Asia: Many Peoples, One Struggle,* edited by Colin Nicholas and Raajen Singh, 157–76. Bangkok: Asia Indigenous Peoples Pact.

Nowak, Barbara. 1985. The Effects of Land Loss and Development on the Btsisi' of Peninsular Malaysia. In *Modernization and the Emergence of a Landless Peasantry: Essays on the Integration of Peripheries to Socioeconomic Centers,* edited by G. N. Appell, 85–110. Williamsburg, Va.: Department of Anthropology, College of William and Mary.

Phoa, John. 1996. The Dayaks and Orang Ulu of Sarawak. In *Indigenous Peoples of Asia: Many Peoples, One Struggle,* edited by Colin Nicholas and Raajen Singh, 197–212. Bangkok: Asia Indigenous Peoples Pact.

POASM (Persatuan Orang Asli Semenanjung Malaysia). 1991. *Pembangunan Orang Asli dalam Konteks Wawasan 2020.* Kuala Lumpur: Jawatankuasa Bekerja POASM/Senator Orang Asli.

Robertson, A. F. 1984. *People and the State: An Anthropology of Planned Development.* Cambridge: Cambridge University Press.

Scott, James C. 1985. *Weapons of the Weak: Everyday Forms of Peasant Resistance.* New Haven: Yale University Press.

Sesser, Stan. 1994. *The Lands of Charm and Cruelty.* New York: Vintage Books.

Williams-Hunt, Anthony. 1995. Land Conflicts: Orang Asli Ancestral Laws and State Policies. In *Indigenous Minorities of Peninsular Malaysia: Selected Issues and Ethnographies,* edited by Razha Rashid, 36–47. Kuala Lumpur: Intersocietal and Scientific Sdn. Bhd.

World Rainforest Movement and Sahabat Alam Malaysia. 1989. *The Battle for Sarawak's Forests.* Penang: World Rainforest Movement and Sahabat Alam Malaysia.

Zawawi, Ibrahim. 1996. *Kami Bukan Anti-Pembangunan! (Bicara Orang Asli Menuju Wawasan 2020).* Bangi, Malaysia: Persatuan Sains Sosial Malaysia.

5 Nationalism and Cultural Survival in Our Time: A Sketch

Benedict R. Anderson

Southeast Asia today has a colossal number of "indigenous minorities," though they became such only in this century. Their creation was the result of the interplay between three modern institutions. First and foremost was the arrival of the census, by which all subjects of the colonial state, down to newborn children, were regularly and systematically *counted* within matrices categorizing everyone by racial and usually also ethnolinguistic affiliation (as the Europeans saw it). And on the basis of these census-imaginings a vast range of mostly new state institutions (police, immigration bureaus, tax authorities, land registrars, schools, etc.) penetrated, shaped, channeled, oppressed, favored, and isolated the colonies' inhabitants. Second was the popularization—through colonial propaganda and Western-type schools, as well as newspapers and magazines—of the state's terrain as a quasi-physical entity, a single-colored jigsaw-puzzle piece next to all the other puzzle pieces making up the world map of modern sovereignties. It became possible to recognize "Burma" simply by its drawn silhouette, without any identifying place-names inserted within it. The colony thus was turned into what Thongchai Winichakul describes as a "geo-body," with "its" own ancient, unitary history and contemporary absolute sovereignty.[1] Finally came mainstream anticolonial nationalism, shaped by and reacting to the census and to the geo-body's history and sovereignty, carrying them powerfully forward into the postcolonial era.

In this process, some crucial transformations took place. Under late colonialism, anticolonial nationalists had few weapons against a well-armed, rich, and highly organized imperial apparatus, beyond those of sheer numbers. It was in their interest to forge broad popular coalitions if they could, and there was not yet any question of "minorities." The very idea of minorities was typically regarded as a divide-and-rule tactic in the hands of the "white" rulers, used to instigate suicidal

165

conflicts among the "people." Furthermore, nationalism was itself regarded as a necessary part of the struggle for the "cultural survival" of the natives in the face of imperial power. But when nationalism triumphed after the Second World War and nationalists came to state power, popular coalitional mobilization was very often replaced by an authoritarian "official nationalism" imposed from the center. "Minorities" thus reappeared—as the objects of state policy, as in colonial times. The ways in which these "minorities" have responded to the enormous pressure put upon them by homogenizing nation-state elites have varied so substantially that it would be impossible to consider them all in this essay. I will therefore concentrate on one end of the spectrum of possibilities: the extremely high-stakes "strategy" of rejecting minority status and going national, that is, seceding from the postcolonial nation-state in the name of an oppressed nationality. High physical risks aside, this strategy always involves a later mimicking of the history of the colonial-era nationalist movement itself—its coalitional character, its re-creation of a "people," its transformation of consciousness and the past, and its profoundly homogenizing instincts. The key question in such cases is typically this: what will survive this kind of radical movement for new "national" cultural survival?

One has to begin, I believe, where the relevant historical process started—with minoritization itself, which was a late colonial program and reflected the new gaze of the colonial state.[2] I say "new" advisedly, if one considers the cases of the two oldest major colonial powers in the region. The Dutch began their conquests in the Indonesian archipelago at the beginning of the seventeenth century but carried out their first census only in 1921. The Spanish arrived in the mid-sixteenth century and barely got round to a primitive census a few years before they were kicked out of Southeast Asia for good at the end of the nineteenth. The British and French censuses came late in the nineteenth century, the American early in the twentieth. These censuses are of great ethnographic and textual importance.[3] With the extremely interesting exception of the Spanish, to which I will turn in a moment, all these censuses were conceptually organized around axes of putative race and ethnicity and, here and there, religion (sometimes the confused census-makers found religion and ethnicity difficult to sort out from one another). Furthermore, opposite these racial and ethnic categories were columns of figures specifying to the state and the public how many persons, including children, belonged to each. These categories may have seemed authoritative at their first appearance, but they proved anything but stable. If one read successive censuses as if they were chapters in a muddled book, one would see the erratic disappearance of some characters who had appeared in earlier chapters and the emergence of new ones later on. The Spanish case is particularly important because right up to the end, Manila failed to make the full transition to ethnoraciality. No Spanish population count mentioned, let alone quantified, any ethnolinguistic group; the categories were anchored in ancient Iberian religious and juridical traditions.[4] It was an astonishing contrast with the first American census in 1903, which was strictly modeled on domestic U.S. ethnoracial ideology and practice.

Two aspects of these public censuses seem particularly worthy of discussion. The first and most obvious is that by their quantificatory procedures, the censuses informed their publics' members of their status within majorities or minorities as the state conceived of them. "Burmans" in Burma, "Vietnamese" in Indochina, learned that they were numerical majorities—at least so long as these categories held. "Javanese" in the Netherlands Indies and "Malays" in British Malaya were very large minorities. Others were middling, and many were very small. But—and this is really important—the abstract percentages were, in the census format, taken colonywide, so that even if there were very few "Javanese" in Sulawesi and hardly any "Burmans" in the vast Kachin hills, this did not matter in the least: their majority-ness or big-minority-ness was never anchored to regional territorial specificities. The only territoriality that mattered to the census was that of the colony itself. Hence, Batavia counted Malays in the Indies but not in Malaya, and Rangoon counted Mons only in Burma, not in Siam. In effect, the census-makers were acting, unself-consciously, as proto-nationalists even as they repressed nationalist activities.[5]

In an age, however, when semidemocratic electoral politics had become mostly normal in the imperial centers, the political implications of census counts back home began to filter through to Southeast Asia, and in time indigenous peoples started to reflect on what the censuses could mean to them: not least that their white rulers were infinitesimally tiny "minorities," who could not possibly win any honest elections.[6]

The second decisive aspect of the census-imagining was its deeply aggregative impulse. The most vivid example I know comes not from Southeast Asia but from the Himalayan fringes of the Raj, the remote Buddhist terrain of Ladakh.[7] In 1911, in a moment of bureaucratic madness, Delhi permitted the young makers of the first Ladakhi census to encourage their subjects to write in the caste to which they thought they belonged. (The fact that caste was assumed to be the relevant central category for a Buddhist community is interesting in itself.) To the census-makers' horror, this license unleashed an astonishing flood. No fewer than 5,934 names were returned as principal castes, tribes, and races, and 28,478 as subcastes and minor divisions. Needless to say, the error was not repeated in 1921, when Delhi insisted that everyone decide among the fifty-four castes it had boiled down, or aggregated up, from the delirious "mess" of ten years earlier. In Southeast Asia such aggregations took place in three related ways: (1) virtually all the censuses were based on a racial grid separating the colonies' populations into, say, whites, foreign Asians, and natives; (2) very substantial differences within putatively large ethnic groups—historical attachments, dialects, agricultural/urban distinctions—were firmly overridden (thus generic millions of aggregable "Sundanese" or "Ilokanos" suddenly appeared on the horizon); (3) even more bizarre aggregations were created of imagined mini-minorities under a territorial designation that was read as if it were ethnoracial. The most striking example is the case of the western half of New Guinea, where a welter of more than two hundred small groups speaking often unrelated languages were aggregated up first as New Guineans, or Papuans, and later— under Indonesian rule, when the region was called West Irian—as Irianese. (It was as if Papua/Irian derived its names from a singular ethnic group inhabiting it.)[8]

All three kinds of bureaucratic-anthropological aggregations were to have crucial long-term consequences. For the colonial state did not carry out censuses for fun, but rather to create the objective database for the implementation of an ever-widening set of policies in a dozen fields and for a deepening surveillance of, and penetration into, the everyday lives of its subjects. The first aggregation pointed forward to the new macrocategories of "Indonesians" and "Burmese"; the second to "we Burmans benignly directing our Burmese Burma/Myanmar"; the third toward, at the outer limit, postcolonial secession. At the same time, these aggregations were, and are, all related to one another.

We are so accustomed today to viewing with a jaundiced eye the practices of postcolonial rulers that it is easy to overlook the real historical character of anticolonial nationalism when it was still a virginal force against the state and had not yet got married to it. Even those groups such as the "Burmans" and the "Vietnamese" who in the early twentieth century could imagine themselves as natural and huge majorities, entitled one day to rule, were extremely weak compared to the might of the state they opposed. Not a single colonial state in Southeast Asia was in any serious trouble in early 1942, when, out of the blue, Hirohito's armies obliterated almost all of them in a few paltry weeks. The nationalists—ex-natives, so to speak—read in their collective nativeness the one resource the white colonial state did not have: very large numbers of people. Their task was therefore to build and mobilize the widest popular coalition against that state—exactly on the juridical and census basis of that nativeness. This aggregated nativeness shows up in the creation, around 1898, of "the Filipino" and, around 1920, of "the Indonesian."[9] It is a pattern that is exactly isomorphic with the subsequent appearance of "the Moro," "the East Timorese," and "the Papuan," with which the bulk of this essay is concerned.

Such changes did not occur without costs: here we come for the first time to the question of cultural survival. It is easy these days to forget or underestimate the enormous and violent shock that high imperialism brought to the colonies in Southeast Asia. In 1870, there were barely forty thousand Dutch people (perhaps only twenty-five thousand adult males) in the Indies, and most natives probably never saw a white face. But by 1900 their numbers had hugely increased, and railways and motor roads were taking them everywhere. Missionaries were pouring in alongside gigantic agribusiness, schoolteacher propagandists, surveyors, tax collectors, open and secret police, urban planners, anthropologists, professional linguists, geologists, and so on.[10] What we can think of as evidence of cultural-survival crises shows up everywhere by the late nineteenth century: peasants burning the cane fields of encroaching Dutch plantations, *ulama* leading small rural rebellions against the inroads of Christianity, aristocrats hugging "tradition" to their velvet-coated chests as they were incorporated into the steepening colonial bureaucracy, hill peoples fleeing deeper into fading forests. And dozens of new kinds of people were also making their appearance—collaborators, urban bandits, brokers, informers, activists, strike makers and breakers, sect leaders, race rioters, journalists, operetta singers: the list is endless. All represented responses of a sort to a cultural typhoon, and in many instances attempts to rescue whatever could be rescued of what had been there "before." But "what was there before" typically proved to be something that was also new: "Tradition" with a capital T, which could only be imagined retrospectively.[11]

All this is by way of a schematic preface to a consideration of a set of three cases of what might be called "nationalism as cultural survival" in Southeast Asia—a minority set, to be sure, but which illuminates the more general difficulties and possibilities of survival. I will proffer a brief sketch of each before turning back at the end to the larger questions I have raised so far. These nationalist movements are the more to be compared in that all emerged for the first time in the decade between 1965 and 1975, and each is well aware of the others.

Bangsa Moro

In their 350 years of rule in the Philippines, the Spaniards were never able effectively to subjugate the Islamic populations inhabiting the southernmost part of the archipelago they named after Felipe II. Coming to the islands in the age of Torquemada, and within two lifetimes of extruding the Moors from the Iberian Peninsula, they called their tough and wily antagonists on the other side of the globe also Moors (Moros), and this name strangely stuck—so that today the descendants of some of those distant sixteenth-century Muslims are guilelessly happy to call themselves Moros.[12] But the term now denotes above all a nationality. It is striking that, to the end, these people never showed up—as Muslims—in any Spanish-era census (the Americans included them in their first one, because by that time Washington had actually broken their local military power). The reason was that in the Spanish era, the axes of differentiation and antagonism were fundamentally religious, not ethnic—Catholicism versus Islam (with Basque, Catalan, and Castilian as unimportant as Tausug, Maranao, and Maguindanao). In the aftermath of the American conquest, Moroland was for a time ruled independently from the rest of the archipelago, and it was not at all a foregone conclusion that it would not become a separate colony. As late as the 1920s, Governor-General Leonard Wood was seriously inclined to that alternative. So it was only about sixty years ago that the Moros started to be integrated into the Philippines, as we know it now.

The biggest cultural innovation of the American colonialists is clear in the 1903 census, which for the first time imagined, categorized, and publicized the real existence of the "tribal" groups of Maguindanao, Maranao, and Tausug and gave them numbers alongside the Catholicized Tagalogs, Cebuanos, and Ilokanos, merely italicizing them in the alphabetically arranged list of fifty-two "tribes" to indicate their savagery and backwardness. But American rule was too short and chaotic to make these anthropological census distinctions overriding. The overwhelmingly Catholic cacique politicians who ran first the Commonwealth and then the independent Philippines shared with their constituents the Spanish-era undifferentiated view of these new "ethnics" as dangerous and benighted Muslims. Nonetheless, the political system set up by the Americans—on the model, in many ways, of the post-Reconstruction South—made possible a certain accommodation between all parties. A regime dominated by congressmen residing in their single-member electoral districts permitted enterprising (and venal) Muslim bigmen (*datu*) to become elective brokers between Catholic Manila and the far South. The authority of the capital reinforced their local power with pork-barrel funds and locally recruited police forces, while their periodic presence in Manila allowed them to claim with some conviction that they were genuinely representing and defending Tausug, Maranao, or Maguindanao—and Muslim—interests. "Moroland," however, did not exist as a political or administrative unit, so that in practice, Maranao bosses ran Maranao electoral districts and Maguindanao bosses ran Maguindanao. Their power was buttressed by widespread illiteracy, a very restricted suffrage, firearms, and the fact that until the late 1950s, Manila had very little interest in its remote southern periphery.

After independence, however, Manila was faced with a major Communist insurgency in the northern island of Luzon, where overpopulation and *hacendado* abuses were rife. In an effort to "solve" the social problem, it decided to give poor Catholic/Communist Luzon tenants and agricultural laborers lands in the "empty" South; soon after, mining and agribusiness corporations moved into the South as well, bringing a huge wave of non-state-sponsored migrants in their wake.

The Muslim bigmen proved incapable of halting this flow—or, bought off, they barely tried—and their prestige and power steadily declined. At the same time, the postindependence state regarded it as its duty to uplift the Moros by public education of a unified national type, so that by the mid-1960s there were, for the first time, Muslim students studying at the University of the Philippines in Manila, mastering English and Tagalog and reading history, too. By the late 1960s, Muslim–Catholic armed conflicts were already rife in Moroland, and when, in the wake of his declaration of martial law in 1972, Ferdinand Marcos attempted a general disarmament of all political groups except his own, a full-scale insurrection in the name of the Bangsa Moro broke out.[13]

It broke out because the dictatorship eliminated the only residues of independent Muslim representation in Manila by closing down the Congress, because the *datu* had become discredited, because losing their guns meant losing the Moros' last defense against Christian Manila, and because a young leadership had appeared from the ranks of Manila-educated Muslim students. These new leaders rejected any further integration with the Philippines, and in the (anachronistic) name of the religious, cultural, economic, and political "survival" of the (new) Bangsa Moro—the Moro Nation—they went to war for independence, just as Bonifacio, Aguinaldo, and Mabini had done seventy years earlier several hundred miles to the north.

For more than two decades the Moro Nation, which is also a strategic coalition of smaller, historically often mutually hostile groupings, fought fiercely for independence—at horrific cost to themselves, but also to their antagonists. By the end of the first four years of the fighting, an estimated 100,000 Moros had been killed, and a further 250,000 fled to Sabah in neighboring East Malaysia; at least 11,000 of Marcos's troops had also died, and the war was costing Manila $150,000 a day.[14] Violence on this massive and brutal scale had not been seen in the islands since Japanese and Americans fought over it in the Second World War and since the savage American pacification at the turn of the century. Both sides received extensive external help in the form of money, guns, and propaganda—Manila from the Americans, the Moros from different regimes in the OPEC-boom Muslim states to the west. After two decades of brutalities, both sides became exhausted, and a shaky compromise is now in place with the creation of an autonomous Moro/Muslim region at least superficially controlled by former Moro Nation leaders. In effect, the Moroland imagined by the Spaniards, Americans, and Filipino cacique elites and created by the Moro insurrectionaries now has real administrative and jural form. Furthermore, with the end of the Marcos dictatorship, electoral congressional government has been restored, which again ensures locally based Muslim representation in Manila. But it remains to be seen whether, after all the bitterness, this compromise will last.

The features of this historical sketch that I would like to emphasize are as follows.

(1)   The terrifying, two-decade armed conflict was largely the outcome of the high-stakes strategy of the Bangsa Moro leaders, who demanded UN-status national independence and thus, in the eyes of Manila, the dismemberment of the American-era Philippines. But these leaders assumed the risks in part to attract international attention and support because of the holy status of the right to self-determination in the post–Woodrow Wilson world.

(2)   If nationalism and self-determination are effective claims in many external quarters, so is Islamic solidarity in others (not, needless to say, in the nominally Christian and Jewish West). The beauty of

"Bangsa Moro" is that it combines both sources of sympathy and support. Nations "matter"—especially if they are seen as the victims of genocidal killing—in a way that mere minorities (such as the Maranao) normally do not.

(3) The fusion of religious and nationalist claims and identities represented by Bangsa Moro does not mean the complete eclipse of local cultures and attachments, but, in combination with the upheavals and displacements of the last quarter of a century, it does mean their subordination and transformation. The youngsters who have laid their lives on the line have been doing so in the name of something—the Bangsa Moro—that was beyond their grandfathers' cultural ken.

East Timor

The story of East Timor is today, thanks in part to the Nobel Peace Prizes justly awarded to Bishop Carlos Ximenes Belo and José Ramos Horta in 1997, rather better known internationally than that of the Bangsa Moro.[15] The semi-island was the last and most remote acquisition of the ancient Portuguese maritime empire, which began its penetration there in the sixteenth century. Portugal's early international decline and later poverty, stagnation, and depopulation meant that East Timor suffered almost no "development" until after the Indonesian armed forces invaded it in early December 1975. The interminable Salazarist clerico-fascist regime, in power from the late 1920s until 1974, simply confirmed a long-standing pattern. East Timor's rulers were a tiny group of Portuguese officials, clerics, and planters, supported by a scarcely less tiny layer of mestizos.[16] The bulk of the population consisted of quite distinct ethnolinguistic communities with little systematic contact between them, although in this century Tetun, as a lingua franca, spread substantially through local trading networks. Some of these communities were related to groups that ended up corralled in the Dutch colonial western half of the island. Illiteracy was overwhelming (90%); what towns existed were poor and small; and even after four centuries, Catholicism had reached only a minority of the people.

In April 1974, when a radicalized Portuguese military overthrew the Salazarist regime, East Timor had a secret police, the notorious PIDE, but no political parties or parapolitical associations, no legislature, and no real press: a typical old-style colonial autocracy. The Lisbon regime fell because it had failed disastrously to fight three Vietnam Wars at the same time—in Angola, Mozambique, and Guinea-Bissau. So the new left-wing rulers of Portugal hastily transferred sovereignty to the guerrilla opposition in these three territories, paying little attention to remote East Timor. Some of the top military leaders seem to have assumed that it would have to be absorbed by Big Indonesia, as Portuguese Goa had been absorbed by Nehru's Big India in 1961: East Timor was, they imagined, socially, politically, and economically "unviable."[17]

But almost immediately, and certainly stimulated by Lisbon's extraordinary change of regime and the successes of their African cousins in gaining UN-recognized nationhood, small groups of educated mestizos and indigenous elites began to organize politically. In short order, three political parties emerged—Fretilin, UDT, and Apodeti, all of which included "Timor" in their names and thus made explicit claims to represent a (new) supra-ethnolinguistic totality.[18] Although each in fact had its local bases of support, none claimed to "stand for," say, the rights of the Mambai or the Atoni. All implied that they stood for grand coalitions of once disparate communities.

Jakarta initially appeared ready to accept a future independence for East Timor parallel to that of Mozambique, Angola, and Guinea-Bissau. But soon, for reasons too complex to discuss here, it changed its mind and began extensive meddling, culminating in a brutal and incompetent invasion of the territory in late 1975. "Legal" incorporation into Indonesia quickly followed, although Jakarta then controlled barely one-third of the territory. (This legality has still to be accepted by any significant external power two decades later.)[19] In the course of the next five years, during which East Timor was closed off not merely to the outside world but even to most Indonesians, a savage effort was launched to bring the population to heel. It is widely accepted that about two hundred thousand people, or one-third of the country's population, died in the fighting or from the famine and epidemic diseases that resulted from it. It was a catastrophe even greater, proportionately, than that suffered by the Bangsa Moro.

The Indonesian regime's initial calculations were as follows: (1) East Timor was so economically backward, so ethnolinguistically and religiously heterogeneous, and so illiterate that whatever nationalism had sprung into view in the twenty months between April 1974 and December 1975 could have no solid popular roots. All that needed now to be done was to suppress any opposition, pour money into development projects that would dwarf those of the Portuguese, and spread the Indonesian language (and culture) through a massive investment in the eradication of illiteracy and the construction of a full hierarchy of educational institutions on the standardized state pattern. Within a generation, so the fancy went, the population of East Timor would have become Indonesian. (2) At a time when Indochina was "falling," the West would support the actions of Indonesia—a huge, strategically situated, resource-rich, anticommunist state—without serious reservations.[20]

Most of these calculations proved to be mistaken, and it is important to see why. The basic reason was the regime's colonial gaze, which from the start saw East Timor as a single entity filled with "East Timorese." (The Jakarta press also, up to this moment, when speaking of various East Timorese notables, never mentions their "ethnic" origins.) The policies pursued—educational, economic, medical, and so on—were all standardized to fit this conception. The people on the receiving end of these policies, treated violently and indifferently as "East Timorese," increasingly saw themselves as just that.

Few of the leaders in Jakarta clearly understood that they were pursuing policies that mirrored those earlier Dutch colonial policies that had created the Indonesian nationalist movement, of which they were the contemporary beneficiaries.[21] The extreme violence of the war meant that almost every Timorese family lost one or more of its members. The long and finally unsuccessful counterinsurgency campaigns made the countryside so dangerous that tens of thousands of rural people poured into the towns, where, as migrants, they were exposed, along with everyone else, to the tumultuous, homogenizing influences of urban life. They could move so massively because the funds that Jakarta poured into the colony—in an effort to persuade international and national opinion—created a network of roads and motor transportation that for the first time linked the whole country from one end to the other. The forcible introduction of Indonesian as the language of all state educational institutions paradoxically gave the young, postinvasion generation of East Timorese a second lingua franca—one that gave them opportunities for intellectual access to Jakarta's colonial project, for alliances with Indonesian oppositionists, and for links with the outside world in a way that Tetun was not positioned to do. Here was an exact parallel with the way that the colonial inauguration of Dutch-language education at the very end of the nineteenth century produced within a generation a Dutch-fluent nationalist movement against Dutch colonialism. Finally, the implementation of an Indonesian-wide policy of compulsory affiliation with a "great" religion, a policy inaugurated in the wake of the great anticommunist *matanza* of 1965–66, soon boomeranged. Within two decades, the overwhelming majority of the East Timorese population had become Catholic, attached to a hierarchy almost entirely East Timorese in character and, thanks to the Vatican's refusal to accept the legality of Indonesia's annexation, not subordinated to Indonesian cardinals but directly linked to the Curia.[22]

By the time of the notorious Santa Cruz massacre of 1991, film clips of which were shown around the world, Jakarta began to realize that, far from destroying a thin veneer of East Timorese nationalism, it had unwittingly deepened and widened its appeal. Indonesia now had nowhere to go: more of the same policies would only continue their subversive effects, while retreating would mean moving toward an acknowledgment of East Timor's independence. No wonder that, in an unguarded moment, Indonesia's capable foreign minister Ali Alatas confessed publicly that East Timor "is like gravel in our shoes."[23]

From the preceding sketch, let me underline three points that lend themselves to comparison with the fate of Bangsa Moro.

(1)   The unbelievable sufferings inflicted on the people of East Timor are inseparable from their claims to their own nationhood and their rejection of Indonesian-ness. Ethnic or religious rebellion would probably have been suppressed more lightly.

(2)   At the same time, it is precisely the East Timorese claim to nationhood that has helped gradually to create a complex web of international supporters. That the country's few months of virtual nation-statehood in 1975 coincided with the independence of Angola, Mozambique, and Guinea-Bissau was crucial at the start. More recently, the punishment of Saddam Hussein for doing in Kuwait what Suharto did in East Timor, the successful emergence of Eritrea from the ruins of Old Ethiopia, and the disintegration of the Soviet Union into a multiplicity of new UN members all worked to help the East Timorese cause. Beyond that, the full Catholicization of the people hooked them firmly up with the enormously influential worldwide network of Roman Catholicism, giving them a hearing in, for example, the United States that Muslim Moroland could never achieve.

(3)   Indonesia's extremely violent, money-rich, and dull-witted colonialism combined with the sudden appearance of East Timorese nationalism to make of East Timor an utterly different place from what it was a quarter of a century ago. The nationalist movement became dominated by a generation of youngsters mostly born after the Indonesian annexation; they are urban, schooled, multilingual, and quite aware of the cultural divide that separates them from many of their elders.[24] East Timoreseness, which also means a removal from older, local cultures, is at the center of their consciousness and is the engine of the new pasts that they are in the process of imagining for

themselves. It is also precisely because they are nationalists that they have had the organized courage to take spectacular actions against a murderous military machine, rather than fleeing or hiding from it. Most important, they are confident that eventually their day of freedom will come, and that confidence seems historically well placed. At the same time, there are good reasons to think that the Mambai culture, studied by anthropologist Elizabeth Traube twenty-five years ago, is, after years of repression and effective deportations, close to being gone for good.[25]

Papua

The nationalist movement in Papua—or Irian Jaya, as it appears on Indonesian maps today—is less well known and much less "successful" than that in Moroland or East Timor, but it is of the same general type.[26] The relevant history does not take us back to the sixteenth century but to 1836, when the Dutch Crown claimed sovereignty, on the basis of very little on the ground, over that part of the huge island of New Guinea lying west of the 141st degree of longitude. In 1901, the region was formally incorporated into the Netherlands Indies, but only a tiny scattering of Dutch colonial officials and missionaries resided there until well after the Second World War.

The incorporation was an administrative convenience. West New Guinea could easily have become yet another Dutch colony on its own, like Surinam and Curaçao; if this had happened, the subsequent fate of its more than two hundred small indigenous peoples (amounting to perhaps no more than seven hundred thousand human beings in the 1960s), most of whom spoke mutually unintelligible languages, would now be completely different. The country was so remote, so backward ("Stone Age"), as the colonialists saw it, that they decided, when the Indonesian nationalist movement got seriously underway, to treat it as a kind of tropical Siberia to which serious troublemakers could be internally exiled for the duration. This happenstance brought "West New Guinea" deep into the martyrology of the Indonesian nationalists, since a fair number of them suffered years of imprisonment there, and not a few died in the malarial conditions that prevailed.[27] But it entered under the sign of the colonial state's gaze. This state regarded the miscellany of populations as generic "Papuans," distinguished from other Netherlands Indies subjects by their "Melanesian physiques" and their "primitiveness." No matter that the Asmat would one day become world famous for their colossal sculptures. Even today, if one asks Indonesians to name any of the two hundred ethnocultural groups in West Irian, few can summon up more than one or two.

The country was left much to itself until the Second World War, when American, Japanese, and Australian armed forces fought their bloody way along its northern shores. When, after four bitter years of war and diplomacy, The Hague was finally forced to concede independence to the Republic of Indonesia (1949), the future status of West New Guinea remained undecided. Indonesians insisted that it join their new republic. The bitter Dutch refused to give it up, fantasizing it first as a refuge for Eurasians fleeing the new Indonesia, later as a last chance to do modern colonialism right. Jakarta's saber rattling and a Cold War environment that encouraged Washington finally to intervene on the Indonesian side brought the country under brief UN supervision in 1962, after which it was unceremoniously taken over by Jakarta.

In the years between 1949 and 1962, however, the Dutch had changed things vastly, for the first time investing sizable sums in transportation networks through the truly formidable terrain, in schools, and in supra-"tribal" councils, which were designed to prepare the indigenes for their own independence one distant day. Missionaries also stepped up their various denominational efforts, with substantial success. By a peculiar irony, however, the Dutch continued in West New Guinea the strange, indeed unique, Netherlands Indies practice of using a form of Malay as a supralocal language of administration and education—a Malay that in Indonesia proper had meantime turned itself into the national language, Bahasa Indonesia. Had West New Guinea become an independent nation-state—which happened to the eastern half of the island in September 1975, just two months before East Timor declared its independence on the eve of the Indonesian invasion—its national language would still have been effectively the same as the national languages of Indonesia and Malaysia.[28]

Incorporation into Indonesia in 1963 came at an exceptionally bad time. The populist Sukarno regime was beginning to unravel, and it disappeared in an orgy of organized violence in 1965–66, out of which emerged the highly militarized dictatorship of General Suharto. Like many other parts of the sprawling archipelagic state, West Irian was put under Javanese military rule; Papuans suspected of hankering for the balmier days of Dutch colonial rule or working for independence were treated brutally as potential subversives and secessionists. The population in general suffered from military abuses and near-racist contempt for its "primitive ways." These misfortunes were later compounded by the arrival of large numbers of carpetbaggers from western and central Indonesia who occupied most of the bureaucratic positions and dominated local trade. When giant American mining corporations and later vast Indonesian-Chinese logging conglomerates moved in, the local military made it their business to protect these interests at whatever cost to the local peoples. The long-standing links of some of West Irian's communities with related communities over the wild border with Papua-Niugini, which has remained a reasonably open and unmilitarized polity, offered a neighboring example of how things might have been and might still be.

Thus, from the late 1960s there appeared a first (illegal) nationalist and secessionist organization—the OPM (Organisasi Papua Merdeka, or Organization of Free Papua). In spite of severe and sometimes barbaric repression,[29] this organization has survived for thirty years, even conducting periodic successful military operations—without, however, posing any fundamental threat to Jakarta's control. And, as in East Timor, the passage of time has changed the composition of the local activists, making them the products of Indonesian, rather than Dutch colonial, education.

The case of "Papua" is especially illuminating by comparison with that of East Timor and Moroland. No previous history of "foreignness" (as in East Timor) or ancient religious antagonism (as in Moroland) marks off Papua ideologically from Indonesia. A mild form of racism is common among ordinary West Indonesians toward the "Irianese," but its thrust is relatively benign, since all Indonesians are taught that the Papuans are also fellow Indonesians and part of the multicultural, multiethnic web of modern Indonesia. Papuans are visible nationally as writers and journalists, as excellent football players, and even as popular transvestite television comedians, mainly in Jakarta. But they appear as "Irianese"—a colonial administrative fiction that has gradually become a social reality—instead of as Baudi, Asmat, or Dhani. Brutal as the regime has been in Irian, this brutality is not too different from that inflicted on other troubled provinces in Indonesia, and it pales by comparison with the horrors endured by East Timor.[30] This means that while the OPM has considerable support in West Irian, it does not command the kind of loyalty on which the resistance in East Timor could rely. Furthermore, so-called tribal or ethnolinguistic conflicts among the OPM have been visible all along, so that an authoritative long-term leadership has not really emerged. Hence, the OPM has been incapable of the kind of spectacular protest actions in Jakarta that young East Timorese managed.[31]

Finally, there is the question of external allies. In some ways, West Irian is more favorably situated geographically than either Moroland or East Timor, neither of which immediately abuts any politically sympathetic nation. The government (and parts of the population) of Papua-Niugini has at various times given some public and private support, particularly in the form of assistance to resistance fighters and terrified families fleeing across the 141st meridian. But Indonesia has been able to enlist the help of Australia, on whom Papua-Niugini is heavily dependent, and deploy intimidation of its own in order to keep Port Moresby's support very low-key. The religious heterogeneity of West Irian's peoples has precluded the kind of sustained concern that Moroland could elicit from the world of Islam and the East Timorese from world Catholicism.[32]

Again, for the purposes of formal comparison with Moroland and East Timor, one can note the following.

(1)   Harshly as West Irian has been treated, it has not suffered the vast violence visited on Moroland and East Timor. It is likely that this relative, and I emphasize *relative,* "lenience" can be attributed to two main factors. First, the OPM has been unable to make the kind of international waves produced by its companions-in-struggle, despite its high-stakes nation-state aspirations; nor has its resistance struck the kind of body blows that the Timorese and Moros have inflicted on the Indonesian and Philippine armed forces. As mentioned earlier, the UN itself effectively turned West Irian over to Indonesia in 1962–63 and is unlikely to make any volte-face in the stance that this transfer implied. Second, West Irian is far more solidly ensconced in the national mythology of Indonesia than are the East Timorese, or the Moros in that of the Philippines.[33] Indonesians think of themselves as in some sense the heirs of the Netherlands Indies, of which, in this century, West Irian was a part, and it is rare to find the kind of visceral hostility toward its people that one can find in the Philippines toward Muslims.

(2)   The OPM's nationalism, though older than that of the East Timorese and no younger than that of the Moro, has faced greater difficulties in creating a widespread, supralocal community consciousness. The sheer size of the territory, into which one could fit five East Timors and five Morolands, the extreme ruggedness of much of its terrain, and the sparseness, dispersion, and heterogeneity of its two hundred linguistic communities have been the primary obstacles. No overriding religious identification has been available to consolidate internal support and leverage external sympathies. There are certainly a sizable number of Irianese who for a variety of reasons have accommodated

themselves to the Indonesian Republic and have done well for themselves in so doing, not merely in West Irian itself but also in the national capital.

(3) West Irian is being generally transformed by the penetration of the Indonesian state and, in mainly coastal enclaves, by the operations of corporate capital. But the processes have been slower than elsewhere, and the sheer size of the territory means that there is more room to evade the onslaught than is available in East Timor or Moroland. Nonetheless, in some ways "cultural survival" is more deeply at stake in West Irian, since the traditional communities are much smaller and less politically sophisticated than their counterparts in the other two countries under discussion. In other words, disintegration is more in the cards than transformation.

Most of the relevant comparisons between these three cases have been adduced in the course of the preceding pages, and it should be needless to repeat them. By way of a conclusion, I would therefore like to return to the special status that links them: their unusual (in a world context) demand for their own UN-seated nation-state.

These days, such demands represent a very bold and dangerous gamble, though perhaps less so than a decade ago. In the age that began with the formation of the League of Nations in 1919, the nation-state has been the only fully legitimate world-form of polity. This is one reason why in this century so many empires collapsed one after another, and why the Soviet Union, which did not regard itself as a nation-state, came to its final, partly-to-be-lamented end. The enormous attraction and legitimacy of the nation-state has three main grounds: (1) its undergirding, certainly formally and in most cases practically, by a solid popular basis in nationalism, which remains the most potent political force in the world two centuries after its first appearance; (2) its internationally accepted jural claims to near-absolute sovereignty within a cartographically delimited geographical space; and (3) its proven capacity to build deep-founded, transformative coalitions between older, and quite often hierarchical, local communities on a basis of ideological equality.

Precisely because of these enormous attractions, existing nation-states normally put up the most violent resistance to any organized movements that break down its popular base by seceding from it, that undermine the doctrine of absolute sovereignty, and that frontally contest the reality of an ideological equality on the basis of common citizenship. So to speak: "We are not Indonesians, and we do not accept the absolute sovereignty of the Republic of Indonesia because we never have been and never will be treated on a basis of respectful equality."

In recent years—by contrast with the high Cold War era, when nationalist secessions were almost never successful (Bangladesh was an extraordinary exception)—there have been spectacular successes, though it must be said that they have occurred in supranational polities, such as the Soviet Union, or in empires disguised as nation-states, such as Old Ethiopia. Nonetheless, people are well aware that today the UN has four times as many members as did the League of Nations at its founding. They are also aware that the possibility of the UN one day extending membership to such entities as Kurdistan, Palestine, and Tibet is by no means chimerical. Self-determination, with all its ambiguities, remains a powerful international clarion call.

Attacked at its core, the nation-state is sorely tempted to respond to secessionist nationalism with extreme violence: the cases of Moroland and East Timor show just how violent the response can be. Yet today, the absolute claims of the nation-state are under assault from a multiplicity of directions, as the pace of international migrations accelerates, as electronic communications instantly cross all national boundaries, as international financial capital roams capriciously and massively across the globe, and as the prestige of universalist conceptions and organizations—promoting human rights, women's rights, indigenous peoples' rights, gay and lesbian rights, the environment's rights, and so on—seems to be steadily rising. Furthermore, in Europe, the core zone of the old League of Nations, the creation of the European Community, despite its many warts, shows concretely how sovereign nation-states can be partially bonded together in subsovereign ways; and how, under this larger umbrella, Scottish, Catalan, and other nationalists can achieve most of their objectives without necessarily taking the high-risk secessionist path. (One cannot doubt that, in the event of East Timor, Bangsa Moro, or the OPM achieving nation-state status, they would soon become members of that distinctly homely family called ASEAN—Association of Southeast Asian Nations.)

But "going national," aside from the severe dangers involved for the populations concerned, is beset by natural conditionalities and is accompanied by two complicated transformations. The most important conditionality is simply geography. It is commonplace today, such is the prestige of nationalism, to speak of the Gypsy Nation, Black Nationalism, Queer Nation, and so on; but the truth is that, politically speaking, these remain chimeras without a demarcatable space in which a "sovereign" nation-state could be established for their constituents. In the Philippines, there is no such space for, say, an aboriginal (*negrito*) nation-state, nor in Indonesia for, say, a Minangkabau nation-state: the relevant populations are simply too geographically scattered and mixed in with others.

More important still are the transformations required. The terrible beauty of nationalism lies in exactly its transformational capacities. Deep down, all nationalist movements are to some degree, even if they do not fully realize it, coalitions of much older and more rooted communities and cultures. Ethnic groups, regional groups, tribal groups, religious groups, lineage groups, caste groups—all have in some measure to be both overridden and agglutinated. One central fashion in which this deep agglutination takes place is through a radical change of consciousness, which of course means a radical change of culture.

Nationalism achieves this end by a fundamental realignment of time, in a process with which we are familiar. Profoundly novel, it nonetheless requires, in our epoch, an anchorage in History.[34] This new ancient history snips up bits of earlier local memories, genealogies, folktales, cosmologies, and so forth, melts them down, and tries to recast them into a powerful, structurally singular narrative. One could say that these snippets "survive," but one feels that that is stretching the meaning of the word. No less important, the nation, because it is birthed and bathed in History, thinks of Futures, as no traditional cultural communities were accustomed to do. National culture is embedded in a general idea of human progress, and it is just this that marks it off from older cultures, creates its special attractions for the young, and makes the sacrifices that it demands so seemingly rational and rosy-fingered.

This transformation of time is a force at least as demonic as it is salutary. It hollows out pasts and it destroys presents. The Hagia Sophia in Istanbul, with its majestic Byzantine cupola and murals, with its fabulous Muslim minarets and ornamental calligraphy, was still, at the end of the nineteenth century, a place for unself-conscious Islamic prayer. Today, it is necessarily a museum for tourists, because no one can now imagine the culture that made that extraordinary combination of different religious arts a part of everyday religious life. The Asmat still (barely) produce their astonishing sculptures, but they are made for a market of art lovers who neither know nor care about Asmat culture as it was even thirty years ago. Museumification and commodification of cultures can take place only when hollowing out is well advanced.

So much for the past. And what about the present? It falls hostage to the tense that I like to call the Future Perfect. This tense summons the present to make sacrifices, both mundane and extraordinary, for the future. The last thing that East Timorese, Bangsa Moro, or OPM activists look forward to is a return to the cultural past or even a continuation of the cultural present. The folk dances and folk arts will be there, not for themselves but as signs of something of which their original creators were innocent: nation-ness. The liberator San Martín decreed in 1821 that "in the future the aborigines shall not be called *indios* or natives; they are children and citizens of Peru and they shall be called Peruvians."[35] These words were not penned cynically, but we can read them today as saying that the natives have no future without a Future.[36] The sentence is perfectly translatable into the worlds of Moroland and East Timor. It means that, for the culture of nationalism, things as they are—survival—cannot be enough. The costs of nationalism as a means to cultural survival we can predict from what we know of nationalism's two-hundred-year world history.[37] Not enormously agreeable—until we reflect on the alternatives.

Notes

This essay was completed before the downfall of the Suharto dictatorship in Indonesia in May 1998. Some of the ideas outlined in this essay are developed more elaborately in my recent book (1998).

1. See Thongchai Winichakul's brilliant and pathbreaking study (1994).

2. See my introduction to Clay's *Southeast Asian Tribal Groups* (Anderson 1987) for an elaboration of this argument.

3. They are discussed and analyzed at length in my recent (1997) article in *Genèses*.

4. See the detailed data set out in the long "demographic" appendix to Corpuz 1989. In the Philippines, the Christian population was juridically and hierarchically divided into *peninsulares* (Spain-born Spaniards), *criollos* (Spaniards born outside Spain), *mestizos* (people of mixed Spanish-native, Spanish-Chinese, and Chinese-native descent), and *indios* (natives), with a small side category of *chinos* (Chinese). No ethnolinguistic community had any juridical or political status.

5. This argument is developed more fully in the section "Census" of chapter 10 in my *Imagined Communities* (1991).

6. Here the term *indigenous peoples* is used in the matter-of-fact sense of populations regarded by the colonial power as anciently settled within the territorial bounds of the colonial state. It therefore excludes Europeans, children of mixed European-native descent, and putative descendants of immigrants from southeastern China, the Hadramaut, and the Raj. It should not be taken as necessarily corresponding to any strict empirical reality.

7. The following account I owe to an unpublished paper by van Beek (1994).

8. In the erratic development of these serious comedies, bizarre conflicts can be detected between official statisticians, territorial bureaucrats acting as amateur anthropologists, professional academic anthropologists, and missionaries. Martijn van Beek has a mordant account in the opening chapters of his Ph.D. thesis (1996).

9. It is possible to be rather precise about these dates. The only people described as *filipino* in José Rizal's great nation-imagining novel *Noli Me Tangere* (1887) are *creoles*, or non-Spain-born Spaniards. But "the Filipino" in the modern sense is pervasive in the earliest surviving writings (1898) of the revolutionary statesman Apolinario Mabini. The first political organization to have "Indonesia" in its name was created by young Communists, who in 1920 named it the Partai Komunis Indonesia.

10. The 1930 census recorded the residence of a quarter of a million "Dutch." But "Dutch" was also a legal category to which the acknowledged children and further descendants of mixed marriages belonged, so that the real increase from 1870 was substantially less than 350 percent.

11. The typhoon did not blow itself out with the fall of colonialism. When the great Indonesian writer Pramoedya Ananta Toer, after almost fifteen years in the prisons and penal colonies of President Suharto, emerged on December 21, 1979, into an Indonesian society drastically transformed by mass murder, dictatorship, OPEC oil billions, and colossal Japanese, American, and European Community investments, he said, "I feel as if I am in a foreign country."

12. The standard sources on the Moros and the rise of the Bangsa Moro are Majul 1973; Che Man 1990; Gowing 1979; George 1980; and Kiefer 1972. See also the very recent, probing study by Abinales (1997).

13. *Bangsa*, an old Malay form, was purposely used in opposition to *bansa*, the Tagalog analogue, to demarcate linguistically the break with the Philippine nation and its (Pilipino/Tagalog) official national language.

14. *Manila Chronicle*, October 7, 1989. The savagery involved is well illustrated by the practice of then Colonel Gregorio "Gringo" Honasan—later to become the most famous putschist against Cory Aquino's presidency—of occasionally sporting a belt on which dried Muslim ears were strung. Though the Marcos regime fought a bitter counterinsurgency war against the revived Communists, it is hard to imagine a comparable belt of dried Communist ears around Honasan's waist. The Communists came from the Christian Philippines.

15. There is a comprehensive multilingual bibliography on East Timor in Carey and Bentley 1995, as well as some important essays. Basic reference texts in English are Jolliffe 1978 and Taylor 1991. Horta's autobiography (1987) is a valuable personal account. Saldanha's text (1994), an English translation of an Indonesian-language original, is impressively documented.

16. Saldanha gives a table of the composition of the territory's population

in 1950: 434,907 indigenes; 3,128 Chinese; 2,022 mestizos; and a mere 568 Europeans (1994, 77).

17. It is striking that Douglas Porch's detailed, first-class account of the "revolution" of 1974 and its aftermath amply discusses Mozambique, Angola, and Guinea-Bissau but passes over East Timor in utter silence. General Costa Gomes, who was President of the Republic in the crisis days, said in a later newspaper memoir that this was his group's thinking at that time. See Arnold S. Kohen, *From the Place of the Dead: The Epic Struggle of Bishop Belo of East Timor* (New York: St. Martin's Press, 1999), 81. It will be remembered that when Salazar refused to negotiate with Nehru over the decolonization of Goa, the Indian apostle of peace sent his well-disciplined troops to seize the little colony. No blood was shed, since the tiny Portuguese garrison folded without a fight (Porch 1977, 35–36).

18. Perhaps not entirely new. The Portuguese organized what population counts they made along a racial gradient and completely ignored American-style ethnicities. It is also striking that although Saldanha is an outstanding East Timorese social scientist, he makes virtually no mention of any ethnolinguistic groups in his four-hundred-page volume (1994).

19. The least significant external power is Australia, whose mercenary leaders have had their eyes on joint exploitation with Indonesia of the huge oil deposits off the East Timorese coast.

20. Jakarta was right at least on this second point. Ninety percent of the Indonesian weapons used in the invasion were American. Though this blatantly violated the terms of the 1958 U.S.-Indonesian arms agreement, not a peep was heard from Washington. But the United States never accepted Indonesia's de jure right to be in East Timor, and Western Europe, partly out of deference to Portugal, followed suit.

21. Nothing better shows the conceptual muddle in Jakarta than its inability over twenty years to provide intelligible history textbooks for East Timorese—and indeed Indonesian—schoolchildren. All "traditional" textbooks are organized on the basis of the coalitional struggle against Dutch colonialism—from which the East Timorese never suffered. Indonesia's own constitution explicitly states that the boundaries of the country are those of the former Netherlands East Indies—of which East Timor was never a part. This means that the annexation of East Timor was clearly unconstitutional! It is striking, also, how often senior officials complain about the "ungratefulness" of the East Timorese, a language they never use about real Indonesians but that was constantly on the lips of senior Dutch officials in colonial times, referring to their native (Indonesian) subjects.

22. The church, local and global, thus can offer the East Timorese population at least some protection against the Indonesian military's oppression. It is revealing that Suharto consistently picked Catholic and Protestant generals to command the troops stationed in the country—not that this lessened in any way the violence they deployed.

23. See Anderson 1995 for a fuller description and discussion of Indonesian colonial policy and Alatas's admission.

24. The population of Dili, the country's capital, has increased well over 500 percent in the last twenty years. Urban youngsters will be fluent in the language of their local origin, Tetun, and Indonesian and may have a smattering of English and Portuguese. By 1990, illiteracy had been reduced to 53 percent, but this ratio was still more than double that of the "worst" province in Indonesia and almost four times the Indonesian national average. See Saldanha 1994, 275. Most of the illiteracy is in rural areas.

25. See, for example, Traube's instructive contribution in Carey and Bentley 1995.

26. Basic references for Irian Jaya in this context are Lijphart 1969 and Osborne 1985. Also, from a Jakarta perspective, see Djopari 1993 and the splendid recent work of anthropologist Danilyn Rutherford (1997). How far Irian Jaya is ignored by scholarship on modern Indonesia is evidenced by the fact that the best general book on the latter subject, Schwarz's *A Nation in Waiting: Indonesia in the 1990s* (1994), mentions it only in passing, while devoting a full chapter to East Timor.

27. Among the internal exiles were future vice president Mohammad Hatta and Indonesia's first prime minister, Sutan Sjahrir. For fine texts on their experiences and their perceptions of it, see Mrázek 1994, 138–52; and Shiraishi 1996.

28. This is why the name of the contemporary militant "Papuan" nationalist movement is in Indonesian/Malay: Organisasi Papua Merdeka (Organization of Free Papua).

29. A particularly sadistic example is offered by General Abinowo, who commanded the Eighth (Irian Jaya) Military Region between February 1989 and August 1992. According to the courageous and well-informed head of the local Legal Aid Institute at the time, Abinowo had his men send him the hacked-off heads of suspected rebels and, on at least one occasion, burned a portion of a village along with its inhabitants in their homes—later forcing the rest, returning from work, to eat the flesh of their charred loved ones.

30. The repression has, overall, been less grisly than that dealt out to the strongly Muslim West Indonesian province of Aceh, where in the late 1980s the Acehnese Independence Movement emerged. Aceh is not off the beaten track; it lies at the gateway to the Straits of Malacca and very close to Malaysia. Acehnese have long-standing and extensive contacts with the larger world of Islam. Hence, the secessionist movement there has been regarded as more dangerous than that in West New Guinea.

31. The most remarkable of these was the occupation by East Timorese students of the front yard of the American embassy on the morning of November 12, 1994, when Suharto was welcoming many heads of state (including U.S. president Bill Clinton) arriving for a summit meeting of APEC (Asia Pacific Economic Cooperation) leaders.

188 At the Risk of Being Heard

32. The very large in-migration of outsiders, especially from Java, Sulawesi, and Maluku, also provides Jakarta with an interested local political base. It is precisely the fear of such demographic swamping that has driven young East Timorese to considerable violence against a recent flow of civilian carpetbaggers into Dili and smaller towns.

33. As mentioned earlier, late Dutch colonialists used West Irian as a sort of tropical Siberia to which they exiled the most recalcitrant of their native opponents. The penal colony of Tanah Merah in the swamps of southeastern Irian quickly assumed high nationalist significance.

34. I say "in our epoch" because this was not the case with the very earliest, New World nationalisms. The question of why the subsequent turn to History occurred is examined in the final chapter of *Imagined Communities* (Anderson 1991).

35. John Lynch, *The Spanish American Revolutions, 1808–1826* (New York: Norton, 1973), 276.

36. The brilliance of Mario Vargas Llosa's nationalist novel *El Hablador* (1991) lies in part in his decision to exclude the future tense from those portions that simulate the narratives of the Machiguenga storyteller. The other portions, where the narrator is the author's alter ego, are all meditations on the past and future of his "malhadado país" (unfortunate/ill-fated/accursed country)—Peru. Unfortunate, yes, but the grammatical form of *malhadado* has about it the flavor not of the future, but of the past.

37. In this regard, there is an instructive contrast between strongly nationalist Indonesia and the much less nationalist Philippines. "Small" local languages in Indonesia are dying out all the time in the presence of a hegemonic Bahasa Indonesia, which fifty years ago almost no one but local Chinese mestizos spoke in their homes . Linguistic diversity is surviving much better in the Philippines, because the state has been too weak, and too mestizo, to ensure for Pilipino/Tagalog a comparable position of overweening dominance.

References

Abinales, Patricio. 1997. State Formation and Local Power in Southern Mindanao, 1900–1972. Ph.D. diss., Cornell University.

Anderson, Benedict. 1987. Introduction to *Southeast Asian Tribal Groups and Ethnic Minorities,* edited by J. Clay, 1–15. Cambridge, Mass.: Cultural Survival.

———. 1991. *Imagined Communities: Reflections on the Origin and Spread of Nationalism.* London: Verso.

———. 1995. Gravel in Jakarta's Shoes. *London Review of Books,* November 2.

———. 1997. Recensement et politique en Asie du Sud-est. *Genèses* 26:55–76.

———. 1998. *The Spectre of Comparisons: Nationalism, Southeast Asia, and the World.* London: Verso.

Carey, Peter, and G. Carter Bentley, eds. 1995. *East Timor at the Crossroads: The Forging of a Nation.* London: Cassell.

Che Man, W. N. 1990. *Muslim Separatism: The Moros of Southern Philippines and the Malays of Southern Thailand.* Quezon City: Ateneo de Manila University Press.

Corpuz, Onofre. 1989. *The Roots of the Filipino Nation.* Vol. 1. Quezon City: Aklahi Foundation.

Djopari, John. 1993. *Pemberontakan Organisasi Papua Merdeka.* Jakarta: Gramedia.

George, T. J. S. 1980. *Revolt in Mindanao: The Rise of Islam in Philippine Politics.* Kuala Lumpur: Oxford University Press.

Gowing, Peter G. 1979. *Muslim Filipinos—Heritage and Horizon.* Quezon City: New Day Press.

Horta, José Ramos. 1987. *Funu: The Unfinished Saga of East Timor.* Trenton, N.J.: Red Sea Press.

Jolliffe, Jill. 1978. *East Timor: Nationalism and Colonialism.* St. Lucia: University of Queensland Press.

Kiefer, Thomas M. 1972. *The Tausug: Violence and Law in a Philippine Muslim Society.* New York: Holt, Rinehart and Winston.

Kohen, Arnold S. 1999. *From the Place of the Dead. The Epic Struggle of Bishop Belo of East Timor.* New York: St. Martin's Press.

Lijphart, Arend. 1969. *The Trauma of Decolonization: The Dutch and West New Guinea.* New Haven: Yale University Press.

Lynch, John. 1973. *The Spanish-American Revolution, 1808–1826.* New York: Norton.

Majul, Cesar Adib. 1973. *Muslims in the Philippines.* Quezon City: University of the Philippines Press.

Mrázek, Rudolf. 1994. *Sjahrir: Politics and Exile in Indonesia.* Southeast Asia Program, Studies on Southeast Asia No. 14. Ithaca: Cornell University.

Osborne, Robin. 1985. *Indonesia's Secret War: The Guerrilla Struggle in Irian Jaya.* Sydney: Allen and Unwin.

Porch, Douglas. 1977. *The Portuguese Armed Forces and the Revolution.* London: Croom Helm.

Rutherford, Danilyn. 1997. Raiding the Land of the Foreigners: Power, History, and Difference in Biak, Irian Jaya, Indonesia. Ph.D. diss., Cornell University.

Saldanha, Joaõ Mariano de Sousa. 1994. *The Political Economy of East Timor Development.* Jakarta: Pustaka Sinar Harapan.

Schwarz, Adam. 1994. *A Nation in Waiting: Indonesia in the 1990s.* Boulder, Colo.: Westview Press.

Shiraishi, Takashi. 1996. The Phantom World of Digul. *Indonesia* 61:93–118.

Taylor, John. 1991. *Indonesia's Forgotten War: The Hidden History of East Timor.* London: Zed Books.

Thongchai Winichakul. 1994. *Siam Mapped: A History of the Geo-Body of a Nation.* Honolulu: University of Hawai'i Press.

Traube, Elizabeth. 1995. Mambai Perspectives on Colonialism and Decolonization. In *East Timor at the Crossroads: The Forging of a Nation,* edited by Peter Carey and G. Carter Bentley, 42–55. Honolulu: University of Hawai'i Press.

van Beek, Martijn. 1994. Who Framed Tsering Phuntsog? Construction of Race/Caste/Class/Tribe/Community in Ladakh. Unpublished paper.

———. 1996. Identity Fetishism and the Art of Representation: The Long Struggle for Regional Autonomy in Ladakh. Ph.D. diss., Cornell University.

Vargas Llosa, Mario. 1991. *El Hablador.* Barcelona: Biblioteca de Bolsillo.

6 Indigenous Autonomy in Mexico

Lynn Stephen

While many have focused on how transnational capitalism and globally driven policy initiatives have negatively affected indigenous peoples and the rural poor in Mexico and elsewhere (Harvey 1998; Collier 1994), few have explored the ways that culture and history are deployed at local levels in response to economic restructuring policy initiatives. This essay focuses on how indigenous peoples in southern Mexico are redeploying nationalism from below in order to redefine their place in the Mexican nation in the wake of economic restructuring undertaken to facilitate free trade.[1] This challenge involves local cultural forms that rework top-down nationalism and create a sense of local nations that offer an alternative to the marginalized position of many indigenous communities in national and regional politics and economic development schemes. In southern Mexico, this challenge has been formalized through the creation of autonomous indigenous communities and municipalities (*municipios*) in the state of Chiapas and in other states, such as Oaxaca.

In the process of creating a national network of local and regional movements for indigenous rights, usually unified around the concept of "indigenous autonomy," the homogenizing influence of the category "Indian" is both embraced by those participating and simultaneously challenged from within through regional cultural differences, as well as by women who have questioned the implications of "traditions" that marginalize them in economic, cultural, and political processes. Indigenous autonomy is understood as respect for the internal practices and decision-making modes of indigenous communities and nations. Autonomy also means that indigenous communities participate in the various levels of economic, political, cultural, and legal decision making associated with the state (see Stephen 1997b, 2000; and Regino 1996).

Indigenous communities, groups, organizations, and coalitions

Map 6.1.   Area of the Zapatista rebellion and the location of
Chiapas in Mexico. (Reprinted from Lynn Stephen, *Zapata
Lives!* Copyright © 2001 The Regents of the University of Cali-
fornia by permission of the University of California Press.)

have rallied in support of the San Andrés peace accords signed by the
Zapatista Army of National Liberation (EZLN) and the Mexican federal government in 1996 as the basis for identifying certain unifying
ideas as shared rights that should be accorded to all indigenous peoples
in Mexico. Yet the differing realities of local nations provide a challenge not only to the peace accords, but to building a national network
out of disparate experiences. Furthermore, the Mexican state has seriously opposed the movement for indigenous autonomy, embarking on
a sustained effort to disable the legislative process for implementing
the peace accords and engaging in a brutal and highly visible campaign

Map 6.2. Towns in Chiapas mentioned in the text. (Reprinted from Lynn Stephen, *Zapata Lives!* Copyright © 2001 The Regents of the University of California, by permission of the University of California Press.)

to put an end to autonomous municipalities in Chiapas. In particular, the Mexican state disapproves of the establishment of self-declared autonomous governments in opposition to counties and town councils run by those affiliated with the Institutional Revolutionary Party (PRI) in Chiapas. This campaign to dismantle autonomous communities with the combined force of the state security police and the army was waged in the spring and summer of 1998. In addition, local paramilitary groups have collaborated with local PRI members to harass, intimidate, and murder activists involved in autonomous parallel governments that are sympathetic to the EZLN. Such a paramilitary group was responsible for the massacre of forty-five Tzotzil men, women, and children in December of 1997 in Acteal.

A series of nested contradictions exists among competing definitions of autonomy: (1) the federal government of Mexico feels threatened by indigenous autonomy and hence creates a homogenizing discourse about how it is a threat to Mexican national sovereignty; (2) a wide range of indigenous counties, communities, and organizations have relied on the notion of autonomy to create a national network dedicated to indigenous rights; and (3) these notions of autonomy are inflected by local and gendered variation and disagreement about the meaning of this concept. In this essay, I outline the Zapatista rebellion and the emergence of the ideology of indigenous autonomy in Chiapas, trace its development at the national level, and highlight its internal contradictions reflected in debates raised by indigenous women's concerns and by regional differences.

Nations, Nationalism, and Indigenous Movements

Understanding the evolution of movements for indigenous autonomy in Mexico involves a brief foray into debates about the relationship between nationalism and local processes of identity construction centered on ethnicity (see Anderson 1983; Chatterjee 1993; Joseph and Nugent 1994; Mallon 1995; and Rubin 1997). I am especially concerned with how local nationalisms (Anderson's "imagined communities" in the plural) produce different interpretations of the larger nation. These different interpretations are part and parcel of the construction of local nations—what Florencia Mallon (1995) has called "community hegemonies." In addition to showing how "the nation" may be differently constructed from varied subject positions tied to specific regions, it is also important to show that even local visions of the nation are contested. While particular regions may construct a local sense of nation along a particular model—such as the Tzeltal and Tojolabal communities of the Lacandón jungle of eastern Chiapas—some have put forward models of multiethnic autonomy (discussed below), though there are differences reflected within this model.[2] Often these differences are articulated along lines of gender, political affiliation, or class. Thus, even "community hegemonies" can be fractured:

> Rural communities were never undifferentiated wholes. . . . The discourses of gender and ethnicity combined and wove together a series of struggles and transformations. While there were periods of greater change or continuity, the creation and transformation of the sociopolitical identities associated with the community were part of an open-ended process that never achieved closure. (Mallon 1995, 11–12)

Mallon outlines how a particular group of local intellectuals—political officials, teachers, elders, and healers—can provide mediation with the larger world and "supervised communal hegemonic processes, organizing and molding the different levels of the communal dialogue and conflict into a credible consensus" (12). In the process of building both regional and national networks and organizations committed to indigenous autonomy in Mexico, local intellectuals have emerged. What is noteworthy is that they are talking together for the first time at both local and Mexican national levels. This unique development can be tied directly to the political opening created through the Zapatista rebellion.

The Zapatista Opening and the Emergence of Indigenous Autonomy in Chiapas

On January 1, 1994, many people in Mexico, as well as around the world, woke up to a surprise: on the first day of the North American Free Trade Agreement (NAFTA), a rebel army of Tzotzil, Tzeltal, Tojolabal, and Ch'ol indigenous peoples took over four county seats in southeastern Mexico and issued a proclamation demanding work, land, housing, food, health care, education, independence, freedom, democracy, justice, and peace.[3] The Mexican government declared a unilateral cease-fire within twelve days of sending more than twelve thousand troops into Chiapas. In March 1994, the government and the Zapatistas sat down in the cathedral in San Cristóbal de las Casas to begin face-to-face peace talks. In the meantime, the Zapatistas maintained de facto control over a significant amount of Mexican territory in Chiapas. Within that territory, as well as elsewhere in Chiapas, citizens seized town halls, deposed PRI officials, invaded thirty thousand to fifty thousand hectares of land (between 1994 and 1996), and began to assert themselves in a variety of political arenas.

The high public profile of the Zapatistas in the initial peace talks in San Cristóbal in 1994 provided a critical opening for the assertion of indigenous autonomy within the framework of the Mexican nation. The second communiqué from the Clandestine Revolutionary Indigenous Committee—General Command (CCRI-CG) makes very specific reference to the indigenous composition of the EZLN, in part to quell rumors spread by the government that the Zapatistas were not indigenous and were controlled by foreign operators:

> The commanders and the troops of the EZLN are mostly indigenous people of Chiapas because the indigenous are the poorest and most dispossessed of Mexico, but also, as now can be seen, because they are the most dignified. We are thousands of indigenous people up in arms, and behind us are tens of thousands of people in our families. Add it up; we amount to many thousands of indigenous people in struggle. The government says that this is not an indigenous uprising, but we think that if thousands of indigenous people have risen up in struggle, then it must be an indigenous uprising.

In our movement are also Mexicans of varied social origins and from different states of our country. They agree with us and have united with us because they are opposed to the exploitation that we suffer. Just as these non-indigenous Mexicans have united with us, more will do so in the future because our struggle is national and not limited to the state of Chiapas. Currently, the political leadership of our struggle is completely indigenous. One hundred percent of the members of the indigenous revolutionary clandestine committees in the combat zones belong to the Tzotzil, Tzeltal, Chol, Tojolabal, and other ethnic groups. (CCRI-CG 1994a, 6)[4]

The clearest early articulation of the EZLN's position on ethnically based politics comes in the indigenous leadership's thirty-four-point document released at the Meetings for Peace and Conciliation in Chiapas that began in March 1994. Key demands are found in points 4 and 12–17, which call for self-government; political, economic, and cultural autonomy; an end to racism and discrimination against indigenous peoples; mandatory indigenous-language instruction; respect for indigenous culture and traditions; and administration of indigenous justice systems according to customary practices and without government interference (CCRI-CG 1994b, 13). This document clearly laid out the primary demands of indigenous communities supporting the EZLN and served as a working plan for civil resistance campaigns that took place following the peace talks. While at one point in 1994 it appeared that the EZLN and the Mexican government might agree on peace accords (they reached tentative agreement on thirty-two of thirty-four points on March 2), the assassination of PRI presidential candidate Luís Donaldo Colosio Murrieta on March 23 shocked the nation and made the Zapatistas back away from negotiations. On June 12, the Zapatista rank and file rejected the peace accords. The leadership began to prepare an alternative organizing strategy built on mobilizing civil society in Mexico and internationally and began establishing de facto local governments in the regions they controlled.

Right before Ernesto Zedillo of the PRI was elected president of Mexico in August 1994, the Zapatistas brought together thousands of politicians, intellectuals, and representatives of indigenous, peasant, student, and labor organizations as part of the Convención Nacional Democratico (CND), which was to become the civilian base of the Zapatista movement. This organizational effort marked the first attempt to build a national network around the issue of indigenous autonomy. Before this network—the National Indigenous Convention—took shape, there was a massive campaign for indigenous autonomy within the state of Chiapas.

In the fall of 1994, almost half of the municipalities in Chiapas declared themselves part of multiethnic autonomous regions and pledged their allegiance to Amado Avendaño's government of transition. Avendaño had run for governor as the candidate of the Party of the Democratic Revolution (PRD) but, according to official results, was not elected. Embracing the ballot box as a way to induce change, thousands of Tzotzil, Tzeltal, Ch'ol, and Tojolabal people voted for the first time in their lives. Charging the PRI with fraud, the PRD and Zapatistas who had voted for Avendaño stated that they couldn't trust the electoral process and began setting up governments in community assemblies. As part of this process, all federal government aid and institutions were rejected. Hundreds of schools were shut down, as were health clinics, city halls, and other government facilities. In some areas, alternative governing systems were created consisting of elected community parliaments; regional councils were also established, as well as a six-hundred-member general council of autonomous multiethnic regions (Stephen 1997b, 2002).

After February 1995, when the Mexican military launched the first of several major incursions into Zapatista territory (initially in the Lacandón area), the situation changed significantly. The Zapatistas, who had had de facto control of a broad territory, were now being gradually pushed further back into the Lacandón, and Zapatista communities were becoming increasingly isolated. During this time, the EZLN continued to slowly build on the concept of autonomous indigenous communities that appointed their own authorities. However, as the Mexican military carried out a strategy of low-intensity warfare, the possibility of living in resistance became increasingly hard to realize.

As a result of the government's 1995 military operation, whole communities were dismantled and forced into the mountains. Those who eventually returned found their lives marked by the permanent presence of the military. Many communities now faced the daily experience of being surveyed by machine-gun-toting troops who drove slowly through town in American-made humvees while photographing and videotaping local residents.

While militarization became an increasingly common aspect of daily life in the Lacandón, elsewhere in the highlands the strength of Zapatista base communities was growing. For example, the Tzotzil township of San Pedro Chenalhó was split into pro- and anti-Zapatista factions that were even further splintered with time. The pro-Zapatista faction then divided into those who were self-declared Zapatistas and those who were part of civil society (*sociedad civil*) and supported the demands of the Zapatistas but did not want to take up arms. Initially, both pro-Zapatista factions were supporters of the PRD. In 1995, however, a split occurred within the party related to the differing Zapatista and civil society positions after a PRD candidate beat the PRI candidate for town mayor. "Rather than wait until fall elections, a Zapatista sympathizer group composed of members of the bases of support for the Zaptistas within the PRD forced the incumbent president out of office and instated the PRD president elect" (Eber 1999, 24). The PRI group called in the federal police to remove the PRD mayor from office. Once this was done, the Zapatista base group withdrew and formed their own autonomous township government. The two governments have coexisted into the present. In 1997, supporters began to arm themselves against the Zapatistas and the civil society group known as Las Abejas (the Bees). From May to November 1997, twenty-nine indigenous members of the Bees and from the Zapatista base groups were assassinated (Eber and Rosenbaum n.d., 8). The horrific finale to this conflict occurred in December 1997 when forty-five members of the Bees were massacred in Acteal.

In other areas of the highlands, such as in San Andrés Larraínzar, a similar process occurred. In both instances, there were parallel governments that coexisted—the PRI government and the autonomous government (often, but not always, affiliated with the PRD). In San Andrés Larraínzar, the coexistence of the parallel governments began to break down during the July 1997 elections. At this time, PRI sympathizers began tormenting the community by shooting off their guns, damaging the municipal building occupied by the Zapatista-PRD government, and later openly declaring themselves part of an anti-Zapatista paramilitary group. In both cases, early assertions of autonomy led to increasing political factionalism, the introduction of paramilitary activities, and finally massacres, such as that in Acteal. In its dismantling of local autonomous governments in several hamlets of El Bosque (known as San Juan de la Libertad), the Mexican army and state security police killed nine Zapatista sympathizers.

As militarization increased to include the highlands, as well as the Lacandón jungle, harassment of indigenous women became routine in many areas, as did the importation of sex workers and eventually the employment of local women and girls in some communities as prostitutes for the military (see Stephen 2000). By 1998, there was one soldier for every three or four people in Zapatista-sympathetic communities. Communities of only six hundred people had military encampments of up to three hundred soldiers parked right at the entrance to their town.

The Mexican State's Position on Indigenous Rights after the Zapatista Rebellion

The government's initial response to the Zapatistas laid the foundation for a national articulation of regional movements of indigenous autonomy that had already existed in many parts of Mexico. By bungling its own attempt to proactively formulate a new relationship between the state and indigenous people, the Mexican government unwittingly promoted the emergence of a national network of indigenous organizations, communities, and regions committed to indigenous autonomy.

After the 1994 rebellion, President Carlos Salinas de Gortari created two entities to oversee indigenous affairs. One was the Commission for Indigenous Affairs of the House of Representatives, headed by Beatriz Paredes, and the other was the National Commission for Integral Development and Social Justice for Indigenous Peoples (see Stephen 1997a, 1997b and Hindley 1995 for a discussion of the state's indigenous policy up to this point). The latter was chaired by Heladio Ramírez, governor of the state of Oaxaca. The two commissions issued a call for forums to consult with Mexico's indigenous citizens, "to ponder the interests and ideas of the indigenous peoples" (Díaz 1994, 36).[5]

But these indigenous "consultations" were compromised by several factors. First, President Salinas had already written a draft of the "General Law of Cultural Plurality and the Social Patrimony of Indian Peoples" to regulate the implementation of Article 4 of the Mexican constitution, which specifies that the country is a multicultural nation.[6] With the law already drafted, the consultations appeared to many observers to be simply a publicity stunt. Second, many organizations and communities were given only forty-eight hours' notice of the consultation meetings. Finally, the document that indigenous communities received to study did not deal with the key issues of self-governance and autonomy. Indeed, it reiterated and consolidated the state's position: indigenous communities were under the protection and supervision of state agencies; access to rights claimed on the basis of indigenous ethnicity was to be mediated by the state; and, finally, academic and institutional experts had the authority to determine which individuals and communities were authentically indigenous.[7] The Mexican state's response in 1994 foreshadowed the government's reluctance to implement the 1996 peace accords on indigenous rights on the grounds that the rights of self-determination granted to indigenous communities would threaten Mexico's sovereignty.

In many parts of Mexico, including Oaxaca, San Luis Potosí, Hidalgo, Chiapas, and the Federal District, the consulting meetings with indigenous communities were boycotted, but later on they served as a springboard for further forms of organizing that articulated local and regional organizations into larger coalitions. In other states, where indigenous representatives did show up for the consulting meetings, they complained that most of the seats were occupied by officials from the government-run National Indigenous Institute (INI), the Agrarian Attorney's office, and other government agencies. Overall, the Mexican state's attempt at consulting the country's indigenous peoples was unsuccessful. Many indigenous communities simply did not participate, and the idea was quietly dropped.

Indigenous Autonomy Goes National: Different Experiences of Autonomy

In December 1994, a new national indigenous network held its first congress as the National Indigenous Convention (Convención Nacional Indígena, or CNI), with the goal of taking the model of indigenous autonomy from Chiapas and moving it to a national level. The particular model of autonomy that the convention proposed was built in part on the experience of eastern Chiapas and also involved some intellectuals who had participated in building autonomous indigenous regions in Nicaragua following the 1979 Sandinista revolution. In some areas of the Lacandón jungle, Tzeltal, Tzotzil, Tojolabal, and Ch'ol settlers who had colonized the interior regions had participated in the formation of an impressive range of peasant, indigenous, and religious organizations between the 1960s and 1990s.[8] They worked with liberation theology priests, who trained them as catechists and helped to organize the First Indigenous Congress in 1974 as well as with Maoist advisers to the Indigenous Congress, who later organized several regional organizations drawing together two or more *ejidos* (agrarian reform communities who share access to common lands and engage in governance of these lands).

In 1980, an umbrella organization known as the Union of Ejido Unions and Solidarity Peasant Organizations of Chiapas (UU) was formed. This organization devoted its efforts to gaining greater control over the production process, improving the terms for coffee marketing, and working periodically with state agrarian ministries to receive funds for credit, technical assistance, and other activities. In many communities, the UU became the sole intermediary between the local *ejido* community and the state (Nigh 1996). It was the first and largest independent campesino organization in Chiapas, representing 12,000 mainly indigenous families from 156 communities in 11 municipalities. In 1988, after some internal divisions, the group was converted into the Rural Association of Collective Interest—Union of Unions (ARIC-UU). This organization became the de facto subterranean government in many of the valleys of the region, with ARIC delegates formally included in community administrative structures (Leyva Solano and Asencio Franco 1996, 116).

The experiences of the ARIC-UU and other regional organizations were influential in the subsequent conceptualization of multiethnic autonomous regions. In the municipalities (*municipios*) of Las Margaritas, Altamirano, and Ocosingo, not only were many *ejidos* made up of people from two or more ethnic groups, but regional meetings of the ARIC-UU brought together people from several different ethnic groups. Many of the delegates were multilingual. Discussions were held in several languages, with Spanish and Tzeltal serving as lingua francas, and all documents and decision-making processes were translated and built around consensus (Leyva Solano and Ascencio Franco 1996, 218–19). Thus, the organizational experience of Chiapas encouraged a multiethnic model of indigenous collectivity rather than the monoethnic model found in many regions, such as in Oaxaca and other parts of the country.

The Tojolabal experience in Las Margaritas was also an important influence in the National Indigenous Convention's proposal for multiethnic autonomous regions, which became the centerpiece of one branch of the autonomy movement. As noted by one researcher, Shannon Mattiace, "the multi-ethnic autonomous region model drew heavily from the experiment with Tojolabal regional government in the late 1980s when the Unión de Ejidos Y Pueblos Tojolabales (Union of Ejidos and Tojolabal Peoples, members of a strong regional peasant organization) acted as an instance of regional government for all its members living in communities within the *canada* Tojolabal (a geographical region between Altamirano and Comitán)" (1997, 53). The Tojolabal experience, as well as that of eleven municipalities in the northern region of Chiapas (including Simojovel, Bochil, and Soyaló, which were declared a multiethnic autonomous region in the fall of 1994), became the focus of attention. In both the Tojolabal and northern regions, the declaration of autonomous regions was strongly tied to the historical presence of regional peasant organizations that were members of the Independent Central of Agricultural Workers and Peasants (CIOAC) (Mattiace 1997, 54–55).

In other regions of Chiapas that identified themselves primarily as Zapatista, thirty-two autonomous municipalities were declared in December of 1994 in protest of the installation of PRI candidate Robledo Rincón as governor. The Zapatistas, along with Amado Avendaño (who was sworn in by some sectors of Chiapas as state governor), began to call for the creation of free, autonomous municipalities (Mattiace 1997, 45). Some of these autonomous municipalities combined towns and hamlets with different ethnic and linguistic affiliations, though others did not follow this pattern. The multiethnic experience of organizing in Chiapas was influential in the Mexican indigenous movement's proposal for multiethnic autonomous regions.

The second source of influence on the multiethnic model of autonomy was the link between a number of indigenous leaders in Chiapas and some intellectuals serving as advisers there who had also been active in mediating conflicts between the Miskitos and the Sandinistas in Nicaragua. The Miskito autonomy proposal, signed in 1987 and written into the Nicaraguan constitution, called for multiethnic assemblies. It "granted political autonomy for the entire coastal population, divided into two autonomous regions. In each autonomous region there would be an election to pick a regional assembly that would legislate regional matters" (Diskin 1991, 164–65).

In Mexico, the multiethnic autonomous region model was formulated to create a fourth level of governance that adds to existing links between the government and citizens at the federal, state, and municipal levels. In essence, the proposal was aimed at promoting a new relationship between indigenous peoples and the state, increasing indigenous peoples' political power, and overcoming the colonial legacy of fragmentation. The initial document produced by the National Indigenous Convention (CNI) in 1994 alludes to this structure but also emphasizes that autonomy does not mean secession from the Mexican nation; rather, it means the creation of political spaces for all ethnicities. The document states in part:

> We demand constitutional recognition of the right of Autonomy. This right must be clearly established in the constitution, in a chapter specific to Indigenous Rights. As a consequence, we consider as insufficient the content of Article 4 . . . this article must be amplified to include recognition of our political and territorial

rights. We shall continue pursuing the Autonomy of our *Pueblos*,[9] communities, municipalities, and regions in spite of the government and their cacique bosses. We shall recoup and reinforce our autonomy in each of our decisions, whether at the communal, municipal, or regional level. . . .

Autonomy is not secession; on the contrary, autonomy is the first opportunity that our indigenous *pueblos* would have to become true Mexicans for the first time. Mexico's indigenous pueblos desire and hope to become integrated completely into Mexico, but without assimilation.

The delegates of the CNI conclude that the recognition of the rights of our *Pueblos* will not result from a struggle isolated from the rest of society, but only within a comprehensive process of national democratization. . . . The CNI acknowledges our willingness to establish respectful alliances with all those mestizos who also struggle to build a new Mexico. In a very special way we unite our efforts with our fellow campesinos to struggle to recuperate lands and territories, to fight against poverty, economic exploitation, and the lack of democracy that oppresses us. . . . Unity among indigenous peoples and mestizos is a necessary, basic condition for the changes that Mexico requires. (CNI 1994)

The National Indigenous Convention met again in February 1995 in Juchitán, Oaxaca, home of one of the first municipalities where the ruling PRI government was unseated by a Zapotec organization of workers and students who had suffered years of repression and confrontation with the government and the army (see Rubin 1997). There and in subsequent meetings, a specific legislative proposal was formulated for promoting multiethnic autonomous regions at the national level. Delegates at the second meeting in Juchitán proposed the creation of communal, municipal, regional, state, and national indigenous councils.

In the spring of 1995, a joint statement by the Executive Council of the Autonomous Multiethnic Regions of Chiapas, two nongovernmental organizations, and the Secretariat of Human Rights of the PRD was released proposing constitutional reforms aimed at "the creation at the national level of autonomous multiethnic regions that would function as a fourth level of government in addition to municipal, state, and federal. These regions would serve as regional indigenous organizations that would allow indigenous peoples to take part in their own processes of economic development and would also serve as the seats of self-government" (GARRI 1995). According to the document, autonomy could only be guaranteed as long as the diverse social groups found within one region could live in harmony and agreement. Therefore, the autonomous region was conceived of in terms of multiethnic power sharing. As stated by one of the authors of the proposal in an earlier discussion, "autonomy starts with the assumption that, as a rule, in these distinct regions all of the different sociocultural groups would have to coexist" (Hector Díaz Polanco, cited in Hernández Navarro 1998b, 29). Carried forward by the National Assembly of Indigenous Peoples in Support of Autonomy (ANIPA), a group that developed out of the National Indigenous Convention, this proposal became the centerpiece for future activities. ANIPA met several times during 1995. Its macrolevel proposal calling for the establishment of regional multiethnic governments influenced the 1996 San Andrés Accords on Indigenous Rights and Culture.[10]

The experience of eastern Chiapas, however, did not reflect the reality of most of Mexico. The proposal for multiethnic autonomous regions was heavily debated in two subsequent congresses of the National Indigenous Convention.[11] Both congresses had significant participation from indigenous peoples whose historical experiences were quite distinct from the colonial legacy of eastern Chiapas. The creation of *multiethnic* autonomous regions did not make sense to many of them because they came from monoethnic regions. During a congress in Sonora in May 1995, Yaquis took over the assembly and questioned the basic principles of multiethnic regions. They stated that autonomy could be monoethnic or multiethnic (Stephen 1997b, 30).

The Mixe and Zapotec of Oaxaca, who were important participants in the emerging network of groups, communities, coalitions, and organizations dedicated to the national movement for indigenous autonomy, also had a historical experience very different from that of peoples in eastern Chiapas. After the Mexican Revolution, a "monoethnic" Mixe district was formed that is still part of the governance structure of the state of Oaxaca. Because of the experience in their district, which dates to 1935, the Mixe practice of autonomy is much more "monoethnic" than multiethnic.

Mixe concepts of autonomy are also based on communal practices of governance. This strand of autonomy, called communal, emerged as a countercurrent to the notion of multiethnic autonomous regions that eventually developed in Chiapas. While there are at least two significant multiethnic organizations in Oaxaca (the Mazatec, Chinantec, and Cuicatec Coordinator—Independent Front of Indigenous Pueblos, or ORECHIMAC-FIPI; and the Union of Indigenous Communities of the Northern Zone of the Isthmus, or UCIZONI), the majority of political organizational spaces are still based at the community level. Most important in the Oaxacan communities was the long-standing form of choosing community authorities through local assemblies, rather than voting by ballot for candidates tied to formal political parties.

During the past twenty years, indigenous communities and organizations in the northern Sierra of Oaxaca have combined the struggle for political autonomy with the struggle for land and social services. As pointed out by Luis Hernández Navarro (1998b, 28), eighteen out of the nineteen Zapotec and Mixe municipalities in the Sierra Juárez region of Oaxaca have formed organizations that have generated communally based authorities and are also organizations that have actively promoted the idea of autonomy.

Based on the different experiences brought to the meetings of the National Indigenous Convention by ethnic groups such as the Mixe and the Yaqui, a more flexible version of the autonomy proposal developed that allowed for autonomous communities and hamlets, as well as municipalities—each to be defined according to the specific local and regional experience. During July and August 1995, ANIPA representatives met with the government negotiating team for the EZLN peace accords (the National Commission of Concord and Pacification, or COCOPA) and the advisory team led by Bishop Samuel Ruiz (the National Intermediation Commission, or CONAI) in an attempt to get their proposals endorsed by the state and the EZLN. They also brought their proposal to the Mexican Congress. Their efforts bore some initial fruit; ANIPA's plan for indigenous autonomy was included in the first round of talks in preparation for the peace accords, which gave the issue of indigenous rights national legitimacy and involved dozens of organizations and indigenous peoples in the process. While many of the actors from the National Indigenous Convention and ANIPA participated in the first and second round of talks on indigenous rights and culture that led up to the accords, the ANIPA leadership was marginalized, and other leaders came forward. Prominent in this new constellation was a proposal for the adoption of "customs and traditions" and "communal autonomy," which was based on the experience in Oaxaca.

The notion of Oaxacan communal autonomy is predicated on collective institutions, such as communal work obligations (*tequio*), methods of selecting local authorities, and the preservation of language and ritual. In recognition of the indigenous autonomy movement, the Oaxacan state legislature in 1995 approved the election of municipal authorities through "traditions and customs" (*usos y costumbres*) (Hernández Navarro 1998a, 95).

The governor of Oaxaca had tried in 1992 to impose the election of indigenous community authorities by forcing candidates to affiliate with political parties. This failed attempt generated a reaction that culminated in the change in Oaxaca's state constitution. This process was stimulated further after the government tried to organize local consultations in Oaxaca in 1994 regarding the modification of Article 4 of the Mexican constitution. These meetings were boycotted, and an alternative set of forums was held dedicated to developing a proposal for implementing local "traditions and customs." In late 1997, this proposal was implemented by the Oaxacan state legislature, despite the initial opposition of the ruling PRI and the right-leaning National Action Party (PAN). What the Oaxacan legislature approved was the right of communities to name their municipal authorities in accordance with local traditions and without the intervention of political parties.

In January 1996, the Zapatistas organized a forum on indigenous rights in San Cristóbal de las Casas in which the notions of autonomous regions, "customs and traditions," and "communal autonomy" were discussed and debated. The forum resulted in a series of proposals that the EZLN brought to its negotiations with the Mexican government, which were in turn influential in the San Andrés Accords on Indigenous Rights and Culture, signed by the government and the EZLN in February 1996. Even though the model of multiethnic autonomous regions was not included in the EZLN proposals, indigenous groups, organizations, and communities from throughout Mexico participated in the forum. They provided input about the range of specific regional realities that the accords on indigenous rights would have to address.

Local and regional differences were one aspect of the challenge to achieve consensus in the national indigenous movement. Another significant challenge facing the movement has been the issue of gender equity.

What Is the Meaning of "Autonomy" and "Indianness" for Women?

The Accords on Indigenous Rights and Culture laid the groundwork for significant changes in the areas of indigenous rights, political participation, and cultural autonomy. Most important, they recognize the existence of political subjects called *pueblos indios* (indigenous peoples/nations/communities) while validating the terms *self-determination* and *autonomy* by using them in the signed documents. The accords emphasize that the state takes responsibility not only for reinforcing the political representation of indigenous peoples and their participation in legislatures, but also for guaranteeing the validity of internal forms of indigenous government. The accords further note that the state promises to create national legislation guaranteeing indigenous communities the right to (1) freely associate themselves with municipalities that are primarily indigenous in population; (2) form associations between communities; and (3) coordinate their actions as indigenous peoples.

In addition, the accords establish that it is up to the legislatures of individual states to determine the best criteria for self-determination and autonomy. These criteria should accurately represent the diverse aspirations and distinctions among indigenous peoples. It is important to note, however, that the peace agreement does not deal with the key issues of land redistribution, indigenous homelands, indigenous control over natural resources—and gender inequities. What follows is the story of how indigenous women attempted to influence the San Andrés accords.

In the development of these accords and in the workings of a new national network called the National Indigenous Congress in meetings held in Mexico City in October of 1996 and 1997, indigenous women participated in broadening the notion of indigenous autonomy. They attempted to influence several arenas of citizenship at once and to integrate concerns of ethnicity and gender with those of nationalism. The notion of autonomy articulated by indigenous women and their advisers during the years of meetings and workshops in Chiapas and elsewhere is expansive. They refer to economic autonomy, defined as women's rights to have access to and control over modes of production; political autonomy, defined as their basic political rights; physical autonomy, defined as the right to make decisions concerning their own bodies and the right to a life without violence; and sociocultural autonomy, defined as the right to assert their specific identities as indigenous women (Hernández Castillo 1997, 112).

In documents produced by women in the congresses, reproductive decision making and the physical and psychological integrity of women's bodies are linked to the right to land, property, and participation in political decision making in all arenas of social life. This integrated vision makes visible the systematic marginalization of indigenous women and suggests specific remedies for correcting it. The most

contentious issue for women during the forums leading up to the
Accords on Indigenous Rights and Culture was the meaning of the
term "traditions and customs" (*usos y costumbres*) that came from the
proposal from Oaxaca. While one of the central facets of the proposals
for autonomy involved legitimizing indigenous systems of customary
justice and decision making, some of the "traditions" included under
the loose terminology of *usos y costumbres* did not promote gender
equity.

While the inclusion of men, women, and children (over twelve years
old) in community assemblies is standard practice in Zapatista base
communities (see Eber 1998, 1999; and Eber and Rosenbaum n.d.), this
is not common in Chiapas or in other indigenous communities in Mexico. "Traditional" political decision making in many Zapotec communities in Oaxaca, for example, involves community assemblies attended
by men between the ages of eighteen and seventy. In such assemblies,
the majority of men present do not speak but rather listen and vote
silently with their hands if a specific resolution is put forward. There
may also be times when the meeting breaks down into looser and more
participatory discussion.

Thus, for many indigenous women, "traditional" community decision-making processes exclude them. Other "traditions" can include
men beating women, parents negotiating the marriages of their daughters (and sons) without respecting their wishes, and divisions of labor
in which women work many more hours than men. While these patterns are not universal, I found them to be common in a significant
number of households in rural Oaxaca and rural Nayarit and in some
parts of Chiapas where Zapatista base communities are not operating.
I conducted fieldwork in indigenous rural communities in these states
from 1986 until the present (see Stephen 1991, 1997c, 2002).

In a national forum on indigenous rights held in October 1995,
indigenous women from Chiapas, Oaxaca, Puebla, Querétaro, México,
Hidalgo, and Mexico City, along with their advisers, put forward a key
modification of the term *usos y costumbres*. They declared, "We
demand that our customs and traditions be respected if and when they
do not violate women's rights" (Grupo de Trabajo 4 1995, 22). This
wording, more or less, was adopted in the signed accords.

However, other important issues highlighted in the women's round-
tables that were part of the preparatory meetings—including women's
rights to land, unequal divisions of labor in households, combating
domestic violence, and rape—were downplayed in the accords signed
by the EZLN and the Mexican government. The signed accords do not

address women's demands concerning the democratization of the home nor issues of sexual violence; they only address women's status at the level of the community by stating that they should participate in all legislative processes and be involved in choosing local leaders.

For many indigenous women who participated in the process leading up to the signing of the accords, the act of coming together with other indigenous women from throughout the nation has provided networks that have taken on lives of their own. Ultimately, these networks may prove to be more important for women than the accords themselves. Indigenous women's unity against those men who wished to silence them no doubt helped to facilitate the building of these networks. The women's internal dialogue around a wide range of issues speaks to their multiple identities as primarily rural, indigenous, and female. This process did not create a homogenous identity out of many but, rather, provided a discursive field within which women participated from different positions.

Conclusion

Let me end with some reflections on the implications of the San Andrés peace accords for indigenous rights and on the relationship of these rights to larger issues of nationalism and ethnic identity. A key force in the creation of the accords was the emergent national movement for indigenous autonomy, which has pulled together local and regional indigenous movements as well as previously unorganized authorities in indigenous communities. The goal of the movement in pushing for the implementation of the accords is not secession from Mexico, but inclusion as part of a multicultural state, one that embraces multiple nations and grants regional and local autonomy. This vision of indigenous autonomy projected from Mexico provides a hopeful alternative to ethnic conflict, which often results in either ongoing war or secession. While postcolonial theorists, such as Partha Chatterjee, have wonderfully outlined the process by which nationalism and nations can be created before the emergence of an independent state, they give a bleak prognosis for the ability of multiple nations—or what Chatterjee calls "communities"—to exist within one state. This Chatterjee attributes to the relationship between modern states and capital.

> The modern state, embedded as it is within the universal narrative of capital, cannot recognize within its jurisdiction any form of community except the single, determinate, demographically enumerable form of the nation. It must therefore subjugate, if

necessary by the use of state violence, all such aspirations of community identity. These other aspirations, in turn, can give to themselves a historically valid justification only by claiming an alternative nationhood with rights to an alternative state. (1993, 238)

Certainly Chatterjee's outlook accurately captures the state of affairs in southern Mexico in the late 1990s, where the government used violence to remove four autonomous governments in Chiapas and to jail activists in Oaxaca for working toward a similar goal. In June of 1998, nine Zapatistas and two government soldiers died during a raid to remove autonomous authorities from the municipality of El Bosque in Chiapas; the operation involved fifteen hundred soldiers and state security police. What Chatterjee's prediction does not mention, however, is the possibility for communities or nations claiming alternative nationhood to coexist within the same state.

The heart of the national proposal for recognizing indigenous autonomy in Mexico is based on a tripartite cultural-political model that brings together multiple indigenous nations (*pueblos*), the Mexican nation (as a multiethnic and diverse entity), and the state as a political and legal framework. The glue holding this tripartite model together is indigenous Mexican nationalism. This nationalist vision builds a common identity around being Mexican and indigenous, but within a multiethnic state. According to this model, the national political boundaries of Mexico should promote the internal plurality of cultural boundaries—not through assimilation, but through granting self-defined cultural entities autonomy in regional and local decision-making processes. Thus, the *pueblos indigenas* (indigenous peoples/nations/communities) are autonomous within the Mexican state, yet they have a shared sense of participation and inclusion in the Mexican nation.[12] In their analysis, indigenous leaders sever the "nation" from the state and liberate the concept of nation to be reappropriated from below, in relation to particular regional and historical circumstances. Such a reinterpretation also allows for the simultaneous existence of a larger nation tied to a state political structure, as well as multiple local and regional nations with unique historical constructions. Such a multidimensional understanding of the meaning of "nation" is what confounds and frightens some representatives of the Mexican government.

The reason offered by the Mexican government in the late 1990s for refusing to implement the accords it signed is that it would not be fair to grant indigenous people particular or special rights when they are equal to all Mexicans. Indigenous peoples, the argument goes, should be granted the same rights as everyone else. This same basic position was ultimately reflected in the watered down version of the accords passed by the Mexican Congress in 2001. The legislation is part of an ongoing process of internal debate. This deliberate invocation of universal rights for all, however, assumes that everyone is playing on a level field. This is obviously not the case for Mexico's indigenous population, particularly in states such as Oaxaca and Chiapas, where on any index of well-being or standard of living the bulk of indigenous people rank near the bottom of the scale. Equality under the law bears grim material results, particularly under current policies of neoliberal economic restructuring, which clearly favor the well-off. Thus, shifting the discourse onto the field of individual equality and rights both ignores the historically disadvantaged position of Mexico's indigenous peoples and undercuts the notion of collective rights and processes inherent in communally based models of indigenous autonomy.

Challenges to economic restructuring in Mexico have come from many quarters. The most sustained challenge has come from indigenous peoples in the form of local cultural nationalism, whereby indigenous people claim the right to decide for themselves how their resources should be used, what model of development they should work with, how to pick their own leaders, and who will represent them at the national level. While the outcome of the struggle for indigenous autonomy in Mexico is uncertain, what will endure is the alternative model of relationships between local communities and nations, the larger Mexican nation, and the state, which is now being experimented with in Chiapas, Oaxaca, and other regions of the country. Thanks in part to the Zapatista political opening, indigenous people in Mexico have begun to move from the political margins and now have a seat at the table of national power.

Notes

1. The 1980s reform measures aimed at privatizing government enterprises and loosening federal regulations regarding foreign investment and ownership found their logical conclusion in the 1992 reformation of Article 27 of the Mexican constitution. Designed to support the North American Free Trade Agreement, this reform ended the government's obligation to redistribute land to those who need it.

2. The four major ethnic groups represented in the Clandestine Revolutionary Indigenous Committee of the Zapatista Army of National Liberation

(EZLN) are Tzeltal, Ch'ol, Tzotzil, and Tojolabal. The "Lacandón" are a very small ethnic group that is the source of vigorous debate. The Lacandón have been in conflict with Tzeltal, Tzotzil, and other settlers who have migrated to the jungle from other parts of Chiapas. As George Collier notes, the Lacandón's style of cultivation, which involves thinning but not destroying the multitiered canopy, contrasts with the intensive style of agriculture favored by highland Tzotzil and Tzeltal migrants, who introduced cattle and cash crops such as coffee (1994, 44). A major point of tension between the Lacandón and other indigenous migrants came in 1968 when the Mexican government set aside a third of a million hectares in the Lacandón jungle as the Montes Azul bioreserve. This would have forced the relocation of eight thousand people already living in twenty-six settlements within the reserve and would have disregarded their land claims. The government set up a logging firm "to manage the bioreserve's timber on behalf of 400 Lacandón individuals" (Collier 1994, 49). Many of the eight thousand Tzeltal and Tzotzil settlers refused to leave, and tensions with the Lacandón continued. The Lacandón, with their history of conflict with Tzeltal and Tzotzil migrants in eastern Chiapas, never participated in the independent peasant and religious organizations that politicized many people in the region and that became the support base of the EZLN. Hence, it is no surprise that the Lacandón are not represented in the Zapatista political structure.

3. See Stephen 1997a, 1997b, 2002; Harvey 1998; and Collier 1994 for accounts of how and why the Zapatista rebellion emerged in eastern Chiapas.

4. The English translations of Zapatista communiqués used in this essay are taken from a special issue of the Mendocino County, California, newspaper *Anderson Valley Advertiser,* vol. 42, no. 31, published on August 3, 1994. Copies can be ordered for $2.00 each by writing to AVA, Box 459, Boonville, CA 95415.

5. Unless otherwise noted, all translations of quotations from Spanish-language sources are mine.

6. Article 4 recognizes Mexico as a pluricultural nation and confers cultural rights on indigenous peoples. It reads: "The Mexican nation has a multicultural composition originally founded in its indigenous peoples. The law protects and promotes the development of their languages, uses, customs, resources, and specific forms of social organization and guarantees their members effective access to the full range of the state's legal authority (jurisdiction). In the agrarian judgments and legal proceedings they are part of, their own legal practices and customs shall be taken into account in establishing the law." As pointed out by Jane Hindley (1995, 11), the fact that Article 4 is contained within a chapter titled "Individual Guarantees" immediately dilutes the concept of indigenous rights as collective. It should also be noted that Article 4 stands alone; no laws had been passed to implement its suggestions until the Mexican Congress legislated a very watered down version of the San Andrés Accords that undermined indigenous self-determination; recognition of col-

lective rights to land, territory, and natural resources; and the right of indigenous communities to regional affiliation.

7. The Salinas document featured familiar themes:

(1) It reiterates Article 4 and identifies who is indigenous in terms of their language, culture, uses, customs, resources, and specific forms of social organization.

(2) Three articles of the document specify that indigenous communities would be under the guardianship of the National Indigenous Institute (INI) and the Secretary of Social Development (SEDESOL).

(3) The document states that indigenous groups can declare themselves to be "indigenous" through a communal statute or a law elaborated in a community assembly and must give their declaration to the National Agrarian Registry (RAN). In order to obtain the rights to the territory they inhabit, indigenous communities are required to offer proof of their forms of organization, representation, traditional authority, and land inheritance. When they want to declare rights over an ancestral territory, they have to take their demand to an agrarian court, which "will determine its legitimacy in consultation with academic institutions of known prestige."

(4) The document states that all agrarian conflicts will be mediated by the INI and the Procuraduría Agraria or Agrarian Attorney and that the impartial rendering of justice will be expedited by the presence of a translator whenever necessary. Judicial authorities are to take into account indigenous judicial forms and customs in rendering their judgements. (Díaz 1994, 36–38)

8. Tzeltal and Tzotzil settlers who came to the Lacandon were not always from multiethnic towns. In some areas of the highlands, prior to migration, inhabitants were more generally from monoethnic municipalities and communities. In the 1980s and 1990s, many municipalities became increasingly indigenous—even the *cabeceras,* or head townships—as ladinos (non-Indians supposedly of mixed Spanish and indigenous descent) moved into larger cities.

9. *Pueblos* (peoples/nations/communities) may range in size from a small number of people in a few hamlets to larger numbers of people in a municipality or a region who share a common ethnic identity and history. See also n. 12.

10. In the ANIPA proposal, "ethnicity" in the context of Chiapas refers to language-based ethnicity. But among the Tojolabal and the younger people of both Tzeltal and Tzotzil migrant communities, Spanish is also commonly used. Hence, the notion of basing "ethnicity" only on linguistic affiliation is questionable. See Stephen 1997b, 32.

11. Details of the debates about the proposal for multiethnic autonomous regions (known in Spanish as RAPs, or *regiones autónomas pluri-etnicas*) can be found in Hernández Navarro 1998b and in a series of essays published in 1995 in *Ojarasca* ("Autonomía, madre de todos los derechos"). For other discussions of the process with opposing views, see Díaz Polanco 1997 and Esteva 1998.

12. The term *pueblos indigenas* has multiple meanings in Spanish. It can refer to peoples, nations, or, at a more localized level, communities. In fact, some ethnic groups in Mexico are no more than a few hundred or a few thousand people spread over several hamlets. Many such groups argue that in order to maintain their ethnic integrity and sense of cohesion, they should be considered small nations. Similar assertions are being made in the United States by small indigenous groups. In an interesting article questioning the utility of the multiethnic autonomous model, Miguel Alberto Bartolomé (1995, 60n.11) asks what happens to smaller ethnic groups such as the Huave, Chontales, and Zoques, who have been historically dominated economically, politically, and culturally by the Isthmus Zapotec in a multiethnic autonomous region. Who would be the representatives of this region?

References

Anderson, Benedict. 1983. *Imagined Communities: Reflections on the Origin and Spread of Nationalism.* London: Verso.

Autonomía, madre de todos los derechos. 1995. Essays by Eugenio Bermejillo, Ramón Vera Herrera, Gustavo Esteva, Fransisco López Bárcenas, and Miguel Alberto Bartolomé. *Ojarasca,* no. 45 (August–November): 21–60.

Bartolomé, Miguel Alberto. 1995. La elocuencia como servicio. *Ojarasca,* no. 45 (August–November): 53–60.

CCRI-CG (Comité Clandestino Revolucionario Indígena, Comandancia General del Ejército Zapatista de Liberación Nacional). 1994a. #2—Declaration of the Lacandón Jungle: Today We Say "Enough." *Anderson Valley Advertiser,* August 3, p. 6.

———. 1994b. #43—EZLN Demands at the Dialogue Table. *Anderson Valley Advertiser,* August 3, p. 13.

Chatterjee, Partha. 1993. *The Nation and Its Fragments: Colonial and Postcolonial Histories.* Princeton: Princeton University Press.

CNI (Convención Nacional Indígena). 1994. Declaración de la Montaña de Guerrero. December. Mimeo.

Collier, George, with Elizabeth Lowery Quaratiello. 1994. *Basta: Land and the Zapatista Rebellion in Chiapas.* Oakland, Calif.: Institute for Food and Development Policy.

Díaz, Gloria Leticia. 1994. Los foros de consulta indígena, "farsa para legitimar lo ya conocido." *Proceso,* no. 911 (April 18): 36–39.

Díaz Polanco, Hector. 1997. *La Rebellión Zapatista y la autonomía.* Mexico City: Siglo XXI Editores.

Diskin, Martin. 1991. Ethnic Discourse and the Challenge to Anthropology: The Nicaraguan Case. In *Nation States and Indians in Latin America,* edited by Greg Urban and Joel Sherzer. Austin: University of Texas Press.

Eber, Christine. 1998. Seeking Justice, Valuing Community: Two Women's Paths in the Wake of the Zapatista Rebellion. Working Paper No. 265, Women in International Development Series, Michigan State University.

————. 1999. Seeking Our Own Food: Indigenous Women's Power and Autonomy in San Pedro Chenalhó, Chiapas (1980–1998). *Latin American Perspectives,* 26 (3): 6–36.

Eber, Christine, and Brenda P. Rosenbaum. n.d. Making Souls Arrive: Enculturation and Identity in Two Highlands Towns.

Esteva, Gustavo. 1998. Alcances y perspectivas de la lucha indígena de Oaxaca. Paper prepared for the Twenty-first International Congress of the Latin American Studies Association, September 24–26, Chicago.

GARRI (Grupo de Apollo a la Autonomía Regional Indígena), Consejo Executivo de las Regiones Autónomas Pluriétnicas, Comisión Mexicana de Defensa y Promoción de los Derechos Humanos, and Secretaría de Derechos Humanos y Pueblos Indios del PRD. 1995. Iniciativa de decreto que reforma y adiciona los artículos 4, 73, y 115 de la constitución política de los Estados Unidos Mexicanos para la creación de las regiones autónomas pluriétnicas. Mimeo.

Grupo de Trabajo 4. Situación, derechos y cultura de la mujer indígena. Declaración de asesores e invitadas del EZLN. 1995. *Ce-Acatl,* no. 73 (November 7): 21–27.

Harvey, Neil. 1998. *The Chiapas Rebellion: The Struggle for Land and Democracy.* Durham, N.C.: Duke University Press.

Hernández-Castillo, Rosalva Aída. 1997. Between Hope and Adversity: The Struggle of Organized Women in Chiapas since the Zapatista Rebellion. *Journal of Latin American Anthropology* 3 (1): 102–20.

Hernández Navarro, Luis. 1998a. *Chiapas: La nueva lucha india.* Madrid: Talasa Ediciones.

————. 1998b. Ciudadanos iguales, ciudadanos diferentes. In *Acuerdos de San Andrés,* edited by Luis Hernández Navarro and Ramón Vera Herera, 15–32. Mexico City: Ediciones Era.

Hindley, Jane. 1995. Towards a Pluricultural Nation: The Limits of Indigenismo and Article 4. In *Dismantling the Mexican State,* edited by Rob Aiken, Nicki Craske, Gareth A. Jones, and David Stansfield. London: Macmillan.

Joseph, Gilbert, and Daniel Nugent, eds. 1994. *Everyday Forms of State Formation: Revolution and the Negotiation of Rule in Mexico.* Durham, N.C.: Duke University Press.

Leyva Solano, Xochitl, and Gabriel Ascencio Franco. 1996. *Lacandonia al filo del agua.* Mexico City: Fondo de la Cultura Economica.

Mallon, Florencia. 1995. *Peasant and Nation: The Making of Postcolonial Mexico and Peru.* Berkeley: University of California Press.

Mattiace, Shannon. 1997. Zapata vive! The EZLN, Indian Politics, and the Autonomy Movements in Mexico. *Journal of Latin American Anthropology* 3 (1): 32–71.

Nigh, Ronald. 1996. Transformation of Peasant Organizations in Las Cañadas Region, Selva Lacandona, Chiapas. Research proposal presented at Planning Workshop of Project on the Transformation of Rural Mexico, Centro de Investigaciones y Estudios Superiores en Antropología Social del Occidente (CIESAS) Guadalajara, August.

Regino Montes, Adelfo. 1996. Los derechos indígenas, en serio. *La Jornada,* October 22.

Rubin, Jeffrey. 1997. *Decentering the Regime; Ethnicity, Radicalism, and Democracy in Juchitán, Mexico.* Durham, N.C.: Duke University Press.

Stephen, Lynn. 2002. *Zapata Lives! Histories and Cultural Politics in Southern Mexico.* Berkeley: University of California Press.

―――. 2000. The Construction of Indigenous "Suspects": Militarization and the Gendered and Ethnic Dimensions of Human Rights Abuses in Southern Mexico. *American Ethnologist* 26 (4): 822–42.

―――. 1997a. Redefined Nationalism in Building a Movement for Indigenous Autonomy in Southern Mexico. *Journal of Latin American Anthropology* 3 (1): 72–101.

―――. 1997b. The Zapatista Opening: The Movement for Indigenous Autonomy and State Discourses on Indigenous Rights in Mexico, 1970–1996. *Journal of Latin American Anthropology* 2 (2): 2–41.

―――. 1997c. *Women and Social Movements in Latin America: Power From Below.* Austin: University of Texas Press.

―――. 1991. *Zapotec Women.* Austin: University of Texas Press.

7 At the Margins of Power: Gender Hierarchy and the Politics of Ethnic Mobilization among the Urarina

Bartholomew Dean

This essay examines the dynamics of political mobilization among the Urarina of Peruvian Amazonia. It considers the practical and ideological dimensions of Urarina women's exclusion from commerce and the public sphere of supralocal politics. The tidy division of social life into two distinct spheres does not hold up under empirical observation: social life is composed of multiple and overlapping public and private spheres whose boundaries are illusory and constantly imploding. These multiple spheres of social life are culturally constructed regimes of exclusion and participation.[1]

In light of Urarina women's active participation in and control over key aspects of the kin economy, I examine the tensions arising from their virtual absence from public transactional spheres. Urarina gender roles are being formulated and enacted in response to debt peonage and a clientelist political agenda mediated in part by the emergent indigenous rights movement.

Analysis of the Urarina's gendered disempowerment contributes to a broader understanding of the linkages between other social inequalities and forms of domination in indigenous Amazonia. In particular, recognition of the gendered nature of Urarina power relations alerts us to the challenges facing the Amazonian indigenous rights movement.

Urarina Society

The Urarina reside in a region of Peru that has long been portrayed in official and elite discourse as *territorium nullius*—a vast and empty frontier simply awaiting incorporation into the nation. Living in small, kin-based longhouse settlements, the Urarina have enjoyed dominion over the Chambira Basin, a vast and ecologically varied tropical watershed, since the Spanish conquest (see map 7.1).[2] While I want to dispel the image that the Urarina are an isolated "rain forest society" with

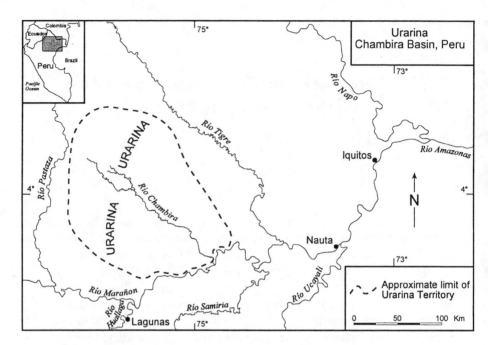

Map 7.1.   Chambira Basin, Peruvian Amazonia

timorous links with the outside world, the seclusion and inaccessibility of their territories have afforded local communities a greater degree of flexibility to determine the terms and scale of their interactions with non-Urarina peoples. Linguistically distinct from neighboring societies,[3] the Urarina are a cultural island in a diverse ethnic archipelago that includes the Tupian-speaking Cocama-Cocamilla living to the south and southwest; the Jivaroan-speaking groups living to the northwest and northeast; and the Candoshi and Zaparoan speakers residing to the west (Dean 1999c).

Numbering about five thousand people, Urarina society is characterized by its political fluidity and structural simplicity. In contrast to other lowland South American societies, the Urarina lack elaborate communal and supralocal organizations, like the Central Brazilian Gê's "dialectical" age grades and moieties or the complex sib and parity segmentation of Northwestern Amazonia. Ostensibly, "[t]he most striking feature of Urarina social life is the separation of the sexes" (Kramer 1979, 45; see also Dean 1995a; Tessmann [1930] 1987; and Ferrúa Carrasco, Linares Cruz, and Pérez 1980). Prescriptive uxorilocality organizes dense kinship ties between extended family groups, or what Pierre Clastres (following Murdock 1949) called *demes* ([1974] 1987, 55ff.) and the Urarina call *kaj laitjíra.* In addition to normative patterns of uxorilocality, the widespread practice of sororal polygyny facilitates the creation and perpetuation of solidaristic female groups, which provide continuity for the local longhouse group.

Urarina communities typically consist of forty to one hundred members of bilateral kindred (*kanarai kíri*) living in a combination of multifamily longhouses, single-family *ribereño* (peasant)-style dwellings, and temporary shelters perched along the region's immense blackwater river system. Longhouses, or *luderí,* are the nexus point for the circulation of goods, labor power, and knowledge. *Luderí* are semipublic assemblages subject to the androgynous mobilization of power. They are at once domestic and public spaces sheltering familial hearths. Longhouses provide the Urarina with their primary forums for the articulation of everyday political discourse. *Luderí* also serve as the principal venue for the Urarina's episodically convened community assemblies.

At the local level, kinship, co-residence, and common natal rivers denote affiliation, loyalty, and obligation. Urarina social life is characterized by a mercurial balance of power between semiautonomous longhouse groups united through affinal ties, political alliances, exchange relations, and disputation. Political power is authorized through personal prestige, rather than jurally sanctioned.

Men garner prestige and influence by negotiating exchanges, distributing goods and information, and promoting intra- and interdemic associations. Successful men of renown do not command, they persuade—often by way of personal example. Urarina headmen, or *kurana,* are followed only as long as people think it is advantageous to do so. While the importance of ritual life in influencing gender conceptions can be readily acknowledged, attention to transcultural exchange challenges the assumption that the relative valuing of gender is simply derivative of control over ritual activities (see, e.g., Langdon 1984, 18).

Female prestige is sanctioned through women's roles as mothers, as senior wives in polygynous households, and as postmenopausal mothers-in-law. Urarina women's power is culturally recognized through their participation in gender-specific productive activities—such as weaving palm-fiber goods (hammocks, fabric, net bags, etc.), pottery making, and beer fermentation—and through their primary roles in critical aspects of horticulture, fishing, and foraging. Women possess their own oral genres, most notably ritual wailing. Like men, they are also recognized as having the capacity to heal, and they can bewitch through their active participation in *ayahuasca* (*Banisteriopsis caapi*) shamanism (Dean 1994b, 1994c).

Much like the Uanano of the Northwest Amazon (Chernela 1984, 29), Urarina women's participation in "village-level" political life manifests itself in the circulation of rumors, hearsay, and innuendo. More generally, Urarina women convene audiences in three semipublic discursive spaces within the longhouse: ritual wailing following the death of a hearth-group member, formal disputation, and informal "gossip" to express their sentiments. These discursive forums are characteristically unstable and often deeply charged instances of social interaction within the *luderí*. For instance, an unexpected death can trigger witchcraft accusations and hostilities, which find expression in ritual wailing, hushed whispers, and venomous gossip. These can in turn develop into full-blown disputes that are eventually aired in formal arbitration sessions, which can result in the fragmentation and eventual splintering of the *luderí* along the lines of hearth-group membership. More serious cases can end in the actual rupture of the *kaj laitjíra,* or local longhouse group.

While Urarina women do have a number of resources to use in asserting their interests, local longhouse groupings and territorial alignments emphasize the prerogatives of prestigious and mature headmen, as is common in western Amazonia (see Hugh-Jones 1993, 110). The authoritative power of an Urarina *kurana* is sustained through his expertise in arcane fields of knowledge and shamanic practices and through his management of multiple indebted relationships of peonage, referred to colloquially as *habilitación.* Relations between Urarina extended family groups are publicly identified with affinal ties and with competitive political relations mediated primarily by socially mature men. As the head of temporally stable residential groups, *kurana* manage the affairs of a number of allied longhouse groups. *Kurana* leadership is predicated on personal attributes that the Urarina deem especially suitable: social maturity, munificence, oratory skill, hunting prowess, and shamanic knowledge.

Politically ambitious men elect themselves as exchange interlocutors, which enables them to compete for political positions in the nascent indigenist movement. Largely indifferent to—or unconvinced by—the "benefits" of assimilation in a society that disparages indigenous peoples, and impatient with the proselytizing efforts of missionaries and evangelists within their midst, the Urarina have instrumentally formed relationships with non-Urarina in order to gain access to basic social services and necessary trade items. This enables the Urarina to fulfill their own consumerist desires and to further their personal and collective political ambitions (McKinley 1994). Since trading relationships are used strategically by *kurana* in their quest to gain access to resources from the state, as well as from nongovernmental organizations (NGOs) and advocacy groups, those communities able to produce more (typically in the form of lumber, forest goods, and crops) are clearly better situated to claim their rights to education, land tenure, health care, and retributive justice.

Gender Hierarchy, Exchange, and Political Mobilization

Urarina men and women do not participate equally in the activities of the *luderí,* nor in the public intrademic affairs of prestation, politicking, and feasting that link *kaj laitjíra* in a complex web of alliance, competition, and rivalry. This is evident from the Urarina's notions of gendered place. Gender segregation is readily apparent in their well-defined patterns of visiting, in their sense of architectural space, and in their acute awareness of the natural landscape, which all influence patterns of social etiquette. When visiting, men are the first to approach the longhouses. Women and juniors will linger in the dugout or at the footpath leading up to the settlement. After being received by the *kurana,* mature men sit near the host in the male domain of the longhouse. It is only then that the visiting children and women will begin approaching the host's longhouse. Facing outward, the female visitors position themselves on bark mats (*jau*) made of plaited palm-fiber or bamboo (*huacrapona*) which are spread along the outer fringes of the hostess's domestic platform and hearth space. This behavior initially establishes respect for men's and women's appropriate social spaces. Within a short while, the visiting becomes somewhat more animated, especially if there is ample cassava beer (*bardigüe*), the consumption of which alleviates initial moments of awkwardness. Notions of gendered space nonetheless continue to implicitly structure relations between men and women of different longhouses.

The productive elaboration of Urarina gender distinctions can be detected in terms of sociospatial attachments and "architectural discourse" (Wigley 1992, 329). The spatial organization of the longhouse is conceptually partitioned according to the space-defining elements or boundaries of family and gender (see Norberg-Schulz 1980, 11). The male-oriented province is the bamboo slat platforms (*adánah*) and the wooden stools (*üfuiufhua,* made from *cedro* or *itauba* wood) or roughly hewn benches that encircle this slightly elevated space. The fulcrum around which women's activities revolves is the cooking fire, adjacent domestic platform, and kitchen lean-to (consisting of a palm-thatch roof of a single pitch with the higher end abutting the longhouse's truss). Whether reclining on the bamboo dais, sitting on mats, or squatting on the ground, women spend considerable amounts of their time inhabiting the area adjoining their hearths. Wooden stools, once the shaman's cathedrae, are now commonly used by women laboring at their hearth fires (cf. Girard 1958, 174–75; and Tessmann [1930] 1987).

Mature men and women of the same generation who belong to different longhouses do not speak publicly to one another (see Kramer 1979, 48). By keeping their backs to each other, men and women avoid direct eye contact, which further emphasizes gendered alterity. Substantial overlap between men's and women's spaces occurs during festive cassava beer drinking and dancing sessions. Accompanied by panpipe, flute, and rhythmic drumming, these exuberant affairs can last for days on end. They are periodic moments that unite the sexes in what is one of the Urarina's most volatile social contexts.

Beyond the homestead, men and boys frequent the surrounding forest when stalking game or fishing or when working at extracting lumber for the regional timber market. Although women work in small groups away from the longhouse in their gardens and make short excursions into the surrounding forest to make use of valuable natural resources, their geographical mobility is somewhat restricted. A favorite wife will occasionally accompany her husband on infrequent trips to regional centers, such as Concordia, Nauta, and even the regional capital, Iquitos. Women do regularly call on kin in a nearby *luderí,* either on foot or in canoes. In the company of their mature kinsmen, women will attend social and work gatherings in surrounding settlements (both with Urarina and *ribereño* groups). Males will invariably escort women during distant scavenging excursions or when they enter palm swamps to collect coveted palm leaves for cordage used for weaving. Aside from accompanying their husbands when visiting other local longhouse groups, or on subsistence and hunting expeditions, women seldom venture far from their homestead and its associated garden and fishing sites. Above all, this includes avoidance of mestizo settlements, as well as cosmically charged locales such as the spirit-endowed palm swamps (*ajláca*) and turbulent whirlpools (*nesamuná*) in the bends of rivers, which are said to unite the terrestrial world of the living with the riverine underworld of dangerous spirits.

Fig. 7.1.   Urarina young woman and girls in longhouse. (Photograph by Bartholomew Dean.)

The separate gendered geographies of place, and Urarina social life more broadly, are critical components in the constitution, enactment, and mediation of translocal economic and political relationships. As with the Panoan-speaking Cashinahua (Kaxináwa) (McCallum 1990, 417; Kensinger 1995, 11), Urarina men's agency links them with the "external world," where they deal with the *anazairi* (foreigners) on behalf of all members of their local longhouse group.[4] This gendered division of labor also logically extends beyond situations of intercultural commerce into "public" discursive relations—namely, political and retributive forays beyond the Urarina's territory in their attempts to secure services or to air grievances to indigenous advocacy groups and state agencies. Although contemporary commercial negotiations appear at first sight to be largely about "goods," they can also be interpreted as attempts to establish monopolistic alliances with traders, indigenous advocates, and state actors. The Urarina communities with whom I have worked tend to frame much of their intercultural encounters in acquisitive terms using the rhetoric of exchange and peonage.

In the Chambira Basin, commercial exchange and social mobility are closely associated. The principal clients of a mestizo labor boss or trader will typically become creditors in their own right to other Urarina individuals within their immediate spheres of influence. Urarina debt (*rebeukön*)—symbolized by the exchange of trade goods— assumes a life of its own. "Debt servicing" is reproduced according to the exigencies of local political alliances (Dean 1994a). Urarina public life is precarious, and the fortunes of *kurana* are made and broken swiftly in this society with limited surplus accumulation. Political prestige is contingent on the continuation of unstable trading networks. By extension, political careers are sometimes very short-lived. Those few headmen who dominate are able to deliver to their constituents under vastly inequitable circumstances.

In a society that vacillates uneasily between hierarchical and egalitarian inclinations, the asymmetry that accompanies transcultural commercial and political negotiations helps determine the transitory careers of *kurana*. Urarina political fluidity is linked to women's ability to assert themselves by maneuvering resources (wealth items, approval, sexuality, etc.)[5] in their efforts to forge alliances with up-and-coming headmen. Women may pool their resources with one headman and retract their collaboration during another round of trade if they are displeased with the management of their affairs. Women regularly call in favors and make claims on the men who are indebted or obliged to serve them in some way, either through mobilizing kinship bonds or through ties of affiliation. These efforts collude with the ambitious machinations of self-aggrandizing *kurana*. As the managers of supralocal affairs, headmen are the mediators between internal relations of socioeconomic production and the external market economy. Recognition of how the redistribution and allocation of trade goods within Urarina settlements reinforces local hierarchies raises the issue of women's agentive capacities, particularly as political actors in supralocal affairs.

Women's negotiations are integral to the status of those considered

Fig. 7.2.   Urarina women and children. (Photograph by
Bartholomew Dean.)

to be *kurana,* but here it is hard to distinguish between men's and
women's prestige orders that are themselves interdependent and complementary. Men's prestige is dependent on their access to the fruits of
women's labor power, whereas women's prestige in the form of their
access to barter goods—particularly cloth and beads—derives from
their alliances with efficacious and fearsome male negotiators. Despite
the separation of gender roles in interethnic exchange, women promote
commercial alliances and make decisions that benefit the men and
women of their hearth group as a whole. Women's reliance on mature
men to manage the commercial exchange of female wealth has reinforced Urarina patterns of inequality, namely, gerontocratic impulses
and male dominance.[6] While patterns of social inequality—both internally and externally generated—are mutually replicated within the
context of debt-peonage relations, women activate a number of
options to optimize their transactional positions. Among other things,
this includes reliance on male kin; marriage; divorce; mobilization of
fictive-kin ties; and/or relocation of residence.

Even though Urarina women instrumentally select those men who they know are both reliable and shrewd to negotiate on their behalf, they must mobilize filial obligations by appealing to the very norms that prohibit their interactions with outsiders. In so doing, women reinforce those normative assumptions that constrain their agency. Accordingly, it is necessary to explicitly demarcate the abbreviated terrain of female political spheres, particularly as commerce becomes coterminous with the larger struggle for resources, such as secured land tenure, education, and health care—from a state disinclined to support the aspirations of indigenous peoples. In this regard, Urarina women are becoming marginalized in relation to socioeconomic and cultural practices that are construed as exclusively public-sphere activities.

Marginality indicates that some forms of human experience are inconsequential and peripheral. I adopt the term to underscore Urarina women's positionality—defined not in geographical terms, but rather with reference to their limited access to power. One cannot claim, however, that Urarina women are all marginalized, nor are they always marginalized. Moreover, their marginality does not derogate from their ability to determine essential aspects of the present, nor does it erase the control that they exert over essential aspects of production, consumption, and reproduction. As Bruce Knauft has recently argued, indigenous women in Amazonia (and Melanesia) have been actively redefining "gendered practices to gain more direct access themselves to agents and objects of perceived modernity" (1999, 347; see also Knauft 1997 cf. Dean 1998). Notwithstanding the pervasive imagery that dissimulates their significance, women are actively present at the core of Urarina social life.

I have underscored the restricted nature of the spheres that Urarina women inhabit in an effort to highlight their limited range of options in dealing with outsiders. But as other anthropologists working in societies with marked gender segregation have indicated, such restrictions on women's interactions do not necessarily derogate from their ability to move and function autonomously within their own domains, which are located within a spectrum of social participation and exclusion.[7] The strategic negotiations and claims that Urarina women must make with the men who are their interlocutors give insight into this continuum of social participation and exclusion. While reliance on men is not by itself an indication of women's impuissance or subordination, in my view it is important to trace the discursive formation of gender relations by taking into account mythologically inspired narratives that help to frame social life.

The Discursive Formation of Urarina Gender Relations

The Urarina authorize their gendered segregation of production, exchange, and consumption by relying on an ideology that obfuscates cultural power and thus facilitates its exercise. Indeed, the circumscribed roles of women do not occur ex nihilo. They are celebrated and legitimated by an elaborate mythological discourse. This is readily apparent when examining Urarina notions of the sacred past, through which cosmology and gender relations are continually reasserted. More broadly, the encoding of Urarina gender is dispersed over a variety of social loci and modes of action and entails oral narratives, music, rituals, material culture, "and all the ways the earth itself is perceived as patterned with [gendered] lines and significant points" (Rowe and Schelling 1991, 53–54).

Urarina men, women, and children not only resist the encroaching outside worlds by engendering society in terms of cultural categories refracted through a mythologized conception of their own past, they also engage with the "fronts of national expansion" (Dean 1990) through these discursive formations. The strategic recounting of myths alludes to Urarina sexual differentiation and helps to legitimate women's exclusion from the public and semipublic spheres of transcultural exchange (cf. Rojas Zolezzi 1992). Popular narratives, such as the elders' story of "the time when there were no women," are discursive formations that establish as a given Urarina sexual differentiation, including women's exclusion from the most public of all social arenas: those exterior relations with non-Urarina men and women where engaged citizens deliberate about their common affairs (see Fraser 1994a, 75).

As a myth of precursory sociology, the Urarina's narrative of "the time when there were no women" establishes men's social importance, while also emphasizing women's ancillary role in life beyond the longhouse. A masculinist perspective is similarly reinforced in the Urarina's myth of postdiluvial creation, which asserts the primacy of men in structuring supralocal social relations (see Dean 1994b). The masculine subtext of popular myths about the origin of barter goods and personal narratives about the circulation of scarce commodities position men as the principal interlocutors with the "outside world"—that is, the mestizo universe of the *Anazairi,* or foreigners; and the Bakagá, who are the Urarina's archrivals—the Jivaroan-speaking Achuar peoples (see Descola 1994).

In their talk about affinal responsibilities and gendered production, the Urarina frequently say that men are obliged to "maintain" their wives and children, whereas their creator deity Kuánra "made women to serve men" (*Kana kuánra enecuaignele*). As Ujkuaiziri, a key informant, self-assuredly remarked to me several years ago, "Women serve us—that is why we have wives . . . we men are not going to be serving them food." When pressed on the issue of the gendered division of labor, exchange, and authority, Urarina adult informants told me that women are incapable of maintaining or supporting men. This view was evident from the words of one particularly vocal female informant, Arúba, who told me that Urarina women "do not speak Spanish, so how are we going to obtain the trade goods we all need?" This sentiment was also echoed in the words of Raguiti, a prominent *kurana* who heads a large and imposing *luderi:* "Women do not know how to speak Spanish; men are the ones who learn to speak Spanish." His senior wife, Masará, reiterated this point by chiming in, "Women's tongues are heavy; we cannot learn to speak. We only live here in the *luderi,* we do not travel far from here, and we never leave our longhouses."

By equating women with an architectonically circumscribed space and with a restricted linguistic register (Kachá eje, spoken Urarina),[8] the Urarina's hierarchical gender discourse privileges men's interlocutory status, which in turn enhances their access to trade goods and claims to prestige. Male patterns of extensive visiting, coupled with their experience of geographic mobility, help them to command public forums, both interdemically and transculturally. This dominance politically eclipses women's less extensive social networks (Dean 1999b).

Men's narrative accounts of their experiences with notoriously evil labor bosses (*patrones*) and traders (*regatones*) bolster their image as adept and fearless negotiators. As noted, Urarina *kurana* rely on their reputations for commercial acumen, bravery, and munificence in constructing their social networks and public personae. Men of renown routinely recount stories of cunning flights from avaricious *patrones.* Men's narratives about debt peonage are framed by a broad geographical landscape that encompasses distant geographical points and diverse experiences. In contrast, women's dramatic self-presentations and narrative accounts do not, as a rule, reference extensive geographic knowledge nor personal experiences of cultural encounter. When negotiating the terms of trade, Urarina men regularly make *encompassing* assertions of not only acting on behalf of their longhouse, but also representing the interests of their deme.[9] Conversely, women make *encompassed* claims with respect to their own desires for trade goods.

Compared with men's negotiations, women's encompassed claims operate at a more localized site of action, namely, the hearth (*isinéja*) and the longhouse (*luderí*), rather than the deme (*kaj laitjíra*) or Urarina (Kachá) society as a whole.[10]

As the Urarina become more enmeshed in the regional and national political landscapes, the discursive legitimization of women's silence and translocal political exclusion is of vital consequence for the future. What will this circumscribed participation in formal politics mean for women's prestige and life opportunities as they are thrust into increased interaction with mestizo national society? This question is particularly salient when we consider that trade and political negotiations with non-Urarina take place in spoken Spanish. As a result, Urarina women's monolingualism is one of the most formidable of all imposed silences.[11] Given that political participation is enacted through the medium of speech, how then can Urarina women assert their claims and ensure that their demands will be met in an increasingly diversified linguistic context? Will the future replicate the mythical, timeless past when, the Urarina say, "there were no women"?

Despite the patina of legitimacy that Urarina mythological narratives bestow upon gendered segregation and male dominance in exterior political relations, "real" life situations attest to marked gender complementarity and female autonomy in hearth-group politics. The degree to which Urarina men claim to speak for the women of their *kaj laitjíra* obfuscates women's active participation in the institution of debt peonage, not to mention other fundamental aspects of social life. One need only mention women's contribution in the form of cassava beer and labor-intensive, elaborate food preparation to realize their involvement in facilitating socially conducive contexts for barter and for interdemic relations.[12] Similarly, by foregrounding the transactional moment at which specific items of female wealth—such as palm-fiber goods, garden crops, or poultry—enter a commodity state, we may in fact do injustice to women's participation in other critical junctures of production, circulation, and consumption that are animated by different cultural logics.

Engaging Women's "Public" Silence

In highlighting Urarina women's silence in the episodic yet crucial negotiations that implicate them in broader, supralocal public affairs, I consciously privilege those transactional moments in which men articulate women's interests. Invariably, a simple focus on those instances of exchange that link the Urarina to national and international markets through mestizo or *ribereño* (peasant) intermediaries elides other fundamental aspects of subsistence and petty-commodity production that indicate gender complementarity.[13] Notwithstanding the existence of gender complementarities in social domains that afford women a marked degree of power and autonomy, their dependence on men to advance their interests in supralocal political arenas invites provocative questions regarding the allocation and elaboration of power relations between the sexes and generations.

A recent slew of ethnographies attests to Knauft's claim that gender is a particularly salient category "in postcolonial, late modern, and transnational arenas of cultural contestation" (1997, 233; see also, among others, Tice 1995; Abu-Lughod 1993; Povinelli 1993; and Kondo 1990). However, the continuing inattention to the gendered nature of power in Amazonia[14] and its relationship to larger structural forces means that areas of significant analytical and practical consequence remain unexplored. In contributing to the emerging trend of ethnography that draws upon the critical insights and concerns of feminist social theory,[15] my aim is to help reverse the androcentric trend of considering political life in native Amazonia as solely a male-dominated activity (cf. Kracke 1993).

Urarina women do actively assert their demands within an encompassed domestic sphere whose boundary is normatively delimited to preclude sustained interaction with non-Urarina peoples, particularly mestizos. In the disturbingly familiar panorama of indigenous engagement with national society, it is a legitimate concern that Urarina women will increasingly lose their political voice without men to represent them in the political spaces now being opened, thanks in large part to the emergence of the indigenous rights movement. To understand the various ways in which localized initiatives and microlevel gender politics intersect larger political processes, one must situate the Urarina's recent political mobilization in the context of the contemporary indigenous rights movement in Amazonia.

Amazonian Pan-Ethnic Confederations

The past two and a half decades have seen an unprecedented rise in political organization and activism in Amazonia by indigenous federations and their advocates. National indigenous organizations—such as AIDESEP of Peru, CIDOB of Bolivia, and CONFENIAE of Ecuador—and the transnational, pan-ethnic confederation COICA (Coordinadora de Organizaciones Indígenas de la Cuenca Amazónica, or Coordinating Body of the Indigenous Peoples of the Amazon Basin) have emerged as vibrant political forces (see, among others, Dean 1999a, 2000; Montoya Rojas 1998; Maybury-Lewis 1997a; Varese 1996a, 1996b; Brysk 1996; Sponsel 1995; and Conklin and Graham 1995).[16] Given the limited successes achieved at the national level, struggles for local and regional autonomy have often been transported to the international arena, where transnational indigenous organizations are finding greater political space for asserting their claims for cultural autonomy, self-determination, and sovereignty.[17] In alliance with environmentalist groups, development organizations, and human rights NGOs, the pan-ethnic movement has been successful at getting the world to turn its attention to the plight of Amazonia's indigenous peoples.[18]

In the ceremonial contexts of so-called native Amazonia, the elaboration of personhood and the performance of collective identities attain "a multimedia apotheosis" (Roe 1995, 98). Throughout the entire region, "myth, oration, dance, music, sartorial and corporeal art, architecture and the organization of private and public space make of life the stuff of performance and theatre" (Roe 1995, 98). Postcolonial identity formation in the area also entails what some analysts have aptly dubbed "the invention of Amazonian autochthony" (see Morin and Saladin d'Anglure 1997, 180; cf. Brown 1993; Jackson 1989, 1994; Caiuby Novaes 1997; and Knauft 1999, 171–72). The strategic deployment of oral-based tradition and the performance of sacred rites and mythical histories reaffirm indigenous peoples' ostensibly legitimate ties to flora, fauna, and—most importantly—land (Chirif et al. 1991).[19] Local and national indigenous leaders marshal discourses that situate indigenous peoples as the authentic and rightful caretakers of the tropical rain forest (COICA 1990).[20]

Indigenous peoples regularly make claims to their lands, because, as Maybury-Lewis notes, "they were there first or have occupied them since time immemorial" (1997b, 8; see also Herlihy 1997). This assertion enhances the credibility of indigenous peoples' various demands for political, cultural, and economic self-determination. Since the 1970s, indigenous federations and their political allies have taken the "land question" as a mere starting point for a number of divergent concerns. Leaders of the Amazonian pan-ethnic alliance routinely invoke a mythic past to articulate their complex and often contradictory demands. Throughout the region, calls for the affirmation of indigenous citizenship have converged with pleas for cultural survival and self-determination. Indigenous peoples' proposals for "ethnodevelopment" based on putatively traditional, autarkic modes of production regularly accompany impassioned pleas for the cessation of foreign (i.e., nonindigenous)-dominated extractive economies common throughout Amazonia, such as gold mining, logging, and oil prospecting (see, among others, Arhem 1998; Gray 1997; Rival 1997; and Sawyer 1996). At the local level, many community leaders advocate for greater regional integration in the market economy, decentralized government, increased access to social services, and the protection of their basic human rights (Sarasara 1997; Smith, Tapuy, and Wray 1996).

For their part, the Urarina have weathered centuries of interethnic conflict and colonial violence through self-imposed isolation and strategies of passive resistance to the presence of outsiders in their midst. The primary threat to the Urarina peoples and their traditional homelands arises from socioeconomic forces exerted by politically and technologically more potent interest groups wanting to establish a foothold in the region. Throughout Peruvian Amazonia, the implementation of extractive modes of production, coupled with the state-sanctioned "civilizing" project, has led to a devastating impoverishment of the region's social and ecological communities. Implicit in the Peruvian state's neoliberal and at times populist "civilizing" project is a political philosophy whose imperative is the creation of a national citizenry out of a heterogeneous mass of culturally, linguistically, and historically diverse ethnic communities (see, e.g., Eusebio Castro 1994; and Varese 1972). Not surprisingly, Amazonia's relatively small and politically vulnerable indigenous societies have been extremely susceptible to the social and demographic distortions associated with colonial and national penetration (Dean 1999c).

The creation and maintenance of ethnic federations that allow politically peripheral societies such as the Urarina to defend their human rights has been a slow process. The political consolidation of Urarina society has been hindered by its geographical isolation, by the nature of its dispersed residential settlement pattern, and by its long history of inter-longhouse factionalism. Moreover, the "egalitarian" character of the Urarina's social relations militates against hierarchical models of political organization (see Clastres [1974] 1987; cf. Dean 1999a). This has been a perennial challenge not only to the Urarina, but also to indigenous political organizations that ideally "seek to permit maximum participation with a minimum of concentration of power" (Smith 1984, 29).

Despite the Urarina's historical reluctance to embrace incorporation into a pan-ethnic confederation, political mobilization has occurred in the Chambira watershed (Dean 1997a, 1997b; Dean and

McKinley 1997; CEDIA 1996a, 1996b). Influenced by their travels to urban and periurban Amazonia, the presence of pro-indigenous NGOs, and the general appeal of *indigenismo,* a new generation of Urarina leaders has come to realize that national multiethnic confederations, such as AIDESEP (Asociación Interétnica de Desarrollo de la Selva Peruana, or Interethnic Association for the Development of the Peruvian Amazon), may be one of the most appropriate mechanisms for indigenous societies to use in articulating and defending their human rights before regional, national, and international groups.

Lessons from the Margins: Engendering Power in Amazonia

Membership in an indigenous federation is not without its attendant problems. In spite of the many successes it has had in securing the social, political, and economic rights of Amazonian peoples, Peru's indigenous movement was until recently characterized by a top-down style of personalized politics. Review of the Amazonian case does indeed support Fredrik Barth's claim that "some of the institutionalized mechanisms of democratic politics may exacerbate, rather than resolve conflict, by mobilizing broad ethnic constituencies in antagonistic competition" (1997, 9). Given the entrenched nature of patron-clientelism in western Amazonia, perhaps the biggest challenge for pan-ethnic indigenous confederations is to ensure that customary political ideals—namely, "a broad consensus" and "absence of political authoritarianism"—are maintained in the transnational political arena (Morin and Saladin d'Anglure 1997, 181).

Urarina social formations, cultural practices, and self-identifications are generally at odds with what some observers have called the indigenous movement's "ideology of dependence and hierarchical order" (Hendricks 1988). The indigenous rights movement's insistence on internal coherence fortifies the dominant universalist paradigm, whose relentless homogenization ultimately destroys or castigates those elements of alterity that it cannot accommodate (McKinley 1995). As Blanca Muratorio has recently argued, "the homogeneous character of ethnic identity projected by the indigenous federations silences the complexities of group and gender differences internal to local societies" (1998, 411). The illusion of an atemporal past and internal social cohesion intimated by the indigenous federations' reliance on a discourse of ethnic primordialism allows its leaders to conceal very real resistance to an imposed, authoritarian organizational structure, particularly by newcomers to pan-ethnic political mobilization.

While the Amazonian indigenous rights movement has been characterized as hierarchical and as dominated by a few ethnic groups and individuals, the emergent personalization of power and attendant patron-clientelist style of leadership have come under fire. Calls for reform peaked with COICA's general congress in 1992, which ratified a series of structural reforms aimed at decentralizing power and enhancing organizational accountability, both political and economic (see Inoash Shawit 1997, 71). In spite of concerted efforts to address problems surrounding the lack of equal participation and direct representation, the indigenous rights movement has been slow to respond to the voices at the margins of power.[21]

There are unquestionably many good reasons to be uneasy about contemporary *indigenismo,* particularly when it continues to conceal the endurance of systematic social distinctions (such as gender inequality) through its appeals to a putatively universal indigenous subjectivity. In its current guise, Amazonian *indigenismo* tends to essentialize culture and fails to adequately recognize cultural difference, social inequality, and gendered disempowerment. All too often, the indigenous movement's intelligentsia rely on an "essentialist conservatism that naturalizes women's identities, most commonly by stereotypical female identification with Mother Earth" (Muratorio 1998, 411). Nevertheless, *indigenismo* carries an enormous moral weight capable of mobilizing collective social action—as seen in the 1990s uprisings in Ecuador or the revolts in Chiapas (Díaz Polanco 1997; cf. Tamayo Herrera 1998; Hill 1996; and Whitten 1996). Indeed, *indigenismo* continues to be identified—at least in the industrialized West—with a discourse of equality, and it has also been responsible for advancing the recognition of the rights of indigenous peoples.

Indigenous Rights, Gender Equity?

Rights are radically contingent on the local moral worlds in which they are embedded. Urarina rights are subject to local notions of relatedness that range from flexible or more relativistic criteria that define a person or group, to the fixed or more absolute criteria—such as names or ethnonyms—that refer to specific persons or groups. Urarina notions of rights, or what I here prefer to call obligations of interconnectedness, are based on a sense of communal belonging that legitimizes the *kaj laitjíra.* Urarina ideas about rights differ from occidental perspectives that emphasize individual liberties. This is obvious in terms of the Urarina's recognition of land rights. As among other indigenous peoples of Amazonia, Urarina cosmology and daily practice suggest an interactive relationship between humanity, divinity, and the natural habitat.[22]

Rather than fully embracing localized notions of morality and political authority, the organized indigenous movement in Peruvian Amazonia regularly champions Western human rights discourse. When it comes to protecting the rights of women, the indigenous rights movement all too often perpetuates the notion of the separation of public and private spheres. Pro-indigenous human rights activists employ a discourse emphasizing state violations (of which there are many instances to cite), while gendered inequalities and intimate violence within the putatively domestic or private sphere are largely disregarded. The linkage of first-generation rights (i.e., civil and political rights as codified in the UN's 1948 Universal Declaration of Human Rights and its 1966 International Covenant on Civil and Political Rights) to the public sphere of citizenship activities is obviously problematic for Urarina women. Similarly, by endorsing cultural beliefs and practices that systematically devalue women and deny the possibility of gender equity, second-generation rights can in fact exacerbate women's vulnerability. As a result, the exclusions, restrictions, and ill treatment associated with women's lives in Amazonia are largely ignored by the indigenous rights movement. In Peru, a country where the masculine citizen-subject is privileged, the indigenous rights movement is predictably devoid of women, even in titular positions. Few women actively participate in community assemblies, and until recently, none had been elected to serve in any of the ethnic federation's primary political offices (Smith 1996, 120; see also Kensinger 1995, 16; and Heise Mondino and Landeo del Pino 1996, 15).[23]

Intra- and intergroup asymmetries are a manifestation of enduring gender hierarchies, which naturalize or depoliticize the subordination of the feminine. Lacking a public voice in the definition of group interests, Urarina women are denied the authoritative status of full personhood accorded to those men who are empowered to make decisions and represent the group in supralocal political forums. The indigenous rights movement's protagonists have rationalized the absence of women in the indigenous political hierarchy through recourse to citing the "traditional" cultural roles that prohibit women from participating in external political activities. Meanwhile, the emphasis on ethnic "authenticity," direct representation, and cultural brokerage checkmates contemporary *indigenismo* by the moves of its very own players (McKinley 1995).

This is the scenario in which Urarina men seek political engagement. In their desire to be assimilated into the ethnic-federation structure, some have eagerly embraced the fetishized hierarchies and gender discrimination that confine women to a restricted domestic sphere (in this case, excluding them from educational opportunities,[24] travel, employment, etc.). Under the guise of deference to "tradition," women and other less powerful indigenous groups are denied direct political representation. This in turn allows the federation structure to continue along narrow, clientelist lines, rather than opening up the movement to a more democratic, dialogic process with greater possibilities for participation and access to resources for all groups.

All too often, Peruvian Amazonia's indigenous rights movements bear the determinist imprimatur of their indigenist predecessors. Their leaders mistakenly assume that "ethnic" identification can either suppress or overcome the multiple constellations of identity, such as gender, class, and hybridity (or, in this "racialized" instance, *mestizaje*), that constitute social being. Proponents of pan-ethnic *indigenismo* distinguish it as a truly authentic, self-directed "native" movement thoroughly grounded in the Amazonian reality. But, like the colonial and republican formulations of the "Indian Question," modern *indigenismo* involves appealing to externally fashioned identities and social practices. How, then, can contemporary *indigenismo* in Peruvian Amazonia embrace the margins without losing the centrifugal pull of the core? Can the Amazonian indigenous rights movement make strategic accommodation for multiple political and intellectual agendas while still retaining its collective strength and unified voice? Similarly, how can an indigenous identity politics recognize or respect cultural diversity—not to mention gender equality—without retreating into an effete relativism?

Schooling for the Future: Establishing Voice and Gendered Authority?

These questions assume urgency in light of the gendered dimensions of political authority and the recent introduction of educational opportunities for the Urarina. As rates of literacy increase, political authority will increasingly be tied to the ability to read and write. Not surprisingly, the "new" generation of politicized Urarina men (*líderes*) has had access (albeit very limited) to literacy through their active involvement with nonindigenous extractive entrepreneurs and traders (*patrones*), missionaries (particularly the Summer Institute of Linguistics), and the Peruvian military. As in other indigenous societies of

Amazonia, schools and the provision of literacy programs will continue to play a significant role in the future development of Urarina political leadership.[25]

While a fundamental part of community life, schools have a lengthy and checkered history for many indigenous peoples in Amazonia. From the time of the establishment of Jesuit missions in the sixteenth and seventeenth centuries to the contemporary period of labor bosses and predatory extractive entrepreneurs, schools have been a way of immobilizing indigenous societies. In Peruvian state-run schools, the forced imposition of Spanish—Castilianization through literacy—separates indigenous peoples from their customary means of socialization and from their traditional modes of expression. This is especially evident for those students, such as the Urarina, who are not part of the hegemonic language community nor national mestizo culture. Influenced by an urban, monolingual-based model of pedagogy, daily instruction is often hierarchical in its organization and intensely authoritarian in practice. Not only do indigenous students assimilate skills that are often not appropriate for their particular socioeconomic and historical situation, they are also indoctrinated into becoming ashamed of their own sociolinguistic and cultural heritage (Dean 1999c; see also Montoya Rojas 1990).

In spite of these very real problems, schools are being embraced by indigenous peoples as a necessary means for addressing issues of communal well-being, cultural autonomy, and self-determination. At the behest of Urarina community leaders and pro-indigenous advocates such as the nongovernmental organization APRI (the Amazonian Peoples' Resources Initiative), a small number of state-backed schools have been established over the past few years in the Chambira Basin.[26] Urarina longhouse communities are now beginning to see the many advantages of establishing a local school. Perhaps most importantly, schools are viewed by many Urarina leaders as a virtual prerequisite for gaining recognition of their longhouse settlements as officially designated indigenous communities (*comunidades nativas*), following the corporatist model of political integration initiated by General Juan Velasco Alvarado's military regime (1968–75).[27]

Many Urarina longhouse communities now see the establishment of a local primary school as an effective way of valorizing their political claims to territory and achieving cultural autonomy vis-à-vis a decidedly hostile national society. Despite low rates of literacy among the Urarina (which I estimate at less than 10% of the total populace), access to formal schooling has become fundamental to the creation and ongoing stability of their communities. Indeed, many Urarina leaders see schools as more than an institutional conduit for formal education. The new generation of male leaders credits the introduction of schools in the Chambira Basin with the Urarina's emergence from the ignorance, ineptitude, and cultural primitivism of their forebears, whom they see as enslaved debt peons helplessly incapable of establishing or maintaining culturally autonomous communities.

While there is a wide range in Urarina men's linguistic capacities, women are predominately monolingual. The recent introduction of formal schooling has tremendous implications for the gendered nature of political power. Urarina women's prestige, unlike that of their male counterparts, has not been sanctioned in terms of their capacity to speak Spanish, orchestrate commercial transactions, or forge supralocal alliances, but rather through their "customary" roles as mothers, matriarchal senior wives in polygynous households, and post-menopausal mothers-in-law. Though it is impossible to escape the socializing effects of the discursive forces that give rise to human subjectivity, conscious subjects can countermand, if not subvert, the ways in which discourse constitutes, valorizes, and undermines social life. The introduction of intercultural bilingual education is a fine example of this process in Peruvian Amazonia (see AIDESEP/ISP 1998; and AIDESEP/ISP/PFMB 1998).

Throughout much of rural Amazonia, women never finish their primary schooling. AIDESEP's intercultural bilingual teacher training program in Iquitos has faced similar problems in the recruitment and retention of women. By 1998 only three of the thirty-three graduates of the program were women.[28] The challenge remains how to formulate educational opportunities in a manner that gets girls and women engaged with questions of social and political consequence—such as land tenure, health care, natural resource management, and cultural survival. As Kenneth Kensinger suggests for the Cashinahua, those women who have attended school "show a propensity to interact directly with Peruvians rather than depending on male kinsmen as was the case in the past" (1995, 11).

By no means is this to suggest that the provision of intercultural bilingual education is without its attendant problems (Montoya 1998, 1990). Beatriz Fabían Arias and Oscar Espinosa de Rivero give a poignant example of the painful fissures of emergent classism and racism in their study of the impact of political violence among the Asháninka of the Peruvian *selva central* (central jungle). A formally educated Asháninka woman referred to her uneducated "sisters" as

Fig. 7.3.   Members of the intercultural bilingual teacher training
program, Iquitos, Peru. (Photograph by Bartholomew Dean.)

"real Asháninka who eat grubs" (*verdaderas campas come-gusanos*). In
response, uneducated Asháninka women defend themselves by saying
that educated women are arrogant because they no longer wear the
customary skirts (*cushmas*) and now know how to speak Spanish
(Fabían Arias and Espinosa de Rivero 1997, 85; cf. Townsley 1994,
350).

Conclusion

The circumscription of women to the realm of home and hearth is not
unique to Peruvian Amazonia; the conservatives' deployment of "tradition" against women in other indigenous societies need not be
recounted here. However, the point of this essay has been to raise, even
if tentatively, the issue of the future prospects for the Urarina while
painting a more detailed picture of women's active involvement as
transactional agents within a political-economic complex that privileges men. The examination of the Urarina's gender hierarchy alerts us
to the need to assess social inequalities in terms of the discursive formations, cultural contexts, and political economies in which they are
elaborated (see Tsing 1993, 96–97).

I have argued that the internal dynamics of political mobilization and exchange in Urarina society can be extrapolated from the overall network of interethnic relations and appear to be a real index of power given the localized factors described here. I do not think that the virtual absence of women in communal-assembly meetings (which are ritually and episodically convened) and translocal political life indicates that Urarina women are powerless. Indeed, close attention to their participation in debt peonage demonstrates their capacity to wield power in, and thereby redefine, the contexts from which they are putatively excluded. Hence, mythology or current social practices cannot be seen as completely determinative of women's ability to assert themselves in novel contexts.[29]

Urarina men and women negotiate the terms of gender equality, intergenerational relations, and political accountability on a daily basis. While the Urarina conceive of the distinction between male (*kicha*) and female (*ene*) in absolute, biological terms, daily life reveals more relativistic distinctions in which elements of maleness and femaleness are continually juxtaposed. Numerous contexts associate gender with fundamental aspects of social life and individual personhood, ranging from kinship terminologies and age distinctions to ritualized behavior and mythology.

Since gender is itself a socially enacted cultural construct, one should not regard the present and future political capacity of Urarina women in predictably fatalistic or overly deterministic ways. Just as we embrace the lability of ethnic and kinship categories, we must insist as thoroughly on regarding gender as a site of negotiation and disjunctive contestation (see, for instance, McCormack and Strathern 1980; Haraway 1989; Butler 1993; and McKinley 1997). In so doing, we need to provide a counterresponse to the supposedly predestined script according to which indigenous women inevitably lose out in situations of accelerated contact with the encroaching "outside world."

But we should also acknowledge the painfully hard fact that Urarina women do not hold political positions in the regional, national, or transnational indigenous organizations and are not likely to do so in the near future. As the Urarina become better placed to establish a voice in supralocal politics, the troubling issues remain those that pose challenges to women's ability to retain power, articulate their concerns in public spheres, and ostensibly have greater control over the enjoyment of all of their human rights—civil, political, economic, social, and cultural.

Notes

Versions of this paper were originally presented at the Annual Meeting of the American Anthropological Association in 1997, the Annual Meeting of the American Ethnological Society in 1998, and the International Studies Faculty Seminar at the University of Kansas in 1998. Thanks to the participants in these events for all their constructive feedback. I am indebted to the following for their many insights: Mauro Arirua, Manuel Burga, Gisela Cánepa-Koch, Johnny Davila, Eliana Elías, Paul Gelles, Ken George, Luis Gonzalez, Olivia Harris, Peter and Laura Herlihy, Jean Jackson, Kenneth Kensinger, Jerome Levi, David Maybury-Lewis, Sally Falk Moore, Tom Myers, Joane Nagel, Jaime Regan, Santiago Rivas, Raul Romero, Jacoba Sucher, and Akira Yamamoto. I have benefited from the collective energy and intellectual vitality of my students and colleagues at the University of Kansas and the Universidad Nacional Mayor de San Marcos. My soul partner and colleague, Michelle McKinley, has been a boundless source of wisdom and critical reflection; I gratefully acknowledge her endless contributions.

The research on which this chapter is based was conducted over thirty-four months between 1988 and 1998. Grants from the following institutions and organizations have supported my research among the Urarina: the Department of Anthropology, Harvard University; Sheldon Traveling Fellowship, Harvard University; Peabody Museum of Archaeology and Ethnology, Harvard University; Mellon dissertation award, Harvard University; IIE-Fulbright Fellowship; Fulbright-Hays Fellowship; Wenner-Gren Foundation; Emslie Hornimam Scholarship, Royal Anthropological Institute; 1998–99 Fellowship in Urgent Anthropology, Royal Anthropological Institute and Goldsmiths College, University of London; Tinker Foundation; the Sigma Xi Research Society; the MAPFRE America Fundación; New Faculty Research Grant, University of Kansas; Faculty Travel Grant, Hall Center for the Humanities, University of Kansas; Tinker Field Research Grant, Latin American Studies Center, University of Kansas; and the General Research Fund, University of Kansas. This essay is dedicated to my children, Maxwell, Isadora, and Gideon.

1. Like Nancy Fraser, I contend that "there are a number of different 'publics' in which groups and individuals act" (1994b, 10; see also Fregoso 1999). My demarcation of public and private sociopolitical and economic domains is linked to ideologies of power rather than to "any existing divisions of social life" (Gill 1994, 9). I also concur with Lynn Stephen's evaluation (1995) of feminist social movements in El Salvador in which she challenges the gendered dichotomy of public/private spheres. In an effort to avoid portraying human experience simply in terms of essentialist categories, Stephen explores the multiple facets of gendered identities, which, as she notes, "all influence the interpretation and experience of political, social, and cultural events" (1995, 824). Stephen persuasively illustrates how Salvadoran women's identities

"both accommodate and resist dominant ideologies of gender hierarchy and national security" (807).

2. Additional information on the Urarina and the Chambira Basin can be found in Dean 1994a, 1994b, 1995a, 1995b, 1999b, 1999c, 2002; and Myers and Dean 1999.

3. The Urarina language, Kachá eje, has been variously categorized as Tupian, as Panoan, as Macro-Tucanoan, as related to the Andean-Equatorial family, and as a linguistic isolate belonging to the Simaco family. There are various dialects of spoken Urarina, all mutually intelligible (Dean 1999c).

4. Shipibo women's control of the elaboration and marketing of handicrafts, such as necklaces, ceramic ware, and ornately sewn skirts (*chitonte*), provides an important exception to this trend in Peruvian Amazonia (Heise Mondino and Landeo del Pino 1996, 46–48). Similar trends have been noted among Aguaruna women, where a recent women's training and empowerment initiative (ODECOFROC) has successfully combined gardening, child nutrition, and pottery making (APRI-MINGA 2000, 11).

5. Janet Siskind recounts that Sharanahua have sexual relations with *patrones* (labor bosses) for merchandise such as cloth and kerosene ([1973] 1977, 179). However, among Urarina women, exchange of sexual favors for trade goods with *patrones* seems to be a relatively rare occurrence.

6. On the comparable situation among the Ashāninka, see Rojas Zolezzi 1992, 208.

7. As Nikki Craske notes in her study of poor women's political participation in Guadalajara, Mexico, it makes more sense to think of public and private political domains as a continuum, to "allow for different degrees of participation between the two extremes and the unlikelihood that a woman is completely immersed in the private with no participation in the public" (1993, 114).

8. See Cajas Rojas et al. 1987; Cajas Rojas 1989; Ferrúa Carrasco et al. 1980; and Espinosa Perez 1955.

9. The idea of encompassing/encompassed gender hierarchies follows from Ortner 1990.

10. Similarities to Urarina gender asymmetry in political life are found in "marginal" communities throughout the globe. In his commentary on gender relations in an upland community in Sulawesi, Kenneth George notes that "[t]he village politics of men encompass the socially and residentially limited politics of women" (1996, 53). Whereas the gender asymmetries in the political life of the upland Sulawesi village are "a matter of political scope," among the Urarina they are also embedded in an ideology of hierarchical value.

11. I estimate that about 40 percent of the Urarina male population is conversant in Spanish, in comparison to less than 10 percent of the female population.

12. The Urarina's symmetrical and complementary regimes of food ex-

change fit with Peter Gow's description of circulation of cassava beer and bush meats among the Piro of the Central Peruvian Amazon. Meat is procured by men and distributed by women, while cassava beer is made by women and generally circulated by men (Gow 1991, 127). The production, distribution, and consumption of these wealth items is central to Urarina social and political life. Given the importance of cassava beer in ritual and political affairs, those men who can rely on large, productive cassava gardens and multiple wives or daughters to make beer are at a distinct advantage in their ability to mobilize attendants at a communal work party (*minga*) or political assembly (Dean 1995a, 13).

13. On Urarina gender complementarity, see Dean 1995a. On gender complementarity in other areas of indigenous Amazonia, see Johnson and Johnson 1975; and McCallum 1990.

14. There are obvious exceptions to this claim. See, for instance, C. Seymour-Smith's important analysis (1991) of Jivaroan gender relations; Blanca Muratorio's analysis (1998) of the contemporary dilemmas of cultural reproduction and gendered identity politics in lowland Ecuador; and recent contributions to our understanding of gender relations in Peruvian Amazonia, including Dean 1995b, 1998; Kensinger 1997; Veber 1997; and Heise, Landeo, and Bant 1999.

15. Some figurations include Behar and Gordon 1995; Tice 1995; Kane 1994; Tsing 1993; Abu-Lughod 1993; di Leonardo 1991; Moore 1988; Ong 1988; and Strathern 1987.

16. COICA is a transnational organization that represents the political interests of about one and a half million people from more than four hundred indigenous societies in the Amazonian regions of several countries. COICA includes the following pan-ethnic national confederations: AIDESEP (Peru), APA (Guyana), CIDOB (Bolivia), COIAB (Brazil), CONFENIAE (Ecuador), CONIVE (Venezuela), FOAG (French Guyana), OIS (Surinam), and OPIAC (Colombia).

17. A case in point is the ethnic nationalism that Jean Jackson (1995) describes among the Tukanoan peoples of northwest Colombia's Vaupés Basin. Invoking Edward Sapir's (1924) famous phrase "culture, genuine and spurious," Jackson explores how the Tukanoans—in concert with local and national indigenous rights groups and international NGOs—have instrumentally mobilized their "indigenousness."

18. For instance, Beth Conklin and Laura Graham (1995) have highlighted the convergence in Brazil over the last decade between international environmentalism and pro-indigenous human rights concerns, which has given rise to the unprecedented internationalization of local indigenous concerns. While beneficial to both parties, the strategic alliance between pro-indigenous advocates and environmentalists is unstable and fraught with political risks for indigenous people (see also Conklin 1997).

19. Special claims to territory are a common feature of the indigenous

rights literature. For instance, Akiwenzie-Damn's study (1996) of identity formation among Canada's First Nations peoples asserts that the fundamental cultural distinction between Aboriginal peoples and Canadians is the relationship each group has with the land.

20. For the case of the national indigenous movement in Peruvian Amazonia, see AIDESEP 1985, 1987, 1992, 2000.

21. In the fashionably new social context of pan-ethnic mobilization, leaders of historically marginal communities such as the Urarina face many challenges to effective supralocal political consolidation. Barriers include the absence of any real historical precedence, not to mention the intensely subjective and at times deeply personalized nature of pan-ethnic identity politics, where indigenous leaders do not necessarily represent their ostensible constituencies (Montoya Rojas 1998; Kearney 1996; Smith 1996). Commentators have noted that Amazonia's pan-ethnic movement suffers from an organizational incapacity to effectively represent the region's culturally and economically diverse constituencies (Varese 1996b). Besides addressing the need for improved horizontal communication between the various constituent elements, the pan-ethnic federation movement must ensure a much greater degree of grassroots community participation at all levels of policy formulation and implementation (Varese 1996a, 1996b; Leon 1987).

22. For the Urarina, flora and fauna are anthropomorphized. In contrast, when *ribereño* or mestizo representatives of Peruvian "national culture" argue about land rights, they practically anthropomorphize the rights and interests in the land. Sometimes they do not even refer to the land itself. Urarina property rights are defined by communal knowledge, itself responsive to various pressures along a series of "interactive 'fronts' among neighbors" (Rose 1988), including mestizo labor bosses, traveling merchants (*regatones*), lumber extractors (*madereros*), and state and NGO actors. Customary rules regarding use-rights exist as stated norms, but all Urarina know that they have multiple means at their disposal to adapt the "rules" in actual practice.

23. During the AIDESEP annual national congress held in Iquitos in June 1998, it was decided that women should be included in the organization's formal power structure. At AIDESEP's next general national assembly, held in Lima in October 1999, a secretariat for indigenous women's affairs was created. At this time, Teresita Antazú López, a Yánesha woman, was elected to serve on AIDESEP's National Council (Consejo Directivo), composed of five members (including the association's president). Antazú is the first woman to occupy such a position of national prominence within Peru's formal indigenous movement (AIDESEP 2000).

24. A 1996 survey by the Peruvian National Institute of Statistics indicates that 21 percent of women between the ages of fifteen and twenty-four in the department of Loreto (population 798,646) never complete their primary-school education, due in large part to pregnancy, child-care obligations, and economic necessity (INEI 1997b, 21). While this figure corresponds with

national trends throughout Peru (INEI 1997a, 22), it occludes the actual figures in indigenous Amazonia, where the majority of women never complete their primary schooling (see Fabían Arias and Espinosa de Rivero 1997, 84). For a review of the situation among the Asháninka, Yagua, Shipibo, and Chayahuita, see Heise Mondino and Landeo del Pino's comparative study (1996) of gender in Peruvian Amazonia.

25. The revalorization of language through educational programs is a means of ensuring cultural survival. With this in mind, Urarina leaders—in collaboration with the Amazonian Peoples' Resources Initiative (APRI)—have recently decided to explore educational opportunities for the Urarina by working directly with the national indigenous federation, AIDESEP, and its bilingual intercultural education program headquartered in Iquitos (Dean 1997a, 1997b, 1999c). This initiative is aimed not simply at "teaching literacy" but also at retaining orality while heightening indigenous self-awareness and political savoir faire (see Campbell 1996, 163; Aikman 1995; and Barclay 1980).

26. APRI has been working in Peru since early 1996. It was originally conceived as a pilot community-defense project among the Urarina peoples of the Chambira Basin. The objectives of the project are to provide geographically isolated Amazonian communities access to appropriate health care and educational opportunities and to facilitate the process of political mobilization among these groups. APRI sponsors initiatives in three areas: reproductive health, intercultural bilingual education, and resource management. Through a combination of radio education (to an audience of more than eight hundred thousand) and community-based training programs, APRI enables a network of locally respected women to provide culturally appropriate health services in their communities. Research into the communities' traditional extractive practices is also being undertaken, due to concern over resource sustainability. These customary practices are being used as the basis for developing improved resource-management strategies aimed at enhancing community welfare. Now in its seventh year, APRI's program combines technical training with a leadership-development curriculum designed around individual reflexivity, skill building, and resource-mobilization strategies. APRI has also cosponsored the creation of the graduate program in Amazonian studies at the Universidad Nacional Mayor de San Marcos, Lima (see Dean and McKinley 1995a, 1995b, 1997; Dean et al. 2000; and Dean 2001).

27. The rise of the so-called Military Radicals (including Velasco) to power (1968–75) heralded a number of changes in the state's traditional posture toward indigenous peoples and the Amazon Basin. The military government embraced an Amazonian development strategy that was tempered by a strong *indigenista* sentiment. The most palpable result of this shift in national development policy was the 1974 promulgation of the Native Communities Law (Ley de Comunidades Nativas). In essence, this legislation was a half-hearted attempt to extend agrarian reform to the tropical lowlands, the *selva.*

The Native Communities Law marked the first time in Peruvian history that the state recognized the right of Amazonia's indigenous peoples to hold communal title to land. This law supplanted legislation passed in 1909 that had rendered the tropical forest territories (*tierra de montaña*) the exclusive property of the state (Uriarte 1985, 40). Under the joint direction of the Ministry of Agriculture and the state's corporatist popular-mobilization agency, SINAMOS (Sistema Nacional de Apoyo a la Movilación Social), a process of indigenous land entitlement began. However, legislation entitling native communities to communal ownership of territory did not stipulate the amount of lands to be granted to specific groups. The Native Communities Law recognized mobile residential patterns and thereby conceded communal rights to territories used for foraging, fishing, hunting, and swidden agriculture. Yet a primary issue not stipulated in the law was how much "migratory" territory the state is obliged to deed to specific *comunidades nativas.*

For a comprehensive evaluation of contemporary indigenous rights legislation in Peru, see Roldán and Tamayo 1999.

28. In 1998, AIDESEP's bilingual teacher training program enrolled 132 students, 18 of whom were women. Relative to previous years, this represents a significant increase in women's participation, yet it falls short of the program's objective of diversifying enrollment (Dean 1999c).

29. The active participation of Asháninka women in Women's Clubs (los Club de Madres) and Health Committees (los Comité de Salud), in spite of their limited social impact, supports this observation (see Heise Mondino and Landeo del Pino 1996, 28; and Fabián Arias and Espinosa de Rivero 1997, 83–85). To date, the Urarina have no comparable communal organizations.

References

Abu-Lughod, Lila. 1993. *Writing Women's Worlds: Bedouin Stories.* Berkeley: University of California Press.

AIDESEP (Asociación Interétnica de Desarrollo de la Selva Peruana). 1985. Indigenous Peoples of the Peruvian Amazon: Land, Natural Resources, and the Definition of Indigenous Peoples. *IWGIA Newsletter* 41:16–41.

———. 1987. Co-ordinadora Leaders Visit IWGIA: Evaristo Nugkuag Ikanan, Interethnic Association of the Development of the Peruvian Rainforest. In *IWGIA Yearbook,* 139–41. Copenhagen: International Work Group for Indigenous Affairs.

———. 1992. *Directorio de Comunidades Nativas: Region Loreto.* Iquitos, Peru: AIDESEP/Oficina Regional Iquitos.

———. 2000. Proyecto: Promoción para la participación de la mujer en el proceso de desarrollo de los pueblos indígenas. Manuscript, Lima.

AIDESEP/ISP. 1998. 10 años construyendo educación intercultural bilingüe. *Kuúmu: Publicación del Programa de Formación de Maestros Bilingües* (Iquitos, Peru).

AIDESEP/ISP/PFMB. 1998. *Programa curricular diversificado de educación intercultural bilingüe para los pueblos indígenas amazónicos.* Iquitos, Peru: ISP "Loreto"/AIDESEP/PFMB.

Aikman, Sheila. 1995. Language, Literacy, and Bilingual Education: An Amazonian People's Strategies for Cultural Maintenance. *International Journal of Educational Development* 13 (4): 411–22.

Akiwenzie-Damn, Kateri. 1996. "We Belong to This Land": A View of Cultural Difference. *Journal of Canadian Studies* 31 (3): 21–29.

APRI-MINGA (Amazonian Peoples' Resources Initiative—Minga Perú). 2000. *Perspectives* 2 (1).

Arhem, Kaj. 1998. *Makuna: Portrait of an Amazonian People.* Washington, D.C.: Smithsonian Institution Press.

Barclay, Frederica. 1980. Educación bilingüe: Por qué y para qué? *Amazonía Indígena* 1 (2): 3–7.

Barth, Fredrik. 1997. Review of *Indigenous Peoples, Ethnic Groups, and the State,* by David Maybury-Lewis. *Cultural Survival Quarterly* 21 (3): 9.

Behar, Ruth, and Deborah Gordon, eds. 1995. *Women Writing Culture.* Berkeley: University of California Press.

Brown, Michael. 1993. Facing the State, Facing the World: Amazonia's Native Leaders and the New Politics of Identity. *L'Homme* 33 (126–28): 307–26.

Brysk, Alison. 1996. Turning Weakness into Strength: The Internationalization of Indian Rights. *Latin American Perspectives* 23 (2): 38–58.

Butler, Judith. 1993. *Bodies That Matter: On the Discursive Limits of "Sex."* New York: Routledge.

Caiuby Novaes, Sylvia. 1997. *The Play of Mirrors: The Representation of Self Mirrored in the Other.* Translated by I. M. Burbridge. Austin: University of Texas Press.

Cajas Rojas, Judith. 1989. Nasalización en Urarina. In *Temas de Lingüística Amerindia,* edited by R. and G. S. F. Cerrón-Palomino. Lima: CONCYTEC.

Cajas Rojas, Judith, Angel Corbera, Beatriz Gualdieri, and Gustave Solis. 1987. *Bibliografía etnolingüística Urarina.* Documento de Trabajo, no. 54. Lima: Instituto de Lingüística Aplicada (CILA), Universidad Nacional Mayor de San Marcos.

Campbell, J. 1996. *Getting to Know Waiwai: An Amazonian Ethnography.* London: Routledge.

CEDIA (Centro para el Desarrollo del Indígena Amazónico). 1996a. Primer Congreso de Comunidades Nativas de la Cuenca del Río Chambira: Resultados de la discusión de los grupos de trabajo. Centro para el Desarrollo del Indígena Amazónico, Lima.

———. 1996b. Reglamento del Primer Congreso de Comunidades Nativas Urarinas del Río Chambira. Centro para el Desarrollo del Indígena Amazónico, Lima.

Chernela, Janet. 1984. Female Scarcity, Gender Ideology, and Sexual Politics in the Northwest Amazon. In *Sexual Ideologies in Lowland South America,* edited by K. M. Kensinger, 28–32. Working Papers on South American Indians, no. 5. Bennington, Vt.: Bennington College.

Chirif, Alberto, Pedro García, and Richard Chase Smith. 1991. *El Indígena y su territorio son uno solo: Estrategia para la defensa de los Pueblos y territorios indígenas en la cuenca Amazónica.* Lima: Oxfam and COICA.

Clastres, Pierre. [1974] 1987. *Society against the State: Essays in Political Anthropology.* Translated by R. Hurley. New York: Zone Books.

COICA (Coordinadora de Organizaciones Indígenas de la Cuenca Amazónica). 1990. We Are Concerned. *Orion Nature Quarterly* 9 (3): 36–37.

Conklin, Beth A. 1997. Body Paint, Feathers, and VCRs: Aesthetics and Authenticity in Amazonian Activism. *American Ethnologist* 24 (4): 711–37.

Conklin, Beth A., and Laura R. Graham. 1995. The Shifting Middle Ground: Amazonian Indians and Eco-politics. *American Anthropologist* 97 (4): 695–721.

Craske, Nikki. 1993. Women's Participation in Colonias Populares in Guadalajara, Mexico. In *"Viva!": Women and Popular Protest in Latin America,* edited by Sarah A. Radcliffe and Sallie Westwood, 112–35. London: Routledge.

Dean, Bartholomew. 1990. The State and the Aguaruna: Frontier Expansion in the Upper Amazon, 1541–1990. M.A. thesis, Harvard University.

―――. 1994a. Multiple Regimes of Value: Unequal Exchange and the Circulation of Urarina Palm-Fiber Wealth. *Museum Anthropology* 18 (1): 3–20.

―――. 1994b. The Poetics of Creation: Urarina Cosmogony and Historical Consciousness. *Latin American Indian Literatures Journal* 10 (1): 22–45.

―――. 1994c. Review of *Portals of Power: Shamanism in South America,* by E. Jean Matteson Langdon and Gerhard Baer, editors. *Latin American Indian Literatures Journal* 10 (2): 175–78.

―――. 1995a. Chanting Rivers, Fiery Tongues: Exchange, Value, and Desire among the Urarina. Ph.D. diss., Harvard University.

―――. 1995b. Forbidden Fruit: Infidelity, Affinity, and Brideservice among the Urarina of Peruvian Amazonia. *Journal of the Royal Anthropological Institute* 1 (1): 87–110.

―――. 1997a. APRI Develops a Dynamic Bilingual Education Program among Indigenous Peoples in Peruvian Amazonia. *APRI Info* 1 (summer): 2.

―――. 1997b. Speaking for Ourselves: The Politics of Urarina Language Preservation. *KU Anthropologist,* 9 (1): 1–6.

―――. 1998. Brideprice in Amazonia? *Journal of the Royal Anthropological Institute* 4 (2): 347–45.

―――. 1999a. Critical Re-vision: Clastres' *Chronicle* and the Optic of Primitivism. *Anthropology Today* 15 (2): 9–11.

―――. 1999b. Intercambios ambivalentes en la amazonía: Formación discursiva y la violencia del patronazgo. *Anthropologica* 17:85–115.

―――. 1999c. Language, Culture, and Power: Intercultural Bilingual Education among the Urarina of Peruvian Amazonia. *Practicing Anthropology,* special issue, Reversing Language Shift in Indigenous America: Collaborations and Views from the Field, edited by L. Watahomigie, T. McCarty, and A. Yamamoto, 20 (2): 39–43.

———. 2000. Respeto a los derechos de los pueblos indígenas. *El Comercio* (Lima), August 4, p. A20.

———. 2001. Digitizing Indigenous Sounds: Cultural Activists and Local Music in the Age of Memorex. *Cultural Survival Quarterly* 24 (4): 41–46.

———. 2002. State Power and Indigenous Peoples in Peruvian Amazonia: A Lost Decade, 1990–2000. In *The Politics of Ethnicity: Indigenous Peoples in Latin American States,* edited by David Maybury-Lewis, 199–238. Cambridge, Mass.: Harvard University Press.

Dean, Bartholomew, Eliana Elías, Michelle McKinley, and Rebecca Saul. 2000. The Amazonian Peoples' Resources Initiative: Promoting Reproductive Rights and Community Development in the Peruvian Amazon. *Health and Human Rights: An International Journal* 4 (2): 219–26.

Dean, Bartholomew, and Michelle McKinley. 1995a. Amazonian Peoples' Resources Initiative. *Cultural Survival Quarterly* 19 (2): 8.

———. 1995b. The Project: Amazonian Peoples' Resources Initiative (APRI). *Indigenous Knowledge and Development Monitor* 3 (3).

———. 1997. Building Partnerships in Health, Education, and Social Justice (Notes from the Field: Amazonian Peoples' Resources Initiative). *Cultural Survival Quarterly* 21 (3): 14–15.

Descola, Philippe. 1994. *In the Society of Nature: A Native Ecology in Amazonia.* Translated by Nora Scott. Cambridge: Cambridge University Press.

Díaz Polanco, Héctor. 1997. *Indigenous Peoples in Latin America: The Quest for Self-Determination.* Boulder, Colo.: Westview Press.

di Leonardo, Micaela, ed. 1991. *Gender at the Crossroads of Knowledge.* Berkeley: University of California Press.

Espinosa Perez, Lucas. 1955. *Contribuciones lingüísticas y etnograficas sobre algunos pueblos indigenas del Amazonas Peruano.* Vol. 1. Madrid: Consejo Superior de Investígaciones Cientificas, Instituto Bernardino de Sahagun.

Eusebio Castro, Mino. 1994. Peruvian State Targets "Abandoned" Lands of Asháninka. *Abya Yala News* 8 (4): 24–25.

Fabían Arias, Beatriz, and Oscar Espinosa de Rivero. 1997. *Las cosas ya no son como antes: La mujer Asháninka y los cambio socio-culturales producidos por la violencia política en la Selva Central.* Lima: CAAAP.

Ferrúa Carrasco, Freddy, Joel Linares Cruz, and Oscar Rojas Pérez. 1980. *La sociedad Urarina.* Iquitos, Peru: Organismo Regional de Desarrollo de Loreto (ORDELORETO).

Fraser, Nancy. 1994a. Rethinking the Public Sphere. *Social Text* 25–26:56–90.

———. 1994b. *Unruly Practices: Power, Discourse, and Gender in Contemporary Social Theory.* Minneapolis: University of Minnesota Press.

Fregoso, Rosa Linda. 1999. Re-imagining Chicana Urban Identities in the Public Sphere, Cool Chuca Style. In *Between Woman and Nation: Nation-*

alisms, Transnational Feminisms, and the State, edited by C. Kaplan, N. Alarcón, and M. Moallem, 72–91. Durham, N.C.: Duke University Press.

George, Kenneth. 1996. *Showing Signs of Violence: The Cultural Politics of a Twentieth-Century Headhunting Ritual.* Berkeley: University of California Press.

Gill, Lesley. 1994. *Precarious Dependencies: Gender, Class, and Domestic Service in Bolivia.* New York: Columbia University Press.

Girard, Rafael. 1958. *Indios selvaticos de la Amazonía Peruana.* Mexico City: Libro Mex.

Gow, Peter. 1991. *Of Mixed Blood: Kinship and History in Peruvian Amazonia.* Oxford: Clarendon Press.

Gray, Andrew. 1997. *Indigenous Rights and Development: Self-Determination in an Amazonian Community.* Providence: Berghahn Books.

Haraway, Donna. 1989. *Primate Visions: Gender, Race, and Nature in the World of Modern Science.* New York: Routledge.

Heise, María, Lilian Landeo, and Astrid Bant. 1999. *Relaciones de género en la Amazonía peruana.* Lima: CAAAP.

Heise Mondino, María, and Lilian Landeo del Pino. 1996. *Relaciones de género en la Amazonía peruana.* Lima: CAAAP.

Hendricks, Janet Wall. 1988. Power and Knowledge: Discourse and Ideological Transformation among the Shuar. *American Ethnologist* 15 (1): 87–103.

Herlihy, Peter. 1997. Indigenous Peoples and Biosphere Reserve Conservation in the Mosquitia Rain Forest Corridor, Honduras. In *Conservation through Cultural Survival,* edited by S. Stevens, 99–129. Washington, D.C.: Island Press.

Hill, Jonathan. 1996. Introduction: Ethnogenesis in the Americas, 1492–1992. In *History, Power, and Identity: Ethnogenesis in the Americas, 1492–1992,* edited by J. Hill, 1–19. Iowa City: University of Iowa Press.

Hugh-Jones, Stephen. 1993. Clear Descent or Ambiguous Houses: A Reexamination of Tukanoan Social Organisation. *L'Homme* 33 (2–4): 95–120.

Inoash Shawit, Gil. 1997. Perspectivas generales de la situación indígena. In *Desarrollo y participación de las Comunidades Nativas: Retos y posibilidades,* 65–73. Lima: Defensoría del Pueblo/CAAAP.

Instituto Nacional de Estadística e Informática (INEI). 1997a. *Encuesta demográfica y de salud familar, 1996: Resumen.* Lima: INEI.

———. 1997b. *Población, Mujer y Salud.* Lima: INEI.

Jackson, Jean. 1989. Is There a Way to Talk about Making Culture without Making Enemies? *Dialectical Anthropology* 14:127–43.

———. 1994. Becoming Indians: The Politics of Tukanoan Ethnicity. In *Amazonian Indians: From Prehistory to the Present,* edited by A. Roosevelt, 383–406. Tucson: University of Arizona.

———. 1995. Culture, Genuine and Spurious: The Politics of Indianness in the Vaupés, Colombia. *American Ethnologist* 22 (1): 3–27.

Johnson, A., and O. Johnson. 1975. Male/Female Relations and the Organization of Work in a Machiguenga Community. *American Ethnologist* 2: 634–48.

Kane, Stephanie. 1994. *The Phantom Gringo Boat: Shamanic Discourse and Development in Panama.* Washington, D.C.: Smithsonian Institution Press.

Kearney, Michael. 1996. Indigenous Ethnicity and Mobilization in Latin America. *Latin American Perspectives* 23 (2): 5–17.

Kensinger, Kenneth. 1995. Battle of the Sexes in an Amazonian Society: Changing Gender Relations among the Cashinahua, 1955–1995. Jane Dwyer Memorial Lecture, Haffener Museum of Anthropology, Brown University, Providence, R.I., September 24.

————. 1997. Cambio de perspectives sobre las relaciones de género entre los Cashinahua desde 1955 a 1994. In *Complementariedad entre hombre y mujer: Relaciones de género desde la perspectiva amerindia,* edited by M. Perrin and M. Perruchon, 109–40. Quito: Abya-Yala.

Knauft, Bruce. 1997. Gender Identity, Political Economy, and Modernity in Melanesia and Amazonia. *Journal of the Royal Anthropological Institute,* n.s., 3:233–59.

————. 1999. *From Primitive to Postcolonial in Melanesia and Anthropology.* Ann Arbor: University of Michigan Press.

Kondo, Dorinne. 1990. *Crafting Selves: Power, Gender, and Discourses of Identity in a Japanese Workplace.* Chicago: University of Chicago Press.

Kracke, Waud, ed. 1993. *Leadership in Lowland South America.* South American Indian Studies. Bennington, Vt.: Bennington College.

Kramer, Betty-Jo. 1979. Urarina Economy and Society: Tradition and Change. Ph.D. diss., Columbia University.

Langdon, E. Jean Matteson. 1984. Sex and Power in Siona Society. In *Sexual Ideologies in Lowland South America,* edited by K. M. Kensinger, 16–23. Working Papers on South American Indians, no. 5. Bennington, Vt.: Bennington College.

Leon, Lydia. 1987. AIDESEP—The Inter-ethnic Development Association of the Peruvian Jungle. *Cultural Survival Quarterly* (4): 70.

Maybury-Lewis, David. 1997a. *Indigenous Peoples, Ethnic Groups, and the State.* The Cultural Survival Studies in Ethnicity and Change. Boston: Allyn and Bacon.

————. 1997b. World System, Local Peoples. *Cultural Survival Quarterly* 21 (3): 27–29.

McCallum, C. 1990. Language, Kinship, and Politics in Amazonia. *MAN,* n.s., 25:412–33.

McCormack, C., and M. Strathern, eds. 1980. *Nature, Culture, and Gender.* Cambridge: Cambridge University Press.

McKinley, Michelle. 1994. Contested Exchanges: Habilitación and the Politics of Urarina Social Mobility. Manuscript, Harvard Law School.

————. 1995. Beyond the Indian Question: The Indigenous Social Movement in International Law. Third-year J.D. paper, Harvard Law School.

————. 1997. Life Stories, Disclosure, and the Law. *Political and Legal Anthropology Review* 20 (2): 70–82.

Montoya Rojas, Rodrigo. 1990. *Por una educación bilingüe en el Perú: Reflexiones sobre cultura y socialismo.* Lima: CEPES/Mosca Azul.

————. 1998. *Multiculturalidad y política: Derechos indígenas, ciudadanos y humanos.* Lima: Sur Casa de Estudios de Socialismo.

Moore, Henrietta. 1988. *Feminism and Anthropology.* Minneapolis: University of Minnesota Press.

Morin, Françoise, and Bernard Saladin d'Anglure. 1997. Ethnicity as a Political Tool for Indigenous Peoples. In *The Politics of Ethnic Consciousness,* edited by C. Govers and H. Vermeulen, 157–93. New York: St. Martin's Press.

Muratorio, Blanca. 1998. Indigenous Women's Identities and the Politics of Cultural Reproduction in the Ecuadorian Amazon. *American Anthropologist* 100 (2): 409–20.

Murdock, George P. 1949. *Social Structure.* New York: Macmillan.

Myers, Thomas, and Bartholomew Dean. 1999. Cerámica prehispánica del río Chambira, Loreto. *Amazonía Peruana* 13 (26): 255–88.

Norberg-Schulz, Christian. 1980. *Genius Loci: Towards a Phenomenology of Architecture.* New York: Rizzoli International Publications.

Ong, Aihwa. 1988. Colonialism and Modernity: Feminist Re-presentations of Women in Non-Western Societies. *Inscriptions* 3–4:79–93.

Ortner, Sherry. 1990. Gender Hegemonies. *Cultural Critique* (winter): 35–80.

Povinelli, Elizabeth. 1993. *Labor's Lot: The Power, History, and Culture of Aboriginal Action.* Chicago: University of Chicago Press.

Rival, Laura. 1997. Oil and Sustainable Development in the Latin American Humid Tropics. *Anthropology Today* 13 (6): 1–3.

Roe, Peter. 1995. Arts of the Amazon. In *Arts of the Amazon,* edited by B. Braun. London: Thames and Hudson.

Rojas Zolezzi, and Enrique Carlos. 1992. Concepciones sobre la relación entre géneros: Mito, ritual, y organización del trabajo en la unidad doméstica Campa-Asháninka. *Amazonía Peruana* 22:175–220.

Roldán, Roque, and Ana María Tamayo. 1999. *Legislación y derechos indígenas en el Peru.* Lima: CAAAP/COAMA.

Rose, C. 1988. Crystals and Mud in Property Law. *Stanford Law Review* 40:577.

Rowe, William, and Vivian Schelling. 1991. *Memory and Modernity: Popular Culture in Latin America.* London: Routledge.

Sapir, Edward. 1924. Culture, Genuine and Spurious. *American Journal of Sociology* 29: 401–29.

Sarasara, César. 1997. La defensa de los derechos y el desarrollo sostenible de los pueblos indígenas de la Amazonía Peruana. In *Desarrollo y participación de las Comunidades Nativas: Retos y posibilidades,* 75–86. Lima: Defensoría del Pueblo/CAAAP.

Sawyer, Suzana. 1996. Indigenous Initiatives and Petroleum Politics in the Ecuadorian Amazon. *Cultural Survival Quarterly* 20 (1): 26–30.

Seymour-Smith, C. 1991. Women Have No Affines and Men No Kin: The Politics of the Jivaroan Gender Relation. *MAN,* n.s., 26:629–49.

Siskind, Janet. [1973] 1977. *To Hunt in the Morning.* New York: Oxford University Press.

Smith, Richard Chase. 1984. Amazonian Indians Participate at UN. *Cultural Survival Quarterly* 8:29–31.

———. 1996. Las politicas de la diversidad: COICA y las Federaciones Etnicas de la Amazonía. In *Pueblos indios, soberanía y globalismo,* edited by S. Varese. Quito: Abya-Yala.

Smith, R. C., C. Tapuy, and N. Wray. 1996. *Amazonía: Economía indígena y mercado: Los desafíos del desarrollo autónomo.* Quito: Coordinadora de as Organizaciones Indígenas de la Cuenca Amazónica and Oxfam America.

Sponsel, Leslie. 1995. Relationships among the World System, Indigenous Peoples, and Ecological Anthropology in the Endangered Amazon. In *Indigenous Peoples and the Future of Amazonia,* edited by L. Sponsel, 263–93. Tucson: University of Arizona Press.

Stephen, Lynn. 1995. Women's Rights Are Human Rights: The Merging of Feminine and Feminist Interests among El Salvador's Mothers of the Disappeared (CO-MADRES). *American Ethnologist* 22:807–27.

Strathern, Marilyn. 1987. An Awkward Relationship: The Case of Feminisms and Anthropology. *Signs* 12:276–92.

Tamayo Herrera, José. 1998. *Liberalismo, indigenismo y violencia en los países andinos (1850–1995).* Lima: Universidad de Lima.

Tessmann, Günther. [1930] 1987. Los Simacos. Partial translation of *Die Indianer Nordost-Perus.* In *Bibliografía etnolingüística Urarina,* edited by J. Cajas Rojas, et al. Lima: Instituto de Lingüística Aplicada (CILA), Universidad Nacional Mayor de San Marcos.

Tice, Karin. 1995. *Kuna Crafts, Gender, and the Global Economy.* Austin: University of Texas Press.

Townsley, Graham. 1994. Los Yaminahua. In *Guía etnográfica de la Alta Amazonía,* edited by F. Santos and F. Barclay, 241–361. Quito: FLACSO/IFEA.

Tsing, Anna Lowenhaupt. 1993. *In the Realm of the Diamond Queen: Marginality in an Out-of-the-Way Place.* Princeton: Princeton University Press.

Uriarte, Luis. 1985. Los nativos y su teritorio: El caso de los Jívaro Achuara en la Amazonía Peruana. *Amazonia Peruana* 6 (11): 39–64.

Varese, Stefano. 1972. *The Forest Indians in the Present Political Situation of Peru.* IWGIA Document 8. Copenhagen: International Work Group for Indigenous Affairs.

———. 1996a. The Ethnopolitics of Indian Resistance in Latin America. *Latin American Perspectives* 23 (2): 58–72.

———. 1996b. The New Environmentalist Movement of Latin American

Indigenous People. In *Valuing Local Knowledge: Indigenous People and Intellectual Property Rights,* edited by S. Brush and D. Stabinsky, 122–42. Washington, D.C.: Island Press.

Veber, Hanne. 1997. Pájaros Pintados: Complementaridad entre hombres y mujeres en la vision de los Ashéninka del Gran Pajonal. In *Complementariedad entre hombre y mujer: Relaciones de género desde la perspectiva amerindia,* edited by M. Perrin and M. Perruchon, 125–40. Quito: Abya-Yala.

Whitten, Norman. 1996. The Ecuadorian Levantamiento Indígena of 1990 and the Epitomizing Symbol of 1992: Reflections on Nationalism, Ethnic-Bloc Formation, and Racialist Ideologies. In *History, Power, and Identity: Ethnogenesis in the Americas, 1492–1992,* edited by J. Hill, 193–217. Iowa City: University of Iowa Press.

Wigley, Mark. 1992. Untitled: The Housing of Gender. In *Sexuality and Space,* edited by B. Colomina. Princeton Papers on Architecture. New York: Princeton Architectural Press.

8 Indigenous Rights and Representations in Northern Mexico: The Diverse Contexts of Rarámuri Voice and Silence

Jerome M. Levi

> Then the gods searched for silence in order to reorient them-
> selves, but they could not find it anywhere; they did not know
> where it had gone. And the gods became desperate because they
> could not find the silence which held the path, and so in an
> assembly of gods they came to an agreement, which was very
> difficult because of all the noise. They finally agreed that each
> should seek a silence in order to find themselves, and they began
> to look to the sides and could find nothing above and there was
> nothing below, and since there was no other place to find the
> silence, they looked inside themselves, and there they sought
> silence and found it there and found one another and found
> their path once again, those great gods who birthed the world,
> the first ones.
> —EZLN spokesman Subcomandante Marcos,
> February 14, 1997

> The Tarahumara is not by nature a talkative person. Even at
> gatherings, such as the Sunday meeting, the men sit around at
> some distance from each other and say little.
> —Wendall C. Bennett and Robert M. Zingg (1935, 187)

As the North American Free Trade Agreement (NAFTA) went into effect on January 1, 1994, Maya Indians in the southern Mexican state of Chiapas burst onto the global scene, making the international media flock to the same part of the world that had captivated tourists, bohemians, and anthropologists for decades. Landless Maya and

255

other peasants emerged as rebel insurgents, members of the Zapatista
Army of National Liberation (EZLN), struggling for recognition and
their rights—for dignity, land, and inclusion in a political process from
which they had long been marginalized (Burgete Cal y Mayor 2000;
Collier and Quaratiello 1994; Gossen 1994, 1999; Harvey 1998; Levi
2000, 2002; Nash 1997, 2001; Rus 1994; Stephen 1997b, 1997c, 1999,
2002; Wilson 1998).

Discourse about the identity and rights of Mexico's indigenous peoples, who are stereotypically associated with the south, is also crucial
for understanding the north. Yet with the notable exception of the
Yaqui, who have been a prominent force in Sonoran politics for more
than a century (Hu-Dehart 1984; McGuire 1986; Molina 2000; Spicer
1985), indigenous peoples of northern Mexico have been relatively
invisible actors in the political arena. As David Frye (1996, 1–6)
observes, they typically are portrayed as wholly extinct, as in northeastern Mexico, or as traditionalists residing in a few refuge regions in
the deserts and mountains of the northwest. The Tarahumara—or
Rarámuri, as they call themselves—are the largest indigenous group in
Mexico north of the capital, with a population of approximately seventy thousand. They occupy a region that is being impinged upon by
many regional and global forces. Given the current interest in indigenous rights in Mexico, why have we not heard more about the Rarámuri as political actors?

In this essay, I examine the differential visibility of the Rarámuri as
political players at local, state, national, and international levels of representation and suggest some reasons why there exist contradictory
images that alternately mask or reveal their presence at each level. The
Rarámuri generally have remained silent and "invisible" when it comes
to the assertion of their rights, employing various forms of passive
resistance to register their discontent. Recently, however, some individuals and communities have begun speaking out and making their
plight known. I assess the range of responses exhibited by the Rarámuri to the multiple problems facing them and consider the interplay
between silence and voice as political tactics sensitive to multiple contingencies and contexts. Silence is a communicative display that should
be explored and understood in cultural terms, particularly when it has
been elected as a strategy of resistance. When indigenous individuals
and groups begin asserting their rights or start forming coalitions with
others, it is important to make known such efforts to an international
public concerned with their welfare. Among the Rarámuri, diverse
responses to outside encroachment reflect significant cultural varia-

tion. This is often obfuscated by homogenizing nationalist discourses and static ethnographic orientations privileging descriptions of "tradition" over new or hybrid forms of social action.

The Sierra Tarahumara: Portraits and Pressures

Since the late sixteenth century, when the first Europeans entered their territory—a rugged region in southwestern Chihuahua commonly known as the Sierra Tarahumara (see map 8.1)—the Rarámuri have persevered against enormous odds, using multiple social, political, material, and symbolic means for their cultural survival (Levi 2001).[1] During the first part of the colonial period, Rarámuri resisted European expropriation of their land and resources through a series of bellicose rebellions (Merrill 1993; Molinari and Merrill 1995; Sheridan and Naylor 1979). By the eighteenth century, however, their pattern of response to the incursion of outsiders had largely changed to one of passive resistance and geographical retreat into more rugged and geographically isolated terrain. Since then, the Rarámuri have refined techniques of veiled communication as stratagems for their cultural survival (Burgess 1981; Levi 1999b). They have masterfully deployed what James Scott (1990) has called "hidden transcripts," making known their grievances in subtle ways through arts of quiet resistance. Nevertheless, given the critical situation threatening the peoples of the Sierra, the viability of this historically successful Rarámuri survival strategy is being tested in new ways.

The adversaries who have beleaguered the Rarámuri in recent years are many and varied. Environmental pressures in the form of demographic shifts, commercial deforestation, and overgrazing have resulted in ecological degradation and soil erosion. Often the best arable lands in the region have been expropriated by non-Rarámuri, primarily mestizos—known in Rarámuri as Chabochi (Whiskered Ones)—who dominate the region politically, economically, and numerically. Today, the Rarámuri find themselves a minority in their own homelands.

Mining, forestry, and tourism are big businesses in the Sierra Tarahumara, providing opportunities for some but difficulties for others. Silver and gold deposits—the proverbial "treasure of the Sierra Madre," which fired the imaginations of colonial Spaniards and Hollywood filmmakers—continue to attract multinational mining firms to the western canyons. For instance, around Basaseachic, 150 mining projects were being developed in 1997 by the Tonto, Peñoles, and Fresnillos mining companies.[2] The spectacular mines scattered through the

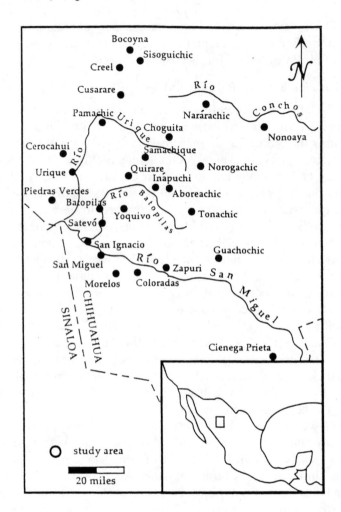

Map 8.1.   Sierra Tarahumara in southwest Chihuahua, northern Mexico

Batopilas canyon, deep in the Sierra Tarahumara, have drawn out-siders since their first silver bonanza in the 1740s. Rarámuri will occa-sionally pan in the rivers, but most avoid mining operations and dis-avow knowledge of the many defunct mines in the gorges. This is hardly surprising, given a past in which mineral-rich veins often meant that either Rarámuri land or labor was required for Chabochi-owned mines.

Although mining historically has been the main economic activity in the Sierra, logging has become increasingly important. The state of Chihuahua is now the leading producer of wood in Mexico. While a source of revenue, extractive forestry has been a major source of conflict for the Rarámuri, who too often have been cheated in the removal of their timber (Lartigue 1983; Petrich 1996a).[3] Roads, originally built for the lumber industry and mineral exploration, now have been improved for passenger travel. The once isolated region is today accessible via a major road-building project known as the Gran Visión, a highway system totaling 911 kilometers in and about the Sierra Tarahumara (González Rodríguez 1985, 20). Meanwhile, new logging roads and dirt tracks to mining sites fan out to distant reaches of the Rarámuri's homeland. The opening of new roads in the Sierra is a mixed blessing for the Rarámuri. On the one hand, roads provide new arteries of communication to remote communities; on the other, they facilitate exploitation of the Rarámuri's natural resources.

The Rarámuri's problems, however, have not been confined to encroachments on their lands. Even the sky has not been giving in recent years. During the last decade of the twentieth century, the Sierra suffered the worst drought in living memory. Many Rarámuri blamed the drought on the wholesale logging that was robbing the mountains of their pine forests. Rarámuri regard these pines as the highlands' sacred sentinels that annually call the rains, thus restoring a green mantle each summer to *wichimoba,* "the surface of the earth." I often heard Rarámuri elders say that as the forests disappear, the land and its people will grow increasingly thirsty. By 1999, the severity of the drought compelled Mexico to declare Chihuahua, as well as four other northern states, disaster zones. In the Sierra, where Rarámuri maintain themselves as subsistence farmers, the situation was desperate. To combat malnutrition—especially acute among children under five— famine relief from domestic and international organizations such as the UN's World Food Program remains vital to many Rarámuri communities (Petrich 1996b).

Conflicting reports over whether the number of Rarámuri deaths caused by the drought was a double- or triple-digit annual figure became a political football between federal authorities and the opposition-party state government in Chihuahua (Darling 1994; Prado Calahorra 1998; Robles 1996).[4] When news of starvation and startling death tolls appeared in the international press (DePalma 1994; Marks 1994), *Los Angeles Times* correspondent Juanita Darling astutely observed that the Rarámuri's plight had the same deeper significance as the uprising in the southern state of Chiapas: "How can a nation aspiring to be a world power, and presumably proud of its rich pre-colonial heritage address the dire poverty of its indigenous population numbering about 8 million?" (Darling 1994, 2).

The seizure of Rarámuri lands for illegal logging or to grow marijuana and opium poppies has been reported widely in numerous venues (Alvarado Licón 1996; Burnett and Raimond 1996; DePalma 1995; Estrada Martínez and Vega Carrillo 1993; Salopek 1989, 1996; Shoumatoff 1995; Raat and Janacek 1996; Weinberg 1998; Weisman 1994).[5] Environmental and human rights activists advocating on behalf of the Rarámuri have been attacked, outspoken indigenous leaders killed, and some logging companies allegedly operated as fronts for laundering profits from illicit crops (Hitt and Gingrich 1995). Military blockades and patrols have been active in the Sierra since the 1980s, but their growing presence and their intimidation of indigenous people have prompted protests from local priests, bishops, and human rights organizations (Alvarez 1998; Romero Ruíz and Villapapando 1996). According to the president of the National Commission on Human Rights for the State of Chihuahua, whom I interviewed in April 1997, Rarámuri are displaced not only because they are physically pushed off their lands, but because their labor is forcibly co-opted for the purposes of cultivation. Given this environment of fear, it is not surprising that some Rarámuri are abandoning their homes.[6]

Not all portraits of the region, however, are as grim as the one I have painted. Since the completion of the Chihuahua al Pacifico Railway in 1961, the Sierra Tarahumara has been depicted as a site for visitors searching for "unspoiled" places off the beaten path (Fabricant 1997; Myerson 1997; Schwartzman and Melia 1996). Besides cultural attractions, the region has spectacular canyons that lure tourists from around the world. Calls for conservation and management of the prominent biological diversity of the Sierra Tarahumara, which includes both tropical dry forests at the lower elevations and the "sky islands" of conifer-oak forests in the highlands, are gaining increasing support from the scientific community (Bye 1994, 1995, 1997) as well as the tourist industry (Fisher 1996). Promotion of ecotourism and the creation of a biosphere reserve have been discussed. For the Rarámuri, tourism provides another source of income through handicraft sales (Burns 1996; Levi 1992; Sheridan 1996) and the occasional collection of small entry fees at designated sites. Unlike environmentally degrading extractive industries such as mining and forestry, tourism has potential benefits, although if implemented without cooperation from the local community, it too may become exploitative. Respect for Rarámuri customs is also sometimes compromised, especially during Christmas and Easter celebrations, when droves of tourists descend on Rarámuri villages to witness the dramatic ceremonies.[7]

In the absence of electoral clout, economic prowess, or military might, the "symbolic capital" accompanying the visual display of indigenous identities, via the ethnic badge of "traditional" body imagery, represents one of the most influential political resources available to indigenous peoples—in the Sierra Tarahumara and elsewhere (Conklin 1997). It, too, is easily co-opted by others. The attractiveness of the visually striking but politically passive Rarámuri has made the Sierra Tarahumara a customary stopover on political campaigns. The photograph of a politician alongside a group of Rarámuri community leaders dressed in traditional headbands, loincloths, and distinctive puffy-sleeved shirts signals indigenous endorsement. Here, indigenes constitute a conspicuous sector of the rural poor in Mexico's postcolonial "imagined community" (Anderson 1991). Superficial but symbolically important encounters such as these between Rarámuri and party candidates for high office also represent a low-risk political gesture toward an indigenous people who until recently were unable or unwilling to press their demands. Commenting on this, several residents in Chihuahua City told me that in their opinion, Rarámuri had become valuable chiefly as a "political banner" for Mexican politicians.

Each of these portraits of the Sierra Tarahumara—a volatile site of drought, drugs, and hardship; a land rich in forests, minerals, and economic opportunities; and a tourist destination encapsulated in stable worlds of unparalleled natural beauty, picturesque Indians, and colonial charm—strives for dominance. Such divergent visions of the region have caused the international media to shine an interested spotlight on formerly hidden recesses within some of North America's deepest and most serpentine canyons. The Rarámuri themselves, however, have seldom sought this publicity. Although rebellions are not unknown among them (Boudreau 1986; Neumann 1991; Sheridan and Naylor 1979), far more common has been their practice of withdrawing—but today there is no place left for them to go. Not surprisingly, some Rarámuri have decided they can no longer struggle in silence. Instead, one now encounters a range of responses to the global forces impinging on the Sierra.

Interest in the human rights of Mexico's indigenous peoples has been growing in recent years, and there have been several works that discuss these issues among the Rarámuri from historical or legal perspectives (Estrada Martínez and Vega Carrillo 1993; González Rodríguez et al. 1994; Molinari and Merrill 1995; Robles O. and Vallejo N. 1995). Little attention, however, has been paid to the diverse stratagems employed by contemporary Rarámuri in responding to adversity. Analyzing the relationship between environmental problems and human rights worldwide, Barbara Rose Johnston notes that there exists a continuum of "responses to human environmental crises that include: passive resistance (efforts to renegotiate conditions in subtle ways), organized efforts to adjust to conditions and effect change within existing systems, confrontational and violent efforts aimed at transforming both conditions and structures of power, and efforts to rebuild in the aftermath of structural transformations of power" (1997, 330). Not only has each of these responses been evidenced in the Sierra Tarahumara, but, just as there exist different types of responses, so too are there different ways in which these responses are displayed, either by the people themselves or by others. Much of the indigenous rights literature either relies on a homogenizing discourse that does not theorize the variety of a people's responses given different contexts and contingencies or, conversely, manages to capture ethnographic particularities but does so with a politically loaded terminology. Commenting on this dilemma in the indigenous rights discourse, Andrew Gray suggests that "[p]ossibly a task for the future is to build a new decolonized vocabulary which reflects particular contexts and circumstances" (1997, 131).

Silence as Cultural Resistance, Reproduction, and Self-Representation

James Weiner (1997, 1999) astutely observes that among many indigenous peoples—particularly in Melanesia, North America, and Australia—culturally appropriate modalities of communication often require them to conceal, rather than reveal, certain kinds of knowledge as a demonstration of political agency and cultural competence. When indigenous people represent themselves in testimonials, organize protests, or avail themselves of modern media, "Western" understandings automatically see empowerment, political assertion, and cultural vitality reflected in these activities (Ginsburg 1997). Yet we seldom consider that such displays sometimes may obscure the very conventions of self-representation and cultural reproduction that we as anthropologists seek to understand. Our job, therefore, is to attend more closely to the "hidden transcripts" (Scott 1990), detecting political agency not only by what is seen and said, but also by what is sequestered and kept quiet, in ellipses and veiled allusions, and all those contexts where the retention of knowledge is the mark of power and virtue. Indeed, this is precisely why we have called our edited collection *At the Risk of Being Heard,* for the phrase expresses the paradoxical predicament that, in our media-saturated world, many indigenous peoples are having to break traditions in order to keep them.

Silence is a particularly noteworthy aspect of the Rarámuri's response to the encroaching "outside world." It is not just the meaningless absence of sound, but a *transmissive* modality of resistance guided by cultural insiders. Not being contingent on attracting the support or attention of citizens, groups, or coalitions outside the immediate region, this tactic of cultural maintenance and conflict management is historically grounded in local conventions of social performance, interaction, or avoidance.

That silence marks culturally meaningful behavior is illustrated by studies from many perspectives.[8] Significantly, recent struggles for indigenous autonomy in Mexico have been marked not only by vocal demands for the recognition of indigenous rights and cultures, but also by a political appreciation of quiescence. Imposed by the indigenous leaders of the EZLN, the intermittent use of silence as a weapon has been an important component of the organization's strategy since its inception. The most noteworthy example of this came between March and July 1998, when no word came from Subcomandante Marcos—spokesman for the EZLN, who normally issued several communiqués each month—giving rise to speculations that the rebels may have been disbanding. Then, breaking six months of silence, Marcos issued several communiqués making clear that rather than preparing for surrender, they instead had been gathering inner strength. The Fifth Declaration of the Lacandón Jungle constitutes one of the most eloquent statements on the conscious use of silence as a form of military and political resistance. In it, Marcos makes explicit how, incorporating defensive techniques of the indigenous peoples themselves, the EZLN confused the government by confronting its lies and weapons with their decisive use of "silences as soldiers" and a quiet that became "a protective wall." Moreover, according to Marcos, the silence enabled them better to listen, watch, and organize "from below," while at the same time preserving their dignity—in contradistinction to the government's shameless deceit and continuing mendacity.

For the analysis of indigenous rights, the relevant point is the recognition that in addition to speech, silence is also deployed situationally as a strategy of communication, and even resistance. It sometimes is a group's socially preferred form of interaction as a sociolinguistic code used in unpredictable contexts or to manage emotion or conflict (Basso 1970; Saunders 1985; Sommer 1991; Tannen 1985, 1990). Moreover, although silence is usually considered to be a sign of powerlessness and passivity, it can also be deployed strategically, according to Susan Gal (1991, 176), "as subversive defense and even political protest," especially in situations when people normally are expected to speak (see also Bauman 1983; Herzfeld 1991; Trosset 1996; and Warren 1993). Consequently, such responses need to be not only respected, but understood as tactical displays directed by cultural insiders sensitive to the contextual cues dictating which among various responses is the most appropriate to a particular setting. Awareness of the context-dependent dialectic between speech and silence enhances understanding of indigenous rights discourse.

Given palpable differences in local histories, environments, educational levels, and intensities of interaction with, or separation from, organs of church, state, and formal political economy, there exists substantial variation among Rarámuri communities, and among individuals within those communities, as to what constitutes the best form of response to adversity. Representations of a static and homogenous Rarámuri culture, therefore, not only amount to dated, overgeneralized stereotypes but conceal the political significance of internal cultural diversity (Kummels 2001). In fact, the absence of a united front among the Rarámuri reflects the empirical reality of geographical dispersion, flexible political structure, regional variation, and economic self-reliance (Levi 1998), which these people have likewise relied upon as everyday forms of resistance and stratagems for their continued survival. Taking this variation into account, I now turn to a discussion of the diverse contexts in which one observes the tactical manipulation of Rarámuri voice and silence.

The Cultural Construction of Silence and Voice at the Local Level

Ethnographers have remarked that, outside of ritual drinking contexts, Rarámuri interpersonal styles are quiet and withdrawn, especially, though not exclusively, when interacting with mestizos (Bennett and Zingg 1935; Champion 1962, 503; Kennedy 1996, 256; Lumholtz 1902). During the course of my own fieldwork, on many occasions Rarámuri were quite talkative, yet on others I, too, found them to be taciturn, shy, or reserved.[9] I was particularly struck by this latter behavior when I saw it manifested in their passive resignation toward and acceptance of abuses committed against them and in their reluctance to report injustices to mestizo authorities. For example, during one period, Rarámuri I knew were being made to sell livestock against their will to mestizos. Rarámuri talked among themselves about how the latter were "thieves" (*chigórame*) who took their sheep and goats at unfair prices. When I suggested that the situation be brought to the attention of municipal authorities, Rarámuri responded by preferring not to lodge a complaint. On another occasion in a neighboring community, I learned that Rarámuri were being charged grazing fees by a local political boss (*cacique*) to pasture their animals on their own land. When I suggested that a complaint be registered with suitable government institutes or nongovernmental organizations (NGOs), my Rarámuri companions felt that, for the time being, it was best to remain silent. On these and other occasions, I followed the lead of my Rarámuri interlocutors and refrained from reporting the injustices to the appropriate agencies. I was, however, frustrated, because I wondered whether my silence, like theirs, was unwittingly empowering the very forces that were victimizing the Rarámuri.

I eventually learned that Rarámuri employ silence among themselves as a discourse strategy in a wide range of situations that often have nothing at all to do with passivity or reticence to take political action. I noticed that silence was associated with emotional comfort or ease as friends and relatives would sit for long periods beside each other without uttering a word, quietly waiting for an event or silently working on their own projects. I had the impression that, confident in their relationships, they did not need to push words between them in order to keep each other company. Here, silence was referencing social intimacy. At other times, silence was observed as a way to manage conflict or volatile emotions, often in situations of great ambiguity or deep unpredictability. Rarámuri are noticeably silent when they meet strangers, even if they are other Rarámuri. Similarly, when going visiting or trading, people will customarily wait some distance from the house before approaching. After being invited forward, they will pause until they are enjoined to converse with the residents. Silence is also used as a way of showing deference or marking status. People refrain from speaking to someone involved in a curing ceremony (Levi 1999a) or while authorities deliver sermons (*nawésari*). The positive evaluation Rarámuri give silence is corroborated by the observations of others. According to Romayne Wheeler, if a Rarámuri person "feels drawn to someone, he also knows he can remain silent with him. For the Rarámuri, someone who talks too much is regarded as untrustworthy and is branded as a gossip for the rest of his life. They say of him that a cricket jumped into his mouth when he was a child and has remained on his tongue for his entire life" (1993, 132).

Indeed, Rarámuri regard highly a person's ability to maintain an emotional state they describe as *kirí,* meaning still, quiet, leisurely, or calm. Similarly, normative behavior was modeled through noninvolvement with a person unable to control his or her emotions. Instead of scolding fussy children, parents more often tended to silently ignore the scene caused by a cranky child, just as troublesome adults were likewise sanctioned by being shunned by other community members. Rarámuri regard for personal autonomy, social distance, and the desire not to be imposed upon by others is eloquently manifested not only in their dispersed settlement pattern and loose sociopolitical organization, but also in the way nonverbal communication is structured through what Erving Goffman (1967) has termed avoidance rituals. By unobtrusively pointing with one's chin or lips, avoiding eye contact, speaking back-to-back, averting one's face, or picking at an object while talking, Rarámuri structure interaction through gestures of nonconfrontation. Whereas non-Rarámuri may interpret Rarámuri who use these behaviors as being secretive, withdrawn, or shy, Rarámuri say these are ways of being polite and showing respect, a point that also has been made by Don Burgess (1981, 14).

These instances represent Rarámuri use of silence and minimal interaction as conventions for the management of deference, emotion, conflict, or uncertainty. As a political strategy, this cultural style was most notably evidenced in the first cases I described, in which Rarámuri chose to absent themselves from channels of power. The following case, conversely, illustrates the visible reappropriation of Rarámuri identity and voice in its ostensible absence.

In the village of Satevó, some mestizos now emphasize their racial and cultural hybridity, as well as grinding poverty, which link them with the Rarámuri who reside in the nearby mountains. The formerly denigrated and submerged Rarámuri branches of their genealogies are now being reclaimed. Their town is a colonial Rarámuri mission that gradually "whitened" over the years through intermarriage. Some elders of the town, however, point out that their grandparents spoke Rarámuri and dressed in indigenous garb. More importantly, the residents of Satevó still collaborate with Rarámuri neighbors to coproduce dances and rituals focused on their ancient church, yielding a distinctive bi-ethnic religious syncretism unlike that of mestizo or Rarámuri communities located elsewhere in the Sierra.

When the peasants of Satevó request famine relief because the

Fig. 8.1.   A ritual venue for the negotiation of interethnic relations. Mestizos (carrying staffs) and Rarámuri (painted black)
collaborate in the performance of Holy Week ceremonies in the
village of Satevó. (Photograph by Jerome Levi.)

drought parched their cornfields as much as the Rarámuri's, or when
they say they deserve a clinic because they are closer to the Rarámuri,
indigenous rights activists must be cautious not to essentialize cultural differences. Mestizos argue that they have rights too, and
whether *mestizaje* is viewed conventionally as racial mixing or more
radically as ethnocidal "de-Indianization" (Bonfil Batalla 1990,
73–96), drawing sharp boundaries between indigenous people and
their congeners is an invidious task. This has sometimes posed a
problem for "separatist" indigenous rights discourse in Mexico, as
rightly noted in the literature (Gledhill 1997, 96; Gómez 1995, 28–55;
Stephen 1997c), as well as in other regions of the world, given the
ambiguities implicit in defining who is indigenous (Béteille 1998;
Maybury-Lewis 1997, 1–57). Satevó's revaluation of its "Indianness"
is attributable to many forces. Some of these may be economic
motives, since indigenous identity alignments potentially entitle
claimants to periodic material assistance in the Sierra Tarahumara.
But Satevó's willingness to reconsider its indigenity also coincides

with national political trends. That is, it is also a local refraction of the country's recent determination to be a "pluricultural" nation, which officially recognizes indigenous communities in the 1990 reforms to Article 4 of the Mexican constitution (Estrada Martínez and González Guerra 1995, 9), even though these changes have been criticized as vague or superficial (Díaz Polanco 1997, 130–32).

While some Sierra mestizos are beginning to use their hybrid ethnicity instrumentally as a political resource, many Rarámuri continue to hide themselves from the sources of state-based power. However, in other districts—where Rarámuri have experienced more exposure to state bureaucratic government, as well as a more embedded history of relationships with the church, tourism, and the lumber industry—Rarámuri are not only speaking out, but they are also actively seeking access to political offices normally held by mestizos. One example is the highland community of Cusárare, which maintains close ties with the Jesuits who founded the pueblo more than 250 years ago. A twenty-minute ride from Creel, a major commercial center for the Sierra, Cusárare leases a parcel of communal land to outside administrators for the operation of a riverside tourist lodge in its pine-studded highlands. In addition to tourism, the forests of Cusárare have attracted the lumber industry, with the community enduring the presence of a sawmill that has benefited investors in paper mills outside the Sierra far more than the Rarámuri whose resources supply it. The exploitation of the local forest by national and transnational interests helped María Elena Quintero become the first Rarámuri woman ever to seek the office of *comisaría ejidal* (commissioner of the local agrarian reform community). Her political position is simple yet powerful. Asserting that Rarámuri are capable of administrating their own natural resources, she wants to rectify a situation in which her people have been absent from those bureaucratic bodies—such as the Secretary of Agriculture and Hydraulic Resources (SARH) and the State Coordinating Office of the Tarahumara (CET)—whose agencies have planned and benefited from the utilization of the Rarámuri's forest. Community support for her position was demonstrated on February 13, 1997, when local Rarámuri closed the sawmill for fifteen days until police removed them (Gil Olmos 1997).

While some Rarámuri are absenting themselves from political arenas, then, others are voicing their concerns through political mobilization. Meanwhile, some local mestizos are reflecting on their own hybrid ethnicity, reappraising what value there may be in situationally claiming Rarámuri or indigenous identity.

Representations at the State Level

Similar counterprocesses that alternately mask or reveal a Rarámuri presence are also evident at the level of the state. In April 1997, I met in Chihuahua City with the state directors of the National Indigenous Institute (INI), the National Institute of Anthropology and History (INAH), and the National Commission of Human Rights (CNDH) in order to gain a clearer understanding of the conflicting information I was getting about the current difficulties the Rarámuri were facing. Each representative demonstrated genuine concern and outlined effective programs for their Rarámuri constituencies, and while each agency approached the issues from its own unique perspective, shedding light on different facets of a difficult situation, overall I came away with a better sense of how these complexities were being manifested at the level of the state.

Most scholarship and national and international media have conventionally defined the plight of the Rarámuri as a rural problem. Geographically, this makes sense, because the Sierra is still where most Rarámuri live. Nevertheless, this focus on the countryside runs the risk of perpetuating romantic and reified visions of Mexican "Indian tradition," consequently blinding us from recognizing a different Rarámuri population—one that is urban and steadily growing (Urteaga 1993). For many years, some Rarámuri have followed a pattern of seasonal migration to nearby cities, including the state capital, often during winter and times of hunger. But customarily they returned to their homes in the mountains for the Easter ceremonial and the beginning of the summer planting season.[10]

Now, however, there are three permanent colonies of Rarámuri in Chihuahua City and another population of Rarámuri as far north as Ciudad Juárez, on the Mexican-U.S. border across from El Paso, Texas. Yet even in these urban centers, the Rarámuri are managing to survive culturally, replicating in miniature social organizations that characterized their life in the Sierra. One of the colonies in Chihuahua recently chose its own *siríame,* or "indigenous governor," as if it were a traditional pueblo in the Sierra. Other customary practices have fared less well in the city, however. They have become, like many things in late modernity (Appadurai 1996), simulations rather than conventionally grounded forms of sociality. The increased alienation of life in the city can only be offset through more strenuous attempts at cultural intimacy. Whereas in the Sierra Rarámuri gather for large occasions only periodically, in Chihuahua about a hundred now congregate every weekend to run races, visit, and drink. Furthermore, I learned that rather than imbibing *tesguino,* their sacred fermented maize beer, urban Rarámuri now consume bottles of commercial beer and hard liquor, drinking it in prodigious amounts as if it were their own traditional low-alcohol beverage—a change inviting the possibility of health and other risks.

How many Rarámuri are urban dwellers? Some of the agencies I spoke with estimated that there was a permanent population of several thousand Rarámuri in the state capital.[11] Estimates indicate that nearly one-fourth of the Rarámuri population was living outside the Sierra by 1980, most of them having settled in just two cities. In addition to the thousands of Rarámuri who are now urban dwellers, the indigenous agencies in Chihuahua informed me that there is a floating population of approximately seven hundred Rarámuri in the state capital without any fixed residence. The INI responded by recently constructing for these people thirty-four *asentamientos irregulares,* or shelters, with forty people housed in each.

Why are ever more Rarámuri coming to the cities, and why is the rest of the world unaware of their existence there despite a heightened concern for the welfare of this ethnic group? Like other Mexican peasants, they are drawn to cities by the prospect of finding markets for their handicrafts or work as laborers in construction, in factories, or in domestic service. In recent years, a combination of ecological degradation, unrelenting hunger, and pervasive fear has driven large numbers of Rarámuri from their homes. These are "environmental refugees"— constituting a little-recognized but growing category of displaced persons who are caught between environmental change and violent conflict in developing regions throughout the world (see Homer-Dixon, Boutwell, and Rathjens 1993; Swain 1996; and Westing 1992).

Not all Rarámuri, however, are invisible occupants of marginal urban landscapes. Some are coming explicitly to be seen and heard—as happened in Chihuahua City on May 19, 1997. Clearly, this was not the first time Rarámuri had come to demonstrate in front of government offices in the state capital, but it was the first time in more than twenty years that indigenous demands for human rights had met with such aggressive force from a Chihuahua government. On that day, about one hundred indigenous people—Rarámuri as well as Tepehuan— came to the capital from the community of Monterde in the western Sierra seeking an audience with Governor Francisco Barrio, a member of the opposition PAN (Partido Acción Nacional, or National Action Party) (Desaloja la policía 1997). They wanted him to intercede on their behalf with the state office of the federal attorney general (Procuraduría General de la República, or PGR), which had failed to investigate claims filed six months earlier against a local cacique, or rural political boss, accused of having stolen indigenous lands. When there was still no response from state authorities after three days, an indigenous delegation was sent to the PGR office demanding the resignation of the attorney general. Meanwhile, outside the attorney general's office, the demonstrators blocked traffic on one of the main thoroughfares in Chihuahua until the order came for the protesters to be removed by force.

The ensuing confrontation lasted more than an hour. Protesters defended themselves with rocks as they were gassed and brutally attacked by the judicial police. Twenty indigenous people were wounded, eleven were hospitalized, and fifty were detained, including children along with their parents. The state directors of the PRI (Partido Revolucionario Institucional, or Institutional Revolutionary Party) and the PRD (Partido de la Revolución Democratica, or Party of the Democratic Revolution) denounced the excessive violence of the state authorities. There also were attempts to limit media coverage. Journalists were beaten, photographs showing Rarámuri bathed in blood were censored in the state press, and a reporter accused of having sent photographs of police aggression to *La Jornada* for circulation in the national press was dismissed from her employment with a Chihuahua newspaper (Foto censurada 1997). The events prompted a second protest late the next day, when about three hundred people, including human rights activists, marched to demand the release of the jailed protesters, many of them Rarámuri who spoke no Spanish. In the state of Chihuahua, then, some Rarámuri are finding the courage to break their silence, despite sometimes violent attempts to censure them; equally significant is the fact that even more people are joining these Rarámuri in a chorus of support.

The Nation and Beyond

At national and international levels of representation, one still finds counterprocesses similar to those examined at local and state levels, which alternately mask or reveal Rarámuri identity and rights. In what follows, I cite several examples illustrating both the visibility and invisibility of Rarámuri in supralocal fields of interaction and how they engage in different forms of social display.

One of the most dramatic recent illustrations of the "virtual identity" of the Rarámuri as political players at the national level occurred during the meetings of the National Indigenous Congress (Congreso Nacional Indígena, or CNI) held in Mexico City in October 1996. This is a new national indigenous coalition that evolved from another network—motivated by the experience of the Zapatistas in Chiapas—known as the National Indigenous Convention (Convención Nacional Indígena), which first met in December 1994 (Stephen 1997c, 29). At the 1996 National Indigenous Congress, a man who claimed to be an "adviser" to and "leader" for the Rarámuri called a press conference inside the building where the meetings were being held. Asserting that he was speaking on behalf of the National Indigenous Congress, which he had not been authorized to do, he proceeded to lambaste and denounce the meetings as a subversive and neocommunist attempt at manipulation by outsiders. Furthermore, he added that the Rarámuri wanted nothing to do with such fraud. "We're passive people," he said—before rushing off, saying he was going back to Chihuahua. Rather than representing the sentiments of the Rarámuri people, it is more likely that this individual was a plant of the reigning PRI. By co-opting the Rarámuri's voice and capitalizing on their stereotypic silence, this political ventriloquism allowed him to speak for the government, yet ostensibly through an indigenous people. In any event, the next day the incident was reported in Mexico City daily newspapers with headlines announcing "CNI Un Fracaso!"—that is, the meetings were denounced as a failure. The articles went on to describe the disturbance caused by this one high-profile individual who had walked out, "in the name of" the Rarámuri.[12]

Another perplexing case of differential visibility exists in relation to one of the most vital human rights and environmental agencies assisting the Rarámuri: the Chihuahua-based Advisory Council of the Sierra Madre (Consejo Asesor de la Sierra Madre, A.C., or CASMAC), founded in 1992. Of the nongovernmental agencies working with the Rarámuri, this one is among the best known and most highly regarded outside of Mexico; it has received prestigious awards and funding from environmental agencies, such as the Biodiversity Support Project, managed by the World Wildlife Fund, the Nature Conservancy, and the World Resources Institute. In 1995 CASMAC's founder, Edwin Bustillos, garnered the Condé Nast Environmental Award and was a finalist for the Robert F. Kennedy Human Rights Award; in 1996 he won the Goldman Environmental Prize for North America, the equivalent of a Nobel Prize for environmental activists. Bustillos, along with Randy Gingrich of the Tucson-based Forest Guardians, has worked tirelessly to create broad-based support for the establishment of a biosphere reserve to protect old-growth forests and remote indigenous communities in the Sierra Madre. By April 1996, CASMAC had received proposals from more than thirteen communities wanting to be integrated into the biosphere project. Moreover, Bustillos has spoken at educational and environmental organizations in the United States and has been featured on National Public Radio and television broadcasts, as well as appearing in other interviews with the popular press. It therefore struck me as odd that despite CASMAC's international visibility, the organization seemed to be virtually unknown in Chihuahua itself—with one exception (the Chihuahua office of the National Institute of Anthropology and History (INAH), even among those people and agencies working most closely with the Rarámuri. Perhaps CASMAC's willingness to publicize the threat posed to the Rarámuri's human rights and the environment by the illegal logging and drug business contributed to the organization's apparent invisibility in the eyes of Chihuahua officialdom. To be sure, it is a delicate situation when activists spotlight abuses while the people themselves typically use silence and retreat as forms of protest, even though such passive resistance has evidently become ineffective in some areas—a complex situation of which CASMAC is aware.[13]

Other cases, however, contradict the virtual or hidden existence of Rarámuri identity and rights at national and international levels. Eight months prior to the incident at the 1996 National Indigenous Congress, the Supreme Council of the Tarahumara (Consejo Supremo Tarahumara, an organizatin meant to represent the collective interests of the Rarámuri people at the level of the state and nation), together with the *siríame* of Bocoyna, Chihuahua, joined their signatures with those of hundreds of other indigenous authorities, communities, and organizations in a letter to Mexican president Ernesto Zedillo published in the national press. Urging Zedillo to fulfill his promise as chief of the federal government, the letter stated that on February 16, 1996, the signatories were witnesses to the signing of the first San Andrés Accords on Indigenous Rights and Culture "to reach a peace with justice and dignity between the representatives of the EZLN and the Federal Government" (Rosas Blanco 1996). Furthermore, there were Rarámuri representatives at the 1997 assembly of the National Indigenous Congress as well as Rarámuri marchers who joined the historic Zapatista caravan that entered Mexico City on March 10, 2001.

The discernible presence of Rarámuri as political actors can also be noted in their involvement as candidates in national elections and the publicity these historic races are generating. The May 1997 headline

"Tarahumara Native Runs for Congress" in the *Frontera Norte/Sur,* a monthly electronic news digest covering the borderlands of north-central Mexico, signaled a new and important level of political participation. No longer were Rarámuri using silence and circumvention as forms of political action. Now, at least some of them were assuming full roles as players in the arena of national electoral politics. María Soledad Batista Espino, the first Rarámuri woman to run for the Mexican National Congress, ran in District 3 in Chihuahua State. A candidate for the opposition Green Party (Partido Verde Ecologista Mexicano, or PVEM), Batista already had an impressive record working to defend the rights of her people.[14]

Although Batista ultimately lost in the congressional elections that year, the stage is now set for further displays of political voice at supralocal levels. Whether Rarámuri are participating in the national indigenous movement or as candidates in political parties, what is noteworthy is that they are not making news just as victims of natural disasters or economic machinations. No longer content to passively accept a precarious history at the margins of power, many Rarámuri are now becoming proactive in having a voice in community welfare. As shown by Batista, stratagems using mass media, existing political structures, and emerging social coalitions to assert the rights of indigenous constituencies can create important openings for the participation of other Rarámuri.

In the despatialized and virtually global environment of the Internet (Escobar 1994), one finds a plethora of Web sites claiming to represent the Rarámuri's world. These range from the tourist industry's romantic and enticing portrayals of the Sierra to the disturbing bulletins posted by human rights organizations, environmental institutes, church organizations, and indigenous news groups advocating on the Rarámuri's behalf. Some Web site masters are located in Chihuahua, some in Mexico City, and others in various parts of the United States, especially in the Southwest. All have their own particular vision, agenda, or philosophy about how best to represent the Rarámuri. There are disagreements among these agencies regarding which aspects of the Rarámuri's plight should be highlighted and which should be publicly downplayed. Most, however, have plural alliances allowing them to connect in various ways with each other or with similar groups working toward common goals.

The Jesuit-run Fundación Tarahumara—José A. Llaguno, inspired by the late bishop of Chihuahua, has an extensive Web site that meticulously reports its programs assisting the Rarámuri in the areas of nutrition, education, health, and orchard planting. Although the Committee for Solidarity and Defense of Human Rights (Comisión de Solidaridad y Defensa de los Derechos Humanos, A.C., or COSYD-DHAC)—a Chihuahua-based NGO that has been a zealous watchdog for human rights abuses committed against Rarámuri and other indigenous peoples in the Sierra—does not have its own Web site, it has gained the support of international indigenous rights organizations, such as the South and Meso American Indian Rights Center (SAIIC) in Oakland, California, which regularly posts messages for COSYDDHAC on its own Web site. CASMAC, via its connections with a ramified network of environmental and human rights organizations, has also used the Internet to publicize problems in the Sierra.

Other groups concerned with Rarámuri well-being have also secured a place in cyberspace. The recently formed Sierra Tarahumara Diversity Project, linked with multiple environmental organizations in both the United States and Mexico, looks promising (Maffi 2001). Over the years, Native Seeds/SEARCH of Tucson has taken a leading role in developing environmentally sustainable horticulture and handicraft projects and in curtailing deforestation, joining with others in the early 1990s to block the multimillion-dollar World Bank Sierra Madre Forestry Project loan (see n. 3). Capitalizing on the publicity they received after winning in the Leadville hundred-mile marathon in Colorado in 1993, the Tarahumara Famine Relief and Racing Team, with the aid of their U.S. promoters, have delivered tons of food to Rarámuri communities while reporting on their efforts and soliciting tax deductible contributions in cyberspace. Workers for the Tarahumara Relief Project of the Tucson based Drylands Institute, a research and education organization dedicated to the conservation of plants, animals, and human cultures in arid environments, reached even more remote locales at the height of the 1996 drought. The plight of Rita Quintero, a Rarámuri woman who was found wandering about in Kansas in 1983 and was then held in a mental hospital for twelve years, although she was never even seen by anyone who spoke Rarámuri until about 1993, has been publicized by NativeNet, an electronic news and information forum dedicated to protecting the rights of indigenous peoples worldwide. On the World Wide Web, one may join the Global Prayer Digest and "plead for the hidden peoples," thereby allowing one to "pray for the 52,000 Cristo-Pagan Tarahumaras of Mexico."[15] Beginning in 1999, one could even go to www.tarahumara.org, whose mission is, "to integrate a community via Internet promotion of and services to the Tarahumara culture." Notwithstanding the apparently good intentions of the webmaster, such an authoritative URL makes it look as though this is an official publication of the Rarámuri people, rather than a private commercial endeavor. In fact, tarahumara.org is just a mirror site for tarahumara.com.mx, a fancy multimedia Web site sponsored by the Chihuahua Pacifico Railway meant to promote tourism to the region. There is no indication that the domain name "tarahumara.org" was registered for this site with the permission of Tarahumara or Rarámuri leadership. Ironically, while many Rarámuri defend themselves through tactics of withdrawal and silence on the ground, cyberspace displays of the Rarámuri that are activated or largely created by non-Rarámuri people give their plight a relatively high profile.

Conclusion

Since the 1994 uprising of the Zapatista Army of National Liberation in Chiapas, debate on indigenous rights and Zapatista discourse have had important reverberations for people throughout Mexico. Ethnographic analyses of these issues, however, have tended to concentrate on southern Mexico, largely although not exclusively on Chiapas (see Stephen 2002, and in this volume). Shifting the focus on indigenous rights to northern Mexico, I have here examined some of the pressures on the Rarámuri—one of North America's largest indigenous groups—as well as differing portraits of this people and the responses they have exhibited to the pressures upon them. In particular, I have explored contrasting images of Rarámuri identity and experiences of human rights abuses at local, state, and national levels of representation.

Why do some images portray Rarámuri as withdrawn, passive traditionalists, while others depict them as self-conscious agents engaged in the politics of change? There are several reasons for this ambiguity and seeming contradiction. First, by theorizing heterogeneity not only between cultures but also within them (Abu-Lughod 1991; Warren 1999), we can see how Wendall C. Bennett and Robert M. Zingg's assertion that "the Tarahumaras present a remarkably uniform culture" (1935, 181) is no longer true, if it ever was. The Rarámuri do not constitute a homogenous society; different representations are therefore required to reflect differing contexts, regional variations, and individual proclivities. The introduction of roads, schools, health facilities, missionaries, local cooperatives, and several major industries is further differentiating Rarámuri along the lines of literacy, wealth, worldview, and participation in wider national Mexican society. Some Rarámuri stand ready to mobilize and openly move into the political arena, while others, perhaps reticent about the consequences

such mobilization may have, prefer to rely on conventional stratagems of circumspection, which I have explored in terms of the cultural
construction of silence.

Another reason accounting for the existence of conflicting representations has to do with the interests of government and business. The
image of the Rarámuri as people who register their resistance through
stoic silence is infinitely more appealing to the state—not to mention
the industries of tourism, logging, mining, and other forms of capital
investment, which naturally recoil from images of angry indigenous
demonstrators demanding recognition of their rights. Small wonder,
then, that the former view has long predominated, although as situations have become intolerable, media attention has begun to shatter
the stoical stereotype and report on a more restless Rarámuri populace. If a prerequisite for being heard is the capacity to communicate
effectively in a lingua franca, then the inability of many Rarámuri to
speak Spanish fluently has also played a role in the historic absence of
their voice from arenas of power. Yet this constitutes only part of the
explanation, for it also must be recalled that Rarámuri regard silence
positively in a wide range of settings. In addition to referencing contexts of ambiguity and uncertainty, silence is prescribed as appropriate
sociolinguistic behavior for the management of emotion and conflict,
as well as being a way of showing respect, intimacy, politeness, and
tranquility. Silence, therefore, cannot be taken a priori as a sign of passivity or powerlessness.

Analysis of Rarámuri displays of resistance shows that women are
assuming a new level of prominence in leadership roles. This phenomenon may be due to some combination of relative gender equality in
Rarámuri society—albeit not in the "traditional" political structure,
where men hold the positions of authority—and an increasing recognition of the rights of women in the national indigenous movement
(Hernández Castillo 1997; see also the essays by Bartholomew Dean
and Lynn Stephen in this volume). The presence of Rarámuri women
as leaders at local, state, and national levels represents not only new
voices in these domains, but new stratagems whereby Rarámuri are
breaking their customary silence—through women who are challenging conventional roles and modes of communication they believe have
disempowered their people.

Rarámuri culture, like all cultures, is still in the making. Static,
essentialist representations of a monolithic Rarámuri culture need to
be balanced by other studies showing how Rarámuri culture is instead
a dynamic, contested site of heterogeneity and negotiation. The case

material I have presented illustrates the flexibility of Rarámuri culture, as well as a range of sites and modalities for its display. At the same time, I have considered the role of silence and withdrawal as a political strategy. In a wide range of contexts, Rarámuri use silence and retreat as sociolinguistic conventions to manage difficult social relations. Proponents of indigenous rights, therefore, need to not only consider the serious business of techniques that heighten visibility and promote speaking out, but also think carefully about cultural preferences for what I argue is tactical silence. This is especially true when the groups that activists are supporting have historically relied upon these seemingly passive practices as successful lines of defense. Giving voice to abuses does not always accomplish their eradication. Rather, in uncritically drawing attention to sensitive issues, these tactics may exacerbate problems and escalate violence, especially for those who do not have the luxury of leaving. Cues should be taken from indigenous actors, and reporting needs to be sensitive to the contingencies and contextualities of cultural realities.

I am not arguing that we should turn away from those in need of international support. Journalists, advocacy groups, and the informed public all have important roles to play. If activists urge indigenous people such as the Rarámuri to abandon culturally based stratagems that have served them for centuries, they also are morally obliged to present them with viable, durable, and effective alternatives. One alternative is assisting them in the creation of safe havens for the voicing of their political demands. With Jennifer Schirmer (1997), I argue that activists must be concerned with the practical sustainability, not just the philosophical universality, of human rights. Part of that sustainability is, I believe, closely tied to an ethnographic appreciation of the multiple and sometimes contradictory cultural fields in which social displays are embedded, especially at different levels of representation. An equally important aspect of this sustainability has to do with familiarizing Rarámuri with their existing rights as Mexican citizens and their emerging rights as one of the country's indigenous peoples.

Anthropologists who wish to remain relevant and responsible must also engage with these issues. Howard Campbell has enjoined his anthropological colleagues to be active, writing: "Contemporary Tarahumara people face dire threats from drought, famine, environmental degradation, violent drug traffickers, and corrupt politicians. Anthropologists could play a major role in supporting this beleaguered people, but not if they retreat further into the confines of the ivory tower" (1998, 154). I agree with Campbell, but I would add that an unreflexive rush to assist that simply relapses into a naive empiricism—that is, one that does not attempt to refine our modes of analysis or critically engage the paradoxes implicit in "writing culture"—likewise will be of little help. I take inspiration from Kay Warren, who, writing of the links between violence in Guatemala and silence and resistance on the part of Maya, maintains that "[t]his is anthropology's dilemma, and it is heightened when we study situations in which human rights are being violated. For many Latin Americanists, social research needs to address inequalities, local culture, and human rights. Our contribution is to give voice to those who are muted by cultural difference and the politics of marginalization and explore the interconnectedness of U.S. and Latin American political realities. We also have moral commitments to the people with whom we work" (1993, 49–50; see also Warren 1999, 111).

My analysis of the complex situation in the Sierra Tarahumara is offered in an attempt to address the problems and paradoxes of which Campbell and Warren speak. Yet my purpose has not only been to document Rarámuri silence. I have also endeavored to show how Rarámuri responses are changing, how people are coming forward and speaking out, and how these new forms of social action are extensions of contemporary Rarámuri culture. I have, on the one hand, brought to a wider audience the voice of those Rarámuri who have elected to come forward, while on the other hand encouraging respect and understanding for the polyvalent uses of Rarámuri silence. At the same time, I am aware that this essay reproduces, at some level, the dialectic of Rarámuri voice and silence that it is intended to describe—but again, Warren aptly characterizes this situation as an increasingly common anthropological predicament: "Flowing as they do from the paradoxes of our responsibilities, our analyses will embody some of the same silences, uncertainties, and ambiguities we document" (1993, 50).

As to why some Rarámuri are increasingly speaking out at this moment in history, I have argued that part of the answer is to be found in the intensification of the pressures they have faced at local and state levels in recent years. But the tendency for Rarámuri to voice their grievances is also attributable to national trends, since it coincides with the political opening provoked by the Zapatistas and a growing recognition of the pluricultural basis of the Mexican nation. Rarámuri demands, therefore, join those of indigenous peoples throughout the country, who, in the last decade of the twentieth century, demonstrated that they have a vital role to play in Mexico's transition to true democracy.

Notes

This essay is dedicated to the late Juan Carlos Aguirre, whose conscientious work in the Sierra Tarahumara provided the inspiration for me to write it. I thank first those individuals—both Rarámuri and mestizo—who over the years have so generously shared their time and knowledge. Financial support from the following institutions is gratefully acknowledged: Minnesota Humanities Commission; Carleton College (Large and Small Faculty Development Grants); Harvard University (Department of Anthropology, Faculty of Arts and Sciences Sheldon Traveling Fellowship, Peabody Museum of Archaeology and Ethnology, Committee on Latin American and Iberian Studies, Center for the Study of World Religions Senior Fellowship); Fulbright-Hays Doctoral Dissertation Abroad Fellowship; Institute for International Education-ITT; and the Tinker Foundation. I appreciate having had the opportunity to present earlier versions of this essay at the Annual Meeting of the American Anthropological Association in 1997, at the Annual Meeting of the American Ethnological Society in 1998, and at the Resource Center of the Americas, Minneapolis, in 1998. Heliodoro Juárez González, Claudia Molinari, Joshua Paulson, Danny Noveck, and Evon Vogt assisted greatly by plying me with information, articles, and books. I am very grateful to my colleagues Kalman Applbaum, Bartholomew Dean, Jim Fisher, Barbara Rose Johnston, Ingrid Jordt, David Maybury-Lewis, Claudia Molinari, and Lynn Stephen, as well as to my students Miguel Cervantes, Ross Chavez, and Emily Shirbroun, for their help and comments on earlier drafts. For her editorial sense, keen observations, and constant enthusiasm, I am deeply indebted to my wife, Tara AvRuskin. Of course, I alone am responsible for the final form of this essay, including its shortcomings. All translations from Spanish are my own.

1. See Champion 1962; González Rodríguez 1982; Fried 1977; Kennedy 1963, 1996; Kummels 1988; Levi 1992, 1998, 2002; Merrill 1988, 1992; Molinari 1998; Pennington 1963; Robles 1991; Slaney 1997; and Velasco Rivero 1983.

2. See Report on the Rights of Indigenous Peoples in Mexico: For the Committee of Experts of the International Labour Organisation (ILO) December 1997 Session, Presented by Centro de Derechos Humanos "Miguel Agustín Pro Juárez" A.C., Comité Nacional para la Defensa de los Chimalapas, Centro Regional de Derechos Humanos "Tepeyac," Centro Regional de Derechos Humanos "Nu'ujkanií" A.C., p. 10, <http://mixcoac.uia.mx /PRODH/ilo1.htm>, September 17, 1998.

3. When it became known in 1990 that a year earlier the World Bank had approved a loan to Mexico worth U.S.$45.5 million for development of a massive forestry project in the Sierra Madre, conservationists working with policy-study centers and environmental organizations were eventually able to stall the loan (Gibson 1991). Even Great Britain's royal family joined the growing chorus of concern, "alerting public officials of several governments to the true

costs of such 'development'" (Burns 1993, 7). Nevertheless, by 1994 a Chihuahua-based conglomerate had managed to receive a $350 million loan from Chase Manhattan to finance an increase in their pulping capacity and replacement of their old pulping plant, representing a dramatic upgrade that "would bring further pressure on the Sierra Tarahumara's fragile forests and Rarámuri people" (Raat and Janacek 1996, 146). Native Seeds/SEARCH, a Tucson-based environmental organization dedicated to the study and preservation of ethnobotanical resources throughout northern Mexico and the southwestern United States, took a leading role in organizing opposition to the World Bank's Sierra Madre Forestry Project and reported developments in every issue of its newsletter, *The Seedhead News,* from spring 1991 through winter 1993.

4. In 1998, the Chihuahua state government publicly denounced a national television broadcast claiming that 168 indigenous children had died of hunger in 1997, asserting instead that 103 persons had expired due to malnutrition, only 15 of whom were children under the age of five (Prado Calahorra 1998). *Exelsior,* a Mexico City newspaper, reported that 240 Rarámuri died in 1996 due to complications related to hunger (Robles 1996). Darling (1994) cited reports saying that more than forty children had died between July and November of that year, adding, "no one knows the exact toll. Many children die without ever seeing a doctor . . . malnutrition weakens children, making illnesses that would be routine in well-fed children fatal. Starvation may not be listed as the cause of death in such cases. Those ambiguities have led to bitter arguments. . . . Last month, Chihuahua Governor Francisco Barrio angrily and publicly refuted a federal report that only one child had starved to death." At the other extreme, a Reuters article from the town of Creel that made its way through Mexican newsgroups on the Internet in early April 1996 claimed that the Rarámuri "lost 400 people this winter to hunger and bitter cold."

5. Mario Alvarado summarily dubbed the Sierra Tarahumara the "Golden Triangle" of Chihuahua (1996, 68) and noted that residents bear uneasy witness to a pervasive culture of violence, especially in the western municipalities, where there has been a marked rise in homicides. Some reports claim that more than 150 Indians have lost their lives since 1988 because of the drug business (Salopek 1996, 50).

6. Interview with Lic. Heliodoro Juárez González, president of the National Commission on Human Rights for the State of Chihuahua, Chihuahua City, April 4, 1997.

7. The growth of tourism without concern for cultural and environmental impacts will be yet another force exerting pressure on Rarámuri land and resources. Wanting to develop for tourist purposes the land around Lake Arareco, outside Creel, the Ministry of Agrarian Reform served the residents there in 1991 with notice of an Act of Dislocation (Raat and Janacek 1996, 147). In response to protest, however, the act was revoked, and now an ecotourism project is in place. Comparing the development of tourism at Arareco with

that in the neighboring community of Cusárare, where a foreign-owned hotel exists, is instructive. The Arareco Tourist Development Project has been managed largely by outsiders, including a Chihuahua-based human rights group, which Anderson (1994) concludes has hurt the community—in contrast to Cusárare, where tourism has proceeded at a slower pace and according to an indigenous-derived strategy. On the other hand, the vocal presence of the human rights group at Arareco has been able to keep the Rarámuri's land in one piece, whereas at Cusárare there is the risk that pressure from outside investments will fracture land belonging to the *ejido* (agrarian reform community). The latter is of special concern given the 1992 reforms to Article 27 of the Mexican constitution, which liberalized the laws protecting the integrity of *ejido* lands.

Currently, the Sierra Tarahumara draws about fifty thousand tourists a year. However, if the massive Copper Canyon Development Project moves forward, with investments reaching U.S.$380,000 from the Interamerican Development Bank and the World Bank, it will be the largest tourist project in northern Mexico. Hotel capacity and infrastructure are expected to accommodate a staggering 270,000 tourists annually (Petrich 1996a). The cultural and environmental impact of such development would be substantial, although an initial study indicates that tourists would be willing to pay a per-person entrance fee of up to U.S.$115 to finance a biosphere reserve (Breunig 1997).

8. The deployment and interpretation of silence in discourse strategies is institutionally and culturally variable. In a pioneering article on the subject, Basso found that "keeping silent among the Western Apache is a response to uncertainty and unpredictability in social relations" (1970, 227). Silence can have connotations of power. In legal proceedings, the judge is the individual who holds authority while hearing a case, yet he or she is usually a quiet functionary while in the courtroom. Similarly, in sub-Saharan Africa, silence is customarily imposed upon divine kings whenever they appear in public (Peek 1994, 477). Because Finns and Athabaskans have conversational styles that are more silent than that of English speakers, cross-cultural communication with them is often misunderstood. In dialogue with others, it is not uncommon for members of these groups to be negatively, and incorrectly, stereotyped as withdrawn, taciturn, sullen, passive, unfriendly, shy, or uncooperative, when in actuality they are merely evidencing the sociolinguistic conventions of their culture (Lehtonen and Sajavaara 1985; Scollon 1985). Even stereotypically voluble Italians situationally employ silence. Saunders suggests that "where there is ambivalence about the expression of emotion, noise and silence may be used as stylized strategies for its management. Furthermore, in the Italian case, the more serious the potential for conflict, the more likely it is that people will choose the silent mode" (1985, 165). Extrapolating this idea, Tannen (1990) discussed the use of silence as conflict management in literary dialogue. Sommer perceptively analyzed Rigoberta Menchú's deliberate use of secrets and silence

in her testimonial as a rhetorical and cultural strategy that "produces a kind of distance akin to respect" (Sommer 1991, 36).

9. I conducted ethnographic fieldwork, concentrated in the municipality of Batopilas, in the summers of 1985 and 1986 and again from January 1988 to August 1989. I also made brief visits to Chihuahua City and the Sierra in December 1994 and April 1997.

10. Rarámuri seek livelihoods on a seasonal or permanent basis not only in nearby cities, but also across the border into the United States. One report stated that due to the collapse of the peso and to post-NAFTA economic policies, more than five hundred Rarámuri had "appealed for 'economic asylum'" in the United States (*Earth Island Journal,* spring 1995, 22). Static and stereotypic views of the Rarámuri, however, have usually prohibited people from analyzing these processual and transnational changes as modern extensions of the "traditional" culture (Urteaga 1993). Cohen (1997, 52) suggests that Mesoamerican "traditionalism" itself may be one of the "unknowns" in anthropology: "What does it mean to say the Tarahumara are Mexico's most traditional Indians? We cannot measure traditionalism against a metered stick, yet such statements are powerful markers of identity and status, establishing the boundaries of knowledge and organizing data into definable sets."

11. Demographic statistics suggest that this estimate may be too low, because over twenty years earlier an even larger urban Rarámuri population was reported. According to Mexico's 1980 Tenth General Census of the Population, there were 4,331 Rarámuri in Chihuahua City, 6,217 in Ciudad Juárez, and another 5,066 in nineteen other municipalities in Chihuahua outside the Sierra Tarahumara (González Rodríguez 1985, 13).

12. I am grateful to Mr. Joshua Paulson, who supplied me with the information about this incident at the 1996 National Indigenous Congress, as well as the Rarámuri involvement at the 1997 National Indigenous Congress (personal communication, March 14, 1997).

13. The point about the Rarámuri's reliance on silence and retreat as a form of protest, and its lack of effectiveness in some places, was made by Randy Gingrich citing Edwin Bustillos, in an interview concerning CASMAC's origin and goals. The interview was conducted by Albuquerque's Interhemispheric Resource Center (Browne 1995).

14. In 1991, she helped establish the Colonia Tarahumara in Chihuahua City, one of the three permanent Rarámuri colonies in the state capital. In 1993, she managed the State Coordinating Office of the Tarahumara (Coordinación Estatal de la Tarahumara, or CET) in Juárez. In 1994, she became a member of the PVEM and also was appointed to the Supreme Council of the Tarahumara, an organization that represents the collective interests of the Rarámuri at the level of state and nation—though many Rarámuri are, unfortunately, still unaware of its existence. Her positions moved her to be critical of the PANista government in Chihuahua, as reported in *Frontera Norte/Sur:* "'We are poor,' she said, 'and they don't listen to us when we call them. They help many people,

but my people get nothing.' In an interview with *Diario de Juárez* about her historic campaign, she had better things to say about the municipal government where she said she was seeing some movement. Of her campaign, Batista said she believes she is opening the door to those who haven't been able to participate" (*Frontera Norte/Sur,* News Digest, Center for Latin American Studies, New Mexico State University Border Resources, May 1997, <http://www.nmsu .edu/~frontera/old_1997/may97/ 597native.htm>).

15. Global Prayer Digest, <http://www.calebproject.org/nance /n1798.htm>, May 28, 1999; first published in *Global Prayer Digest* (Pasadena, Calif.), September 22, 1984.

References

Abu-Lughod, Lila. 1991. Writing against Culture. In *Recapturing Anthropology: Working in the Present,* edited by R. Fox, 137–62. Santa Fe: School of American Research.

Alvarado Licón, Carlos Mario. 1996. *Tarahumara, una tierra herida: Análysis de la cultura de violencia en zonas productoras de estupefacientes en Sierra de Chihuahua.* Chihuahua: Talleres Gráficos de Estado de Chihuahua.

Alvarez, Jaime. 1998. Pide Obispo de Tarahumara frenar excesos de la milicia. *El Diario de Chihuahua,* August 31.

Anderson, Amy E. 1994. Ethnic Tourism in the Sierra Tarahumara: A Comparison of Two *Ejidos.* Master's thesis, University of Texas at Austin.

Anderson, Benedict. 1991. *Imagined Communities: Reflections on the Origins and Spread of Nationalism.* London: Verso.

Appadurai, Arjun. 1996. *Modernity at Large: Cultural Dimensions of Globalization.* Minneapolis: University of Minnesota Press.

Basso, Keith H. 1970. "To Give Up on Words": Silence in Western Apache Culture. *Southwestern Journal of Anthropology* 26 (3): 213–30.

Bauman, Richard. 1983. *Let Your Words Be Few: Symbolism of Speaking and Silence among Seventeenth-Century Quakers.* Cambridge: Cambridge University Press.

Bennett, Wendall C., and Robert M. Zingg. 1935. *The Tarahumara: An Indian Tribe of Northern Mexico.* Chicago: University of Chicago Press.

Béteille, André. 1998. The Idea of Indigenous People. *Current Anthropology* 39 (2): 187–91.

Bonfil Batalla, G. 1990. *México Profundo: Una civilización negada.* Mexico City: Editorial Grijalbo.

Boudreau, Eugene. 1986. Tarahumara Uprising, 1918. *Password* 31 (4): 175–83.

Breunig, Lydia. 1997. The Economic Benefits of Protected Areas in Relation to Tourism: A Case Study of the Sierra Tarahumara (Copper Canyon Region) of Chihuahua, Mexico. Master's thesis, Duke University.

Browne, Harry, ed. 1995. Sustainability against the Odds. *BorderLines* 11 (3): 1–5.

Burgess, Don. 1981. Tarahumara Folklore: A Study in Cultural Secrecy. *Southwest Folklore* 5 (10): 11–22.

Burgete Cal y Mayor, Aracely, ed. 2000. *Indigenous Autonomy in Mexico.* Copenhagen: International Work Group for International Affairs.

Burnett, John, and Francesca Raimond. 1996. In the Long Run: The Tarahumara Indians of Mexico. *Soundprint, National Public Radio,* November 4.

Burns, Barney. 1993. Concern Grows over Sierra Madre Logging Plans. *Seedhead News,* no. 40 (spring): 7.

———. 1996. Evolving Tarahumara Arts and Crafts. *Journal of the Southwest* 38 (4): 463–73.

Bye, Robert. 1994. Prominence of the Sierra Madre Occidental in the Biological Diversity of Mexico. In *Biodiversity and Management of the Madrean Archipelago: The Sky Islands of Southwestern United States and Northwestern Mexico,* 19–23. Fort Collins, Colo.: The Rocky Mountain Forest and Range Experiment Station, General Technical Report RM-GTR-264.

———. 1995. Ethnobotany of the Mexican Tropical Dry Forests. In *Seasonally Dry Tropical Forests,* edited by S. Bullock, H. Mooney, and E. Medina, 423–37. Cambridge: Cambridge University Press.

———. 1997. A Range Full of Treasures. *Ocelotl: Revista Mexicana de la Conservación* 6:18–23.

Campbell, Howard. 1998. Reading Robert Zingg: Anthropology, Literary Criticism, and Political Correctness. *Sociological Imagination* 35 (2/3): 137–58.

Champion, Jean R. 1962. A Study in Culture Persistence: The Tarahumaras of Northwestern Mexico. Ph.D. diss., Columbia University.

Cohen, Jeffrey H. 1997. Commentary: In the Shadow of the Unknown. 1996–97 AN Theme: The Known, Unknown, and Unknowable in Anthropology. *Anthropology Newsletter* 38 (3): 52.

Collier, George A., and Elizabeth Lowery Quaratiello. 1994. *Basta! Land and the Zapatista Rebellion in Chiapas.* Oakland, Calif.: Food First Books.

Conklin, Beth A. 1997. Body Paint, Feathers, and VCRs: Aesthetics and Authenticity in Amazonian Activism. *American Ethnologist* 24 (4): 711–37.

Darling, Juanita. 1994. Drought Adds to Starvation of Tarahumara Indians. *News* (Mexico City), November 28.

DePalma, Anthony. 1994. Dying Babies Are Witness to Proud People's Crisis. *New York Times,* October 31.

———. 1995. Mexico's Indians Face New Conquistador: Drugs. *New York Times,* June 2.

Desaloja la policía en Chihuahua un plantón indígena ante la PGR. 1997. *La Jornada,* May 23.

Díaz Polanco, Héctor. 1997. *Indigenous Peoples in Latin America: The Quest for Self-Determination.* Translated by Lucia Rayas. Latin American Perspectives Series, no. 18. Boulder, Colo.: Westview Press.

Escobar, Arturo. 1994. Welcome to Cyberia: Notes on the Anthropology of Cyberculture. *Current Anthropology* 35 (3): 211–31.

Estrada Martínez, Rosa Isabel, and Gisela González Guerra. 1995. *Tradiciones y costumbres jurídicas en comunidades indígenas de México.* Mexico City: Comisión Nacional de Derechos Humanos.

Estrada Martínez, Rosa Isabel, and Graciela Vega Carrillo. 1993. *Informe sobre el Programa de Atención a Comunidades Indígenas de la Sierra Tarahumara.* Primera Visitaduría General Coordinación de Asuntos Indígenas. Mexico City: Comisión Nacional de Derechos Humanos.

Fabricant, Florence. 1997. Making Tracks in the Mountains. *New York Times,* January 12.

Fisher, Richard D. 1996. *Mexico's Copper Canyon: Canyon Train Adventure— Sierra Tarahumara.* Tucson: Sunracer Publications.

Foto censurada en la prensa de Chihuahua. 1997. Nota de la redacción (Note from the editorial office). *La Jornada,* May 27.

Fried, Jacob. 1977. Two Orders of Power and Authority in Tarahumara Society. In *The Anthropology of Power: Ethnographic Studies from Asia, Oceania, and the New World,* edited by R. Fogelson and R. Adams, 263–69. New York: Academic Press.

Frye, David. 1996. *Indians into Mexicans: Identity and History in a Northern Mexican Town.* Austin: University of Texas Press.

Gal, Susan. 1991. Between Speech and Silence: The Problematics of Research on Language and Gender. In *Gender at the Crossroads of Knowledge: Feminist Anthropology in the Postmodern Era,* edited by M. di Leonardo, 175–203. Berkeley: University of California Press.

Gibson, Daniel. 1991. Risky Business: Developing the Sierra Madres. *Crosswinds: New Mexico's News Monthly* 3 (10): 14–19.

Gil Olmos, José. 1997. Tensión en la Tarahumara; cómo explotarla, el conflicto. *La Jornada,* April 3.

Ginsburg, Faye. 1997. From Little Things, Big Things Grow: Indigenous Media and Cultural Activism. In *Between Resistance and Revolution: Cultural Politics and Social Protest,* edited by R. Fox and O. Starn, 118–44. New Brunswick, N.J.: Rutgers University Press.

Gledhill, John. 1997. Liberalism, Socio-economic Rights, and the Politics of Identity: From Moral Economy to Indigenous Rights. In *Human Rights, Culture and Context: Anthropological Perspectives,* edited by R. Wilson, 70–110. London: Pluto Press.

Goffman, Erving. 1967. *Interaction Ritual.* Garden City, N.Y.: Doubleday.

Gómez, Magdalena. 1995. *Derechos indígenas: Lectura comentada del Convenio 169 de la Organización Internacional del Trabajo.* Mexico City: Instituto Nacional Indigenista.

González Rodríguez, L. 1982. *Tarahumara: La Sierra y el hombre.* Mexico City: Fondo de Cultura Económica.

————. 1985. *Tarahumara.* Mexico City: Edición Privada de Chrysler de Mexico, S.A.

González Rodríguez, Luis, Susana Gutiérrez, Paolo Stefani, Margarita Urías, and Agusto Urteaga. 1994. *Derechos culturales y derechos indígenas en la Sierra Tarahumara.* Estudios Regionales 8. Ciudad Juárez: Universidad Autónoma de Ciudad Juárez.

Gossen, Gary H. 1994. Comments on the Zapatista Movement. *Cultural Survival Quarterly* 18 (1): 19–21.

————. 1999. *Telling Maya Tales: Tzotzil Identities in Modern Mexico.* New York: Routledge.

Gray, Andrew. 1997. *Indigenous Rights and Development: Self-Determination in an Amazonian Community.* Providence: Berghahn Books.

Harvey, Neil. 1998. *The Chiapas Rebellion: The Struggle for Land and Democracy.* Durham, N.C.: Duke University Press.

Hernández Castillo, Rosalva Aída. 1997. Between Hope and Adversity: The Struggle of Organized Women in Chiapas since the Zapatista Uprising. *Journal of Latin American Anthropology* 3 (1): 102–20.

Herzfeld, Michael. 1991. Silence, Submission, and Subversion: Toward a Poetics of Womanhood. In *Contested Identities: Gender and Kinship in Modern Greece,* edited by P. Loizos and E. Papataxiarchis, 79–97. Princeton: Princeton University Press.

Hitt, Sam, and Randy Gingrich. 1995. Mexico's Tarahumara Fight Drugs and Loggers. *Earth Island Journal* 10 (2): 21–22.

Homer-Dixon, Thomas F., Jeffrey H. Boutwell, and George W. Rathjens. 1993. Environmental Change and Violent Conflict. *Scientific American* 268:38–45.

Hu-DeHart, Evelyn. 1984. *Yaqui Resistance and Survival: The Struggle for Land and Autonomy, 1821–1910.* Madison: University of Wisconsin Press.

Johnston, Barbara Rose. 1997. Conclusion: Crisis, Chaos, Conflict, and Change. In *Life and Death Matters: Human Rights and the Environment at the End of the Millennium,* edited by B. R. Johnston, 330–39. Walnut Creek, Calif.: AltaMira Press.

Kennedy, John G. 1963. Tesguino Complex: The Role of Beer in Tarahumara Culture. *American Anthropologist* 65:620–40.

————. 1996. *Tarahumara of the Sierra Madre: Survivors on the Canyon's Edge.* Pacific Grove, Calif.: Asilomar Press.

Kummels, Ingrid. 1988. Schulerziehung für oden gegen indianische Ethnien? Die Rarámuri von Kabórachi und die Erziehungspolitik der mexikanischen Regierung. Ph.D. diss., Ludwig-Maximilians University, Munich.

————. 2001. Reflecting Diversity: Variants of the Legendary Footraces of the Rarámuri in Northern Mexico. *Ethnos* 66 (1): 73–98.

Lartigue, François. 1983. *Indios y Bosques: Políticos forestales y communales en la Sierra Tarahumara.* Ediciones de la Casa Chata, no. 19. Mexico City: Centro de Investigaciones y Estudios Superiores en Antropología Social.

Lehtonen, Jaako, and Kari Sajavaara. 1985. The Silent Finn. In *Perspectives on Silence,* edited by D. Tannen and M. Saville-Troike, 193–201. Norwood, N.J.: Ablex Publishing Corp.

Levi, Jerome M. 1992. Commoditizing the Vessels of Identity: Transnational Trade and the Reconstruction of Rarámuri Ethnicity. *Museum Anthropology* 16 (3): 7–24.

———. 1998. The Bow and the Blanket: Religion, Identity, and Resistance in Rarámuri Material Culture. *Journal of Anthropological Research* 54 (3): 299–324.

———. 1999a. The Embodiment of a Working Identity: Power and Process in Rarámuri Ritual Healing. *American Indian Culture and Research Journal* 23 (3): 13–46.

———. 1999b. Hidden Transcripts among the Rarámuri: Culture, Resistance, and Interethnic Relations in Northern Mexico. *American Ethnologist* 26 (1): 90–113.

———. 2000. Review of *The Chiapas Rebellion: The Struggle for Land and Democracy,* Neil Harvey. *Journal of Interamerican Studies and World Affairs* 42 (4): 151–57.

———. 2001. Tarahumara (Rarámuri). In *Oxford Encyclopedia of Mesoamerican Cultures: The Civilizations of México and Central America,* edited by D. Carrasco, vol. 3:185–87. Oxford: Oxford University Press.

———. 2002. A New Dawn or a Cycle Restored? Regional Dynamics and Cultural Politics in Indigenous Mexico, 1978–2001. In *The Politics of Ethnicity: Indigenous Peoples in Latin American States,* edited by D. Maybury-Lewis. Cambridge: Harvard University Press.

Lumholtz, Carl S. 1902. *Unknown Mexico: A Record of Five Years' Exploration among the Tribes of the Western Sierra Madre, in the Tierra Caliente of Tepic and Jalisco, and among the Tarascos of Michoacan.* Vol. 1. New York: Charles Scribner's Sons.

Maffi, Luisa. 2001. Toward the Integrated Protection of Languages and Knowledge as Part of Indigenous Peoples' Cultural Heritage. *Cultural Survival* 24 (4): 32–36.

Marks, Scott. 1994. Starvation, Isolation Killing Children of Mexico Indians. *Los Angeles Times,* November 25.

Maybury-Lewis, David. 1997. *Indigenous Peoples, Ethnic Groups, and the State.* Cultural Survival Studies in Ethnicity and Change, edited by D. Maybury-Lewis and T. MacDonald Jr. Boston: Allyn and Bacon.

McGuire, Thomas R. 1986. *Politics and Ethnicity on the Río Yaqui: Potam Revisited.* Tucson: University of Arizona Press.

Merrill, William. 1988. *Rarámuri Souls: Knowledge and Social Process in Northern Mexico.* Washington, D.C.: Smithsonian Institution Press.

———. 1992. The Rarámuri Stereotype of Dreams. In *Dreaming: Anthropo-*

logical and Psychological Interpretations, edited by B. Tedlock, 194–219. Santa Fe: School of American Research.

———. 1993. Conversion and Colonialism in Northern Mexico: The Tarahumara Response to the Jesuit Mission Program, 1601–1767. In *Conversion to Christianity: Historical and Anthropological Perspectives on a Great Transformation,* edited by R. Hefner, 129–64. Berkeley: University of California Press.

Molina, Hilario. 2000. Historic Autonomies: Yaqui Autonomy. In *Indigenous Autonomy in Mexico,* edited by A. Burgete Cal y Mayor, 98–116. Copenhagen: International Work Group for Indigenous Affairs.

Molinari M., Claudia. 1998. Protestantismo y cambio religioso en la Tarahumara: Apuntes para una teoría de la conversión. In *Sectas o iglesias: Viejos o nuevos movimientos religiosos,* edited by E. Masferrer Kan, 191–205. Mexico City: Plaza y Valdés Editores.

Molinari, Claudia, and William Merrill. 1995. Chiapas y Chihuahua: Cuatro siglos de resistencia india. *Ojarasca* 44:14–19.

Myerson, Allen. 1997. All the Roads Are Straight in Mexico. *New York Times,* September 5.

Nash, June. 1997. The Fiesta of the Word: The Zapatista Uprising and Radical Democracy in Mexico. *American Anthropologist* 99 (2): 261–74.

———. 2001. Mayan Visions: The Quest for Autonomy in an Age of Globalization. New York: Routledge.

Neumann, José. 1991. *Historia de las rebeliones en la Sierra Tarahumara (1626–1724).* Edited by L. González Rodríguez. Colección Centenario, no. 8. Chihuahua: Editorial Camino.

Peek, Philip M. 1994. The Sounds of Silence: Cross-World Communication and the Auditory Arts in African Societies. *American Ethnologist* 21 (3): 474–94.

Pennington, Campbell W. 1963. *The Tarahumar of Mexico: Their Environment and Material Culture.* Salt Lake City: University of Utah Press.

Petrich, Blanche. 1996a. Bosque sobre ruedas en la Tarahumara. *La Jornada,* July 8.

———. 1996b. En la Tarahumara: Muerte y silencio. *La Jornada,* July 7.

Prado Calahorra, Edgar. 1998. En 1997 fallecieron 168 menores de 5 años, niegan muertes por hambre en la sierra: Refuta gobierno a televisa y da sus propios datos. *El Heraldo de Chihuahua,* August 6.

Raat, W. Dirk, and George R. Janacek. 1996. *Mexico's Sierra Tarahumara: A Photohistory of the People of the Edge.* Norman: University of Oklahoma Press.

Robles, J. Ricardo. 1991. Los Rarámuri-Pagótuame. In *El rostro indio de dios,* edited by M. Marzal, 43–132. Lima: Fondo Editorial de la Pontificia Universidad Católica del Perú.

Robles, Martha. 1996. Muerte en la Tarahumara: Crimen oficial y privada. *Excelsior,* December 10.

Robles O., Ricardo, and Carlos F. Vallejo N. 1995. Los juicios en el pueblo Rarámuri. In *Tradiciones y costumbres jurídicas en comunidades indígenas de México,* edited by R. Estrada Martínez and G. González Guerra, 71–95. México City: Comisión Nacional de Derechos Humanos.

Romero Ruíz, Alejandro, and Rubén Villalpando. 1996. Protestas por la presencia militar en la Sierra Tarahumara. *La Jornada,* August 13.

Rosas Blanco, Melquiades (Comisión de Seguimiento del CNI). 1996. A Cumplir La Palabra! Nunca Mas Un Mexico Sin Nosotros. Reformas a la Constitución: La Hora de los Pueblos Indios. *La Jornada,* December 20.

Rus, Jan. 1994. The 'Comunidad Revolucionaria Institucional': The Subversion of Native Government in Highland Ciapas, 1936–1968. In *Everyday Forms of State Formation: Revolution and the Negotiation of Rule in Modern Mexico,* edited by G. Joseph and D. Nugent, 265–300. Durham: Duke University Press.

Salopek, Paul. 1989. Harvest of Violence: Narcotics Pistoleros Seize Land of Indians. *El Paso Times,* February 26.

———. 1996. Sierra Madre: Backbone of the Frontier. *National Geographic* 190 (2): 44–51.

Saunders, George. 1985. Silence and Noise as Emotion Management Styles: An Italian Case. In *Perspectives on Silence,* edited by D. Tannen and M. Saville-Troike, 165–83. Norwood, N.J.: Ablex Publishing Corp.

Schirmer, Jennifer. 1997. Universal and Sustainable Human Rights? Special Tribunals in Guatemala. In *Human Rights, Culture and Context: Anthropological Perspectives,* edited by R. Wilson, 161–86. London: Pluto Press.

Schwartzman, Karen, and Bob Melia. 1996. Copper Canyon: Drums Tell the Tale of a Tribe. *Boston Globe,* August 20.

Scollon, Ron. 1985. The Machine Stops: Silence in the Metaphor of Malfunction. In *Perspectives on Silence,* edited by D. Tannen and M. Saville-Troike, 21–30. Norwood, N.J.: Ablex Publishing Corp.

Scott, James C. 1990. *Domination and the Arts of Resistance: Hidden Transcripts.* New Haven: Yale University Press.

Sheridan, Thomas E. 1996. The Rarámuri (Tarahumaras): When We Walk in Circles. In *Paths of Life: American Indians of the Southwest and Northern Mexico,* edited by T. Sheridan and N. Parezo, 141–61. Tucson: University of Arizona Press.

Sheridan, Thomas E., and Thomas H. Naylor, eds. 1979. *Rarámuri: A Tarahumara Colonial Chronicle.* Flagstaff, Ariz.: Northland Press.

Shoumatoff, Alex. 1995. Trouble in the Land of Muy Verde. *Outside Magazine* 20 (3): 56–154.

Slaney, Frances. 1997. Double Baptism: Personhood and Ethnicity in the Sierra Tarahumara. *American Ethnologist* 24 (2): 279–301.

Sommer, Doris. 1991. Rigoberta's Secrets. *Latin American Perspectives* 18 (3): 32–50.

Spicer, Edward H. 1985. *The Yaquis: A Cultural History.* Tucson: University of Arizona Press.

Stephen, Lynn. 1997a. Pro-Zapatista and Pro-PRI: Resolving the Contradictions of Zapatismo in Rural Oaxaca. *Latin American Research Review* 32 (2): 41–70.

———. 1997b. Redefined Nationalism in Building a Movement for Indigenous Autonomy in Southern Mexico. *Journal of Latin American Anthropology* 3 (1): 72–101.

———. 1997c. The Zapatista Opening: The Movement for Indigenous Autonomy and State Discourses on Indigenous Rights in Mexico, 1970–1996. *Journal of Latin American Anthropology* 2 (2): 2–41.

———. 1999. The Construction of Indigenous Suspects: Militarization and the Gendered and Ethnic Dynamics of Human Rights Abuses in Southern Mexico. *American Ethnologist* 26 (4): 822–42.

———. 2002. *Zapata Lives! Histories and Cultural Politics in Southern Mexico.* Berkeley: University of California Press.

Swain, Ashok. 1996. Environmental Migration and Conflict Dynamics: Focus on Developing Regions. *Third World Quarterly* 17 (5): 959–73.

Tannen, Deborah. 1985. Silence: Anything But. In *Perspectives on Silence,* edited by D. Tannen and M. Saville-Troike, 93–111. Norwood, N.J.: Ablex Publishing Corp.

———. 1990. Silence as Conflict Management in Fiction and Drama: Pinter's *Betrayal* and a Short Story, "Great Wits." In *Conflict Talk: Sociolinguistic Investigations of Arguments in Conversations,* edited by A. Grimshaw, 260–79. Cambridge: Cambridge University Press.

Trosset, Carol. 1996. "I Don't Want to Talk about Things I'm Unsure Of": Silence and Advocacy at Grinnell. Paper presented at Associated Colleges of the Midwest Conference on Personal Identity and the College Community, Macalaster College, March.

———. 1995. Aspectos culturales del sistema político Rarámuri. In *El estudio de la cultura política en Mexico,* edited by E. Krotz, 293–323. Mexico City: Consejo Nacional para la Cultura y las Artes—Centro de Investigaciones y Estudios Superiores en Antropología Social.

Urteaga, Agusto. 1993. Raramuri: Su tonada en el desconcierto de las naciones. *Ojarasca* 20–21: 19–23.

Velasco Rivero, Pedro de. 1983. *Danzar o morir: Religión y resistencia a la dominación en la cultura Tarahumar.* Mexico City: Centro de Reflexión Teológica.

Warren, Kay M. 1993. Interpreting *La Violencia* in Guatemala: Shapes of Maya Silence and Resistance. In *The Violence Within: Cultural and Political Opposition in Divided Nations,* edited by K. Warren, 25–56. Boulder, Colo.: Westview Press.

———. 1999. *Indigenous Movements and Their Critics: Pan-Mayan Activism in Guatemala.* Princeton: Princeton University Press.

Weiner, James. 1997. Televisualist Anthropology: Representations, Aesthetics, Politics. *Current Anthropology* 38 (2): 197–235.

———. 1999. Culture in a Sealed Envelope: The Concealment of Australian Heritage and Tradition in the Hindmarsh Island Bridge Affair. *Journal of the Royal Anthropological Institute* 5 (2): 193–210.

Weinberg, Bill. 1998. Agony of the Tarahumara: Mexico's Most Remote Indian Nation Confronts Drug War Militarization. *Native Americas* 15 (3): 44–55.

Weisman, Alan. 1994. Drug Lords vs. the Tarahumara: Traffickers are Invading Mexico's Most Spectacular Forests, Destroying Ancient Trees—and Any Native Who Objects. *Los Angeles Times Magazine,* January 9.

Westing, Arthur R. 1992. Environmental Refugees: A Growing Category of Displaced Persons. *Environmental Conservation* 19 (3): 201–7.

Wheeler, Romayne. 1993. *Life through the Eyes of a Tarahumara.* Chihuahua: Editorial Camino.

Wilson, Richard J. 1998. Environmental, Economic, Social, and Cultural Rights of the Indigenous Peoples of Chiapas, Mexico. In *Human Rights of Indigenous Peoples,* edited by C. Cohen, 201–34. Ardsley, N.Y.: Transnational Publishers.

9 Reconciling Personal and Impersonal Worlds: Aboriginal Struggles for Self-Determination

Ian S. McIntosh

In 1998, the UN Special Rapporteur Miguel Alfonso Martinez completed his report on treaties, agreements, and other constructive arrangements between states and indigenous peoples. The aim of this nine-year study, conducted on behalf of the Working Group on Indigenous Peoples, was to analyze the role of treaties in the history of European overseas expansion, to look at the contemporary significance of such instruments, and to examine their potential value as the basis for governing future relationships between indigenous peoples and states (Martinez 1998). The unanimous opinion of geographically dispersed indigenous peoples is that existing state mechanisms are unable to satisfy their aspirations. Martinez notes that there is a widespread desire among indigenous peoples to establish a solid, new and different kind of relationship with states, quite unlike the acrimonious and adversarial relations of the past. He posits that either there should be full compliance with existing treaty documents, or entirely fresh instruments should be negotiated, with the full participation of indigenous people.

In Australia, no treaty was enacted or even contemplated between the English settlers and the indigenous Aborigines and Torres Strait Islanders. It is estimated that upon the European incursion in 1788, the indigenous population numbered about three hundred thousand, divided into hundreds of linguistic groups (Berndt and Berndt 1975). By 1900, 75 percent of this population had succumbed to introduced infectious diseases, such as smallpox and tuberculosis, or had been killed through the violent acts of convicts and other newcomers on the frontier. However, by 1999, Australia's indigenous population had once again reached the three hundred thousand mark (under 2% of the nation's population), and there is a groundswell of support on the part of the non-Aboriginal majority for the recognition of the property rights of the First Australians. Yet for nearly two hundred years there had been no official recognition of even the presence of Aborigines and Islanders. For instance, it was only in 1967, following a national referendum, that the First Australians received the right to vote and were officially counted in the national census. Is it too late to contemplate a treaty or pact of reconciliation with Australia's indigenous people? What form would such a treaty take, and who would benefit? What perspectives do Aborigines and Islanders bring to this debate?

Perhaps the most undertheorized subject in anthropology, reconciliation poses a great challenge for those working in the applied field. What does reconciliation "look like" in Australia? What are the building blocks of the analytical framework? Who is to be reconciled with whom or what, and why? Descendants of both convicts and free settlers in the colonial period and self-identifying Aborigines? The international development community and traditional landowning Aboriginal language groups? What are the criteria for evaluating the attainment of reconciliation? Improving health, education, imprisonment, and welfare statistics? Aboriginal athletes winning Olympic gold medals? Reconciliation—the possibility of creating a shared vision for the future—is contingent on not only cross-cultural understanding and dialogue, but also compromise.

While there is no shortage of non-Aboriginal commentary on the supposed preconditions of reconciliation, Aboriginal demands, if heard at all, are lumped under the rubric of "land rights" or subsumed within the somewhat vague call for "justice." As Pigg (1997) says in relation to development, indigenous peoples are assumed by the Other not to have development visions. Instead, they are considered culture bearers, holders of sacred knowledge. According to that perception, maintaining "culture" is their sole prerogative and motivation. How, therefore, could Aborigines have a perspective on coexistence or reconciliation? As the victims of unceasing European expansion and oppression, why should they?

The stories that Aborigines tell themselves about themselves and others are not always accessible. Therefore, what they reveal of themselves—their grievances and plans—in a negotiation process is pivotal in the reconciliatory process. There is perhaps no story that a non-Aborigine can tell to justify, to an Aborigine's satisfaction, what has occurred since the arrival of the first settlers in Australia from Europe in 1788. But what of Aboriginal discourse? What stories are being told, retold, invented, and reinvented for public review on the subject of reconciliation?

Coexistence, as envisaged by the UN Rapporteur—a normative arrangement that reconciles the seemingly irreconcilable: the disparate interests of disempowered Aborigines and myriad non-Aborigines—is the subject of a great storytelling tradition by Yolngu (Aborigines of northeast Arnhem Land). Inspired by epic Dreaming narratives of Djang'kawu, Lany'tjun, and Birrinydji (and their counter, the ambiguous, antisocial, and world-destroying adventures of the dingo), this narrative tradition centers on both the principle of "unity in diversity" and the changing nature of the adopter-adoptee relationship—Aborigines and non-Aborigines (Indonesian and European) creating small-scale mutually beneficial partnerships in a model through which many Yolngu examine the broader outlines of a united Australia.

Here is a model of reconciliation held by Yolngu that considers cultural survival and coexistence as codependent objectives. Described by Yolngu as "membership and remembership," this model is a solidly grounded but emerging vision of what reconciliation "looks like."[1] It is a model that considers Aborigines not as "dogs" in the eyes of the newcomers, a feature of so much of colonial and postcolonial thinking on Aboriginal rights, but as people whose knowledge of the land and seascape has sustained them through the millennia, and whose cultures and histories provide vital clues as to what it means to be Australian.

The Jewish theologian Martin Buber (1949) proposes an outlook similar to "membership and remembership" in his essay "In the Midst of Crisis." He describes a community as a circle with a clearly defined center. Members have a common relation to this center that overrides all other relations. The community—that is, the circle—is described by the radii, not by the points along its circumference. The common center must be something concrete, like a sacred text (such as the Torah), a person (such as Jesus Christ), or a set of rituals (as in Confucianism). As people see, study, and come to understand the center, they become aware of the divine, and their attention is turned outward to the world around them, to larger levels of membership, where their work lies, for it is beyond this circle or community that the authority and authenticity of the center is proven. In northeast Arnhem Land, Aborigines look to the Dreaming as the sacred center of their community. In a perspective based on "membership and remembership," they consider their emerging roles and responsibilities in a world lying well beyond their homelands. For them, the achievement of reconciliation will be a testimony to the truth and continuing relevance of the Dreaming.

In this essay, I compare and contrast this "personal," pan-Aboriginal vision of reconciliation of Yolngu community members at Galiwin'ku (Elcho Island) with the largely "impersonal" schemes currently being employed by Australian authorities, and I explain why, after ten years, all attempts by the federally funded Council for Aboriginal Reconciliation to achieve a rapprochement with Australia's indigenous people have ended in stalemate. Despite elaborate conferences, television broadcasts, and numerous public events, the Aboriginal voice is not being heard. It is evident that until the government comes to an understanding of indigenous philosophies such as "membership and remembership," Aboriginal reconciliation will remain nothing more than a pipe dream—fine-sounding words with little substance. The central disagreement is whether Aboriginal reconciliation is a national identity issue or a problem to be solved through practical measures—that is, whether reconciliation is contingent on non-Aborigines' forging their Australian identities in relation to Aborigines and Islanders, or whether it means simply creating the conditions whereby indigenous peoples can solve their own problems in their own ways. It should not be considered an either-or situation.

The Impersonal Dimension of Reconciliation

Since 1984, national parliamentary inquiries into the alarming rate of deaths of Aborigines in police custody and into the fate of those "stolen generation" children removed from the custody of their parents "for their own good," as well as the protracted court battles between developers and Aborigines over the planned destruction of sacred sites, have signaled a growing national commitment for a rapprochement on Aboriginal terms. In 1988, at the Northern Territory Barunga Festival celebrating the survival of Aboriginal culture through forty thousand years, the Labor prime minister, Bob Hawke, made a historic commitment to the negotiation and conclusion of a treaty or compact between the Commonwealth of Australia and the Aboriginal people. He invited Aborigines and Islanders to consider what the terms of such a compact would be. The outcome was the establishment in 1991 of the Council for Aboriginal Reconciliation through a unanimous vote in both houses of the federal parliament.

The year 2001 marked the end of the work of the council. It also marked the centenary of Australia's federation—and there was much soul-searching about the future of the island continent. A significant number of Australians hoped that the new millennium would herald the election of an Australian head of state in place of the nation's titular English monarch. However, whether or not Australia became a republic, the need to achieve a lasting reconciliation with indigenous people ranked high on the national agenda. The Council for Aboriginal Reconciliation, composed of twenty-five members (twelve of whom were Aboriginal, two Torres Strait Islanders), identified eight key goals for the reconciliation process:

1. To promote a greater understanding of the importance of the land and sea in indigenous societies
2. To build better relationships between indigenous people and the wider community
3. To foster the recognition of indigenous cultures and heritage as a valued part of the Australian heritage
4. To share ownership of Australian history
5. To understand the causes of disadvantage that prevent indigenous people from achieving fair and proper standards in health, housing, employment, and education
6. To address the underlying causes of the unacceptably high levels of imprisonment for indigenous people
7. To provide opportunities for indigenous people to control their destinies
8. To agree on whether the process of reconciliation would be advanced by a document of reconciliation or treaty (Council for Aboriginal Reconciliation 1997)

In 1992, Labor Prime Minister Paul Keating set the tone for a reconciliation to come when he signaled the end of the "great Australian silence" on the past mistreatment of Aborigines. In a moving speech heralding the UN's International Year for Indigenous Peoples, he stated that reconciliation was the "litmus test of Australian democracy." He continued:

We took the traditional lands and smashed the traditional way of life. We brought the diseases. The alcohol. We committed the murders. We took the children from their mothers. We practiced discrimination and exclusion. It was our ignorance and our prejudice. And our failure to imagine these things being done to us. With some noble exceptions, we failed to make the most basic human response and enter into their hearts and minds. (Broome 1996, 70–71)

Reconciliation was to be a demonstration of Australia's maturation as a nation, its coming of age. The Australian people would reach an understanding of the Aboriginal experience and come to terms with their responsibility. This was in contrast to the past, when modernity was measured by the notion of progress, and the displacement of Aborigines was considered a necessary precondition.

Notwithstanding an unprecedented groundswell of support for rapprochement during the 1990s, the reconciliation movement foundered because of disagreement over the meaning of the term *reconciliation.* Some non-Aborigines said it was about saying they were sorry for the past and moving on. Others said it was about land rights, compensation, and a treaty. Still others suggested a need for a complete rewriting of Australian history. Most Aborigines still say that all of the above are necessary prerequisites.

In the 1990s, Australia's indigenous people made significant headway in achieving the first of these prerequisites—recognition of their property rights—as a result of two progressive High Court decisions: *Mabo* (1992) and *Wik* (1996) (Bachelard 1998; Brennan 1993). While I say "progressive," in truth these decisions merely brought Australia into line with developments in international law: *terra nullius* ("land without people"), the legal doctrine that had facilitated Aboriginal dispossession, had been discredited by the International Court of Justice in its advisory opinion in the Western Sahara case in the 1970s (Anaya 2000; Martinez 1998). The concept was not similarly rejected in Australia until the 1990s, following the High Court *Mabo* decision. Under the *terra nullius* regime, any and all rights that Aborigines enjoyed were deemed to have been extinguished as a consequence of British colonization. However, in 1992, the Australian High Court affirmed that there is a place in the common law for Aboriginal and Islander customary law. As Reynolds (1999, 224) says, Aboriginal property or native title rights were not rights invented by the courts or a gift of the government to indigenous people. These rights preexisted the courts and the government, being derived from Aboriginal society as it was before settlement. For the very first time since colonization, Aboriginal and Islander native titleholders were able to direct what was to happen on their traditional lands and had an opportunity to negotiate for employment, training, and other benefits accruing from approved development projects. This was the real meaning of reconciliation, many Aboriginal leaders declared.

The Aboriginal victory was short-lived. The *Mabo* and *Wik* decisions fueled fears of an Aboriginal land grab, Reynolds (1999) argues, because they threatened long-accustomed patterns of hierarchy and subordination—leading inevitably to a sustained and bitter backlash. Federal native title legislation facilitating the Aboriginal claims process was deemed unworkable by the mining and pastoral lobbies, and forecasters proclaimed imminent stagnation for the national economy. In 1998 the federal government, incensed with so-called radical High Court decisions, modified the Native Title Act to favor the interests of developers over and above the interests of Aborigines and Torres Strait Islanders. A ten-point amendment plan insisted that indigenous native title claimants have a continuing physical connection with the land of their ancestors, even though the ancestors of a majority of Australia's indigenous people had been forcibly removed from their homelands as a result of colonization. Aboriginal leaders declared this reactionary move to be tantamount to a return to *terra nullius*—and the end of the reconciliation process (Galarrwuy Yunupingu, personal communication, 1998).

In 2001, when Aborigines continued to press the government for a national apology for past dispossession as a sign of good faith in continuing the reconciliation process, Australia's prime minister and Liberal Party leader, John Howard, refused. He argued that an apology would signify an acceptance of guilt, and his generation was not responsible for any atrocities committed against Aborigines. Another setback came with Aborigines' rejection of a draft preamble to a revised Australian constitution that would recognize their place as the past inhabitants of the continent—they were to be honored for their "ancient and continuing cultures." In the draft, the First Australians were relegated to the status of migrants, just like the newer arrivals; and while the wording stressed respect for the human rights of individuals, it made no mention of the group rights of the First Australians. And so the official, state-sponsored process of reconciliation in Australia came to a standstill.

A former high-ranking official in the Australian public service and renowned social commentator (and adoptee of the Yolngu), Dr. H. C. "Nugget" Coombs (1994), argued that reconciliation becomes a meaningful and achievable objective only when non-Aborigines identify and empathize with an Aboriginal agenda—such as the Yolngu concept of "membership and remembership." In this reconciliatory vision, as adopted members of Aboriginal society, non-Aborigines would "remember," acknowledge, and respect the preconditions of their membership in the Aboriginal world—just as Aborigines would uphold the law in all their various levels of belonging, including the law of the dominant non-Aboriginal society.

A Reconciliatory Metaphor

The inevitable blending of saltwater and freshwater in the intertidal zone in the coastal reaches of Australia's remote north Arnhem Land is, for Aborigines, a metaphor for the unity of "saltwater" and "freshwater" peoples: Aborigines are born into clans that are so designated. Freshwater bubbles up through the sand in the intertidal flats, saltwater inundates the freshwater springs of the mainland during king tides, and freshwater streams fed by rain flow unceasingly to the sea. When the waters mix there is a chaotic froth, but gradually a recognizable pattern is established as the waters begin to merge. However, Aborigines believe that at various levels, the diverse streams continue to exist, influencing and changing each other, but they do not lose their identity or integrity (Coombs 1994, 230; Magowan 1997).

This "unity in diversity" is fundamental to the Aboriginal worldview, even though there is no single corresponding term for the concept in Yolngu matha (northeast Arnhem Land languages). In an intercultural setting, however, Yolngu refer to this identity-focused outlook by the English expression "membership and remembership" and apply its reconciliatory logic in their efforts to negotiate with governments and advance their cause.

In the 1950s, the Australian federal government envisaged the total assimilation of Aborigines into mainstream society. This policy never had the support of Galiwin'ku Yolngu such as the late David Burrumarra.[2] But he was also adamant that "membership and remembership" was not the means whereby the totality of "whites" could be assimilated into Aboriginal society or vice versa. Rather, "membership and remembership" would result in each group's enriching the other with sacred values and spirituality and with environmental and technological expertise. Adoptees in an indigenous kinship system would acknowledge the enduring significance of Aboriginal mores but would also recall, seek out, and honor their own origins—just as Arnhem Land Aborigines remember their sacred origins even while living in a world that increasingly marginalizes them from their sacred land (see McIntosh 1999).

Burrumarra believed that "membership and remembership" was the only means for building lasting partnerships between indigenous and nonindigenous peoples. And such a methodology was reliant upon the success of adoption—adoption of Aborigines ("blacks") into the non-Aboriginal ("white") world and vice versa[3]—in affirming the self-worth of both parties. Aborigines had been thrust into a new level of membership, the dominant non-Aboriginal society, in such a way that they were denied their basic human rights to land and to autonomy. Their ability to maintain and cultivate their cultures was constricted in this world. As a strategy for realizing and regaining their rights at this overarching level of membership, and as an avenue for the affirmation

Fig. 9.1.   David Burrumarra, M.B.E., advocates "membership
and remembership" as a nationwide reconciliatory model. (Photograph by Ian McIntosh.)

of the importance of maintaining other extant levels of membership
(language group, clan, family, kinship subsection, etc.)—levels that
each confer certain rights and responsibilities upon members—Aborigines would adopt members of the non-Aboriginal majority and groom
them to work on behalf of these collectives. The object is for both Aborigines and non-Aborigines to acknowledge, or "remember," all the

various levels of belonging relevant to their lives while operating within the confines of the dominant non-Aboriginal society. Aborigines' acceptance of their "membership" in this larger, impersonal domain is contingent upon this "remembership"; and they are unceasing in their attempts to personalize this impersonal world, that is, to make non-Aborigines understand that Aboriginal worlds continue to exist within this greater Australian collectivity. Adoption is therefore a means to an end—and Aborigines believe that by giving a "license," or honorary "membership," in a clan to particular adopted mediators, they are providing the means by which non-Aborigines as a whole can feel a sense of belonging in the island continent and will no longer be considered strangers to it. To Burrumarra, this was the essence of reconciliation.

"Membership and remembership" could be considered as a Yolngu response to the "great Australian silence," or "disremembering," on indigenous-nonindigenous relations that has lasted two hundred years and that still plagues the nation. Simply put, "membership and remembership" involves Aborigines' adopting non-Aborigines into their domain and vice versa, affirming the worth of both parties. Non-Aborigines are landowners as a result of Aboriginal dispossession and must "remember" the rights of the traditional owners of the land. Aborigines are Australian citizens, but they "remember"—or assert—their rights as members of landowning language groups, clans, and families. Burrumarra summarized his ideology when he said that for Aborigines, human rights entail following Aboriginal law, building up one's own clan and homeland, and bringing honor to yourself, other Aborigines, and the nation.

The principal relevance of "membership and remembership" in Australia's reconciliation quest is this willingness of Aborigines to find a place for individual non-Aborigines within the Aboriginal domain and cosmovision and the willingness of non-Aborigines to reciprocate—to find a place for Aborigines within their own worlds. For Burrumarra, adoption was a necessary method of enticing non-Aborigines to adapt to Yolngu ways, while at the same time providing Yolngu with insight into the nature of non-Aboriginal worlds. He was actively involved throughout his life in adopting influential non-Aborigines into his Yolngu family, teaching them to work on behalf of Aborigines in their dealings with non-Aboriginal government agencies. In his view, "membership and remembership" provided the means for Aborigines to build ties with select non-Aboriginal individuals, who become active and supportive members of the moiety, clan, and family. It also enabled strong links to be made with faith communities, which spread the word of unity and reconciliation through shared belief in Christianity. At the international level, it facilitated alliance building with fourth-world peoples, who would plead the case for self-determination and land rights for indigenous peoples at forums such as the United Nations, the World Council of Churches, and elsewhere.

Adoption is achieved simply through recital of a story of traditional significance, revealing a sacred site, or the gift of an Aboriginal name to an outsider. Yolngu acknowledge the importance of non-Aboriginal brokerage, for, as Collmann (1988, 235) argues, if Aborigines are to influence non-Aborigines at all, they must try to bind them within the boundaries of Aboriginal society. Adoption affirms the self-worth of the adopter and also the importance of the Yolngu cultural inheritance: outsiders obey Aboriginal law sometimes even when it conflicts with prevailing non-Aboriginal law.

Adoption, thus described, becomes a means for controlling and influencing the social impact of an otherwise intrusive and unwelcome "white" presence. The adopter takes on the role of mentor and protector. Indeed, in Burrumarra's vision, adoption symbolizes the First Australians' initiation of the new settlers into the ways of the Aboriginal world.

Such "remembership" encompasses both memory and belonging, and it was certainly a widely held Aboriginal notion in the days before European colonization.[4] Today there is often a scramble to adopt a newcomer to a community, particularly if that person is deemed to have specific skills or influence within the broader world. The adoptee in this latter case is expected to discharge a number of functions—as, for example, a defender of the Yolngu when impersonal government agencies are threatening some aspect of their life (e.g., cutting off a pension check); as a mediator, when there is a need to speak with a doctor about an illness; or as a driver, for transportation to and from an airport or favorite hunting ground.

Adoption of non-Aborigines by the Yolngu in Arnhem Land is not adrogation—the gaining of full civic rights, as the term was understood in Roman law. The outsider, whether Aboriginal or non-Aboriginal, is granted certain privileges but never enjoys complete membership status within a clan (or Mala), that most significant level of belonging. In precolonial times, an outside Aborigine, a shipwrecked Indonesian fisherman, or other non-Aborigine might be given a place within an Arnhem Land family and even marry. Rarely would they be given an Aboriginal name, participate in ceremonies, or have access to the inner sanctum of tribal life, and even less frequently would mortuary rites be performed in their honor. More often than not, the outsider would be killed upon reaching old age or before then (Burrumarra, personal communication, 1988). However, today at Galiwin'ku, the nature of the adoptive process has changed to a significant degree, as I detail later.

As a rule, non-Aborigines are referred to as Balanda—an expression derived from "Hollander," that is, Dutch. However, in some cases today, adoptees are referred to as "Yolngu" if they live as members of the community, speak the relevant dialect of Yolngu matha, respect the community's leadership, and fulfill family obligations. If the adoptee's membership is challenged by outside Aborigines, the adopting party will exclaim, "No, he's not a Balanda. He's one of us." To a degree, the adoptee is an "Aboriginal," but such recognition rarely extends beyond the immediate settlement area. *Balanda* is a term indicative of that category of anonymous, "impersonal" non-Aborigines whose mere existence poses a threat to the "personalized" Aboriginal world and Aboriginal law. As an "alien," the adoptee will never acquire the same level of acceptance as a person born through the intervention of totemic spirit beings. The cultural creation of kinship ties is of the utmost significance, but this never trumps Aboriginal identity based on descent.[5] Still, the change from earlier times is dramatic.

In explaining this transition in adoption practices from precolonial times to the present, Burrumarra said: "Today, people live as one group. 'Black' can marry 'White' and vice versa. This is part of the lesson of [reconciliation]. We are different today than before. We live by a new law. Our histories have merged. The law of the past was ['Whites' for 'Whites'] and Yolngu for Yolngu. We do not mix. Outsiders tried to steal the women and steal the land. We would lose everything. But we can share the future if there is equality. . . . We ask . . . [c]an we be equal in your eyes?" (McIntosh 1996, 3).

An Arnhem Land Perspective on Reconciliation

The people of northeast Arnhem Land are referred to in the anthropological literature as Murngin, Wulamba, and Miwatj. They call themselves Yolngu, a word meaning "human being." Galiwin'ku, the largest settlement in northeast Arnhem Land, is situated on the southern tip of Elcho Island and is home to approximately fifteen hundred out of a total Yolngu population of five thousand. Established in 1942 by the Methodist Overseas Mission, Galiwin'ku is the traditional homeland of the Liyagawumirr clan. They share their country with

Fig. 9.2. In the spirit of "membership and remembership," David Burrumarra's reconciliation flag, which incorporates both Aboriginal and non-Aboriginal symbols, is used here in a Galiwin'ku ceremony to honor the Reverend Djiniyini Gondarra, who had received an honorary doctorate from a U.S. university in 1992. (Photograph by Ian McIntosh.)

eleven closely related clans whose territories lie in the immediate vicinity of Elcho Island (Rudder 1993).

Residents of Galiwin'ku claim to speak with authority about the land and sea and everything associated with their territories because the laws that they follow were laid down once and for all at the "beginning of time." Traditional Yolngu law at Galiwin'ku is similar to that reported from other parts of Australia: the Yolngu follow a framework of customs and traditions established in the Dreaming (Wangarr). In a northeast Arnhem Land context, the Dreaming refers to the period when the world was created, along with the responsible creational beings and the framework of laws guiding Aboriginal action.[6]

An Aborigine born at Galiwin'ku is automatically a member of a clan that is affiliated with one of two moieties, named Dhuwa and Yirritja. A map of clan territories in northeast Arnhem Land will show the land to be divided in a checkerboard manner, giving an impression of distinct bands of people spread evenly over the landscape. This is an erroneous impression. Social interaction in northeast Arnhem Land entails a "structure of overlapping, interlocking, and open social networks rather than a segmentary structure of clearly defined groups" (Keen 1994, 63).

"Membership and remembrance" was evidenced in precolonial Australia when Aborigines from distant lands encountered each other. They would clarify their relationship by reference to totems associated with their place of birth, moiety, clan, kinship section or subsection, and so on. One might say, "I call the kangaroo my mother," and the other might reply, "Then you are my brother." When early Australian explorers traversed the Arnhem Land coast, they often had Aboriginal guides who, while unfamiliar with the language of the district, could usually communicate to local Aborigines the intentions of the visitors. An Arnhem Lander would look to see if the unfamiliar Aborigine was circumcised or whether one of his incisors had been ceremonially removed—outward evidence of membership and full initiation—before he would allow the visitor to drink from the sacred waterhole or permit an audience with the elders.[7]

The system whereby individuals and clans relate to one another within and beyond the moiety and that serves as the foundation for these individual and group totemic affiliations has its origins with the Dreaming figures Lany'tjun for the Yirritja moiety and Djang'kawu for the Dhuwa moiety. These figures ascribe to each Mala (clan) certain bodies of law and provide rights in land for the respective groups, as well as strategic "totemic" alliances. While there is no single story by which one can describe the legacy of these ancestral beings that is shared by all within the moiety—and each clan has its own perspective on key events—certain shared understandings and ceremonies allow for moiety-wide cooperation.

"Unity in diversity" is a motto for the Djang'kawu and Lany'tjun legacies. For instance, the Liyagawumirr, like all other Dhuwa moiety clans, are custodians of totems for which they have a primary responsibility, such as the mud crab and goanna; but they also honor emblems that unite the Dhuwa moiety as a whole, such as the sun and the black cockatoo. In a similar way, Burrumarra's Warramiri clan is the primary custodian of the whale and the octopus, but in moiety-wide (Ngarra) ceremonies, they celebrate their joint "ownership" of the barramundi and mangrove worm through Lany'tjun.

Aboriginal law pertaining to intercultural affairs and adoption is central to the narratives of Birrinydji—the third major body of ancestral law in coastal northeast Arnhem Land, which grew out of extended contact between Yolngu and Indonesian seafarers known as Macassans (see map 9.1). This group label comprises a variety of peoples, including Sama Bajau (sea gypsies), Bugis, Macassarese, and perhaps others from Maluku and Papua. From at least the early 1600s until 1907, Macassans fished for trepang (bêche-de-mer) from the port of Macassar (Ujung Pandang) for sale to the Chinese.[8]

According to the Yirritja moiety Warramiri narratives of Birrinydji, at some point in the past, under the tutelage of Birrinydji's workers, Aborigines enjoyed the wealth and privilege of "whites." Macassans worked for them. Then, in a dramatic reversal of fortune (brought about by the antisocial behavior of the totem dingo), non-Aborigines became wealthy and powerful at the expense of Aborigines. Birrinydji's technology and power was now controlled by non-Aborigines.

Contact history, viewed through the Birrinydji lens, reveals two types of people: Aborigines, who possess the sacred songs and dances of Birrinydji, and non-Aborigines, who are ignorant of Birrinydji's law but enjoy the wealth and prestige that arise from access to the minerals found on Aboriginal land. According to the logic of the Birrinydji narrative, non-Aborigines can never totally dominate Aborigines, because Birrinydji is an Aboriginal Dreaming. Non-Aboriginal wealth is contingent upon Birrinydji's pleasure, but also upon Aboriginal compliance with outside agendas. Aborigines desire this same power and influence, and the only way this can be achieved is in partnership with outsiders—that is, those with Birrinydji's technological know-how. For the custodians of Birrinydji narratives, such as Burrumarra, here was a blueprint for reconciliation. Both Macassans and Aborigines needed each other so as to "hold up the universe" in a new and expanded dimension of membership.

Even though the social impact of the Macassan trepang trade was relatively constant along the coast, the role of determining "policy" on relationships with non-Aborigines was the sole province of Yolngu of the Yirritja moiety—Birrinydji's moiety. Yirritja alone would negotiate trade with the visitors and with inland and other coastal clans. Adoption at this juncture was impersonal through the Dreaming and via Birrinydji: the entire group of non-Aborigines became associated with the Yirritja moiety. Most Macassans were classified by Yolngu as Yirritja, as this was the moiety of all things associated with the new, such as the trade goods of the visitors and the wealth that they had generated from Aboriginal land and waters. The object of this large-scale adoptive embrace was the same as for individuals, in that it attempted

Map 9.1. Journey of Macassans to Aboriginal Australia,
1600–1907

to affirm the worth of the adopting party and provided Aborigines
with an avenue for the pursuit of their goals—the reclamation of their
dignity, prestige, and former status. In the later years of the trade, in
the early twentieth century, the adoptive process took on a personal
aspect. Some Macassan captains—those with a basic understanding of
Yolngu language and culture and with a long history of visitation—
were adopted into Yolngu clans, from both Dhuwa and Yirritja moieties; and Aborigines undoubtedly gained deeper insight into the
nature of Macassan society and culture.

Custodianship of the laws of Birrinydji in the Macassan era and
beyond was tantamount to possessing a mandate for asserting pan-
Yolngu rights in relation to non-Aborigines, and the Yirritja clans
inherited this mediating role through several generations right up to

the mission period. In the early days of the Methodist presence at Gali-win'ku in the 1940s, for example, male missionaries were adopted into the Yirritja clans, and their wives into Dhuwa clans. By the 1960s, however, with more than fifty non-Aboriginal mission staff, each individual was developing close relations with one or more Aboriginal families, and it was no longer appropriate or desirable for intercultural relations to be bound by a moiety or Dreaming framework. Missionaries were adopted on an individual basis, and in the aftermath of the mission period, which ended in 1974, there were equal numbers of Dhuwa non-Aboriginal males and Yirritja non-Aboriginal females. Today also, Yirritja Yolngu are no longer the sole brokers in terms of relationships with non-Aborigines. Dhuwa, as always, control Dhuwa land and everything on it—but they also determine the nature of their own relationships with non-Aboriginal authorities.

Dog Consciousness: An Impediment to Reconciliation

The most significant impediment to the realization of equality or reconciliation for Yolngu can be interpreted through "outside," or public, stories pertaining to the Birrinydji legacy—the multitude of dog, or dingo (Warrang), narratives (see McIntosh 1992). Self-categorization as dogs in Aboriginal narratives is an important guide in understanding cross-cultural relations during the Macassan era and in the present. Aborigines were "dogs" in relation to Macassans—a reflection of their technological and material poverty compared to the visitors, and also of their dependence upon Macassans for trade goods such as tobacco and alcohol.

Such self-denigration, one might imagine, would preclude the possibility of relationships of parity between the parties. But when the relationship between Aborigines and outsiders was viewed through the mythological lens of Birrinydji, the reconciliatory blueprint was apparent. The Macassans ("whites") were also considered to be dogs, because of their antisocial nature. They lived outside of the law. But the idea of a partnership at the level of the "dog" was ludicrous and a recipe for chaos. Through the Birrinydji narratives, Aborigines understood that what the Macassans had in the way of material wealth truly belonged to Aborigines, for it was a product of Aboriginal lands and waters (trepang, hematite, pearl shell, etc.). On this basis, and via this law, the two parties could be considered equal and mutually dependent. Aborigines owned the land from which the visitors received benefit, and Macassans would honor their ownership rights; but Macassans had the technology of Birrinydji that Aborigines required

Fig. 9.3. Warramiri leaders with their "membership and remembership" flag incorporating the Union Jack, the Birrinydji image, and octopus designs. From left: Liwukang, Burrumarra, and Wulanybuma. (Photograph by Ian McIntosh.)

and had become accustomed to over the several hundred years of contact prior to the arrival of Europeans. In this manner, the "dog consciousness"—which so overwhelmed the Aboriginal consciousness, as will be seen—could be countered, but only by reference to this sacred body of law.

In order to highlight the transition that was taking place in adoptive practices and "membership and remembership," I turn my attention to the two principal dog myths in northeast Arnhem Land that illuminate intercultural relations. The coping mechanisms Aborigines used to overcome feelings of worthlessness and shame in the face of outside intrusion by what was deemed to be a wealthy and ruthless elite are examined.

The dingo's late arrival in Australia (not more than four thousand years ago) and its innate viciousness and antisocial nature have inspired a wealth of Aboriginal narratives, conveying a profound message about Aborigines' humanity and their relationships with non-

Aborigines. In central Australia, the newcomers were European pastoralists and miners. In northern Australia, they were the Macassans. In both localities, it is the dingo that the bricoleur utilizes when fashioning the narratives of encounter. In central Australia, the story goes that the old Aboriginal men rubbed the sacred dog rock so that the wild dingoes would chase away and kill the invading whites. In the Tiwi Islands, there lived a mythical white man named Murantani, and one day he was killed and partially eaten by wild dogs. Today, the Tiwi refer to non-Aborigines as Murantani. It is a word that implies asociality—that one lives by laws foreign to the rules that should govern humanity.

Unlike the domestic dog, the dingo is somewhat of a trickster. In Aboriginal narratives, it shares some of the characteristics of the Chinese monkey and the North American coyote and rabbit, but any other resemblance to the classical trickster figure is illusory. Jung saw tricksters as primordial figures transcending humankind's conceptual boundaries, moving freely between the worlds of gods and humans and playing tricks on both. But the dingo, in the words of one Aboriginal elder, is a "fully fledged lawman." It institutes Dreaming laws but also breaks them. In various parts of the Australian continent it is considered the ultimate destroyer, disrupting the status quo and bringing disarray to human affairs (Kolig 1978, 106). Some Aborigines in Western Australia credit it with the origin of death.

As a sacred totem, the dingo provides a reference point for Aboriginal customs and social structure. Its behavior, somewhat like that of other tricksters, suggests alternate ways of being that, if implemented, would ultimately subvert the desired order of things. The dog mates indiscriminately, kills for pleasure, and does not share its food. It makes its own camp and follows its own rules—and yet, when young, the pup hankers for human company and is completely dependent upon its Aboriginal masters. Like a child, it is given a name and a place in the kinship system, and it is considered almost a member of the family. But when the pup grows up, it goes astray. As in many areas of Aboriginal Australia, young men before they are initiated are referred to as wild dogs: during this period they know nothing of the sacred laws by which humans must live; to operate in society, they must learn to act according to cultural expectations. The dingo is therefore a powerful symbol for moderation in behavior at both individual and group levels. According to anthropologist Debbie Rose (1992), the dingo makes us human.

At the beginning of time, people and animals were indistinguishable. An Arnhem Land "man-dog" called Umbulka journeys away from its home territory to the far north, where it witnesses an emerging relationship between white "man-dogs" from Macassar and black ones like him. When Elcho Island Aborigines tell this story, they describe Umbulka as shy, secretive, and dangerous—a "real bush blackfella" (Burrumarra, personal communication, 1988). On returning to its home range, the "man-dog" pounces on, kills, and partially eats its Aboriginal masters, the very first black people, and makes a sacred site of their incompletely buried bodies. Umbulka then retreats to the wilderness, transforming itself into the wild dingo we now know, living its life apart from humans—the ultimate symbol of asociality. It is this "dingo asociality" that was a centerpiece of Aboriginal perceptions of non-Aborigines; that is, non-Aborigines did not live by Yolngu law.

Young Aborigines growing up at Galiwin'ku may not become familiar with details of the Umbulka story (Yirritja moiety, Wangurri Mala) until their teens, but from the earliest age they will learn the story of the related totemic dog-hero figure Djuranydjura. This is the most intriguing of the narratives involving the dingo and also the best known, because it imparts a message to young, impressionable Yolngu not to kowtow to non-Aborigines but to hold their heads up, be proud of their heritage and traditions, and not become dependent upon the non-Aborigine for anything.

In the narrative, the black male dog Djuranydjura (Yirritja moiety, Lialanmirr Mala) had a fateful meeting with Macassans at the "beginning of time." The dog rejects all exotic goods offered it by the visitor for fear that acceptance would mean a loss of its identity. The Macassan says, "Why do you act like this? You could have everything that I have." The dog replies, "I want you to be a Macassar man. I am a black man. If I get these things, I will become a Macassan and you will become an Aborigine." So the Macassan packs up his house and goes away, and the dog retreats to the bushes. Today the sacred rock that is Djuranydjura stands on the beach at Howard Island (see map 9.2). When people look at it, they think about why blacks have so little and Macassans and whites so much: Djuranydjura had rejected these things so many years ago (adapted from Berndt and Berndt 1989, 418; McIntosh 1992; Rraying n.d.; and Warner 1958, 536).

While the land and seascape of Elcho Island is ablaze with totemic significance (parrot fish, whale, crocodile, etc.), it is this dog story that many young children are perhaps most impressed by. It is an "outside," or public, story, but its message is the same as that of the profound and sacred (or "inside") narratives of Birrinydji. These "inside"

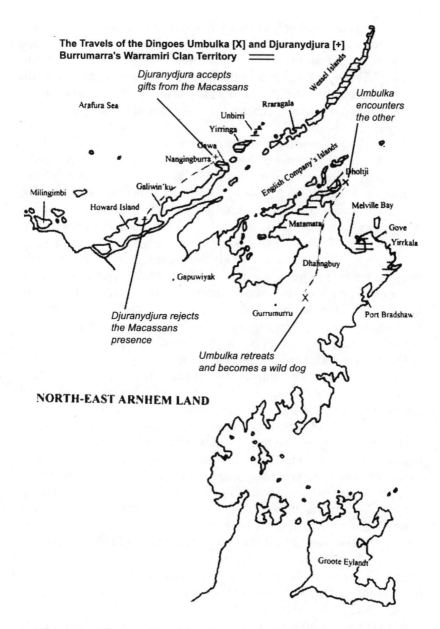

**The Travels of the Dingoes Umbulka [X] and Djuranydjura [+]
Burrumarra's Warramiri Clan Territory** ═══

*Djuranydjura accepts
gifts from the Macassans*

Arafura Sea

Rraragala

Wessel Islands

Unbirri

*Umbulka
encounters
the other*

Yirringa

Oewa

Nangingburra +

English Company's Islands

Dholtji

Galiwin'ku

Melville Bay

Milingimbi

Howard Island

Matamata

Gove

Yirrkala

Dhalingbuy

. Gapuwiyak

X

*Djuranydjura rejects
the Macassans
presence*

Gurrumurru

Port Bradshaw

*Umbulka retreats
and becomes a wild dog*

NORTH-EAST ARNHEM LAND

Groote Eylandt

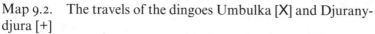

Map 9.2. The travels of the dingoes Umbulka [X] and Djuranydjura [+]

stories the young will only come to understand with experience of outsiders, when they know how the "white" world has oppressed them and threatens to take all that they have. A child, however, knows only the story of Aboriginal defiance in the face of outside intrusion. And the story is told with gusto; the child learns never to give up on what the Aborigines have—they alone are the inheritors of the sacred land, its language, and so on.

In localities along the Northern Territory coastline, other myths highlight the ambivalence of Aborigines toward the newcomers, and it is not only the dingo that rejects them. In one case, the Scrub Fowl (Yirritja moiety, Golpa Mala) uses its powerful legs to kick down the Macassans' bamboo hut and sets fire to their provisions using the Macassans' own matches. In another area, honeybees (Yirritja moiety, Gupapuyngu Mala) sting the Macassan trepangers as they trek overland in search of fresh water, driving them away. In yet another narrative, the trepang (Yirritja moiety, Mildjingi Mala) spurts out a huge torrent of water from its mouth, capsizing an Indonesian fishing craft. But it is the dingo that predominates in Arnhem Land myths telling of the contact with outsiders. Non-Aborigines, as human beings, are a part of the social order; but, being ignorant of Aboriginal law, they are a threat to the social order, just as with the dog.

The Djuranydjura narratives refer to the dingo as an Aborigine, as a representative of Aborigines, on an errand for Aborigines, or representing the "law" of the Aboriginal people. It is the dog that determined the nature of actual relations with the international visitors, for in the area where this mythical rejection took place, the Indonesians did not fish for trepang. The Macassans called that part of the Australian coastline Marege Siki—a dangerous area—and were careful to avoid it. A descendant of one of the last trepang captains, reminiscing in the 1980s, said that if the Macassans tried to land at Marege Siki, the local Aborigines would spear them. In those days, as Burrumarra said earlier, the law was "Black for Black" and "White for White. We do not mix." In other words, there was little scope for reconciliation. But times changed from those early days of confrontation, for Djuranydjura's rebuff of the Macassans did not end the story.

For more than two hundred years, Aborigines benefited greatly from the presence of Macassans. Trade goods such as cloth and knives became indispensable. But how could this be the case if the dog's law, Aboriginal law, demanded the rejection of the visitors? In the vicinity of Howard Island, the Aborigines tell several myth variations on a theme that provide clues: The Macassans see a fire burning in the direction of their homeland across the seas and depart. The dog also sees smoke rising, but it is from the land of its grandfather, the Yirritja moiety Warramiri Mala. Djuranydjura is worried and sets out to investigate, but its canoe sinks as it tries to cross to the next island—a clear statement of the inferiority of its technology compared to that of the Macassans.

In another variation, the dog travels along the beach, drawn by a strange smell, one it has never smelled before. As it gets closer to the source, it is transformed: its color changes from black to white, its sex from male to female, its diet from bush foods to seafood, and its language to that of its grandfather. According to the keepers of this Dreaming narrative, Burrumarra's Warramiri Mala, the transformation was indicative of the newly established trading relationship between Warramiri Aborigines and Macassan "whites." Djuranydjura had arrived at its grandfather's camp to see a Macassan cutting up and cooking a beached whale in the shallows. This was the source of the unfamiliar aroma. Djuranydjura was offered a piece of rotting whale meat, and she ate it; and in a repeat of the meeting with Macassans at her homeland, she was handed a necklace and a fishing line. This time she accepted it, but she added, "I'm only taking this because you want me to. These things still belong to you." Aborigines owned the source material—pearls and hematite—but Macassans had the technology to transform these materials into desired goods. The acceptance of the gift was symbolic of acceptance of a partnership.

The black male dog, now a white female, was in a position to appreciate that there was a new law in the land—the Aboriginal law of Birrinydji. This cosmovision enabled Aborigines to reconcile a dichotomy: the rejection of Macassans as law breakers on the one hand, and the enjoyment of the benefits of contact through an intermediary clan such as the Warramiri on the other—a scenario that Burrumarra says created the conditions for intermarriage between the two collectives. It is this myth/history that has come to facilitate the adoption process now so prevalent in Arnhem Land.

Djuranydjura is therefore integral to the resolution of the paradox. His Aborigines would not tolerate the Macassans' presence and would reject their gifts as a threat to the social order, but they would accept axes, rice, and tobacco through internal trade, through established kin ties with those Aboriginal groups who were followers of Birrinydji, like his grandfather. According to this sacred law, Aborigines were the rightful owners of all that the Macassan possessed. The truth of this was affirmed at the end of the trepang season, for example, when

Macassans would give Aborigines canoes, metals, alcohol, and so forth as payment for their services during the fishing season. But for the followers of Birrinydji, this was not compensation. It was their due. The Macassans were merely acknowledging their debt to the ceremonial landowners—the members of the Yirritja moiety Warramiri, Gumatj, Wangurri, and other Mala. Trade goods were a product of ritual practice associated with Birrinydji, but because of the dog's initial rejection of them, these goods came to Aborigines at a price. The Aborigines were completely subordinate to the visitors, like an Aboriginal woman to an Aboriginal man, like a camp dog to its master (McIntosh 1999). And at night, the Aborigines say, you can hear the barkless dingoes crying for the First Australians, for what happened to them in their subsequent dealings with Indonesians and "whites." Like the Thylacine, or Australian native dog, in many cases Aborigines were dispossessed of their land and disappeared from the face of the earth.

In Australian literature, the dingo is often featured as a symbol of "whites." For instance, in his famous novel *Capricornia,* Xavier Herbert wrote: "When dingos came to the waterhole, the ancient kangaroos, not having teeth or ferocity sharp enough to defend their heritage, must relinquish it or die" (1981:3). The dingo's killing of the Thylacine is equated with the European destruction of Aboriginal Australia. The dingo, stripped of its clan identity and name (as in the Lialanmirr and Warramiri Mala story of Djuranydjura), *is* the "white" man: cowardly, vicious, and revengeful. For an adult Aborigine to be called a dingo (apart from those undergoing initiation) is a great insult. In northeast Arnhem Land, the dingo is called *warrang* or *wakingu,* meaning literally having nothing and belonging to no one, living outside the law. Like a "trickster," the non-Aborigine by its mere presence introduces diseases that destroy Aboriginal populations. It conjures up material goods that, though much desired, inspire jealousy and greed, wreaking havoc on native communities. Djuranydjura's Aborigines feel great bitterness toward outsiders, a fact that explains the continued popularity of this dingo narrative in contemporary northeast Arnhem Land. Galiwin'ku Aborigines resent the fact that so little respect is shown by "whites" for Aboriginal understandings and ways of doing things, and that they have had to make substantial changes in their own ways in order to accommodate outsiders—but not vice versa. But through Birrinydji, there is an avenue to reconciliation.

In the history of relations between "whites" and "blacks," Aborigines viewed themselves as "dogs" and were treated as such, according to these narratives. But the visitors were dogs as well, because of the antisocial behavior they induced and their failure to live by the precepts of Aboriginal law. Aborigines resented their poverty and dependence upon the newcomers.

The eradication of the "dog nature," or "dog consciousness," remains for the Aborigines a priority of reconciliation. Aborigines demand equality. They must be treated as people with rights and not as dogs. Non-Aborigines, too, must understand the antisocial consequences of their actions and their continued negative impacts on Aboriginal societies. As Aboriginal minister and reconciliation advocate Dr. Djiniyini Gondarra has said: "In the old days we followed you. We kept our heads down because we were ashamed. Now we walk with our heads up and we look at you in the eye and say, 'We can be brothers and sisters together'" (McIntosh 1997, 284).

Aborigines and non-Aborigines are members of one community. "Membership and remembership" and adoption lie at the very core of their struggle for rights and coexistence.

The Prospect for Reconciliation at Galiwin'ku

There is overwhelming agreement from both Aborigines and non-Aborigines that face-to-face negotiations are essential ingredients for reconciliation. Many believe that Aborigines in the twenty-first century must pay their own way and not rely upon welfare handouts, and that they must sit down and negotiate a fair deal for opening their land to development. Only then will they begin to enjoy better housing, schools, community centers, gardens, and the like. However, Aborigines, arguing for justice before reconciliation, respond by saying, "Why do we have to have mining in order to enjoy our rights?" Representatives of industry stress that Aborigines and non-Aborigines must be equal before the law and that no special legal provisions should be enacted to favor one segment of society over another. They have argued that Aborigines need viable industries in order to survive and that industry can lend a hand, but, as the Aborigine and academic Marcia Langton points out, Aborigines are still suspected of desiring rights that no one else enjoys. Alternatively, some non-Aborigines assert that Aborigines have lost all contact with the land and do not follow the traditions of old, so it is unreasonable of them to expect compensation if, for example, a sacred site is disturbed during a big-budget project bringing vital export dollars into the national coffers.

Residents of Galiwin'ku live outside the mainstream of Australian politics, and in some sense they represent a special case. They were never removed from their land, as was the case in many other parts of the nation. Under provisions of the Aboriginal Land Rights Act (Northern Territory) of 1976, they have the power of veto over development, a right that few Aborigines in other Australian states and territories enjoy. One might presume that Elcho Islanders should have fewer complaints, but this is not the case. They are not exempt, for example, from the problems endemic to Australia's indigenous populations. Three Elcho Island Mala have become extinct in the past ten years, and more than twenty have become extinct throughout the Arnhem Land region over the past fifty years, according to one estimate (personal communication, S. Davis 1989). School attendance and performance is unacceptably low, and petrol sniffing and substance abuse are rife among teenagers and adults. At communities such as Galiwin'ku, more often than not people do not live beyond the age of fifty. The incidence of disease stemming from unsanitary and overcrowded living conditions is on the increase, and money is always in short supply. Some reconciliation advocates use these statistics as evidence of the need for a better deal for Arnhem Landers.

When Burrumarra spoke of "membership and remembership," he made explicit the various levels of belonging inherent in Yolngu society and the concomitant responsibilities for both Aborigines and non-Aborigines. For instance, members of an extended family have specific duties to fulfill in relation to their father, mother, mother-in-law, grandparents, and so on. There are also those individuals for whom the kinship system requires total avoidance with other indiviudals. When Yolngu come together as a clan, they remember these specific family obligations, but they also acknowledge the importance of their membership in a wider kin group. At those times when clans unite as a moiety to celebrate the legacy of the ancestors, they do not forget their clan totemic affiliations but, rather, bring honor to them. The increasing popularity of Christianity in the community of Galiwin'ku since the 1970s has led to the local consolidation of an entirely new level of membership: the Christian community, which facilitates the building of partnerships with other Aboriginal and also non-Aboriginal congregations. Certain bodies of traditional law—in particular, those associated with the rainbow serpent—reflect principles that are in conflict with values espoused by the church. In such instances, Yolngu Christians attempt to play down differences, but often a clear demarcation results between what they believe and what they respect and honor as their sacred Aboriginal heritage.

When Aborigines and non-Aborigines come together to discuss the possibility of a treaty, there is almost a universal cry by Yolngu elders for unity and an end to the divisions that keep the First Australians locked into poverty on the margins of "white" society. Most traditional Aboriginal leaders, including Burrumarra, stress the need for partnerships, and the model for their reconciliatory pronouncements has its origins with Djang'kawu, Lany'tjun, and especially Birrinydji.

While Yolngu at Galiwin'ku own their own land and to a degree are able to control developments upon it, they are still relatively powerless in terms of determining, or even seriously affecting, the decisions being made about their future. Most businesses at Galiwin'ku, such as the store and take-away restaurants, are owned by non-Aborigines. The few profitable enterprises open to Elcho Island residents are in areas of dubious legality, such as the importation of kava from Tonga or Fiji,[9] the unauthorized hiring and sales of videos, or high-risk "grog running." Some non-Aboriginal advocates of reconciliation accuse Aborigines of expecting a dramatic turnaround in their fortunes without working for it. But there are few opportunities for Aborigines to manage their own viable enterprises.

A majority of Elcho Islanders would argue that reconciliation is not just saying sorry, lending a helping hand in order to get a business started, or even the provision of funding to improve Aboriginal living conditions. Self-determination, an object of the adoption process and implicit in "membership and remembership," would entail the acknowledgment of indigenous property rights and full participation in the management and utilization of natural resources. Of course, a substantial barrier to the achievement of such goals is non-Aboriginal law itself—acts of Parliament that restrict Aboriginal ownership of the land and sea and that limit the involvement of indigenous people in the management of their ancestral heritage—as well as the activities of mining and other development enterprises, which operate with scant regard for the wishes and interests of indigenous people. Australia seems a long way from achieving these prerequisites.

Conclusion

Reconciliation, like self-determination, is a buzzword in indigenous circles. The coexistence of different cultures within a single, pluriethnic modern state is a priority for many nation-states. But reconciliation is a process beset with problems. South Africa's Truth and Reconciliation Commission, for instance, has been heralded as a necessary part of the healing process for a divided nation, but bitterness surrounds the awarding of amnesty to the perpetrators of hate crimes. The Philippines Indigenous Peoples Rights Act of 1997, a landmark piece of legislation acknowledging the rights and freedoms of indigenous tribes, has been ruled unconstitutional by the Supreme Court because it is contrary to the regalian doctrine that once justified Spanish colonial expansion. Guatemala's Historical Clarification Commission, the referendum on independence for East Timor, New Zealand's revamped Treaty of Waitangi Tribunal, and royal commissions in Australia and Canada are also spoken of as groundbreaking reconciliatory acts. In most instances, however, the ruling regime is unwilling to take part in a significant rethinking of internal arrangements with their indigenous populations. Such is the case in Australia; a stalemate has ensued and will not be overcome until there is some sort of federal devolution of power or "remembering" on a national scale.

One of the few avenues for pursuing change at the domestic level is by appeals at international forums in Geneva or New York—this vast new level of membership—and more and more indigenous people are availing themselves of this opportunity. It is often threats to a nation's international standing, through embarrassing revelations of poor treatment of domestic indigenous populations, that inspire reform at home. At the 1997 Aboriginal Reconciliation Convention in Melbourne, for example, indigenous peoples from all over the world rallied together in support of the Australian Aboriginal cause and publicly acknowledged, or "remembered," the rights of the traditional landowners.

Despite the exalted thoughts and actions of the many advocates of reconciliation and the encouraging words of reconciliation-council members and visiting scholars, the future of Aboriginal reconciliation is in the hands of politicians and at the mercy of the political process. Only a minority of Australian parliamentarians have any idea of what Aborigines think, and still fewer care. Pursuing political power and accommodating the agenda of the multinational corporate sector are of uppermost concern. Under the present federal regime, reconciliation appears to be a lost cause. Few existing federal or state laws promote reconciliation, and where they do, they are under threat. The future holds three possibilities:

1. improved relations between Aborigines and non-Aborigines if the Labor Party attains power;
2. a slow erosion of Aboriginal rights and the reconciliation process if a conservative Liberal-National government retains power; or
3. the cessation of the reconciliation process and the extinguish-

ment of Aboriginal native title Australia-wide if extreme right-wing parties such as the One Nation Party ever achieve the balance of power in the Federal Parliament.

For some sympathetic non-Aborigines, reconciliation is a process that aims to promote a much-desired sense of belonging in the knowledge that "white" Australia has a "black" history. Yet for politicians and those with political aspirations, there are few votes to be won in supporting the cause of Aborigines. The search for a new national identity in collaboration with the First Australians is far too risky a proposition for the "white antisocial dog."

Notes

1. The closest approximation of "membership and remembership" in Yolngu matha (Aboriginal languages from northeast Arnhem Land) is the expression *rringitj,* which refers to the sacred bond between people and the land through shared bodies of sacred law; or, alternatively, *djalkirri*—footprint/land/membership/relationship.

2. David Burrumarra is often referred to as the last great leader of Arnhem Land. He was advocating reconciliatory policies in the 1950s, well before it became popular to do so. A tall, stately figure, a diplomat and staunch advocate of Aboriginal rights, Burrumarra had a considerable impact on the way northeast Arnhem Land communities developed. He devoted his life to ensuring that Aboriginal cultural values were preserved in a quickly developing technological world. In 1978 he was awarded an M.B.E. (Member of the British Empire medal) by Australia's governor-general for his achievements in community building and cross-cultural education (McIntosh 1994b).

3. Aborigines and non-Aborigines frequently characterize their relations in misleading and inappropriate "black" and "white" terms—which is unfortunate, because it exaggerates differences and downplays shared interests and concerns.

4. In one recorded instance from the turn of the century, when Warramiri clansmen from Arnhem Land defeated their Wangurri foes in a battle, they raised the children of the deceased "enemy" clansmen with the full knowledge of their Wangurri ancestry. This was a means of rebuilding the sacred bonds that should exist between the two clans, and it is an example of "membership and remembership" (see McIntosh 1994b).

5. For comparative purposes, consider the Lakota Hunkapi, or "making of relatives," ceremony of North America.

6. The English expression *Dreaming* is drawn from the Central Australian Aranda Aboriginal word *Altjiringa,* meaning "to see the eternal," for Aborigines believe that they are in touch with fundamental truths while asleep. In

Yolngu matha, the term for the Dreaming is *Wangarr*. Members of all resident clans at Galiwin'ku have their own unique Wangarr heritage.

7. In one recorded case, however, the Aboriginal visitor was appalled at the Arnhem Land habit of eating stingray, for in his home territory far to the southeast, this was taboo—a detail that may have prevented any free flow of communication (Flinders 1814).

8. While today some Yolngu speak of "Macassans" as being the only group of outsiders involved in the trepang trade, members of several Yirritja moiety Mala, such as Burrumarra's Warramiri, speak of the Macassans as coming at the tail end of waves of visitors, beginning with dark-skinned peoples who respected Aboriginal rights and traded as equals with them. They were followed by "golden-skinned" visitors who introduced Aborigines to trepanging and who had the skills of iron manufacture, pottery production, and weaving but kept these secrets for themselves. Then came "light brown" Macassans and "white" Japanese and Europeans. A change in skin color from "black" to "white" in this reading of the past corresponds to a change in the nature of relations with Aborigines, from reciprocity to a complete absence of it. It was the Dreaming entity Birrinydji who drew all of these outsiders to the coast by the strength of his *marr* (desire). As Burrumarra said: "Although we were different colors, we were one people linked in life, in ceremony, and history" (personal communication, 1989).

9. Kava was first introduced to Arnhem Land by missionaries, who saw it as a preferable alternative to alcohol.

References

Anaya, S. J. 2000. *Indigenous Peoples in International Law*. Oxford: Oxford University Press.

Bachelard, M. 1998. *The Great Land Grab: What Every Australian Should Know About: Wik, Mabo, and the Ten Point Plan*. Melbourne: Hyland House.

Berndt, R. M., and C. H. Berndt. 1975. *The World of the First Australians*. Sydney: Ure Smith.

———. 1989. *The Speaking Land: Myth and Story in Aboriginal Australia*. Melbourne: Penguin.

Brennan, F. 1993. The Law, Politics, and Religion of Land Rights in the Post-Mabo Era. The 1993 Felix Arnott Lecture, St. Francis' Theological College, Brisbane.

Broome, R. 1996. Historians, Aborigines, and Australia: Writing the National Past. In *In the Age of Mabo: History, Aborigines, and Australia*, edited by B. Attwood, 54–72. Sydney: Allen and Unwin.

Buber, Martin. 1949. *Paths in Utopia*. Boston: Beacon Press.

Collmann, J. 1988. *Fringe-Dwellers and Welfare: The Aboriginal Response to Bureaucracy*. St Lucia: University of Queensland Press.

Coombs, H. C. 1994. *Aboriginal Autonomy: Issues and Strategies*. Melbourne: Cambridge University Press.

Council for Aboriginal Reconciliation. 1997. *The Path to Reconciliation: Issues for a People's Movement.* Canberra: Australian Government Publishing.

Flinders, M. 1814. *A Voyage to Terra Australis.* London: G. and W. Nicol.

Herbert, X. 1981. *Capricornia.* Sydney: August Robertson.

Keen, I. 1994. *Knowledge and Secrecy in an Aboriginal Religion: Yolngu of North-East Arnhem Land.* Oxford Studies in Social and Cultural Anthropology. Oxford: Clarendon Press.

Kolig, E. 1978. Aboriginal Dogmatics: Canines in Theory, Myth, and Dogma. *Bijdragen Tot de Taal Land en Volenkunde* 134 (1): 84–115.

Magowan, F. 1997. *A Sea of Song and Law: Preliminary Report on Yolngu Customary Marine Rights and Interests from Cape Wilberforce to Port Bradshaw and Adjoining Seas.* Darwin: Northern Land Council.

Martinez, M. A. 1998. Study on Treaties, Agreements, and Other Constructive Arrangements between States and Indigenous Populations. Final Report of the United Nations Special Rapporteur to the UN Working Group on Indigenous Peoples. Unedited ms.

McIntosh, I. S. 1992. The Bricoleur at Work: Warrang (Dingo) Mythology in the Yirritja Moiety of North-East Arnhem Land. M.Litt. thesis, University of New England.

———. 1994a. The Dog and the Myth Maker: Macassans and Aborigines in North-East Arnhem Land. *Australian Folklore* 9:77–81.

———. 1994b. *The Whale and the Cross: Conversations with David Burrumarra, M.B.E.* Darwin: Historical Society of the Northern Territory.

———. 1996. Can We Be Equal in Your Eyes? Ph.D. thesis. Northern Territory University, Darwin.

———. 1997. Anthropology, Self-Determination, and Aboriginal Belief in the Christian God. *Oceania* 67 (4): 273–88.

———. 1999. *Aboriginal Reconciliation and the Dreaming: Warramiri Yolngu and the Quest for Equality.* Cultural Survival Series on Ethnicity and Change. Boston: Allyn and Bacon.

Pigg, S. L. 1997. Found in Most Traditional Societies: Traditional Medical Practitioners between Culture and Development. In F. Cooper and R. Pockard, eds., *International Development and the Social Sciences,* 259–90. Berkeley: University of California Press.

Reynolds, H. 1999. *Why Weren't We Told? A Personal Search for the Truth about Our History.* Ringwood: Viking.

Rose, D. B. 1992. *Dingo Makes Us Human: Life and Land in an Australian Aboriginal Culture.* Cambridge: Cambridge University Press.

Rraying. n.d. *Macassan and Dingo Give Each Other Fire.* Translated by M. Christie. Milingimbi Literature Center, Milingimbi, Northern Territory.

Rudder, J. 1993. Yolngu Cosmology: An Unchanging Cosmos Incorporating a Rapidly Changing World? Ph.D. thesis, Australian National University.

Warner, W. L. 1958. *A Black Civilization: A Social Study of an Australian Tribe.* Chicago: Harper and Row.

10 From Elimination to an Uncertain Future: Changing Policies toward Indigenous Peoples

David Maybury-Lewis

This concluding essay stems from a paper given to introduce a Presidential Symposium at the meetings of the American Anthropological Association in November 1997. The symposium marked the twenty-fifth anniversary of the founding of Cultural Survival, an organization started by my wife, Pia Maybury-Lewis, and myself to defend the rights of indigenous peoples worldwide. It also celebrated the growing strength of indigenous movements and the progress, albeit hesitant, that had been made in the fight for indigenous rights over the past twenty-five years. Since there is often confusion as to exactly who are indigenous peoples, it is worth clarifying at the outset whom we are talking about. Indigenous peoples are those who have been conquered by populations ethnically or culturally different from themselves and who have been incorporated into states that consider them outsiders and usually inferiors.

The title of my essay refers to a recent and worldwide tendency for states to move away from policies aimed at the elimination of their indigenous populations, while leaving them still facing an uncertain future. The massacre of indigenous peoples was routinely practiced and routinely accepted in the heyday of imperialism. The imperialists enjoyed the advantage of overwhelming power, which enabled them to kill their subjects for a variety of reasons—to emphasize their subjection, to teach them a lesson, to clear them off their lands, or even for the sheer sport of it. There is a sickening literature documenting these abuses, which are familiar enough that they need not be extensively referenced here. One need only remember that the atrocities were committed in all parts of the world, by people of all the colonial powers, and even by people such as Americans (in their treatment of the Indians) who did not consider themselves imperialists.[1] The atrocities rarely evoked outrage, since it was generally assumed in the nineteenth and early twentieth centuries that "more advanced" peoples had the right to dominate "backward peoples" and that such excesses as might be committed in the course of this domination were the "price of progress."

This melancholy history is tragic enough, but equally distressing is the fact that similar atrocities and massacres continue into the present. The immediate reason for the founding of Cultural Survival in 1972 was our realization—a century after the United States, Argentina, and Chile had concluded their genocidal campaigns against the indigenous populations that stood in the way of their advancing frontiers of settlement—that history was repeating itself in the Amazon Basin. In Brazil and other countries of the region, indigenous peoples were being dispossessed, mistreated, and even massacred in the name of progress (see Davis 1977; Hecht and Cockburn 1990; Maybury-Lewis 1991, 1994; and Jobim 1970). Cultural Survival was founded to consider what could be done to prevent such human rights abuses, what were the responsibilities of anthropologists who worked in areas where such abuses were committed, and what courses of action were open to them.

The first task that our organization undertook was to bear witness to these abuses and to publicize them in order to help mobilize both national and international opinion on behalf of indigenous peoples. The *Cultural Survival Quarterly* and our monographs and occasional publications became the vehicles for doing this, as well as for analyzing and debunking the arguments most commonly used to deny indigenous peoples their human rights.

In the course of our work, we discovered that the physical elimination of indigenous peoples was normally denied or explained away by the governments of the countries in which they lived. The authorities usually argued that the reports of massacres were exaggerated or, alternatively, that they were carried out by encroaching pioneers who took advantage of the relative lawlessness of the remote areas in which they lived. As a result, Cultural Survival undertook to publish accurate information devoted to analyzing the context of official negligence, where this was demonstrable, and to showing that such massacres were in fact tolerated, even if they were not actually instigated by the authorities.[2]

We also found that the social elimination of indigenous groups— ethnocide rather than genocide, carried out by alienating their lands and suppressing or undermining their cultures—was routinely practiced and defended as a way of assimilating indigenous peoples into the mainstream national culture. In many instances, it was argued that indigenous peoples could not maintain their own cultures in the "modern" world, and that even if they could, they should not be encouraged to do so, since their cultures were backward and should be abandoned. Indigenous peoples would then no longer act as a brake on modernization, nor would they undermine the mainstream national culture.

Against such contentions, Cultural Survival has consistently argued that indigenous peoples' cultures can and do survive in the modern world. In the Americas, for example, indigenous peoples have for more than five centuries resisted the efforts of their conquerors to systematically eradicate their cultures. Theirs is an incredible story of cultural persistence in the face of overwhelming pressure. Yet against this evidence, it is often argued that indigenous cultures inevitably change, so that in that sense they do not survive. This is, of course, true, but it is a trivial truth based on a misunderstanding of what is meant by cultural survival. No societies maintain their ways of life unchanged over long spans of time. So-called modern societies do not; they are expected to change. It is uninformed and patronizing to assume that "traditional societies" are not likewise constantly changing. Cultural survival, as far as indigenous peoples are concerned, is not a matter of cultural stasis, but rather of cultural control and continuity. Such cultures can be said to survive (and are thought to do so by the people who live in them) to the extent that their members control their own affairs and maintain a satisfactory continuity with the past. Since no society, especially in these days when globalization proceeds apace, has complete control over its own affairs (and indigenous societies, by definition, do not), cultural survival is always a relative matter. Nevertheless, indigenous peoples have struggled for centuries to control their lands and their resources and to maintain the institutions and traditions that are important to them.

Indigenous organizations are now taking the lead in this struggle, and pro-indigenous organizations such as Cultural Survival have a significant role to play in lending them support (see Cultural Survival 1984; and CONAIE 1988). To this end, indigenous advocates have developed two major lines of argument. The first responds to the oft-repeated contention that it would be inequitable to allow indigenous peoples to monopolize what they have traditionally thought to be their own resources. Such resources, the argument runs, should be shared with the wider society for the greater good of the nation. It is ironic that in a world where resources are rarely, if ever, distributed widely and equitably, the argument should be made that the resources of indigenous minorities should be so shared.[3] As is demonstrated throughout this volume, when indigenous peoples are deprived of their lands, of the products that grow on them, or the minerals that lie beneath them, these resources are not normally redistributed to the general public but are instead taken over by nonindigenous concerns for private profit. Even if such redistribution were to be sincerely contemplated, it ought to be carried out only after negotiations with the indigenous stewards of the land, and after agreement has been reached as to what would constitute suitable royalty payments to them.

The other line of argument that pro-indigenous advocacy organizations such as Cultural Survival have developed over the years is that indigenous peoples do not necessarily undermine the state if they fight to maintain their separate cultures within it. Such a struggle is subversive only if the state refuses to accept the legitimacy of multiple cultures within it and insists that minorities give up their own distinctive cultures and join the national mainstream. Yet it can be shown that such a refusal on the part of states is derived from outworn theories of the state, which have been controverted by the evidence from real states (Maybury-Lewis 1997).

From its inception, Cultural Survival assisted the indigenous federations that were forming in the Amazonian countries, and it has done what it can to collaborate with the indigenous organizations that have contributed to the remarkable growth of the indigenous movement in recent decades. The worldwide movement since the Second World War to do away with colonialism raised the consciousness of indigenous peoples and prompted critical reflections on internal colonialism, especially in the Americas.[4] The aggressive efforts of the Amazon Basin countries to tap the putative riches of the rain forest led many of the indigenous peoples of the area to organize to defend themselves. Indigenous federations were helped by Cultural Survival and other pro-indigenous organizations to publicize their grievances internationally.[5]

Indigenous peoples have not been completely neglected in the discussions of human rights that have preoccupied the international community since the Second World War. The International Labor Organization and the United Nations, for instance, have discussed the particular abuses to which indigenous peoples are subject, but they initially sought to deal with them by promoting the integration of indigenous populations into the mainstream of the states that enveloped them. Starting in the 1960s, however, newly assertive indigenous leaders, supported by pro-indigenous organizations and a spate of scholarly and popular writing about the indigenous cause, developed an international campaign in support of the cultural survival of indigenous peoples. In 1982, the UN established a Working Group on Indigenous Populations, which in 1985 approved a Draft Declaration on the Rights of Indigenous Peoples. In 1989, the International Labor Organization, now affiliated with the UN, approved Convention No. 169. This landmark convention recognized "the aspirations of [indigenous] peoples to exercise control over their own institutions, ways of life and economic development and to maintain and develop their identities, languages and religions, within the framework of the states in which they live" (Anaya 1996, 48). Clearly, these documents, drafted after lengthy international discussions, represented a sharp change in the world's attitude toward indigenous peoples. Indigenous peoples' right to maintain their own cultures and to retain a degree of autonomy within the states in which they live was at long last recognized, and there was a growing expectation that states should abide by the principles of the Draft UN Declaration on the Rights of Indigenous Peoples.

The consequences of this worldwide change of attitude are already being felt. In the Americas, after five centuries of denial, country after country is now proclaiming itself pluriethnic, which means that indigenous populations are granted the right to maintain their own cultures without, in theory, being considered second-class citizens. It is noteworthy that the majority of the countries that have now declared themselves pluriethnic—Mexico, Colombia, Ecuador, Bolivia—have sizable, restive indigenous populations, and all are currently afflicted by a great deal of political uncertainty. In Mexico, the Zapatista revolt in the south has inspired uprisings elsewhere and led to a widespread rethinking of the Mexican state. In Ecuador and Bolivia, indigenous federations from both the lowlands and the highlands have coordinated marches on the national capitals, to demand a new order and a new relationship between indigenous peoples and the state. In Colombia, a new constitution has granted local autonomy to indigenous groups and incorporated their indigenous-controlled territories into the table of organization of the Colombian state. However, Colombia is in the throes of civil war, and the state has virtually come unraveled. All of this makes it reasonable to wonder whether the recent popularity of pluriethnicity in the Americas is not part of a desperate effort to co-opt and control situations that are already out of hand. Even so, the moves toward the pluriethnic option constitute an admission that the old system of assimilation has not worked, that the formal recognition of indigenous cultures and their place in society is beneficial for nation building—or is at any rate the least bad option. At the very least, such recognition represents an important break with the past.

It is also noteworthy that the American nations perhaps most resistant to pluriethnic solutions are those with small and scattered indigenous populations, notably Brazil and the United States. Yet the case of the United States is not clear-cut. While the United States does not formally recognize the autonomy of its indigenous peoples, it does recognize certain kinds of limited sovereignty, and it is this recognition that has given some indigenous groups the right to open casinos on the lands they control, even when gambling is forbidden in whichever state surrounds them. At the same time, the United States and Canada both tolerate the issuing of passports by the Iroquois confederacy that spans the international boundary between them. The Iroquois assume the trappings of a sovereign state, not only by issuing their own passports, but also by parading behind their flag and playing their national anthem when the Iroquois team plays "international" lacrosse games. In effect, there are pragmatic arrangements made in the United States that appear to concede limited sovereignty to indigenous groups without formally doing so.

The movement in the direction of recognizing indigenous rights has even affected Australia, a country that had deprived its Aboriginal inhabitants of any rights by declaring the country to have originally been *terra nullius* (no-man's-land) in a legal decision handed down as recently as 1971 (Broome [1982] 1994, 231). Australia has now backed away from that disgraceful fiction and admitted that Aborigines do have rights to land. It is, however, a complicated matter for Aborigines to claim these rights and to have those claims recognized. After all, great efforts were made by the colonists over two centuries to detach Aborigines from the lands they claimed and the cultures by which they tried to live. Aborigines are now required to give evidence of their traditional attachment to given territories if they wish to claim any rights to them. Some Australian judges have tried to ease the burden of proof by accepting Aboriginal evidence concerning land rights—evidence given in songs and song lines, for example, that would not previously have been acceptable in court. Meanwhile, there is a backlash against the current trend toward recognizing Aboriginal rights that is gathering powerful support from ranching and mining interests.

Just as the movement toward recognition of indigenous rights is a worldwide phenomenon, so too is the opposition it provokes from powerful interests. The indigenous movement and its allies try to counter this by mobilizing international pressure on behalf of groups that are suffering, but such pressure is difficult to orchestrate and is often ineffective. In Russia, for example, the rights of the indigenous peoples of Siberia are officially recognized, but the bureaucratic obstacles to claiming them are virtually insuperable (Fondahl and Poelzer 1997). Since Russia is in such desperate financial shape, international pressure in connection with the release of loan funding might be effective in securing indigenous rights, but it is not clear that the funders are interested in applying it. Meanwhile, the financial crisis in Russia's current phase of robber-baron capitalism also has the effect of increasing pressure on indigenous lands and resources.

International pressure is least effective when it is resisted by states that are determined to crush indigenous aspirations and that have little reason to fear international sanctions. Burma (Myanmar) is a classic case in point. When it gained its independence from Britain after the Second World War, it was a federation of distinct peoples governed by the preponderant Burmese majority. These peoples, such as the Shan, Karen, Karenni, Mon, Kachin, Naga, and Arakanese, hesitantly joined the Burmese federation on condition that they would have the right to secede if things did not work out. Things did not. The Burmese have oppressed them and driven most of them into open revolt, while their right to secede became a dead letter long ago (see Cultural Survival 1989). Burma is now boycotted internationally because its military leaders keep Aung San Suu Kyi, the Nobel Prize–winning leader of the party that won the last election, confined to her house and deny her and her followers any role in Burmese politics. The Burmese army keeps up its brutal attacks on the minority peoples of the federation because the international community is unwilling or unable to do much about it.

A similar situation obtains in Indonesia, notwithstanding efforts to live up to its national motto of "Unity in Diversity." The country's official policies of tolerance have not been applied to the Papuans in Indonesia's easternmost province, Irian Jaya, and have been denied until very recently to the people of East Timor. The original defining characteristic of Indonesia was that it comprised the Dutch-ruled territories of the East Indies. The Portuguese colony of East Timor lay outside of it and indicated that it would proclaim itself an independent state when the Portuguese withdrew. Indonesia prevented this by forcibly annexing East Timor. The ensuing repression and slaughter of the East Timorese was documented and denounced for years, yet it was only in the late 1990s that international pressure was put on Indonesia to desist. The United States supported the Indonesian invasion, which it saw as preempting a possible leftist regime in East Timor. There was, by contrast, a flutter of concern in Indonesia when it became known in Jakarta that the World Bank had interrupted loan payments to Brazil because that country had failed to honor its commitment to protect the indigenous peoples of its northwest if the bank invested in the development of the region (see Cultural Survival 1986). The Indonesians understood very clearly that if such actions were indicative of future World Bank policies, then their own loans might be affected. Nevertheless, Indonesia has pursued a policy of suppressing and changing the culture of the Papuan inhabitants of Irian Jaya so that they can become "civilized" and cease to be "nomads running around naked," as the foreign minister put it in 1984. As in Burma, the repression has led to demands for secession and to the growth of a secessionist movement among the Papuans of the province (see Deihl and Gordon 1987).

This brings us back to the central issues of autonomy, self-determination, and secession. Indigenous peoples universally desire autonomy, which, in the vast majority of cases, means that they wish to exercise local control over their own affairs within the framework of the states in which they live. States regularly misinterpret such aspirations as being secessionist and try to suppress them on that score, with the result that national policies often help to create secessionist movements where they did not previously exist. It is clear, though, that a slow change is taking place in the climate of world opinion, which is becoming increasingly favorable to the idea of pluriethnic states; they are seen as preferable alternatives to those in which authoritarian assimilation is the norm or those that are perennially riven by ethnic conflict.

Cynics will argue that the only practical consequences of this change in world opinion are that resolutions are passed at the international level and policy changes approved at the national level, none of which are implemented at the local level. The cynics, for once, will be only partly right. Indigenous organizations, such as AIDESEP (Asociación Interétnica de Desarrollo de la Selva Peruana) in Peru, once scattered and weak, are now collaborating with each other on a worldwide scale, supported by pro-indigenous and human rights organizations. The resulting indigenous movement is now seeking and often finding interlocutors who understand what indigenous peoples want and who are willing to negotiate with them. Clearly, the struggle for indigenous rights is far from over, but it has at least entered a new phase. The indigenous movement and its allies have put indigenous rights on the world's agenda, and the world is, in theory, increasingly sympathetic.

The indigenous movement does need all the help it can get—from nongovernmental organizations such as Cultural Survival and from scholars and activists worldwide. It is here that anthropologists can play an important role. They are especially well qualified to analyze and clarify the issues surrounding indigenous rights and to provide the counterarguments against those who would deny those rights. It is anthropologists who should, and often do, take the lead in showing that indigenous peoples are not archaic but, rather, marginalized; that an indigenous culture is a process, and often one that is used by indigenous peoples themselves in self-defense; that indigenous peoples do not stand in the way of development but can in fact participate in development if it is redesigned to include them; that indigenous cultures do not undermine the state but can be legitimate resources if the state is genuinely pluriethnic. Above all, pro-indigenous scholars and activists have an enormous educational role to play in making the general public aware of these issues so that people may be more willing to live and let live— not just as a matter of justice, but also out of enlightened self-interest.

Notes

1. To give some examples: there is an extensive literature on the brutalities committed against the indigenous peoples of the Americas by Spanish, Portuguese, and other European invaders, which in turn inspired Eduardo Galeano's searing quartet of books entitled *Memory of Fire* (see, e.g., Galeano 1985). Joseph Conrad's *Heart of Darkness* ([1902] 1981) was a similar evocation of Belgian atrocities in the African Congo. German cruelties in South-West Africa are described in Horst Drechsler's *Let Us Die Fighting* (1980). British mistreatment of indigenous peoples is detailed in Richard Broome's *Aboriginal Australians* ([1982] 1994), and their extermination of the Tasmanians in James Bonwick's *The Last of the Tasmanians* ([1869] 1969). Similarly, much has been written about French colonial massacres in Africa and American brutalities against indigenous peoples during what Theodore Roosevelt called *The Winning of the West* (1889).

2. See, for example, *Brazil,* a special report of Cultural Survival (1979).

3. I have elsewhere shown the weakness of this argument when applied to Brazil; see Maybury-Lewis 1985.

4. Internal colonialism is a concept that has been used by leading scholars in the Americas, such as Roberto Cardoso de Oliveira in Brazil (1972) and Rodolfo Stavenhagen in Mexico (1967).

5. In the early 1980s, Cultural Survival invited indigenous leaders from the Amazonian countries to conferences held in South America. These meetings helped them to develop the arguments for indigenous rights that they later presented to the UN in Geneva. See Smith 1984.

References

Anaya, James. 1996. *Indigenous Peoples in International Law.* New York: Oxford University Press.

Bonwick, James. [1869] 1969. *The Last of the Tasmanians.* London: Sampson Low, Son, and Marston.

Broome, Richard. [1982] 1994. *Aboriginal Australians.* St. Leonards, N.S.W.: Allen and Unwin.

Cardoso de Oliveira, Roberto. 1972. *A sociología do Brasil indígena.* São Paulo: Tempo Brasileiro.

CONAIE. (Confederación de Nacionalidades Indígenas del Ecuador). 1988. *Las nacionalidades indígenas del Ecuador: Nuestro proceso organizativo.* Quito: Ediciones Tinkui.

Conrad, Joseph. [1902] 1981. *Heart of Darkness.* New York: Bantam Books.

Cultural Survival. 1979. *Brazil.* Special Report No. 1. Cambridge, Mass.: Cultural Survival.

————. 1984. Organizing to Survive. *Cultural Survival Quarterly* 8 (4).

————. 1986. Multilateral Banks and Indigenous Peoples. *Cultural Survival Quarterly* 10 (1).

————. 1989. Burma, in Search of Peace. *Cultural Survival Quarterly* 13 (4).

Davis, Shelton. 1977. *Victims of the Miracle.* Cambridge: Cambridge University Press.

Deihl, Colin, and Robert Gordon. 1987. The Forgotten Refugees: The West Papuans of Irian Jaya. In *Southeast Asian Tribal Groups and Ethnic Minorities,* 155–63. Cultural Survival Report No. 22. Cambridge, Mass.: Cultural Survival.

Drechsler, Horst. 1980. *Let Us Die Fighting: The Struggle of the Herero and Nama against German Imperialism (1884–1915).* London: Zed Books.

Fondahl, Gail, and Greg Poelzer. 1997. Indigenous Peoples of the Russian North. *Cultural Survival Quarterly* 21 (3): 30–33.

Galeano, Eduardo. 1985. *Memory of Fire.* Vol. 1, *Genesis.* New York: Pantheon Books.

Hecht, Susanna, and Alexander Cockburn. 1990. *The Fate of the Forest.* London: Penguin.

Jobim, Danton. 1970. *O problema do indio e a acusação de genocídio.* Bulletin No. 2, Conselho de Defesa dos Direitos da Pessôa Humana, Ministry of Justice. Rio de Janeiro.

Maybury-Lewis, David. 1985. A Special Sort of Pleading: Anthropology at the Service of Ethnic Groups. In *Advocacy and Anthropology,* edited by Robert Paine, 130–48. St. John's, Newfoundland: Memorial University Press.

————. 1991. Becoming Indian in Lowland South America. In *Nation-States and Indians in Latin America,* edited by Greg Urban and Joel Scherzer, 207–35. Austin: University of Texas Press.

————. 1994. From Savages to Security Risks: The Indian Question in Brazil.

In *The Rights of Subordinated Peoples,* edited by Oliver Mendelsohn and Upendra Baxi, 38–63. Delhi: Oxford University Press.

———. 1997. *Indigenous Peoples, Ethnic Groups, and the State.* Boston: Allyn and Bacon.

Roosevelt, Theodore. 1889. *The Winning of the West.* New York: G. P. Putnam.

Smith, Richard Chase. 1984. Amazonian Indians Participate at UN. *Cultural Survival Quarterly* 8 (4): 29–31.

Stavenhagen, Rodolfo. 1967. *Seven Erroneous Theses about Latin America.* Boston: New England Free Press.

Contributors

Benedict R. Anderson is the A. L. Binenkorb Professor of International Studies in the Government Department, Emeritus, Cornell University. Most of his work has been in the area of Southeast Asia, with special emphasis on revolutionary movements, political culture, and military regimes. He has also written on comparative political history, especially the history of nationalism. In addition to numerous articles on comparative politics and his seminal *Imagined Communities: Reflections on the Origin and Spread of Nationalism,* his many books include *In the Mirror: Literature and Politics in Siam in the American Era; Violence and the State in Suharto's Indonesia* (ed.); *Java in a Time of Revolution: Occupation and Resistance, 1944–1946; Religion and Social Ethos in Indonesia; Mythology and the Tolerance of the Javanese;* and *Language and Power: Exploring Political Cultures in Indonesia.* His most recent book is *The Spectre of Comparisons: Nationalism, Southeast Asia, and the World.*

Marjorie Mandelstam Balzer is Research Professor at Georgetown University in the Sociology/Anthropology Department and at the Center for Eurasian, Russian and East European Studies (CERES), where she coordinates the Social, Ethnic and Regional Issues concentration. A sociocultural anthropologist, she is editor of the M. E. Sharpe journal *Anthropology and Archeology of Eurasia.* She is author of *The Tenacity of Ethnicity: A Siberian Saga in Global Perspective* and has edited two books featuring indigenous Siberian writers.

Bartholomew Dean is Assistant Professor of Anthropology at the University of Kansas. His research and publications have emphasized the kinship, politics, material culture, cosmology, and human rights of Peruvian Amazonia's indigenous peoples. In 1995, he and his wife, Michelle McKinley, cofounded the Amazonian Peoples' Resources Initiative. He is also a founding member of the Graduate Program in Amazonian Studies at the Universidad Nacional Mayor de San Marcos, Lima, and currently serves as the Contributing Editor for Lowland South American Ethnology for the U.S. Library of Congress's *Handbook of Latin American Studies.* He was awarded the Royal Anthropological Institute's Fellowship in Urgent Anthropology in 1998–99. He is currently completing a monograph entitled *Ambivalent Exchanges: Urarina Society, Cosmos, and History in Peruvian Amazonia.*

Kirk Endicott is Professor and Chair of the Department of Anthropology at Dartmouth College. He has studied the Batek people of Peninsular Malaysia since 1971, focusing on their economy, social organization, gender relations, and religion and the effects of development and government programs on their customary ways of life. His numerous publications include *Batek Negrito Religion* and, as coauthor, *Malaysia and the "Original People."*

Richard B. Lee is a University Professor of Anthropology at the University of Toronto. He has worked with the San peoples of southern Africa since the 1960s, spanning the late colonial to the post-Apartheid eras. His numerous books include *Kalahari Hunter-Gatherers; The !Kung San; Politics and History in Band Societies; The Cambridge Encyclopedia of Hunters and Gatherers;* and, most recently, *The Dobe Jul'hoansi* (3d ed.). He is a founding member of the Kalahari Peoples Fund and remains actively involved in indigenous support work.

Jerome M. Levi is Associate Professor and Chair of the Department of Sociology and Anthropology, Carleton College, Northfield, Minnesota. He has conducted extensive fieldwork among indigenous peoples in Mesoamerica and the U.S. Southwest since the 1970s. His numerous publications focus on religion, material culture, interethnic relations, and cultural rights. In the United States, he has submitted congressional testimony on the Hopi-Navajo land dispute and worked with indigenous leaders of southern California on cultural preservation. In Mexico, he has studied the Tarahumara (Rarámuri) of Chihuahua and the Tzotzil of Chiapas, with a research emphasis on symbolism, ethnicity, commoditization, and cultural politics. In 1997–98 he was a Fellow at the University of Chicago's Globalization Project, and in 2001 he was awarded a Technos International Fellowship to Japan by the Tanaka Ikueikai Educational Trust. Working with the Southern California Tribal Digital Village, he recently began locating, copying, repatriating, and digitizing legacy film materials relating to the Kumeyaay people of San Diego County. A contributor to *The Oxford Encyclopedia of Mesoamerican Cultures,* he is currently completing a monograph entitled *Pillars of the Sky: Rarámuri Identity, Religion, and Exchange in Northern Mexico.*

David Maybury-Lewis is the Edward C. Henderson Professor of Anthropology at Harvard University, where he has taught since 1960. His research has focused on indigenous peoples, ethnicity, and development with special emphasis on Latin America, particularly Brazil. In 1972, he and his wife, Pia Maybury-Lewis, founded Cultural Survival, an organization that defends the rights of indigenous peoples around the world. His books include *The Savage and the Innocent; Akwe-Shavante Society; Dialectical Societies: The Ge and Bororo of Central Brazil* (ed.); *The Indian Peoples of Paraguay: Their Plight and Their Prospects; The Prospects for Plural Societies* (ed.); *The Attraction of Opposites: Thought and Society in the Dualistic Mode* (ed.); *Millennium: Tribal Wisdom and the Modern World;* and *Indigenous Peoples, Ethnic Groups, and the State.*

Ian S. McIntosh is the managing director of Cultural Survival, a Harvard University–affiliated nongovernmental organization that promotes the rights, voices, and visions of the world's indigenous peoples. He holds a Ph.D. in anthropology from Australia's Northern Territory University, has many years of experience working with Aborigines and Torres Strait Islanders, and has published more than fifty essays on indigenous issues. His most recent book is *Aboriginal Reconciliation and the Dreaming: Warramiri Yolngu and the Quest for Equality.*

Parker Shipton is Associate Professor in the Department of Anthropology and Research Fellow at the African Studies Center at Boston University. He has done extensive fieldwork in Africa, especially in Kenya and the Gambia, and he has written many articles on topics such as kinship, land tenure, money and finance, symbolism, politics, "development," and food and famine. His ethnographic writings include *Bitter Money: Cultural Economy and Some African Meanings of Forbidden Commodities;* and he has coedited *Seeking Solutions: Framework and Cases for Small Enterprise Development Programs,* as well as a special issue of the journal *Africa* titled *Rights over Land.* He is writing a three-part study on entrustment and obligation in East Africa, and he continues his research on wealth, poverty, religion, and symbolism in African cultures.

Lynn Stephen is Professor and Chair of the Department of Anthropology at the University of Oregon. Her wide-ranging research focuses on gender, ethnicity, political economy, social movements, human rights, and nationalism in Latin America. Her books include *Zapotec Women; Class, Politics, and Popular Religion in Mexico and Central America; Hear My Testimony: María Teresa Tula, Human Rights Activist of El Salvador; Women and Social Movements in Latin America: Power from Below;* and, most recently, *Zapata Lives! Histories and Cultural Politics in Southern Mexico.*

Index

Aborigines and Torres Strait Islanders: and adoption, 300–303, 315, 319; and alliances, 303, 307; and Christianity, 303, 318; and colonialism, 293–94, 298, 299, 302, 303, 307, 332n. 1; demands of, 294; and dingo, 311–12, 314, 316; and future prospects, 320–21; and impersonal reconciliation, 294, 295; and native title law, 298–99, 318; and non-Aborigines as *Balanda,* 304; and reconciliatory metaphor, 299–300; and rights, 293–94, 298, 299, 300, 302, 317, 319; sacred sites, 296, 300; as a social problem, 318; "stolen generation" children, 296; storytelling, 295, 310, 314; voice, 296; and "unity in diversity" worldview, 300, 315

Academy of Sciences Institute for the Problems of Minority Peoples, 123

Aceh, 187n. 30

Achimoa, 101

Achuar, 228

Advisory Council of the Sierra Madre (CASMAC), 272, 273, 275, 283n. 13

African National Congress (ANC), 91, 93, 98, 103–4

Afrikaner Weerstandbeweging (Afrikaner Resistance Movement), 98

aggregations, colonial: bureaucratic-anthropological, 168; Burmans, 167, 168; East Timorese, 169, 175; Filipinos, 169, 172; Ilokanos, 168; Indonesians, 168, 169; Iranese, 168, 179, 180; Javanese, 167; Malays, 167; Moros, 169; New Guineans, 168; Papuans,168, 169, 177, 179, 187n. 28; Sundanese, 168; Vietnamese, 167, 168

Aglukark, Susan, 99

Aguaruna, 242n. 4

Aguirre, Juan Carlos, 280

Akan, 67

Akiwenzie-Damn, Kateri, 244n. 19

Alatas, Ali, 176

Alexander, Benny (Khoisan X), 98

Alexander, Neville, 98

Al Qaeda, 26

Amazonia: and ceremonial contexts, 231; and cultural survival, 231; and extractive economies, 232; and gendered nature of power, 230; and genocide, 325; and human rights, 232; and indigenous movement, 23, 217, 230–31, 327, 332n. 5; and patron-clientelism, 233; and postcolonial identity, 231

Amazonian Peoples' Resources Initiative, 237, 245nn. 25, 26

ambivalence, 32–33n. 11

American Anthropological Association, xi, 4, 63, 65, 324

Anderson, Benedict, 4, 13, 20, 22, 194

/Angn!ao, Kiewiet, 100

Angola, 87, 173, 174, 176

155–56; and Austronesians, 143; and concept of rights, 151–52, 160n. 4; and ecological degradation, 153; and federal government, 155; and gazetting, 152; indigenous peoples of, 144; and Native Customary Land, 151–52; Sabah and Sarawak, 142, 144, 147, 149, 151–52, 153, 172; Sarawak Land Consolidation and Rehabilitation Authority, 153; and sovereignty, 147; and special rights, 145. *See also* Malaysia

Botswana, 84, 85, 88, 102; assimilationist pressures, 87–88; and "Basarwa" (San) as social problem, 86, 87; and Kua (San), 88; and Remote Area Development Program, 87

Brazil, 218, 243n. 18, 325, 329, 331

Bredekamp, Henry, 96, 97

Bretons, 70

British ethnicity, 97

Brooks, Alison, 89

Broome, Richard, 332n. 1

Brown Childs, John, 8

Buber, Martin, 295

Bureau of Indian Affairs, 131–32

Burgess, Don, 266

Burma, 165, 168, 330; and Aung San Suu Kyi, 330; and indigenous peoples (Karen, Karenni, Kachin, Naga, Arakanese, Shan), 330; and Mons, 167, 330; as Myanmar, 168, 330

Burrumarra, David, 300, 318, 319, 321n. 2

Buryats, 115, 116

"Buschmanreich," 89

Bushmen. *See* San

Bustillos, Edwin, 272, 283n. 13

Buterlin, S. A., 120

Cabral, Amilcar, 96, 101

Calabrians, 70

Campbell, Howard, 278–79

Canada, 84, 99, 132, 320, 329; and Métis, 133n. 1

Candoshi, 218

Caribbeans, 61

Carrier, James, 75n. 35

Cashinahua, 238

Castilians, 170

Catalonians, 70, 170, 182

Cebuanos, 170

Central African "Pygmies" (Efe), 7, 61

Chagga, 69

Chatterjee, Partha, 132, 209–10

Chayahuita, 245n. 24

Chechnya war, 113, 119, 130, 132

Chennells, Roger, 93

Chiapas, 2, 23, 25, 30, 191, 194, 200, 201, 202, 204, 207, 208, 210, 211, 212n. 2, 234, 255, 260, 272, 276; and Acteal massacre, 193, 198; and autonomous municipalities (*municipios*), 192, 202; and Institutional Revolutionary Party (PRI), 193; and multiethnic autonomous regions, 197, 201, 202, 203–4; and state, 192–93; and Tojolabal experience, 201. *See also* Mexico

Chile, 325

China, 144, 307

Ch'ol, 195, 197, 200, 212n. 2

Chontales, 214n. 12

Chuckchi, 114

Chuvantsy, 120

Clandestine Revolutionary Indigenous Committee—General Command (CCRI-CG), 195–96, 211–12n. 2

Clastres, Pierre, 219

Cobo, Jose Martinez, 146

Cocama-Cocamilla, 218

Cohen, Jeffrey, 283n. 10

Collier, George, 212n. 2

Collmann, J., 303

Ksenofontov, P. V., 117
Kulakovsky, A. E., 117
Kurdistan, 182
Kurilov, Gavril, 120, 122
Kuwait, 176

Lacandón, 194, 197, 198, 212n. 2,
   213n. 8, 263
Ladakh, 167–68
LaDuke, Winona, ix–x
Laing, Harrison Ngau, 157
Lakota Hunkapi, 321n. 5
Land Claim Committee of the
   Southern Kalahari Bushmen, 93
landholding, 68–69, 76n. 38
Langton, Marcia, 317
language death, 28
Lasimbang, Jannie, 152
League of Nations, 181, 182
Lee, Richard B., 15, 22
Levi, Jerome, 23, 105n. 9, 131, 134n. 8
Lévi-Strauss, Claude, 72n. 12, 73n. 19
Lloyd, Lucy, 83
Locke, John, 49–50, 52–56
Lubicon, 99
Luhya, 69
Lumbee, 105n. 3, 106n. 12
Luo, 62–63, 68, 69, 70, 75n. 34

Maasai, 67
Maguindanao, 170
Mahmud, Abdul Taib, 152
Malays, 97, 142, 143, 145, 148, 149,
   167; as *bumiputera* ("indigenous
   peoples"), 145–46, 149; national
   culture, 148, 156; and special
   rights, 145
Malaysia, 6, 22, 31–32n. 6, 140–62,
   172; and Aboriginal Peoples Act,
   145, 154; and Aboriginal Reserves,
   151; and the British, 142, 143–44,
   146, 147, 151; and the Chinese, 142,
   144, 145, 148, 159; ethnic politics
   of, 142–60; exploitation of indigenous peoples, 150–56, 159–60; Federal Constitution of, 142, 143, 145;
and Federal Land Development
Authority (FELDA), 149; federation, 144, 147; and government,
142, 147, 154, 159; and Hindu
Tamils, 144; and Indians, 144, 145,
148, 159; Internal Security Act
(ISA), 157; land law, 151; and logging, 159, 160; and Malaysian Bar
Council, 157; and Muslims, 143,
148, 156; nation building, 147–48,
159; and New Economic Policy
(NEP), 148; Peninsular, 142; as
"plural society," 142; and religious
conversion, 157; and resettlement,
154; and rights, 148; and Sahabat
Alam, 157; and sultanates, 147,
148. *See also* Borneo; Iban;
Kadazan; Malays; Orang Asli
Mallon, Florencia, 23, 194; and
"community hegemonies," 194
Mambai, 174, 177
Mandela, Nelson, 91, 94–95
Mansi, 115, 124, 125, 129
Marais, Eugène, 83
Maranao, 170
Marcos, Ferdinand, 171, 172, 185n. 14
Marks, Shula, 83, 90, 98
Marshall, John, 87, 94, 100
Marshall, Lorna, 87
Martinez, Miguel Alfonso, 293
Marx, Karl, 55, 72n. 12, 99
Mashpee legal case, 14–15
Mattiace, Shannon, 201
Maya, 25, 255
Maybury-Lewis, David, 24–25, 29,
   231
Maybury-Lewis, Pia, 324
Mbehi, Thabo, 93
McIntosh, Ian, 24
Melanau, 22, 144
Melanesia, 226, 262
Menchú, Rigoberta, 1, 282–83n. 8